The Transformation of American International Power in the 1970s

Barbara Zanchetta analyzes the evolution of American-Soviet relations during the 1970s, from the rise of détente during the Nixon administration to the policy's crisis and fall during the final years of the Carter presidency. This study traces lines of continuity among the Nixon, Ford, and Carter administrations and assesses its effects on the ongoing redefinition of America's international role in the post-Vietnam era. Against the background of superpower cooperation in arms control, Dr. Zanchetta analyzes aspects of the global bipolar competition, including US-China relations, the turmoil in Iran and Afghanistan, and the crises in Angola and the Horn of Africa. In doing so, she unveils both the successful transformation of American international power during the 1970s and its long-term problematic legacy.

Barbara Zanchetta is a Researcher at the Finnish Institute of International Affairs in Helsinki. She is also a Scholar at the Machiavelli Center for Cold War studies in Italy. She is the co-author of *Transatlantic Relations since 1945: An Introduction* (2012).

The Transformation of American International Power in the 1970s

BARBARA ZANCHETTA

CAMBRIDGE
UNIVERSITY PRESS

32 Avenue of the Americas, New York, NY 10013-2473, USA

Cambridge University Press is part of the University of Cambridge.

It furthers the University's mission by disseminating knowledge in the pursuit of education, learning, and research at the highest international levels of excellence.

www.cambridge.org
Information on this title: www.cambridge.org/9781107041080

© Barbara Zanchetta 2014

This publication is in copyright. Subject to statutory exception and to the provisions of relevant collective licensing agreements, no reproduction of any part may take place without the written permission of Cambridge University Press.

First published 2014

Printed in the United States of America

A catalog record for this publication is available from the British Library.

Library of Congress Cataloging in Publication data
Zanchetta, Barbara, 1976–
The Transformation of American International Power in the 1970s / Barbara Zanchetta, the Finnish Institute of International Affairs (Helsinki).
pages cm.
Includes bibliographical references and index.
ISBN 978-1-107-04108-0 (hardback)
1. United States–Foreign relations–1969–1974. 2. United States–Foreign relations–1974–1977. 3. United States–Foreign relation–1977–1981. 4. United States–Foreign relations–Soviet Union–History. 5. Soviet Union–Foreign relations–United States–History. I. Title.
E840.Z36   2013
327.73009'04–dc23   2013024114

ISBN 978-1-107-04108-0 Hardback

Cambridge University Press has no responsibility for the persistence or accuracy of URLs for external or third-party Internet Web sites referred to in this publication and does not guarantee that any content on such Web sites is, or will remain, accurate or appropriate.

To my family

Contents

List of Images		*page* ix
Acknowledgments		xi
Introduction		1
	PART ONE. THE REMAKING OF AMERICAN GLOBAL POWER, 1969–1976	
1	The Nixon Administration and a "Moment of Beginning"	19
2	The Diplomatic Revolution: The China Opening	35
3	An "Era of Negotiation" versus the "Supreme Test": Nixon between SALT I and Vietnam	60
4	"Protect Me": Nixon and the Shah of Iran	86
5	Détente Questioned: Domestic Challenges and International Crisis	116
6	The Ford (and Kissinger) Administration	142
7	Defending the Dual Track: SALT II, Angola, and the Crisis of Détente	158
	PART TWO. RETHINKING THE FALL OF DÉTENTE, 1977–1980	
8	The Carter Administration's Ambitious Agenda	189
9	Initial Shift: The Horn of Africa	204
10	Re-Creating the Strategic Triangle: Normalization with China and SALT II	221
11	The Loss of Iran	243

12 Reaffirming Containment: The Carter Doctrine	271
Conclusion	293
Selected Bibliography	315
Index	325

List of Images

1. President Nixon on a speaker's platform with the shah of Iran, October 21, 1969, White House south grounds — *page* xv
2. President Nixon and Henry Kissinger walking on the White House grounds after Cambodian Minister of National Defense Sirik Matak's departure, August 10, 1971 — xvi
3. President Nixon at the Ba Da Ling portion of the Great Wall, February 24, 1972, Beijing, China — xvii
4. Chinese leader Mao Zedong and President Nixon shaking hands near a doorway, February 29, 1972, Beijing, China — xviii
5. President Nixon and General Secretary Brezhnev signing an agreement between the United States and USSR on "Scientific and Technical Cooperation in the Field of Peaceful Uses of Atomic Energy," June 21, 1973, White House, East Room — xviii
6. President Nixon conversing with Leonid Brezhnev, June 23, 1973, La Casa Pacifica Library, San Clemente, California — xix
7. President Nixon in the Oval Office during a meeting with Henry Kissinger and Gerald Ford, October 13, 1973 — xix
8. President Ford and his golden retriever Liberty, November 7, 1974, White House, Oval Office — xx
9. President Ford and General Secretary Brezhnev sign a joint communiqué following talks on the limitation of strategic offensive arms, November 24, 1974, Vladivostok, USSR — xxi

List of Images

10 President Ford, Secretary of State Henry Kissinger (left), and Secretary of Defense James Schlesinger (right) at a meeting to discuss the situation in South Vietnam, April 29, 1975, White House, Oval Office — xxi

11 President Ford, as the Republican nominee, shakes hands with nomination foe Ronald Reagan on the closing night of the Republican National Convention, August 19, 1976, Kansas City — xxii

12 President Ford and Jimmy Carter meet at the Walnut Street Theater in Philadelphia to debate domestic policy during the first of the three Ford-Carter Debates, September 23, 1976 — xxii

13 President Carter, Secretary of State Cyrus Vance, and National Security Adviser Zbigniew Brzezinski, August 14, 1977, White House — xxiii

14 President Carter and the shah of Iran, November 15, 1977, White House — xxiii

15 President Carter and the shah of Iran toast at a state dinner (the "island of stability" toast), December 31, 1977, Tehran, Iran — xxiv

16 President Carter, former President Nixon, and Chinese leader Deng Xiaoping during a state dinner, January 29, 1979, White House — xxiv

17 President Jimmy Carter and Chinese leader Deng Xiaoping at the signing of the normalization of relations between the United States and the People's Republic of China, January 31, 1979, White House — xxv

18 President Jimmy Carter with General Secretary Brezhnev at the signing of the SALT II agreements, June 18, 1979, Vienna, Austria — xxv

Acknowledgments

As with most books, this book was something very different at the start from the final result. As a student in Italy, I chose Nixon and Kissinger as the topic for my first thesis at the University of Urbino largely because of the controversy and polemic surrounding both figures. However, after visiting the US archives and reading the voluminous literature on the period, I still had not given myself a satisfactory explanation of why these two individuals – and the policy of US-Soviet détente they initiated in the early 1970s – were (and still are) so divisive, both in the United States and around the world. I became all the more intrigued and thus decided to expand my research on American foreign policy throughout the 1970s, which then evolved into my PhD topic at the University of Florence. As my work progressed, I started to ask myself repeatedly the same all-important question: did Nixon and Kissinger's acclaimed, or disdained, policies really make a difference in the history of the Cold War and on the evolution of American foreign policy? Inevitably, the scope, thematic and chronological, of my research expanded seemingly endlessly – as some of my less supportive colleagues and professors, either jokingly or more seriously, admonished – to include an assessment of the crisis and fall of détente, and a link to the 1980s. The practical consequences were that I spent more and more time at various archives, read more and more books, and, ultimately, took much longer to complete this book than ever envisioned. The result of my efforts – *The Transformation of American International Power in the 1970s* – is my attempt to answer the same reoccurring question: did Nixon and Kissinger's policies really make a difference?

During the years it took to complete this book I moved to different institutions and countries, and I was fortunate to find encouragement and support everywhere I went. In Italy (where it all began), I am indebted to the research team at the University of Urbino, skillfully set up many years ago by Professor Max Guderzo. Special thanks to Maurizio Cremasco for his help and friendship at the earliest stages of my career, and to Massimiliano Cricco, Fiorella Favino, Eleonora Guasconi, Matteo Napolitano, and Andrea Pierotti for creating a wonderful and stimulating work environment for a young scholar. At the University of Florence, I would like to acknowledge the History of International Relations PhD team, and in particular Duccio Basosi, Matteo Gerlini, and Angela Romano, who at various moments provided precious input and criticism on my research.

In Italy, however, my greatest thank you goes to my two professors and mentors, Max Guderzo and Ennio Di Nolfo. Without their backing, guidance, and audacity (often diplomatically opposed by others) I could have never undertaken such a broad topic or had the courage to make bold claims, and then the perseverance to transform my findings into a book of this type. Thank you both very much, personally and professionally.

In Finland, I would like to thank the University of Tampere and the Academy of Finland for hosting me as a post-doctoral researcher. Special thanks to the History Department and to those – especially Touko Berry, Miia Ijas, and Katri Sieberg – who made the cultural (mostly climatic) clash (an Italian – from Rome – in Finland) interesting and amusing. At the Finnish Institute of International Affairs in Helsinki (yes, after the exotic province, I had to move back to a capital city) I would like to acknowledge the support of the former and current directors of the Institute, Raimo Vayrynen and Teija Tiilikainen, for embracing the – often not too popular – idea that history does matter for a better understanding of current affairs. Thanks also to my former and current colleagues at the Institute, especially my program directors Mika Aaltola and Matti Nojonen, and the Global Security/Transformation of the World Order research programs for creating a nice, friendly, and stimulating work environment. A special thank you to Hanna Ojanen – for her cooperation and friendship from our first meetings – and to my friends Liisa Kohonen and Noora Kotilainen, who endured more than others my complaints and frustrations (in those dark Finnish days) with encouragement, support, and humor. Those long days in the office would have been unbearable without you both! I would also like to express gratitude to my students, at the Universities of Tampere and of Helsinki, whose curiosity helped stimulate mine.

Acknowledgments

As a historian, the most important – and at times very exciting – part of my work is to see (and touch) original documents. The archivists at the US National Archives at College Park (in the days when the Nixon Presidential Materials were there) and at the Gerald Ford and Jimmy Carter Presidential Libraries deserve a special thank you for their tolerance of a sometimes undisciplined Italian and, most importantly, for making my search for "the needle in stacks of hay" seem simple and easy. I would also like to express my gratitude for the financial assistance granted me by the Ford Library, which enabled me to prolong my stay in Ann Arbor.

At Cambridge University Press, I was extremely fortunate to work with Eric Crahan, who first saw my proposal and helped me understand that, eventually, I could turn my manuscript into this book. Since his departure, I am very grateful for the support of my editor Robert Dreesen, his assistants, and all those at Cambridge who worked to edit and produce my book. I would also like to thank the reviewers, whose comments and suggestions greatly helped improve my manuscript.

A number of friends outside the academic world helped and supported my long journey into the making of this book. A special mention goes to Alain Wallart and his family in Les Saisies, France. I originally went up to those beautiful mountains to learn French and, in addition to doing that with great fun (thanks to Alain's patience and skill), also found refuge in a perfect setting to work on the early stages of this manuscript. Yes, now it is finally done. Another special thank you goes to two very exceptional people, Ed and Renata Louie, who, throughout these years, made my many trips to Washington possible (and much more pleasant) by offering me their home, their friendship, and their love.

Lastly, but most importantly, I would like to deeply thank my family. My parents – Alberta and Francesco – who have always supported, encouraged, and guided me through the various stages of my life and career. Without them, I would have never made it through this and other difficult journeys. Grazie di tutto mami e papi, vi voglio tanto bene. And my husband Jussi, who always (and in this case also) gives me the strength to follow my dreams and ambitions, in spite of all kinds of difficulties, and helps me believe that I can achieve what I want. Here, the book is finally finished and it is also thanks to you (will you read it now?!). Kiitos minun iso rakas.

FIGURE 1 President Nixon on a speaker's platform with the shah of Iran, October 21, 1969, White House south grounds, White House Photo Office, Courtesy of the Richard Nixon Presidential Library and Museum

FIGURE 2 President Nixon and Henry Kissinger walking on the White House grounds after Cambodian Minister of National Defense Sirik Matak's departure, August 10, 1971, White House Photo Office, Courtesy of the Richard Nixon Presidential Library and Museum

FIGURE 3 President Nixon at the Ba Da Ling portion of the Great Wall, February 24, 1972, Beijing, China, White House Photo Office, Courtesy of the Richard Nixon Presidential Library and Museum

FIGURE 4 Chinese leader Mao Zedong and President Nixon shaking hands near a doorway, February 29, 1972, Beijing, China, Source unknown, Courtesy of the Richard Nixon Presidential Library and Museum

FIGURE 5 President Nixon and General Secretary Brezhnev signing an agreement between the United States and USSR on "Scientific and Technical Cooperation in the Field of Peaceful Uses of Atomic Energy," June 21, 1973, White House, East Room, White House Photo Office, Courtesy of the Richard Nixon Presidential Library and Museum

FIGURE 6 President Nixon conversing with Leonid Brezhnev, June 23, 1973, La Casa Pacifica Library, San Clemente, California, White House Photo Office, Courtesy of the Richard Nixon Presidential Library and Museum

FIGURE 7 President Nixon in the Oval Office during a meeting with Henry Kissinger and Gerald Ford, October 13, 1973, White House Photo Office, Courtesy of the Richard Nixon Presidential Library and Museum

FIGURE 8 President Ford and his golden retriever Liberty, November 7, 1974, White House, Oval Office, White House Photographs, Courtesy of the Gerald R. Ford Library

FIGURE 9 President Ford and General Secretary Brezhnev sign a joint communiqué following talks on the limitation of strategic offensive arms, November 24, 1974, Vladivostok, USSR, White House Photographs, Courtesy of the Gerald R. Ford Library

FIGURE 10 President Ford, Secretary of State Henry Kissinger (left), and Secretary of Defense James Schlesinger (right) at a meeting to discuss the situation in South Vietnam, April 29, 1975, White House, Oval Office, White House Photographs, Courtesy of the Gerald R. Ford Library

FIGURE 11 President Ford, as the Republican nominee, shakes hands with nomination foe Ronald Reagan on the closing night of the Republican National Convention, August 19, 1976, Kansas City, White House Photographs, Courtesy of the Gerald R. Ford Library

FIGURE 12 President Ford and Jimmy Carter meet at the Walnut Street Theater in Philadelphia to debate domestic policy during the first of the three Ford-Carter Debates, September 23, 1976, White House Photographs, Courtesy of the Gerald R. Ford Library

FIGURE 13 President Carter, Secretary of State Cyrus Vance, and National Security Adviser Zbigniew Brzezinski, August 14, 1977, White House, White House Photographs Collection, Courtesy of the Jimmy Carter Library

FIGURE 14 President Carter and the shah of Iran, November 15, 1977, White House, White House Photographs Collection, Courtesy of the Jimmy Carter Library

FIGURE 15 President Carter and the shah of Iran toast at a state dinner (the "island of stability" toast), December 31, 1977, Tehran, Iran, White House Photographs Collection, Courtesy of the Jimmy Carter Library

FIGURE 16 President Carter, former President Nixon, and Chinese leader Deng Xiaoping during a state dinner, January 29, 1979, White House, White House Photographs Collection, Courtesy of the Jimmy Carter Library

FIGURE 17 President Jimmy Carter and Chinese leader Deng Xiaoping at the signing of the normalization of relations between the United States and the People's Republic of China, January 31, 1979, White House, White House Photographs Collection, Courtesy of the Jimmy Carter Library

FIGURE 18 President Jimmy Carter with General Secretary Brezhnev at the signing of the SALT II agreements, June 18, 1979, Vienna, Austria, White House Photographs Collection, Courtesy of the Jimmy Carter Library

Introduction

> Whoever wishes to foresee the future must consult the past; for human events ever resemble those of preceding times. This arises from the fact that they are produced by men who ever have been, and ever shall be, animated by the same passions, and thus they necessarily have the same results.
>
> Niccolò Machiavelli

In recent years, the relative decline of the United States has been a central topic in international debates. The economic crisis has put tight constraints on Washington's maneuvering space, with obvious consequences on foreign policy. In the early 1990s the Unites States may have been dubbed the "indispensable nation." In the immediate post-9/11 years America may have enjoyed a seemingly unlimited global outreach. But in the second decade of the twenty-first century the situation appears dramatically different. The decisions on the composition and deployment of US military forces need to be closely balanced against domestic concerns. Moreover, as the crisis of the US economy has deepened, the international competitiveness of the American model has been questioned and its influence and attractiveness to the rest of the world has progressively waned.

This evolution has triggered a wave of distinguished scholarship on the weakening of the United States and of the Western world in general. Such historians as Niall Ferguson, Charles Kupchan, and Alfred McCoy have recently published books on the decline of the West (and of America, still considered the leading exponent and exporter of Western ideals and values).[1] Although they differ on which reasons triggered the

---

[1] The reference here is to these books: Niall Ferguson, *Civilization: The West and the Rest* (New York: Penguin Press, 2012); Charles Kupchan, *No One's World: The West, the*

current crisis and on the prescriptions for the future, these works all focus on the decline and eventual fall of the "American Empire" – a process considered more rapid and imminent than generally acknowledged. In a 2010 article titled "Empires Fall Abruptly, and the American Empire Is on the Brink" Ferguson, for example, argued that the US power position in the world was on the verge of collapsing because of the size of America's economic debt. This would cause cuts in defense spending, ultimately leading to the US withdrawal from global affairs.[2] Expanding the argument to include educational and military as well as negative economic trends, McCoy further asserted that "the American Century, proclaimed so triumphantly at the start of World War II, will be tattered and fading by 2025, its eighth decade, and could be history by 2030."[3] These gloomy scenarios build upon the central arguments of previous seminal works – such as Samuel Huntington's *Clash of Civilizations*[4] and Fareed Zakaria's *The Post-American World*[5] – which pose the question of whether America (and the West) can survive and redefine its power in the face of the "rise of the rest." With the expanding influence of other "civilizations" – Islamic, Chinese, Russian – and the growing economic power of China, India, Brazil, and Russia (the so-called BRICs), is the decline of the United States (and of Western civilization with it) inexorable and inevitable? How can America face these complex new challenges to its predominant power position?

In addition to global negative trends beyond American control, in the last decade the United States – already, allegedly, in decline – has had to deal with the unprecedented consequences of the transnational threat posed by international terrorism. The September 11, 2001 attacks hit and devastated American cities for the first time in their history, causing a widespread sensation of impotence and vulnerability. How could the

---

Rising Rest, and the Coming Global Turn (New York: Oxford University Press, 2012); Alfred McCoy, Joseph Fradera, and Stephen Jacobson (eds), *Endless Empire: Spain's Retreat, Europe's Eclipse, America's Decline* (Madison, WI: University of Wisconsin Press, 2012).

[2] Neil Ferguson, *The Australian*, July 29, 2010. The same argument was made at the 2010 Aspen Ideas Festival in July 2010 (see http://www.eutimes.net/2010/07/harvard-professor-warns-of-sudden-collapse-of-american-empire/).

[3] Alfred W. McCoy, "The Decline and Fall of the American Empire" in *The Nation*, December 6, 2010.

[4] Samuel P. Huntington, *The Clash of Civilizations and the Remaking of World Order* (New York: Touchstone, 1996).

[5] Fareed Zakaria, *The Post-American World. And the Rise of the Rest* (London: Penguin Books, 2009).

only remaining superpower be so surprisingly and shockingly struck by terrorists? Is the power of the United States inherently limited and helpless in face of the new security challenges of the twenty-first century?

The debate about the restraints on American resources and the limits of US power has shaken the country to its core. According to some, this is unprecedented. For the historian, however, the sense of imminent crisis, frantic overstretch, and near exhaustion is reminiscent of the late 1960s, a time when the dilemmas of the Vietnam War and growing strength of the Soviet Union unleashed the dramatic realization of the limits of American power. Those were the days when Democratic Senator William Fulbright denounced what he saw as "the arrogance of those who would make America the world's policeman."[6] Doesn't this theme resound today? What will be the future American role in global affairs, given the Afghan quagmire, the rise of other economic powers, and the domestic crisis in the United States?

Despite the radically different international context (the post–Cold War era obviously poses different types of challenges compared to the bipolar Cold War system), the themes on the decline of the United States sound as strikingly familiar when related to the debates and the issues hindering American foreign policy during the 1970s. The deterioration of the US position following the problematic involvement in the Vietnam War; the rise of other centers of economic power, a consequence of the recovery of Western Europe and Japan; the emergence of China as a potential international partner for Washington after the Sino-Soviet split; the challenge posed to US supremacy by the growth of the Soviet Union's nuclear capabilities; and the sense of crisis these issues created with the consequent need to adjust and redefine America's role in order to face the combination of all these "new" threats to its global power position are all themes that were characteristic of the debates of the 1970s. The American response to the generalized perception of decline – then and in recent years – is also somewhat similar. As will emerge in the pages of this book, the presidents of the 1970s reacted to the weakening of the US position worldwide by seeking new ways to expand the American influence (in order to counter the Soviet one). In response to the post-Vietnam forced acknowledgment of limits, America conceived different means to maintain and at times increase its global outreach. At the dawn of the twenty-first

---

[6] J. William Fulbright, *The Arrogance of Power* (New York: Random House, 1966) quoted in Dana H. Allin and Erik Jones, *Weary Policeman: American Power in an Age of Austerity* (London: Routledge – for IISS, 2012), 15.

century, the United States, far from retreating in face of the terrorist challenge, forcefully reacted and engaged in the so-called war on terror, which could be seen as another way to reassert American power, countering the image of impotence and vulnerability resulting from 9/11.

The search for the origins of some of today's most pressing issues hampering US foreign policy making was the initial trigger for this book. Can the study of America's response to its relative decline in the 1970s inform current debates and help put today's dilemmas into better perspective? Can the US involvement in the same critical "hot spots" of the world – such as Afghanistan and the Horn of Africa – and still problematic relationships – with Iran and, for different reasons, with China – be better understood by turning to the 1970s and unveiling the motivations of America's initial engagement in these areas and countries? Then, a specific interest in the 1970s – a decade which, because of its apparent contradictions and troubled legacy, distinguishes itself within the broad history of the Cold War – further and more deeply motivated this study. In fact, despite the voluminous scholarship dedicated to the Nixon administration, the debate on the objectives, meanings, and intended outcomes of the innovative policies undertaken by President Nixon is still ongoing among historians. Can the early 1970s really be considered a turning point in the evolution of the Cold War, as many scholars have argued?[7]

As pointed out by historian Robert Schulzinger, in 1972 even the critics in the United States and abroad "could only mutter and look embarrassed" as President Richard Nixon and his National Security Adviser Henry Kissinger "rewrote the script of post-World War II foreign policy."[8] However, this new course seemed not to endure the test of time. Only a few years later, Jimmy Carter was elected on the basis of a platform proclaiming far-reaching changes. At first sight, the policies of the Nixon administration – centered on a deemphasis of ideology and grounded on national interests – and those of the Carter administration – linked to democratic ideals and to the promotion and respect of human rights – are radically different. And, by the time Carter left office in 1981, nothing of the path of US-Soviet détente seemed to remain, as Ronald Reagan embraced a new Cold War posture. The evolution of American foreign policy between 1969 and 1981 was thus characterized by many ruptures

---

[7] Jussi Hanhimäki makes this basic point in the chapter "Ironies and Turning Points: Détente in Perspective" in Odd Arne Westad, *Reviewing the Cold War. Approaches, Interpretations, Theory* (London: Frank Cass Publishers, 2000).

[8] Robert Schulzinger, *Henry Kissinger: Doctor of Diplomacy* (New York: Columbia University Press, 1989), 101.

and turning points – 1969 with the election of Nixon and the pursuit of détente, 1975 with the fall of Saigon, 1979 with the Soviet invasion of Afghanistan, for example – and by the consequent calls for change and new beginnings by the incoming presidents. These allegedly abrupt shifts in the American foreign policy lines make the 1970s a particularly interesting and challenging decade to study. Behind the surface of the repeatedly proclaimed changes, did the actual policies of the United States shift accordingly? Or was there, instead, more continuity than may at first sight appear? These are some of the central issues that this book will address. By searching for the legacy of the 1970s, it will also unveil whether there any lessons to be learned from those turbulent years of decline and renewal.

RUPTURES, TURNING POINTS, ... OR MORE?

At the end of the 1960s, the changing dynamics of the international system necessarily imposed a rethinking of the US-Soviet relationship, the central aspect of American foreign policy since the beginning of the Cold War. Moscow's near attainment of nuclear parity introduced a structural change in the balance of power between the superpowers and revolutionized the basic assumptions upon which the United States had based its Cold War posture. This occurred when the bipolarity of the international system, though still fundamentally governing the international scene, appeared to be less rigid – with the emergence of an economically more powerful Western Europe and increased tensions within the Communist bloc (particularly evident after the Sino-Soviet split). At the same time, the unstable nations of the Third World, which had only recently gained their independence, offered a potential new battleground for Cold War confrontations, posing the question of how to assure America's predominant influence on an increasingly global scale. In short, the United States needed to adjust to a context in which its dominance was no longer taken for granted.

In the early 1970s, the Nixon administration responded to the changed realities of the international balance of power with the celebrated, or denigrated, policy of US-Soviet détente. This has generally been characterized as a period of relaxation of tensions between the superpowers that enabled the conclusion of significant agreements (the SALT Agreements above all); an effort that was to a large degree in vain, as the new approach to relations with Moscow started to unravel after 1973. Thus, détente has been viewed as an attempt to chart a different course, which proved unsuccessful when faced with the combination of rising domestic criticism in the United States and a new assertiveness of the Soviet Union, particularly in the Third World.

The first goal of this book is to challenge these orthodox views on détente by setting forth a particular interpretation of the Nixon administration's foreign policy. Then, on this basis, the second objective is to interrelate the policies of the three presidents of the 1970s – Nixon, Ford, and Carter – tracing lines of continuity which, to this date, have been widely ignored (rarely, in fact, have Nixon and Carter been cited as having something in common). The broader scope of the book is to propose a reflection on the meanings and implications of the continuity of US foreign policy throughout the 1970s, while assessing its impact on the overall redefinition of America's international role.

Trying to look beyond the shortcomings of a design that, for a combination of reasons, crumbled only a few years after its celebrated climax, the central questions are: Did détente really mark a "moment of beginning"[9] or were the achievements of the early 1970s merely a series of significant, albeit isolated, diplomatic breakthroughs? More broadly, in Henry Kissinger's words, did the Nixon presidency successfully respond to the challenges it faced and guide "America through the transition from dominance to leadership?"[10] Was American power, in the long run, effectively transformed as a result of the policies pursued during the 1970s? If so, then US-Soviet détente may not have been just a turning point in the evolution of the Cold War, but much more.

PERSONALITIES, IDEAS, AND POLICY MAKING

The 1970s saw the succession of three very unlike individuals to the presidency of the United States. Richard Nixon, Gerald Ford, and Jimmy Carter, in fact, had very different backgrounds, personalities, and worldviews. With extensive experience at the top level of the American government, serving as Eisenhower's vice president for two terms, Nixon had a passion for and a remarkable grasp of international affairs, coupled with an innate conspiratorial mind-set and a penchant for secrecy.[11] At

---

[9] This is a reference to Nixon's 1969 inaugural address: "Each moment in history is a fleeting time, precious and unique. But some stand out as moments of beginnings, in which courses are set that shape decades or centuries. This can be such a moment." *Public Papers of the Presidents, Richard Nixon, 1969.*

[10] Henry Kissinger, *Diplomacy* (New York: Simon & Schuster, 1994), 704.

[11] Christopher Andrew, *For the President's Eyes Only. Secret Intelligence and the American Presidency from Washington to Bush* (London: Harper Collins, 1996), 350–351.

the basis of Nixon's realistic approach to foreign relations was a deep understanding of the dynamics of geopolitics and an almost exclusive focus on the American national interest. The notions of balance of power, as an element producing stability, and of a strong America, as essential to global equilibrium, were central elements of his vision. This explained, at least in part, the choice of Henry Kissinger as his closest aid, given the Harvard professor's studies on the dynamics of the balance of power and its importance in effective foreign policy making.[12] At the same time and to a certain degree, surprisingly, the former president whom Nixon admired the most was Woodrow Wilson. Nixon considered American idealism an important feature in politics and shared Wilson's passionate internationalism. According to Nixon, the task for the American leadership was to redefine a sustainable role for an idealistic America in a new complex international environment, one in which *wilsonianism* and *realpolitik* would have to merge.[13]

This book will confirm Nixon's fundamentally pragmatic and realistic approach to the management of the relationship with the Soviet Union. The American national interest and balance of power considerations were constantly at the basis of policy making, while the idealistic component rhetorically justified the "era of negotiation." Realizing that an acknowledgment of limits was the key to the development of an innovative and effective foreign policy, the Nixon administration elaborated its major initiatives – such as the Nixon doctrine, the China opening, the SALT agreements – by deemphasizing ideology and by pragmatically focusing on America's concrete geostrategic necessities. In this process, Nixon and Kissinger revealed their awareness that geopolitical strength, or vulnerability, had become the central element around which the competition with the Soviet Union would evolve. In the age of nuclear parity, whichever side was capable of posing challenges outside the nuclear-strategic domain would, over time, accumulate enough power and influence in order to, potentially, prevail. Therefore, the Nixon administration's central objective was "to prepare America for a role novel in its history but as old as the state system: preventing the accumulation of seemingly marginal geopolitical gains which, over time, would overthrow the balance of power."[14]

---

[12] The reference here is to Kissinger's first book *A World Restored. Metternick, Castlereagh and the Problems of Peace, 1812–1822* (Boston: Houghton Mifflin, 1957).
[13] Henry Kissinger, *Diplomacy*, 705–707.
[14] Ibid, 751.

Due to the Watergate scandal, in 1974 Gerald Ford assumed the presidency under extraordinary circumstances. He was the first vice president to be appointed, not elected, and then to occupy the White House after a president's resignation. As an individual, Ford's "open and uncomplicated personality could hardly have been more different from that of his predecessor."[15] Also, his political background greatly differed from Nixon's. He had been a member of Congress for more than twenty years, including eight years as the Republican minority leader in the House of Representatives, earning a reputation for integrity and candidness. However, in foreign policy he had an almost complete lack of experience. He was thus to rely heavily on Henry Kissinger as his chief adviser. For the most part, Ford agreed with the fundamental changes at the basis of the revolutionary foreign policy he had inherited.[16] Moreover, considering the rapid and unusual transition period, he chose not to disassociate himself from the policies of his predecessor. Kissinger's initial continued presence as both secretary of state and national security adviser symbolized the general and overall continuity of American foreign policy. However, in contrast to his forerunner (Watergate and the resignation cannot cancel the achievements of the summits in Moscow and Beijing), the Ford administration's foreign policy record is not generally considered successful – with the impasse in the SALT II negotiations and the debacles in the Third World, Vietnam, and Angola in particular. In fact, by 1975 the decline of détente seemed to be inexorable. Nevertheless, this book will point to the fact that, despite the setbacks, the Nixon-Ford-Kissinger years can be treated as a continuum.

While the Ford presidency was necessarily and intrinsically related to the Nixon administration, President Carter's proclaimed intentions instead promised radical changes. Having served two terms in the Senate of the state of Georgia, then becoming governor in 1971, Carter's political career was closely linked to the state, while he was virtually unknown nationwide. However, as the scandals of the Nixon administration had not yet been overcome by the American public, being an "outsider" became an asset during the 1976 presidential campaign. The nation's recovery was the central aspect of Carter's platform, with the promise of a "competent and compassionate" government, responsive and close to

[15] John L. Gaddis, "The Statecraft of Henry Kissinger" in Gordon A. Craig and Francis L. Loewenheim (edited by), *The Diplomats 1939–1979* (Princeton, NJ: Princeton University Press, 1994), 570.
[16] John Robert Greene, *The Presidency of Gerald R. Ford* (Lawrence, KS: University Press of Kansas, 1995), 117.

the expectations of the American people. Themes which, after the election, constituted the leitmotif of the president's inaugural address.[17]

In criticizing the excessive *realpolitik* that had shaped the Nixon-Kissinger-Ford years, Carter sought to restore consensus by reinvigorating the nation's moral purpose. He wanted to lead the country in a new direction, "openly, morally, and with an absolute commitment to human rights."[18] The realistic approach to international relations was rejected. The objective, instead, had to be the creation of a more humane world order, in which the traditional American democratic values were given priority. Furthermore, the obsession with the Soviet Union no longer had to dominate American policy and each nation's distinctiveness had to be recognized and respected. Therefore, while Nixon had placed the notions of balance of power and national interest at the center of his project, Carter sought to reassert American prestige through the restoration and promotion of liberal democratic values in an international context.

The different worldview and approach to foreign policy of the Republican administrations (Nixon and Ford) and of Carter's Democratic presidency are thus indisputable. These differences inevitably influenced the choice of foreign policy advisers and the decision-making mechanisms created by each administration. The absolute centrality of the White House during the first Nixon administration resulted from the president's near obsession with secrecy and reflected a deeply rooted distrust for the departments and, in general, of the bureaucracy. As a consequence, the National Security Council emerged as the main forum for American foreign policy making, with Henry Kissinger exercising a crucial role. All the major achievements of Nixon's first term were negotiated in secret back channels in which Kissinger had unchallenged authority, reporting exclusively and directly to the president. The unfolding of the Watergate drama further enhanced Kissinger's authority, then confirmed during the Ford administration. However, as his influence expanded and he increasingly became a public figure, his freedom to operate with few domestic constraints obviously diminished. As Kissinger himself acknowledged in his memoirs, it was impossible, and not recommendable, to continue with "the Byzantine administrative procedures of the first Nixon administration."[19] To make the foreign policy achievements permanent, they would

---

[17] John Dumbrell, *The Carter Presidency. A Re-evaluation* (Manchester, England: Manchester University Press, 1993), 2.

[18] Gaddis Smith, *Morality, Reason and Power. American Diplomacy in the Carter Years* (New York: Hill and Wang, 1986), 7.

[19] Henry Kissinger, *Years of Upheaval* (London: Phoenix Press, 2000), 6.

have had to be institutionalized, with all the consequences that this would have entailed.

In contrast to the stature and preeminence of Kissinger, which had immediately emerged during the Nixon administration and was (notwithstanding the necessary adjustments) in substance maintained during the Ford years, President Carter initially underlined collegiality and joint decision making. The different viewpoints of National Security Adviser Zbigniew Brzezinski and of Secretary of State Cyrus Vance were seen as balancing and complementary in what Carter hoped would be the overall direction of American foreign policy. Brzezinski's emphasis on the primacy of power and on the containment of the Soviet Union had to be balanced by Vance's penchant for diplomacy and negotiation. The structure set up for foreign policy decision making reflected the importance of collegiality. The Policy Review Committee (PRC) was chaired by the secretary of state and the Special Coordination Committee (SCC) by the national security adviser. Both analyzed issues and assessed the various possibilities for action, which were then passed on to the president at the weekly foreign policy "breakfasts" with the secretaries of defense and state, or during the meetings of the National Security Council.

From this brief snapshot of the Republican and Democratic presidencies of the 1970s asserting that, ultimately, similarities outplayed the differences and continuity prevailed over change seems, indeed, to be a tall order. This book, however, will tackle precisely this issue. In particular, did these apparently opposite and conflicting presidencies have common elements, in terms of concrete choices made and actual policies pursued in the management of the Cold War relationship with the Soviet Union? Did Carter's promise of change translate into actual policy, or did his administration, in the long run, adopt some of the policies initially so bitterly criticized? And, if continuity can be traced, what are its broader implications for the understanding of US foreign policy during the 1970s and beyond?

While in the United States the 1970s saw the succession of three presidencies; in the Soviet Union, Leonid Brezhnev's leadership went unchallenged. Member of the Politburo of the CPSU Central Committee since 1952, Brezhnev, under the patronage of his predecessor Nikita Khrushchev, gradually became a dominant figure in the second half of the 1960s.[20]

---

[20] Odd Arne Westad, "The Fall of Détente and the Turning Tides of History" in Odd Arne Westad (ed), *The Fall of Détente. Soviet-American Relations during the Carter Years* (Oslo, Norway: Scandinavian University Press, 1997), 10.

After Khrushchev's removal from power in 1964, which he had helped orchestrate, Brezhnev assumed leadership of the party and in the course of the 1970s became the central formulator of the Soviet Union's foreign policy.[21] While "stamping his own personality on the regime to a far lesser degree than either his predecessors or his successors," Brezhnev's leadership was longer than any other, with the exception of Stalin's. Described as having an unconcealed love for luxury, an enormous ego and as "no intellectual," he nevertheless proved skillful in managing a long and much-needed period of stability. Furthermore, he succeeded in projecting to the outside world the image of the USSR "as a stable, pragmatic, and responsible superpower."[22]

From the Kremlin's point of view, an innovative and more cooperative relationship with the United States was designed to lead to the long-sought acceptance of the Soviet Union as an equal in the context of the bipolar international system. Moscow's standing in the world and its security could, indeed, only improve through this "validation of the regime."[23] Brezhnev therefore personally and politically committed himself to détente with the United States. At the same time, the Soviet Union's support for Communist-inspired "liberation" movements throughout the world would not necessarily have to diminish. In fact, interventionism to foster the development of socialism and the objectives of US-Soviet détente were not seen as irreconcilable in Moscow. Thus, in the late 1960s, a greater degree of pragmatism in the pursuit of the national interest was placed also at the center of Soviet foreign policy making. This set the stage for a potential convergence with the United States on those issues that both superpowers considered vital for their respective national security.

The chapters of this book will unequivocally confirm the absolute centrality of the Soviet Union – "Subject A" as Nixon called it[24] – in the

---

[21] After the plot against Khrushchev, Brezhnev became the general secretary of the Communist Party and Alexei Kosygin the head of the government (chairman of the Council of Ministers). In foreign affairs, Brezhnev's close political partners were Defense Minister Dimitri Ustinov, KGB Chairman Iurii Andropov, and Foreign Minister Andrei Gromyko. Brezhnev prided himself on his consultative style of leadership, in conscious contrast to his predecessors; Ibid., p. 12. However, as confirmed by all the American documents consulted, by the beginning of the 1970s the United States considered Brezhnev as its only interlocutor.
[22] William Tompson, *The Soviet Union under Brezhnev* (London: Pearson, 2003).
[23] Westad, "The Fall of Détente and the Turning Tides of History," 12–13.
[24] Address by Richard Nixon at the Bohemian Club, San Francisco, July 29, 1967. Full text available at: http://history.state.gov/historicaldocuments/frus1969–76vo1/d2.

making of American foreign policy. The US-Soviet relationship took center stage when dealing with other important world "actors" – from the self-centered shah of Iran, to the ruthless dictators of Ethiopia and Somalia, and the ambivalent Egyptian leader Anwar Sadat. The policies toward these countries were subordinated to the overriding necessities dictated by the relationship between Washington and Moscow. Even the Chinese leaders Mao Zedong, Zhou Enlai, and later Deng Xiaoping – personalities who undeniably left a mark on world affairs in their own right – will emerge in this narrative as actors in a supporting (but crucial) role in the redefinition of America's position *vis à vis* the Soviet Union.

The structure of *The Transformation of American International Power in the 1970s* reflects the chronological evolution of American foreign policy. The book is divided into two parts, the first on the Nixon-Ford years and the second on the Carter administration. An initial chapter introduces the key personalities and the basic worldviews that influenced the foreign policy making of each presidency (including Gerald Ford's). Then, the analysis focuses on some (*not* all) of the initiatives and policies that shaped the fundamental reassessment of America's standing in the world that was taking place in those years.

After an introductory chapter on the Nixon administration and its "moment of beginning," Chapters 2 (on the China opening) and 3 (on SALT and Vietnam) assess the rise of détente and point to the emergence of a complex design for the management of the relationship with the Soviet Union – a dual track in which competitive and cooperative aspects existed together and simultaneously reinforced each other. Chapter 4 analyses Nixon's relationship with the shah of Iran, with particular emphasis on the timing and scope of the president's May 1972 visit to Tehran. This confirmed the continued competitive nature of US-Soviet relations, notwithstanding the concomitant triumphs of détente. The final chapter on the Nixon administration (Chapter 5) focuses on the domestic criticism of détente and interrelates the internal challenges to the questions that surfaced during and after the 1973 October War in the Middle East. All this is set against the background of the Watergate scandal, which weakened the president's authority to defend his innovative design. Chapter 6 introduces the Ford administration and studies the unusual transition period, emphasizing continuity both in terms of personalities (Henry Kissinger above all) and policies (arms control in particular, with the Vladivostok summit). The continued ambivalence of Washington's strategy is the focus of Chapter 7, with the pursuit of a strategic dialogue with Moscow (in the context of the SALT II negotiations), though at the same time seeking to counter Soviet expansionism in Angola. The chapter (the last of Part One) also raises the question of what survived of the revolutionary policies of the early 1970s, despite the crisis of détente. From this perspective, the legacy of the Nixon-Ford-Kissinger years is described and assessed.

In Chapter 8, the personalities of the Carter administration are introduced, while analyzing the incoming presidency's ambitious new agenda. Chapters 9 (on the Horn of Africa) and 10 (on the China normalization and SALT II) analyze the administration's gradual shift from its proclaimed intentions, with the reemergence of an ambivalent dual-track policy toward the Soviet Union. Chapters 11 (on the Iranian revolution) and 12 (on the Carter doctrine) focus on Carter's definite change of stance. The study of the making of the Carter doctrine unveils the unrelenting importance and centrality of the Soviet Union for US foreign policymakers.

It is important to note that this book focuses on the transformation of American power (on the basis of the views of the main US policymakers). The impact and reactions of the policies studied on Moscow are not assessed. Therefore, the book is mainly based on American sources, only recently declassified and available for consultation at the US National Archives and presidential libraries. Moreover, this book does not study the relations between the United States and its Western Allies. In fact, the adjustments taking place within the transatlantic "community" during the 1970s, particularly in the economic-financial domain, are not part of this analysis.[25] Without diminishing the importance of the US search for means to reshape its leadership within the Western Alliance, the scope of this study is to concentrate on the relatively less-explored repercussions of the 1970s on America's even greater ambition to secure for itself the

---

[25] Transatlantic relations have been extensively studied in other contexts, for example: Jussi Hanhimäki, Benedikt Schoenborn, and Barbara Zanchetta, *Transatlantic Relations since 1945. An Introduction* (London: Routledge, 2012); Geir Lundestad, *The United States and Western Europe since 1945. From "Empire" by Invitation to Transatlantic Drift* (Oxford: Oxford University Press, 2003); Geir Lundestad (ed), *No End to Alliance. The United States and Western Europe: Past, Present and Future* (Houndmills, England: Macmillan, 1998). On US economic Cold War strategies: Alan Dobson, *United States Economic Statecraft for Survival, 1933–1991* (London: Routledge, 2002). On the economic adjustments taking place in the 1970s within the West, particularly as a consequence of Nixon's decision on the inconvertibility of the dollar see, for example: Duccio Basosi, *Il Governo del Gollaro. Interdipendenza Economica e Potere Statunitense negli Anni di Richard Nixon, 1969–1973* (Firenze, Italy: Polistampa, 2006).

role of world leader – ultimately prevailing over its global antagonist, the Soviet Union. While the US policies toward Europe during the détente years may have been geared toward maintaining the status quo of the Cold War division, in a number of other regions and areas – that constitute the focus of this book – the American policies were driven by the need and desire to fundamentally reshape the US-Soviet relationship and, with it, the global power position maintained by the United States in world affairs.

This book thus concentrates on Washington's ambivalent policies toward Moscow, with parallel cooperation, in the nuclear-strategic field, and competition, on a broad geopolitical scale. The goal is to convey a global perspective, while underlining the increased importance of the interconnection between Third World actors and great power politics. Two important regions, however, remain outside the main reach of the book: Latin America and Indochina.

Washington's role in Latin America, though crucial in the 1970s, has been left out of this analysis primarily due to the long history of US involvement in the Western Hemisphere, in decades well preceding the emergence of the Cold War.[26] The US-Latin American relationship therefore constitutes a separate story. However, it is interesting to note that many initiatives undertaken by Washington throughout the 1970s substantiate one of the main arguments of this study – that increased (though, in most cases, indirect) presence in the periphery progressively became the central aspect of America's Cold War posture.[27]

---

[26] For an overview of US-Latin American relations: Peter H. Smith, *Talons of the Eagle. Dynamics of U.S.-Latin American Relations* (New York: Oxford University Press, 2000). For a history of US interference in the orientation of the Latin American governments, even before the Cold War: David F. Schmitz, *Thank God They Are On Our Side: The United States and Right-Wing Dictatorships, 1921–1965* (Durham, NC: University of North Carolina Press, 1999). For an edited collection with contributions focusing on both the pre-Cold War and on the 1960s and 1980s: Abraham F. Lowenthal, *Exporting Democracy: The United States and Latin America* (Baltimore, MD: The John Hopkins University Press, 1991). On the US involvement in the destabilization of left-wing governments in Latin America also by tacitly supporting the terrorist subversive activities code-named "Operation Condor" see: Barbara Zanchetta, "La 'special relationship' tra Stati Uniti e America Latina e la sua 'fundamentally repugnant philosophy'" in Cricco, Guasconi, Napolitano (eds), *L'America Latina tra guerra fredda e globalizzazione* (Firenze, Italy: Polistampa, 2010).

[27] Just to cite a few examples – on US involvement in Chile: Peter Kornbluh, *The Pinochet File. A Declassified Dossier on Atrocity and Accountability* (New York: The New Press, 2003) and Jonathan Haslam, *The Nixon Administration and the Death of Allende's Chile: A case of Assisted Suicide* (London: Verso Press, 2005). On US involvement in Nicaragua: Robert Pastor, *Not Condemned to Repetition: The United States and*

The Vietnam War, though constantly remaining in the background of the narrative, and in some cases emerging directly (as in Chapter 3, for example), could not constitute the bulk of analysis for a combination of reasons: first, the motivations leading to the initial US involvement in Indochina predate the period examined here; second, due to the massive scholarly attention dedicated to the subject,[28] an in-depth focus in this context would have appeared superfluous; lastly, but most importantly, because this study is based on the assumption – that is taken as a fact – that the Vietnam trauma was one of the key aspects that triggered the reflections on American vulnerability and relative decline.[29] It is this unprecedented acknowledgment of limits on the part of the American leadership that is at the core of this book.

Nicaragua, Second Edition (Boulder, CO: Westview Press, 2002) and Anthony Lake, *Somoza Falling* (Amherst, MA: University of Massachusetts Press, 1990).

[28] Just to cite a few examples of the massive literature on Vietnam – for the background and general overview of American involvement: George C. Herring, *America's Longest War: The United States and Vietnam, 1950–1975* (New York: McGraw-Hill, 2001); Marilyn Young, *The Vietnam Wars, 1945–1990* (New York: Harper Perennial, 1991); Robert S. McNamara, *In Retrospect: The Tragedy and Lessons of Vietnam* (New York: Vintage Books, 1996). On the Nixon administration and Vietnam: Jeffrey Kimball, *Nixon's Vietnam War* (Lawrence, KS: University Press of Kansas, 2002); Larry Berman, *No Peace, No Honor: Nixon, Kissinger and the Betrayal in Vietnam* (New York: Touchstone, 2002).

[29] The Nixon administration's perception of relative decline has been in part studied by Robert Litwak in *Détente and the Nixon Doctrine. American Foreign Policy and the Pursuit of Stability, 1969–1976* (Cambridge, England: Cambridge University Press, 1984). Differentiating itself from Litwak's, this book offers a more in-depth analysis of Nixon's policies, benefiting from the primary documentation now available. Also, the scope of this study is broader, focusing on a longer time period and on the "legacies" of the Nixon-Ford years.

PART ONE

THE REMAKING OF AMERICAN GLOBAL POWER, 1969–1976

I

The Nixon Administration and a "Moment of Beginning"

> Each moment in history is a fleeting time, precious and unique. But some stand out as moments of beginnings, in which courses are set that shape decades or centuries. This can be such a moment.
> Richard Nixon's Inaugural Address, 1969

> We are not involved in the world because we have commitments; we have commitments because we are involved. Our interests must shape our commitments, rather than the other way around.
> Richard Nixon, *A New Strategy for Peace*, 1970

Was a "moment of beginning" really necessary in January 1969, when Richard Nixon, after a long career in politics and eight years as Eisenhower's vice president, started his first term in office as president of the United States of America? What was so exceptional in the challenges the new administration had to face?

During the first two decades of the Cold War, the United States had enjoyed a uniquely dominant position on the global scene. The Second World War had drained the resources and had devastated both America's industrialized allies and its future Cold War adversaries. Conversely, the US territory had been untouched by the conflict, while the American economy had expanded as a result of the wartime effort. After the war, US military forces remained in Europe and Asia, creating a network of bases from which Washington could project its military and political power worldwide. American ascendancy as the leader of the "free world" had gone unchallenged. The new superpower status of the United States was sustained also by domestic stability and a general popular support for its foreign policy. Therefore, the United States had not only possessed the sinews of power, but it was also perceived as possessing them, an equally if not more important factor. As President Truman's Secretary of State Dean Acheson put it, in addition to its unmatched power and prestige America also enjoyed "the shadow cast by power."[1] Consequently, the expectation – both in the United States and abroad – had been that, as famously stated by President John F. Kennedy, America could "pay any price, bear any burden, meet any hardship, support any friend, oppose any foe, in order to assure the survival and the success of liberty."[2]

However, by 1968 these perceptions of strength had started to waver. The Tet offensive, considered by many the beginning of the end of the Vietnam War; President Johnson's decision to withdraw from the presidential race; the assassinations of Martin Luther King Jr. and of Robert Kennedy; a narrowly won presidential election, which brought Richard Nixon to the White House; and renewed fierce anti-Vietnam War protests were events that signaled the emergence of foreign and domestic challenges unforeseen only a few years earlier. They were symptomatic of a deeper, historic change in America's relative power position in global affairs. Indeed, in the late 1960s a combination of elements challenged the dominant position previously held by the United States: the different power relationships within the Western world; the evolution of the Communist bloc and the end of the alliance between China and the Soviet Union; the consequences of the decolonization process; and the emergence of an economically and militarily more powerful Soviet Union.

With the help of US economic aid, America's industrialized allies had fully recovered from the war. Western Europe and Japan had in fact regained economic strength and had begun to question American commercial predominance. Renewed economic power brought with it a sense of political independence and a diminished willingness to accept American hegemony. Tensions thus surfaced within the Western camp, which necessarily imposed a reflection in Washington on how to maintain its leadership despite the shifting balance of power.[3]

At the same time, the United States had to reassess its relationship with the "other side" – the Communist bloc. In the early Cold War

---

[1] Dean Acheson, *Present at the Creation: My Years in the State Department* (New York: W. W. Norton & Company, 1987), 405.
[2] John F. Kennedy Inaugural Address, January 20, 1961.
[3] For the evolution of the Transatlantic relationship see, for example, Jussi Hanhimäki, Benedikt Schoenborn, Barbara Zanchetta, *Transatlantic Relations since 1945: An Introduction* (London: Routledge, 2012).

years, America had faced a monolithic camp (or at least so it was perceived in Washington) but by the time Nixon entered office the nature of that coalition had radically changed. Several communist countries had become more powerful but communist unity and solidarity had faded away. After 1945, the Red Army had intervened three times against its own allies – in Eastern Germany in 1953, in Hungary in 1956, and in Czechoslovakia in 1968. In addition, and from Washington's viewpoint most importantly, the Soviet Union and the People's Republic of China, tied by an alliance in 1950, had become adversaries. The United States had to adjust its policies to this radically different scenario.[4]

Moreover, by the late 1960s the anticolonial movement had brought the Third World into existence. The new governments were in the hands of nationalist leaders determined to maintain their independence. In some cases this meant a certain distance from the United States, or nonalignment, while in others it led to open anti-Americanism. Membership in the United Nations had doubled, and then tripled, thus destroying the almost automatic pro-American majority of the 1950s. Many of the new countries were economically weak and politically unstable. Their fragility provided opportunities for the expansion of Soviet influence and, from America's point of view, a compromise needed to be found between overextension and neglect.[5]

The decline of America's relative power position, a consequence of these broad shifts in the nature of the international system, was exacerbated by the strengthening of the Soviet Union. Initially with the nuclear monopoly, and then with a clear-cut superiority, the United States had based its Cold War posture on the assumption that it would maintain the lead in the nuclear arms race. Throughout the 1960s, however, the Soviet Union had invested massively in the development of its nuclear arsenal. When Nixon entered office, analysts assessed that the American and Soviet nuclear forces were approaching parity (in terms of destructive power, while obviously remaining very different in their composition). This imposed a broad and wide-ranging revision of America's strategic

---

[4] On the rise and fall of the Sino-Soviet alliance see, for example, Odd Arne Westad, *Brothers in Arms: The Rise and Fall of the Sino-Soviet Alliance, 1945–1963* (Washington, DC: Woodrow Wilson Center Press, 1998).

[5] For a comprehensive analysis of the Cold War in the Third World: Odd Arne Westad, *The Global Cold War. Third World Interventions and the Making of Our Times* (New York: Cambridge University Press, 2005).

posture, ultimately leading to the beginning of arms control negotiations with the Soviet Union.[6]

Added to these systemic changes, largely beyond US control – the recovery of Europe and Japan, the Sino-Soviet split, the birth of the Third World, and the growth of Soviet power – the acknowledgment of the limits of American power was a direct consequence of the Vietnam War. Its effects were so pervasive that it is considered a watershed in the evolution of US foreign policy. The period following the war is in fact referred to as the post-Vietnam era. Domestically, the war drained resources and disrupted US economic growth, thus irreparably damaging one of the foundations of American power. Internationally, Washington's failure to win the war or to bring peace severely damaged US prestige worldwide, leading other nations to question their perceptions of American strength and effective decision making. Vietnam also had traumatic effects on US society, reducing public support for the use of military power as an instrument of foreign policy. The result was a negative attitude in the American Congress on defense spending, which led to cuts in national defense budgets at a time when the Soviet Union was investing in its military buildup. Moreover, Vietnam destroyed the public consensus on the policy of containment, which since the beginning of the Cold War had been the central pillar of US foreign policy.

For the combination of all these reasons, when Richard Nixon entered office in January 1969, American foreign policy called for a comprehensive new design.[7] At the beginning of the administration, both the president and his national security adviser, Henry Kissinger, considered Vietnam the central issue upon which the reestablishment of American credibility and prestige greatly depended.[8] Both in fact "understood that the crucial question was whether the US could emerge from Vietnam strong enough to operate effectively in a changing international environment in which American power was seriously weakened and the power of its principal adversary, the USSR, had grown significantly."[9]

---

[6] On the origins and evolution of arms control negotiations with the Soviet Union, see Chapter 3.
[7] Jussi Hanhimäki, *The Flawed Architect, Henry Kissinger and American Foreign Policy* (New York: Oxford University Press, 2004), 28–31.
[8] Hanhimäki, *The Flawed Architect*, 39; Robert Dallek, *Nixon and Kissinger. Partners in Power* (New York: Harper Collins, 2007), 67–68, 105–106, 169.
[9] William Hyland, *Mortal Rivals. Superpower Relations from Nixon to Reagan* (New York: Random House, 1987), 19.

In short, therefore, the United States had to adapt to a situation in which its dominance was no longer taken for granted.[10] The basic pillars of the strategy of containment that had guided US policy since the late 1940s – American strategic superiority, almost unlimited resources, US predominance in the Western camp, and domestic consensus and stability – were being seriously questioned.[11] As historian Robert Litwak put it, "the end of the postwar era positioned the United States at a political and, perhaps more significantly, a psychological crossroad."[12] A "moment of beginning" was thus a necessity more than a choice.

A NEW "ERA OF NEGOTIATION"

The Nixon administration's foreign policy was, by various standards, ground breaking. Among its achievements were the first visit of an American president to the People's Republic of China, the first arms control treaty with the Soviet Union, and – as a result of Kissinger's shuttle diplomacy – a unique position for the United States in the Middle East. The debate among scholars on the motivations and scope of the Nixon administration's innovative policies is still ongoing.[13] According to some, the era of summit diplomacy and nuclear arms control negotiations between the United States and the Soviet Union was but a passing phase in the history of the Cold War, a momentary pause in the unrelenting tension between the superpowers. For others, détente was simply an American strategy conceived in order to find an acceptable exit from Vietnam. Others still consider the early 1970s an authentic turning

---

[10] John L. Gaddis, "The Statecraft of Henry Kissinger" in Gordon A. Craig and Francis L. Loewenheim (edited by), *The Diplomats 1939–1979* (Princeton, NJ: Princeton University Press, 1994), 570.
[11] Mario Del Pero, *The Eccentric Realist. Henry Kissinger and American Foreign Policy* (Ithaca, NY: Cornell University Press, 2010), Chapter 1.
[12] Robert S. Litwak, *Détente and the Nixon Doctrine. American Foreign Policy and the Pursuit of Stability, 1969–1976* (New York: Cambridge University Press, 1984), 2.
[13] Olav Njolstad has summarized the debate on détente, which rotates around four viewpoints that try to explain its downfall, or "failure": (1) the failure of détente was a consequence of its own contradictions, the flaws in its design and implementation; (2) the collapse of détente was due to the fact that one party, or both, pursued objectives that were incompatible with the rules and spirit of détente; (3) détente ultimately fell victim to the rise of conservatism in the United States; (4) détente was torn apart by more fundamental forces – ideological, socioeconomic, and military and the underlining bipolarity of the international system; Olav Njolstad, "The collapse of superpower détente, 1975–1980" in Leffler and Westad, *The Cambridge History of the Cold War* (Cambridge, England: Cambridge University Press, 2010), 135–136.

point that marked the beginning of the end of the Cold War. In broader terms, scholars have debated on the ultimate goals of the policy. Was it a "conservative"[14] policy meant to stabilize the bipolar relationship, thus indefinitely prolonging the Cold War order? Or was it a revolutionary policy designed to overcome the Cold War divisions?[15]

The interpretation of the Nixon administration's policies set forth in this book shares the view of some of the more recent scholarly works on the period: that the policy of détente was not intended as a means to overcome the Cold War antagonism.[16] As will repeatedly surface in the following chapters, it was evident that Nixon and Kissinger operated within the limits and dynamics of the bipolar system that they had inherited. Their policies were conceived as a means to better manage the rivalry with their long-time adversary, not as a way for overcoming it. Their methods were new, but their mind-set was not.

Acknowledging that détente was in essence a Cold War strategy – and therefore in this sense a conservative policy – does not, however, automatically lead to the assertion that it was uniquely designed to stabilize the international system, or to indefinitely accept the status quo. On this point this book clearly differentiates itself from other accounts of US-Soviet détente because it sets forth a particular interpretation of détente as an inherently dualistic policy. One pillar was designed to accept the Soviet Union's superpower status through negotiations. This resulted in cooperation aimed at stabilizing the nuclear arms race. A second aspect instead assigned greater importance to the American presence or influence in the periphery (most notably in areas of the Third World). This dual-track policy ultimately transformed the nature of the Cold War and, with it, the way in which American power was exercised worldwide. Therefore, according to the interpretation of détente set forth in this book, Nixon and Kissinger tried both to stabilize the superpower relationship and to transform it. Their policies were a response to the realities of the 1970s, a way of adapting to the changed power relationships of the international

---

[14] The reference here is to Jeremi Suri's description of Nixon and Kissinger's policy as aimed at maintaining what he defined as "a conservative world order" in his book *Power and Protest: Global Revolution and the Rise of Détente* (Cambridge, MA: Harvard University Press, 2003), 258.

[15] Particularly because of the impact of détente in Europe – not a topic of this book – scholars have debated on its role in bringing about the end of the Cold War.

[16] Such a view emerges, for example, in Jussi Hanhimäki's article "Conservative goals, revolutionary outcomes" in *Cold War History*, Volume 8, Number 4, November 2008.

system, while effectively restoring American power, prestige, and global leadership.

This leads to the second distinctive feature of this narrative, which is mainly an analysis of the effects of the policy of détente on the United States itself. The rich literature on the Nixon years has focused almost exclusively on the foreign goals of the administration's policy and on its impact on the international system.[17] But how did the innovations introduced by Nixon influence the reconceptualization of US power ongoing in those years?

From the beginning, Nixon and Kissinger's objective was to reestablish the primacy of the United States. Because this could no longer be mainly based on America's strategic superiority, the geopolitical dimension of power became increasingly important. This was the real revolution introduced by Nixon and Kissinger, which brought a whole series of unintended and long-lasting consequences. As Kissinger later stated:

There is in America an idealistic tradition that sees foreign policy as a contest between good and evil. There is a pragmatic tradition that seeks to solve 'problems' as they arise. There is a legalistic tradition that treats international issues as juridical cases. There is no geopolitical tradition.[18]

The Nixon administration tried to fill this "gap" and chose to rely on geopolitics as the main parameter to reassert US power worldwide. This was a way to adjust to the post-Vietnam retrenchment, while acknowledging the unprecedented increase in Soviet power. An essential component of this new approach to foreign policy making was a more realistic definition of American interests. The universalism of the early Cold War years was no longer appropriate in the complex world of the 1970s. Threats to American national interests had to be assessed carefully and pragmatically, and then policies had to be based on the capacity of the United States to respond at an acceptable risk and cost.

This approach shaped the administration's willingness to negotiate with the Soviet Union, the "new era of negotiation" called for by Nixon in his inaugural address. There were to be no illusions: Profound

---

[17] Emblematic in this sense is the special issue of *Cold War History* in which such scholars as Noam Kochavi, Vladislav Zubok, Jussi Hanhimäki, Thomas Schwartz, and Jeremi Suri assess if and in what ways détente impacted on the international system to the point of having played a role in the end of the Cold War: *Cold War History*, Volume 8, Number 4, November 2008.

[18] Quoted in Terry L. Diebel, *Presidents, Public Opinion and Power. The Nixon, Carter and Reagan Years,* Foreign Policy Association, Headline Series No. 280, April 1987.

ideological differences and divergent interests still separated the United States and the Soviet Union. However, Moscow's increased nuclear capability imposed the need to consider the advantages of negotiating for the limitation of strategic nuclear weapons. It was in America's interest to put emphasis on negotiation, and no longer on confrontation.[19]

An American version of *realpolitik* was therefore in the making. The administration's first foreign policy report to Congress summed this up:

> We will regard our Communist adversaries first and foremost as nations pursuing their own interests as they perceive these interests, just as we follow our interests as we see them. We will judge them by their actions as we expect to be judged by our own. Specific agreements, and the structure of peace they help build, will come from a realistic accommodation of conflicting interests.[20]

For the first time, an American administration openly maintained that interests, and not ideals, had to be placed at the center of policy making, even when dealing with communist adversaries. A dose of realism coupled with more energetic, effective diplomacy had to be the key elements of negotiations. Between 1969 and 1972 this enabled the opening of a dialogue with both communist "giants" – the People's Republic of China and the Soviet Union – crucial building blocks of Nixon's "moment of beginning."

THE NIXON-KISSINGER STRATEGY

In order to deal with the decline of American power, the Nixon administration designed a sophisticated strategy, with individual moves orchestrated into an overall framework. The construction of a new relationship with the People's Republic of China (Chapter 2) proceeded in parallel with, and gave impetus to, the elaboration of US-Soviet détente and the signing of SALT I (Chapter 3). The administration's China policy can be interpreted in different ways – as a means to find an end to the Vietnam War; as a dramatic move to convince the US public that America, under Nixon's leadership, once again had the capacity to act impressively on the world stage, with all the related domestic political benefits for the presidency; and as a way of giving concrete substance to the concept of an emerging multipolar world order that the administration had called for. However, Chapter 2 will unequivocally show that the main purpose

---

[19] "A New Strategy for Peace" in *Setting the Course: The First Year. Major Policy Statements by President Richard Nixon* (New York: Funk and Wagnalls, 1970).
[20] Quoted in Hanhimäki, *The Flawed Architect*, 66.

of the China opening was to put pressure on the Soviet Union. China was the Kremlin's most immediate security concern and the prospect of a US-Chinese strategic partnership, which encircled the Soviets on two fronts, was the worst possible scenario for Moscow. Geopolitics at its boldest, the opening to China would reconfigure the global balance of power in favor of the United States.

Nixon and Kissinger's foreign policy vision was, in fact, clearly Soviet-centric. The arms control dialogue – a central piece of US-Soviet détente and of the Nixon-Kissinger strategy – was designed to put limits on the Soviet military buildup. Nixon considered these negotiations crucial and wanted them to succeed but, at the same time, he upheld the competitive part of détente by brutally responding to the North Vietnamese offensive in May 1972 (Chapter 3). Therefore, resisting Soviet geopolitical gains was a constant priority for Washington, even at the height of détente and well before the competitive aspect of détente emerged publicly and dramatically during the October War in the Middle East (Chapter 5).

Another essential element of the dual-track policy pursued by the administration was limiting US commitments abroad without yielding to Soviet expansionism. Until the late 1960s, US foreign policy had been based on America's predominant power and on the undertaking of the primary responsibility as the leader and defender of the free world. Strategies were designed in Washington and then implemented directly, with only a limited role assigned to local or regional powers. Throughout the first decades of the Cold War, this had led the United States into maintaining a strong military presence abroad, and to massive deployments in cases of crisis (the wars in Korea and Vietnam were emblematic). However, the Vietnam debacle had unveiled the dilemmas related to America's overextension. How could the United States maintain its global role while at the same time coming to terms with the limits of American power? How could the United States remain the leader of the Western world even without a direct presence worldwide?

President Nixon's response to these questions was apparently simple: The United States would maintain its major commitment in defense of the free world but each individual country had to assume a greater responsibility in defending its internal security (except in the case of a threat involving nuclear weapons).[21] This was the core concept of what came to be

---

[21] "Edited Excerpts from an Informal Background Briefing and Press Conference on the Island of Guam July 25, 1969" in *Setting the Course: The First Year. Major Policy Statements by President Richard Nixon* (New York: Funk and Wagnalls, 1970).

labeled as the Nixon doctrine: America had no intention of withdrawing or of diminishing its global responsibilities. But it was necessary to define a more balanced role for the United States, one that would allow for more credible and effective leadership. In concrete terms, this meant transferring resources to local leaders in order to boost their capacity to defend themselves, while simultaneously diminishing America's direct presence.[22] This was the logic that would shape the "Vietnamization" of the conflict in Indochina and, subsequently, the US posture in various parts of the world, most notably in the Middle East. As demonstrated by the unique relationship created between Nixon and the shah of Iran (Chapter 4), it was on the basis of this scheme that the United States would continue to resist the expansion of the Soviet Union's influence.

With these three pillars – the opening to China, the arms control negotiations with the Soviet Union, and resisting the Soviet Union's geopolitical expansion through the Nixon doctrine – the administration sought to restore US power and face the new, unprecedented challenges to America's global position. Rather than seeking to establish if Nixon and Kissinger were successful in their endeavor or not, the main scope of this book is to discover if, and how, their innovative approach impacted on the remaking of American international power and on the evolution of US foreign policy.

THE NIXON WHITE HOUSE

On January 20, 1969, Richard Nixon was proclaimed the thirty-seventh president of the United States. The inauguration ceremony took place without the traditional huge crowds, in a climate of evident popular detachment. Around 250,000 people attended the inaugural parade, compared to the over one million present for the inauguration of President Johnson. In order to protect the incoming president and first lady from demonstrators, the secret service invited them to remain inside the presidential limousine (closing the sun roof of the car). Along the route, after a few blocks of friendly cheering crowds, Nixon could see protest signs waving above the double line of police that struggled to keep the protesters back. A group lifted a Vietcong flag, while others shuffled to tear it down.[23] The

---

[22] For reference on the making of the Nixon doctrine: Melvin R. Laird, *The Nixon Doctrine* (Washington, DC: American Enterprise Institute for Public Policy Research, 1972).
[23] Richard M. Nixon, *RN: The Memoirs of Richard Nixon* (New York: Touchstone, 1990), 366.

country was deeply divided, public opinion demoralized and discouraged. A decade that had started under the banner of reasserting American pride was coming to an end in a climate of national tragedy.

In the presidential race, Nixon had defeated rival Democrat Hubert Humphrey with 302 electoral votes out of 538, but with only 43.4 percent of the popular vote – the lowest percentage obtained by a US president since the election of Woodrow Wilson in 1912.[24] In a dramatic moment of its history, America therefore found itself led by a narrowly elected president whose image had been tarnished by a defeat (in 1960 against John F. Kennedy). Apart from voting in favor of a way out of Vietnam – Nixon had promised to have a secret plan to end the war – Americans were confused and distraught. As one observer noted on Inauguration Day, Nixon's future task had to be one of a symphony conductor that would "set a divided people marching to a new music."[25] The public longed for a return to the "normality" of the previous decades. In January 1969, no one could imagine the theatrical high points of the triumphant foreign policy that were to come.

Nor could these have been easily anticipated, considering Richard Nixon's political background. Coming from a poor family – his father owned a gas station and grocery store in the small town of Whittier, California – Nixon had built his career, first in the House then in the Senate, and finally as Eisenhower's vice president, around the image of the ordinary, self-made American. Identifying with the public mood of the early Cold War years, he ably, cunningly, and often deceitfully made his way up the political ladder, building the reputation of a hard-liner who was uncompromisingly anticommunist. Nixon had emerged as a national figure in the early 1950s during the congressional investigation against Alger Hiss, who was convicted of perjury in January 1950 because of his alleged procommunist activities.[26] During the same period, Nixon's bid for the Senate seat (which he obtained) became infamous because of the aggressive charges against rival Helen Douglas, tarred as a communist sympathizer, "pink down to her underwear."[27] The vice-presidential

---

[24] For a comprehensive study of the 1968 presidential election – including the impact of the Vietnam War on the campaign and the election itself – see Melvin Small, "The Election of 1968" in *Diplomatic History*, Vol. 28, No. 4 (September 2004).
[25] Russel Baker, "Observer: Inaugurations are Rededications," *The New York Times*, January 20, 1969.
[26] Conrad Black, *Richard Milhous Nixon: The Invincible Quest* (London: Quercus, 2007), Parts I and II; Steven E. Ambrose, *Nixon: The Education of a Politician*, 1913–1962 (New York: Touchstone, 1987), 34–249.
[27] Cited in Conrad Black, *Richard Milhous Nixon: The Invincible Quest*, 162.

years and the 1960 election campaign did not change Nixon's image. Paradoxically, his reputation – solidly grounded on undisputable anti-communist credentials – would aid him in achieving some of the objectives advocated by his political adversaries (but that had been, until then, unfeasible): an opening to China and successful arms control negotiations with the Soviet Union.

For the Nixon administration, undertaking a courageous foreign policy at a time when national consensus was at a low point in practice meant that the White House had to substitute its will for that of the nation. Nixon's response to the post-Vietnam domestic disarray was, in essence, to ignore it, keeping the bureaucracy and Congress in the dark and assuming that political decisions imposed top down were the best way to defend and reassert US national interests. Policy making was thus centralized in the White House, using methods that were highly personalized, secretive, and authoritarian.

Accordingly, Nixon introduced some structural changes to the US foreign policy-making process.[28] During one of the first meetings with Kissinger, the president-elect stated that in order "to give the people of this country the foreign policy they want" it would be necessary to "revitalize" the National Security Council and shift the decision-making center of gravity away from the State Department in favor of the White House.[29] Consequently, Kissinger designed a plan – which Nixon subsequently approved – that would ensure the White House domination of foreign policy making.[30]

The centrality of the White House entailed a predominant position for the national security adviser, with a diminished role of the two other main foreign policy advisers – the secretaries of state and defense. For the position of secretary of state – traditionally the leading foreign policy post – Nixon appointed William P. Rogers, a New York attorney who had been Eisenhower's attorney general and a Nixon friend and ally during the 1950s. Rogers's lack of expertise and background in foreign affairs was, ironically, the main reason for his appointment. As Nixon told Kissinger, "Rogers's unfamiliarity with the subject was an asset because it guaranteed that policy direction would remain in the White House." To implement his design, the president also needed a reliable secretary of defense.

[28] For a study on Nixon's decision-making process: Asaf Siniver, *Nixon, Kissinger and the US Foreign Policy Making. A Machinery of Crisis* (New York: Cambridge University Press, 2008).
[29] Litwak, *Détente and the Nixon Doctrine*, 64.
[30] Dallek, *Nixon and Kissinger*, 84–85.

He did not search for a figure with high visibility and influence (as had been the case of Robert McNamara during the Kennedy years), but rather an administrator who would aid in the relationship with Congress (which was under Democratic control). Eventually, Nixon picked Melvin Laird, a sixteen-year Republican congressman from Wisconsin, considered an expert on defense appropriations (a topic of crucial importance at a time of increased cuts in defense budgets).[31]

The creation of a secret decision-making system that rotated around an expanded and increasingly influential National Security Council would, in the brief timespan of a few years, enable the NSC adviser – Henry Kissinger – to emerge as the central figure in the shaping of American foreign policy. The influence of the German-born, former Harvard academic would, in fact, expand to an unprecedented degree. Stretching well beyond the mandate of the NSC adviser (and later of the secretary of state), Kissinger's impact on the making of US foreign policy was so great that historians often refer to the Nixon and Ford administrations as "the Kissinger years."[32]

While the expansion of Kissinger's influence – and his ultimate almost total control of US policy – was hardly foreseeable at the start (and no one could anticipate the Watergate scandal, which contributed to further enhancing Kissinger's role), the structure that permitted his rise to power was in place from the beginning. The plan was drafted by Morton Halperin, Kissinger's former Harvard colleague, and approved on Inauguration Day 1969. It created a network of interagency committees below the NSC level. The Interdepartmental Groups and Under Secretaries Committee (both composed of State Department experts), instead of reporting to each other (as was customary under previous presidencies) were placed under the direction of the Senior Review Group, chaired by the NSC adviser. In addition to supervising the activities of the Interdepartmental Groups, that were to produce National Security Study Memoranda, Kissinger also chaired a number of other specialized committees through which the major foreign policy decisions of the Nixon

---

[31] Dallek, *Nixon and Kissinger*, 83–84.
[32] The massive literature on the Kissinger years is summarized by Jussi Hanhimäki in "Dr. Kissinger or Mr. Henry? Kissingerology, Thirty Years and Counting" in *Diplomatic History* Vol. 27, No. 5 (November 2003). Henry Kissinger continues to attract the attention of scholars, who seem to constantly unveil different angles from which to study his policies. The most recent example is Barbara Keys's Bernath Lecture article "Henry Kissinger: The Emotional Statesman," which examines the influence of emotions and beliefs on some of Kissinger's choices; *Diplomatic History*, Vol. 35, No. 4 (September 2011).

administration would be made (such as the Washington Special Actions Group, the Verification Panel, the 40 Committee, and others).[33] It was a highly centralized and hierarchical structure. As a member of the NSC summed it up, "everyone reports to Kissinger, and only Kissinger reports to the president."[34]

Although these formal mechanisms certainly contributed to the unprecedented expansion of the NSC's power and influence, the emergence of Kissinger's unchallenged authority was a consequence of his skilled personal diplomacy and secret back-channel negotiations, obviously initiated with Nixon's consent. In fact, the famous "channel" – the direct line of communication with the Soviet leaders – was called for by Nixon during the first meeting with Soviet ambassador Anatoly Dobrynin in February 1969. It later became the forum for the discussion of the most important issues of the US-Soviet relationship.

The channel operated on two levels: a direct communication line between Nixon and Brezhnev and a second, more frequent one, for the conversations between Kissinger and Dobrynin. The exchanges between Nixon and Brezhnev provided the tone and framework for subsequent negotiations and became increasingly intense during crises. On the American side, the messages were drafted by NSC members (and chief aides to Kissinger) Helmut Sonnenfelt and William Hyland, or by Kissinger himself, and then approved by Nixon. The second and more regular forum was between Kissinger and Dobrynin, who generally met in the Map Room of the White House residence. In Kissinger's words, the location was "sheltered from the outside world by verdant bushes, creating an atmosphere of seclusion." Initially, the discussions focused on the general state of US-Soviet relations, Vietnam and, later, on strategic arms control. Eventually, the channel became the venue for some of the administration's most important breakthroughs, such as the May 1971 agreement to proceed simultaneously with defensive and offensive limitations in SALT; a decision that led to the successful outcome of SALT I

---

[33] The Washington Special Actions Group was created in April 1969 for crisis management and/or contingency planning (it oversaw management of the Jordanian crisis of 1970 and of the Indo-Pakistan War in 1971, for example); the Verification Panel was established in July 1969 as a database for the conduct of strategic arms control negotiations; the 40 Committee was the group authorized to approve covert intelligence operations (similar committees had existed before, Nixon renamed the 303 Committee, operational under the Eisenhower administration, the 40 Committee in early 1970). Other committees chaired by Kissinger included the Intelligence Committee and a special committee to supervise the developments in Vietnam.

[34] Litwak, *Détente and the Nixon Doctrine*, 67–73.

in 1972 (the channel also allowed the conclusion of the negotiations on Berlin, another landmark agreement of the Nixon years).[35]

However, as Kissinger himself later acknowledged, this system was inherently flawed:

> There were precedents for my role in the first Nixon White House in the relationship between Woodrow Wilson and Colonel House or between Franklin Roosevelt and his intimate Harry Hopkins. Undoubtedly, Nixon, with my collaboration, carried the domination of the White House to unprecedented lengths. Much was achieved, but the procedural and human cost was high. It was a pattern that emerged in unique circumstances, not a precedent for the future.[36]

Unfortunately, this "closed, two-man system" ultimately denied the Nixon-Kissinger strategy – and the successes that it achieved – the most important constituency: Congress and the American people.[37]

The Nixon administration entered office with the pledge to transform the theory and the practice of American foreign policy. Scholars have focused widely on the origins of Nixon and Kissinger's innovative design and on how the ideas they had prior to assuming office influenced and shaped the making of US-Soviet détente (and the opening to the People's Republic of China).[38] Suffice it here to underline only a few essentials, such as the importance Nixon assigned to the realistic assessment of the national interest and his passion and deep knowledge of foreign policy (not a typical characteristic of US presidents). These elements had clearly surfaced during his years as Eisenhower's vice president. Nixon's inclinations were well-

---

[35] Douglas E. Selvage and David C. Geyer (eds), *Soviet-American Relations. The Détente Years, 1969–1972* (Washigton, DC: United States Government Printing Office, 2007), forward by Henry Kissinger, xv-xvi.
[36] Ibid, xv.
[37] Litwak, *Détente and the Nixon Doctrine*, 72–73.
[38] The many biographies of Nixon have studied how his early life shaped his views as a politician, for example: Stephen Ambrose, *Nixon: The Education of a Politician, 1913–1962* (New York: Simon & Schuster, 1987); Jonathan Aitken, *Nixon. A Life* (Washington, DC: Regnery Publishing Inc, 1993); Richard Reeves, *President Nixon. Alone in the White House* (New York: Simon and Schuster, 2001). Similarly, the numerous biographies of Henry Kissinger dealt with the topic, for example: Robert Schulzinger, *Henry Kissinger: Doctor of Diplomacy* (New York: Columbia University Press, 1989); Walter Isaacson, *Kissinger* (New York: Simon and Schuster, 1992). In particular, and more recently, Jeremi Suri has comprehensively reassessed how Kissinger's background shaped the views he subsequently applied when in office in *Henry Kissinger and the American Century* (Cambridge, MA: Belknap Press, 2007). Jussi Hanhimäki also studies Kissinger's life before entering office in the opening chapter of *The Flawed Architect*, 1–16. Robert Dallek assesses both Nixon and Kissinger's background in the first two chapters of *Nixon and Kissinger*, 3–59.

complemented by Kissinger's pre-1969 academic studies on the dynamics of power, which clearly revealed a bias for great power diplomacy. Kissinger had also repeatedly called for a focus on "gray areas" – that is, on local conflicts – and on the importance of the geopolitical dimension of the rivalry between nations. Both Nixon and Kissinger (while for different reasons) had an inherent distrust of the bureaucracy and a penchant for secrecy. Both sought to remove the "obstacle" of Vietnam in order to be able to rechart the broader lines of US foreign policy and restore American power and prestige worldwide.

Leaving aside the – in other contexts interesting – discussion on the origins of the Nixon-Kissinger strategy and the debate on which one of the two chief architects of détente had a greater influence on the making of policy, the central theme of this book rotates around these main points: Did Nixon and Kissinger really transform the foundations of US foreign policy? And, if they did even only partially, what was the impact of the changes they introduced on the overall exercise of American power?

2

The Diplomatic Revolution

The China Opening

> Taking the long view, we simply cannot afford to leave China forever outside the family of nations, there to nurture its fantasies, cherish its hates and threaten its neighbors. There is no place on this small planet for a billion of its potentially most able people to live in angry isolation.
>
> Richard Nixon in *Foreign Affairs*, 1967

> We must not forget China. We must always seek opportunities to talk with her, as with the USSR (...). We must not only watch for changes. We must seek to make changes.[1]
>
> Richard Nixon in September 1968, as the Republican candidate to the presidency

On October 1, 1949, standing at the Gate of Heavenly Peace at the entrance of the Old Forbidden City in Beijing, communist leader Mao Zedong proclaimed the birth of the People's Republic of China. As the remnants of Chiang Kai-shek's Nationalist army were driven out of the mainland, the victorious communist revolutionaries declared that the "new China" would support the Soviet camp against the "imperialist" United States.

In Washington, "the loss of China sent tremors throughout the American political landscape."[2] The transformation of the most populous Asian country into a communist state allied with the Soviet Union caused a huge psychological shock and concrete geostrategic repercussions for

---

[1] "Nixon's View of the World – From Informal Talks," in *U.S. News & World Report*, vol. LXV, n. 12 (September 16, 1968), p. 48.
[2] Michael Shaller, *The United States and China in the Twentieth Century* (New York: Oxford University Press, 1990), 127.

the United States. These were further aggravated the following year, with the support lent by the newly born republic to North Korea at the outbreak of the Korean War. Originally rooted in the division of Europe, the Cold War thus spread to the Asian continent with upsetting similarities and China openly became, together with the Soviet Union, the enemy to confront. Consequently, and for the next two decades, the United States refused to grant legitimacy to the People's Republic. American policy aimed at isolating Beijing through the stubborn recognition of Chiang Kai-shek's regime, exiled in Taiwan, as the sole government of China.[3]

Until the late 1960s, this policy had been endorsed also by Richard Nixon. During the Eisenhower administration, he had supported US involvement in Vietnam against the communist influence; during the presidential campaign of 1960, when debating John F. Kennedy, he had attacked the Chinese communists, stating that they "don't just want Formosa. They want the world."[4] And, during the Johnson administration, he had adamantly criticized American ineffectiveness in resisting Chinese and Vietnamese communists in Indochina. Nixon had also been a member and promoter of the so-called China lobby, which advocated a return of the nationalist government of Taiwan to mainland China. Yet, it would be President Nixon, during his third year in office, who was the first US president to visit communist China and to meet with Chairman Mao. How did this personal and, most significantly, diplomatic revolution come about? And, most importantly, what were the motivations of Nixon's trip to China in February 1972?

A "FLIGHT OF FANCY?"

In early 1969, China definitely was not the administration's top foreign policy concern. At the beginning of the presidency, the "issue on which everything else seemed to hinge" was, obviously, the Vietnam War.[5] While the importance of a potential opening to the People's Republic was acknowledged in Washington, "originally," as Kissinger concedes in his memoirs, Nixon and his NSC adviser "had not thought reconciliation possible. We

---

[3] For a history of US-China relations before 1972: Gordon Chang, *Friends and Enemies. The United States, China, and the Soviet Union, 1948–1972* (Stanford, CA: Stanford University Press, 1990). See also Margaret MacMillan, *The Week That Changed the World. Nixon and Mao* (New York: Random House, 2007), 94–109.
[4] Shaller, *The United States and China*, 170.
[5] Jussi Hanhimäki, *The Flawed Architect. Henry Kissinger and American Foreign Policy* (New York: Oxford University Press, 2004), 33.

were convinced that the Chinese were fanatic and hostile."⁶ In fact, during the first year of the administration, US-China relations remained characterized by uncertainty and hesitation. Some signals revealing a potential shift in policy were sent by both sides but overall the contradictions and reservations remained dominant. The bilateral relationship was still hindered by decades of mutual distrust and by a general lack of understanding.

The first positive signs, through which President Nixon sought to distance himself from the past, came from some of his official statements. For example, the Johnson administration had used the specter of Soviet expansionism in Asia, favored by the Chinese government, as a justification for the American intervention in Vietnam. "The deepening shadow of Communist China," had stated Johnson, needed to be resisted because the "rulers in Hanoi are urged on" by Beijing.⁷ The incoming president, instead, refused this formula and neither cited, nor referred to, an anti-Chinese motivation for the American involvement in Indochina.⁸ A less confrontational attitude toward Beijing emerged, moreover, in between the lines of Nixon's Inaugural Address. The reference to China, though implicit, was rather unequivocal:

Let all nations know that during this Administration our lines of communication will be open. We seek an open world – open to ideas, open to the exchange of goods and people, a world in which no people, great or small, will live in angry isolation.⁹

Timid signals of change were sent also by the Chinese. Both *Renmin ribao* and *Hongqi*, the two monthly journals of the Communist Party, published, together with editorials very critical of Nixon, the integral version of the president's inaugural speech. This was unprecedented in the history of the People's Republic. We now know that Chairman Mao himself had ordered the publication of Nixon's entire speech to convey that the president's willingness to develop relations with all countries had been picked up by the Chinese leadership.¹⁰

---

⁶ Henry Kissinger, *White House Years* (London: Phoenix Press, 2000), 163.
⁷ Quoted in Henry Kissinger, *On China* (New York: Penguin, 2011), 205.
⁸ Kissinger, *White House Years*, p. 168.
⁹ "The Inaugural Address" in *Setting the Course: The First Year. Major Policy Statements by President Richard Nixon* (New York: Funk and Wagnalls, 1970).
¹⁰ Chen Jian, *Mao's China and the Cold War* (Chapel Hill, NC: The University of North Carolina Press, 2001), 238–239. Kissinger in his memoirs instead underlines only the criticism of the United States published by the Chinese press after Nixon's inauguration. He states that the Chinese had not picked up on Nixon's overture. This reveals that Mao's gesture had passed unnoticed in Washington; Kissinger, *White House Years*, 168.

Although unnoticed in Washington – which was at the time still single-mindedly engaged in fighting communist expansion in Asia – in 1965 Chairman Mao had tried to signal a shift toward the United States in an interview with American journalist Edgar Snow, who had been a supporter of the Chinese communists since the 1930s. Snow had visited the provinces under communist control and interviewed Mao and other prominent members of the Chinese Communist Party. In 1938, he had published the book *Red Star over China*, which conveyed a positive image of the communist revolution. In 1965, Mao told Snow that he regretted that the "forces of history" had divided the Chinese and American people. "Today the gulf seems broader than ever. However," continued Mao, "I myself do not believe it will end in war and one of history's major tragedies." Moreover, Mao stated that China would not attack the US forces in Vietnam unless they entered Chinese territory – "please rest assured that we won't attack the United States" said the chairman. The world had changed since the Korean War and, as the Soviet Union became increasingly threatening, Mao was starting to change his view of America, his more distant adversary. However, these signals never reached the US leadership and, in any case, given Edgar Snow's reputation in America as a propagandist for Beijing, they would have hardly been considered as evidence of a real shift in Chinese policy.[11]

Therefore, at the beginning of the Nixon administration the overall state of the US-Chinese bilateral relationship remained tense and problematic. The prospect of reinstituting the Warsaw meetings – the only line of communication that had remained between Washington and China after the Korean War[12] – temporarily vanished in early 1969 after the defection of a Chinese diplomat received at the US embassy at The Hague. In protest, Beijing cancelled the meeting scheduled for February 20, 1969. Referring to this episode, Nixon underlined both the potential

---

[11] Kissinger, *On China*, 204–206.
[12] The Chinese and American ambassadors met in Warsaw, starting in 1955, in order to work out the details of the exchange of US prisoners of war detained in China. These meetings were the only official contact between the United States and the PRC. However, this thin line of communication had been broken in the mid-1960s during China's Cultural Revolution. From that moment onwards, the United States and China were deprived of all political and diplomatic contact; James Mann, *About Face. A History of America's Curious Relationship with China, from Nixon to Clinton* (New York: Vintage Books, 1998), 19. On China's isolation during the Cultural Revolution: MacMillan, *Nixon and Mao*, 24–26.

The Diplomatic Revolution: The China Opening

importance of improving relations with China and his doubts on how to concretely achieve this long-term objective:

> Looking further down the road, we could think in terms of a better understanding with Red China. But being very realistic, in view of Red China's breaking off the rather limited Warsaw talks that were planned, I do not think that we should hold out any great optimism for any breakthroughs in that direction at this time.[13]

While the idea of an opening to China may have been present at the beginning of the administration, it was difficult to conceive a strategy capable of achieving that goal. In early February 1969, Nixon asked Kissinger to explore the possibility. The NSC adviser complied, and initiated a broad internal review of US-China policy.[14] But Kissinger was far from enthusiastic. In fact, he told his top aide Colonel (and later General) Alexander Haig that the president had just ordered him to "make this flight of fancy come true."[15]

In less than three years, what had indeed appeared to be pure fantasy was to become reality, with Kissinger himself as one of its main protagonists. Events beyond Washington's control came to favor the United States: The military clashes between China and the Soviet Union along the Ussuri River border, and the consequent realization of the definitive breach between the two former allies, gave the US leadership the opportunity to transform a brilliant, but still abstract, intuition into a concrete policy line. The conflict between the two communist giants opened new prospects and possibilities for American policy and was to constitute the basis of Washington's future "triangular diplomacy."[16]

THE SINO-SOVIET CONFLICT

The armed clashes of the spring and summer of 1969 universally conveyed the depth of the Sino-Soviet rupture. However, the split between Beijing and Moscow had far deeper origins. The less than idyllic partnership between the world's two major communist parties had started

---

[13] "The President's News Conference of March 4, 1969," *Weekly Compilation of Presidential Documents*, vol. V (March 10, 1969), 362.
[14] Raymond Garthoff, *Détente and Confrontation. American-Soviet Relations from Nixon to Reagan* (Washington DC: The Brookings Institution, 1994), 245.
[15] Hanhimäki, The *Flawed Architect*, 32.
[16] This was the term used to define America's simultaneous pursuit of a dialogue with both the Soviet Union and the People's Republic of China, which came to be known as the Washington-Beijing-Moscow triangle.

to fatally crack when in the Soviet Union Nikita Khrushchev succeeded Stalin in 1956.[17] In his drive to discredit Stalin's political heirs and consolidate his leadership, Khrushchev openly attacked the former dictator and his "cult of personality." But considering the public identification of Stalin with Mao, the charges also indirectly touched the Chinese leader, causing personal embarrassment and challenging his authority and prestige within the party.

Throughout the 1950s, the differences between China and the Soviet Union continued to increase and their relationship to worsen due to reciprocal accusations of having abandoned the communist orthodoxy in favor of ideologically less pure policies. In 1960, these divergences became public, as the Chinese newspapers accused the Soviets of revisionism. The Soviet Union responded by withdrawing its advisers and freezing all economic aid.

During the 1960s, the Sino-Soviet split shifted gradually from a political confrontation to a potentially military conflict. The Soviets were suspicious of the Chinese national defense policy, which climaxed with the nuclear tests of 1964. Consequently, Moscow started to intensify its military presence along the Chinese border. Hence, when in 1968 the Soviets invaded Czechoslovakia on the basis of the Brezhnev Doctrine, the Chinese feared that they might become the next victims. Moscow's declared right to use force to compel socialist states that had drifted from the "right" path to remain within the Soviet bloc rendered a Sino-Soviet war conceivable, thus worsening an already critical situation and deepening the break between the two former allies.

While during the Hungarian crisis of 1956 China had been complacent toward Moscow, in 1968 the reaction was one of open condemnation. Chinese newspapers denounced the invasion as "an armed aggression and a military occupation" conducted by the Soviet "revisionists" and defined Brezhnev's limited sovereignty doctrine as a "fascist" theory.[18] Beijing thus openly distanced itself from Moscow. Premier Zhou Enlai stated that the socialist camp, until then dominated by the Soviet Union, no longer existed.[19] The Soviets were accused of "ideological revisionism" and

---

[17] The history of the tensions between Communist China and the Soviet Union from 1949 to 1968 is here revisited on the basis of a memorandum to H. Kissinger from R. Solomon: "Mao Tse-tung and the Sino-Soviet Dispute," December 7, 1971, National Archives (hereafter NA), Nixon Presidential Materials (hereafter NPM), National Security Council (hereafter NSC) files, Henry A. Kissinger (hereafter HAK) Office files, box 91, folder 1.
[18] Kissinger, *White House Years*, 166.
[19] Garthoff, *Détente and Confrontation*, 228–229.

of "social imperialism," the Chinese definition of Soviet expansionism.[20] China then turned to support Rumania and Yugoslavia, whose break with the Soviet Union was already obvious and recognized and, within certain limits, the emerging "eurocommunist" positions, previously ridiculed and insulted.[21]

Although in the context of the Vietnam War the two communist countries were still apparently linked by their common support for Hanoi, the Chinese position vis à vis the Soviet Union had worsened. Until the mid-1960s, China had assumed that Vietnam was on its side in the struggle against Soviet "revisionists." But as the Vietnam War progressed and intensified, Hanoi and Moscow grew closer. After Khrushchev's removal from power in 1964, the Soviet Union began to provide Hanoi with more support and called for a unified stance of all communist countries in support of the Vietnamese struggle. In face of Mao's refusal to tone down his polemic against the Soviets, Hanoi progressively tilted toward Moscow. This, in turn, caused a cooling off of Chinese-North Vietnamese relations.[22] Thus, in 1969 when a communist victory had become a concrete possibility, it was evident that Moscow, and not Beijing, would be the principal beneficiary of the American withdrawal from South Vietnam.[23]

Against this background the clashes along the Sino-Soviet Ussuri River border were particularly relevant. Other incidents resulting in casualties had occurred along this highly contested border, but in the aftermath of the March 2 and 15 episodes,[24] the level of violence, and the corresponding reciprocal accusations, seemed to escalate. The Chinese launched harsh propaganda, calling for extensive preparations in case of

---

[20] Robert Ross, *Negotiating Cooperation. The United States and China 1969–1989* (Stanford, CA: Stanford University Press, 1995), 24.
[21] Garthoff, *Détente and Confrontation*, 229. "Eurocommunism" was the term adopted by the European communist parties in the 1970s intended to convey their independence from the Soviet communist party, in particular to distance themselves from the Soviet move into Czechoslovakia in 1968 in application of the Brezhnev Doctrine.
[22] Jian, *Mao's China and the Cold War*, 229–235.
[23] Ross, *Negotiating Cooperation*, 25.
[24] For a detailed description of the Sino-Soviet border clashes and their impact on the shaping of the US opening to China see also Patrick Tyler, *A Great Wall. Six Presidents and China: An Investigative History* (New York: The Century Foundation, 1999), 45–105. In his recent book *On China*, Kissinger states that already in the aftermath of the March clashes the US leadership had assessed the Soviets as the aggressors. This judgment proved false regarding the first clashes – recent scholarship has in fact revealed that the incidents had been initiated by the Chinese, who were upholding their concept of deterrence; Kissinger, *On China*, 216–217.

a war with the Soviet Union. On its part, Moscow retaliated by threatening a nuclear strike on China and by moving additional troops to the Sino-Soviet border.[25] In April 1969, at the Ninth Congress of the Chinese Communist Party, the strongest criticism targeted the Soviet Union (even if the references to the United States remained).[26] For the first time in the history of the People's Republic of China, the Soviet Union had officially become an enemy.[27]

As a second series of clashes occurred (in April and May, this time along the border between Sinkiang and Kazakhstan), in the United States the perception of an increased aggressiveness of the Soviet Union started to take hold.[28] This coincided with a series of direct threats of a Soviet attack on China, expressed on various occasions between the summer and fall of 1969 – in an editorial in *Pravda* (August 28) and in an interview on the *Evening News* in London (September 16), for example. Moreover, in August 1969, a KGB officer (placed at the Soviet embassy in Washington) met a US State Department official and probed on the possible American reaction to a Soviet attack on China's nuclear facilities.[29] Without knowing whether such a course of action was credible, or even if it was a simple bluff, the sole idea of a Soviet move on China had a deep impact on the making of US policy.

A few days before the revelation made by the KGB officer, at a meeting of the National Security Council, Nixon had already openly stated that he was convinced that the Soviet Union was the more aggressive party in the context of the Sino-Soviet rivalry. And, most significantly, he affirmed that the United States could not tolerate a Soviet attack on China. In sum, as Kissinger later stated, the president had declared that the United States "had

---

[25] Hanhimäki, *The Flawed Architect*, 40–41.
[26] Garthoff, *Détente and Confrontation*, 233.
[27] After April 1969, the Soviet Union, in fact, came to clearly represent the major threat to China's security. However, the Chinese leadership was divided on the issue of the opening to the United States and Mao himself initially wavered. But by September 1969, the chairman became increasingly convinced that an opening to the United States was a strategic necessity, lest China be subject to a Soviet attack. From that moment onwards, a strategy for rapprochement with Washington started to emerge; Hanhimäki, *A Flawed Architect*, 56–60.
[28] In his memoirs, Kissinger reveals that until the April-May clashes he had been convinced that China was the more aggressive of the two communist powers. However, the location of these clashes – close to a Soviet supply route but miles away from any Chinese route – seemed to point to the Soviet Union as the aggressor; Kissinger, *White House Years*, 179.
[29] Garthoff, *Détente and Confrontation*, 237–238.

a strategic interest in the survival of a major communist country, long an enemy, and with which we had no contact."³⁰

Therefore, while in precedence only the United States and the Western bloc had considered the Soviet Union a hostile and threatening power, in the late 1960s China developed the same perception. Chairman Mao had become convinced that in the following decade (the 1970s) Soviet power would be ascending and that sooner or later the Soviet Union would attack China. After 1969, Mao's entire foreign policy would be based on this premise and, consequently, on the need to engage in an alliance with the United States against the rise of Soviet power.³¹ As he reportedly told his doctor in 1969, "didn't our ancestors counsel negotiating with faraway countries while fighting those that are near?"³²

In other words, Beijing and Washington even before having established any form of contact potentially shared the common objective of containing the Soviet Union. In theory, the two sides had a major incentive for rapprochement; they needed only to find a pursuable line of action, a task which evolved with surprising rapidity.

"A MOMENT OF EXTRAORDINARY HOPE"

Although a number of pressing issues were addressed by Kissinger and Dobrynin in their back-channel meetings, during the Nixon administration's first year in office actual progress toward US-Soviet détente was slow. Despite verbal commitments to improving relations, the issues were numerous and inherently complex – the Vietnam War, the tension in the Middle East, the issue of Berlin (and of a possible European Security Conference), and the difficulties in the strategic arms limitation talks. To break this deadlock "something dramatic and substantial was needed."³³ And what could be more dramatic than an opening to communist China? From the start, therefore, the potential rapprochement with Beijing was inserted within the broader context of the US-Soviet relationship. It was the preoccupation with the Soviet Union that was to take center stage in the administration's pursuit of what came to be called triangular diplomacy.

---

[30] Kissinger, *White House Years*, 179; Hanhimäki, *The Flawed Architect*, 58.
[31] Odd Arne Westad, "The Great Transformation: China in the Long 1970s" in Neil Ferguson, Charles S. Maier, Erez Manela, Daniel J. Sargent (eds), *The Shock of the Global: The 1970s in Perspective* (Cambridge, MA: Belknap Press, 2010), 76.
[32] Quoted in Kissinger, *On China*, 208–209.
[33] Hanhimäki, *The Flawed Architect*, 53.

During the second half of 1969 the Nixon administration signaled its intention of moving toward a dialogue with China in two main ways: by initiating the so-called Pakistani channel[34] and by reactivating the only remaining thin line of communication between Washington and Beijing via the diplomatic meetings in Warsaw. In August 1969, Nixon visited Pakistan (as part of a worldwide tour) and met with Pakistani president Yahya Khan. During their conversations, Nixon stated that China could not continue to remain outside the international community and underlined that the United States would never support initiatives or policies targeted against China. The US president then asked that this communication be transmitted to Beijing.[35] A few months later, a representative of the Pakistani government visited Kissinger in Washington and delivered a message on behalf of President Yahya: The US general willingness to improve relations with the People's Republic had been conveyed to high-level Chinese officials. And, considering a forthcoming visit to Pakistan by Chinese premier Zhou Enlai, Yahya asked whether a more specific message had to be passed on.[36] The Pakistani channel was thus activated and, from that moment onward, became crucially important for the successful unfolding of the China opening.

At the same time, Nixon and Kissinger instructed US Ambassador to Poland Walter Stoessel to approach his Chinese counterpart in Warsaw and to communicate the US intention to reinitiate discussions. After some difficulty (Stoessel had to literally run after the Chinese diplomatic representative at a reception in order to convey the message), the Chinese reciprocated and invited Stoessel to the Chinese embassy. It was the first time that a US diplomat had been invited to the embassy of the People's Republic of China. In an atmosphere described as "cordial," the decision to restart the Warsaw meetings was made.[37] The first took place on January 20, 1970. Therefore, exactly one year after the inauguration of President Nixon, the United States and China formally started a dialogue. As Kissinger put it:

We still had a long way to go. But we were at last in the foothills of a mountain range that it would take us another eighteen months to traverse.

It was a moment of extraordinary hope.[38]

---

[34] Nixon also sought a dialogue with Rumania, but it would be the Pakistani channel that was to actually deliver, Hanhimäki, *The Flawed Architect*, 109.
[35] Kissinger, *White House Years*, 180–181.
[36] Kissinger, *White House Years*, 187.
[37] Kissinger, *White House Years*, 188.
[38] Kissinger, *White House Years*, 194.

The Diplomatic Revolution: The China Opening 45

Although only two meetings were held in Warsaw (in January and February 1970), they were significant for at least three reasons: First, the American position revealed some flexibility toward Taiwan and, in particular, referred to the possibility of reducing the US presence on the island if and when the tension in the area diminished. This introduced the link between the issues of Taiwan and Vietnam, which would later become crucial.[39] Second, the idea of holding a high-level meeting was accepted by the Chinese, who revealed their willingness to receive "a special envoy of the United States President for further exploration of questions of principle between the United States and China."[40] Finally, the Warsaw meetings marked the end of the involvement of the State Department in the making of America's China policy. In fact, after the Chinese decision to break the Warsaw meetings, in the aftermath of the US incursion into Cambodia, the opening to China would be managed directly and exclusively by the White House and, personally, by Henry Kissinger.

After the February meeting, and until the end of 1970, the opening to China momentarily stalled. In the United States reservations emerged on the prospect of rapid normalization. The State Department in particular insisted that progress had to be made on bilateral issues, which for decades had hindered the relationship with Beijing, before planning an eventual visit to China. For Nixon and Kissinger, instead, it was crucial to hold high-level talks as soon as possible. Bilateral issues, however important, were marginal compared to the motives that could potentially bring Washington and Beijing together. As Kissinger later stated, he and Nixon "wanted to explore the strategic situation produced by the triangular relationship between the Soviet Union, China, and the United States. We strove for an occasion not so much to remove irritants as to conduct a geopolitical dialogue."[41]

Internal difficulties in China also slowed down the unfolding of the diplomatic revolution. The power struggle between Chairman Mao Zedong and Defense Minister Lin Biao (at the time considered the designated heir to Mao) had emerged after the Ninth Congress of the Communist Party in April 1969. Since then, and until the Plenary Session of the Central Committee of the Party held in Lushan in August and September 1970,

---

[39] James Mann, *About Face*, 23.
[40] Department of State Airgram from US Embassy Warsaw, "Stoessel-Lei Talks: Report of the 136th Meeting, February 20, 1970," February 21, 1970, NA, NPM, NSC Files, box 1031, folder 3. See also: Department of State Airgram from US Embassy Warsaw, "Stoessel-Lei Talks: Report of 135th Meeting, January 20, 1970," January 24, 1970, NA, NPM, NSC files, box 1031, folder 3.
[41] Kissinger, *On China*, 224–225.

Mao was forced to concentrate on domestic affairs, thus delaying decisions on the mode and timing of the pursuit of an opening with the United States.⁴² Then, at the Lushan conference, the opposite views of Zhou Enlai – the promoter of improving relations with Washington to counterbalance the deteriorating relationship with Moscow – and the more conservative approaches led by Lin Biao clashed. But, ultimately, Zhou's stance emerged strengthened. After Lushan the line of the Communist Party gradually shifted toward the position, officially adopted only in 1972, which pointed to the Soviet Union, and not to the United States, as the greatest security threat for the People's Republic of China.⁴³

Domestic constraints both in the United States and in China, therefore, slowed the pace of the opening. Moreover, the process was delayed by the developments in Indochina. After the March 1970 coup in Cambodia, led by US-backed General Lon Nol, the ousted Cambodian prince Sihanouk established an exiled government in Beijing. This created a link between China and Cambodia. Hence, when South Vietnamese and American forces entered Cambodia to encircle the "sanctuaries" of the North Vietnamese forces, the Chinese government retaliated by cancelling the Warsaw meeting scheduled for May 20, 1970. The developments related to the Vietnam War thus negatively impacted on the evolution of the China opening.⁴⁴ They did not, however, mark the end of the process.⁴⁵

In fact, the preoccupations circulating in Washington that the Cambodian incursion would definitely break the dialogue with China would, eventually, prove unfounded. The Chinese (and Soviet) reaction

---

⁴² Jian, *Mao's China and the Cold War*, 253.
⁴³ William Bundy, *A Tangled Web. The Making of Foreign Policy in the Nixon Presidency* (London: IB Tauris, 1998), 165; Garthoff, *Détente and Confrontation*, 254. While Zhou's position did emerge strengthened after Lushan and, consequently, the opening to the United States gradually became a concrete course of action, opposition within the Chinese leadership toward rapprochement with Washington remained strong, particularly among those aligned with Lin Biao; Hanhimäki, *The Flawed Architect*, 106–107.
⁴⁴ Between the spring and the summer of 1970 the Cambodian incursion did have a series of negative repercussions for the United States, provoking severe domestic unrest and opposition to what was perceived as an expansion of the Vietnam War into Cambodia. Moreover, the cancelling of the Warsaw meetings delayed the opening process and gave the erroneous impression that Vietnam was an insuperable obstacle on the road to rapprochement; for more details on the impact of the Cambodian incursion on the unfolding of triangular diplomacy, Hanhimäki, *The Flawed Architect*, 71–82.
⁴⁵ It is important to note that Chinese scholar Chen Jian underlines that the delay in the process of improving relations with the United States was caused more by the internal power struggle within China – which lasted until the fall of 1970 – than by China's intention to retaliate or punish the United States for the incursion into Cambodia, Jian, *Mao's China and the Cold War*, 253.

to the US intervention, in essence rather limited, demonstrated the continued opportunity to develop triangular diplomacy. In the following months it gradually became evident that Beijing was not willing to compromise the potential opening with Washington. Moreover, the events in Indochina further deepened the rivalry between the two communist giants as they competed over influence in Cambodia. And this, clearly, came to Washington's advantage.

In the meantime, President Nixon continued to signal the importance of a renewed policy toward China. In an interview published by *Time* magazine in October 1970 he underlined the need for a constructive role of the People's Republic in world affairs:

> Maybe that role won't be possible for five years, maybe not even ten years. But in 20 years it had better be, or the world is in mortal danger. If there is anything I want to do before I die, it is to go to China. If I don't, I want my children to.[46]

In parallel – though at the time not grasped in Washington – Mao reciprocated. On October 1, during the celebrations for the anniversary of the People's Republic, the chairman invited Edgar Snow and his wife to the annual parade and were photographed next to him. This was an unprecedented gesture; no American citizen had ever been honored in this way. By inviting Snow to the annual parade as "a distinguished guest"[47] and by allowing him to sit next to the highest Chinese authorities, Mao sought to signal – to his domestic constituency and to the United States – that America could be seen differently. It was the first step that paved the way for the future dramatic shift in Sino-American relations.[48]

Therefore, by the end of 1970 both sides had reached the conclusion that a strategic realignment was a vital necessity. Again thanks to the good offices of Pakistan, the general agreement on a high-level US visit to China was reached, even if the Chinese formulation of the invitation still limited the potential future talks to the topic of Taiwan.[49] Then, in early 1971, what came to be labeled as "Ping-Pong diplomacy" confirmed that the tension in the bilateral relationship was slowly subsiding. During the table tennis World Championship held in Japan in late March 1971 the Chinese (considered the best team worldwide) and American players

---

[46] *Time*, Oct. 5, 1970.
[47] Jian, *Mao's China and the Cold War*, 255.
[48] Jian, *Mao's China and the Cold War*, 256. It is important to note that Kissinger in his memoirs concedes that the US leadership had at the time failed to grasp the significance of Mao's gesture, Kissinger, *White House Years*, 698–699.
[49] Kissinger, *White House Years*, 701–702.

exchanged friendly gestures and gifts (reportedly a scarf and a T-shirt). A few days later, the Chinese team invited – an order issued by Mao himself – the American team to visit Beijing.[50] The White House immediately instructed the American players to accept. During the visit of the US team, the Chinese media extensively covered the events. On April 14, 1971, the team was received by Zhou Enlai, who underlined the importance of the moment and stated that a new era had begun in the relations between the Chinese and American people. Afterwards, the American team invited the Chinese team to the United States. Significantly, only hours after the meeting between the players and Zhou, the White House lifted the trade embargo against China that had lasted for twenty-two years.[51]

In the brief timespan of a few days, "Ping-Pong diplomacy" revolutionized the political climate between the two states. The prospect of improved Sino-American relations captured worldwide attention and aroused profound emotions. On the wave of this enthusiasm, both sides accelerated the preparations for the forthcoming visit of a special envoy of the US president to China. Still secretly communicating via the Pakistani embassy in Washington, between April and May 1971 the agreement on Kissinger's secret visit to China was made.[52] What only a little over a year earlier had been defined as an "extraordinary hope" had become reality. As Nixon commented in his memoirs, the agreement on the visit "truly was a moment of historical significance."[53]

"WE HAVE GONE THROUGH THIS FOR TWENTY-ONE YEARS, AND WE HAVE LIVED THROUGH IT"

The events preceding Nixon's historic trip to China (Kissinger's secret visit of July 1971 and his second preparatory visit of October 1971) and the account of the February 1972 summit itself are, today, very well known.[54] In this context it is nevertheless important to highlight two aspects, which would later also characterize the Carter administration's

---

[50] Kissinger, *On China*, 232.
[51] Kissinger, *White House Years*, 709–710; Jian, *Mao's China and the Cold War*, 260–261; Richard Nixon, *RN: The Memoirs of Richard Nixon* (New York: Touchstone, 1990), 548.
[52] By the spring of 1971, in fact, Chinese premier Zhou Enlai had decided that the developments in Vietnam would no longer derail the opening to the United States, Hanhimäki, *The Flawed Architect*, 121.
[53] Nixon, *Memoirs*, 552.
[54] The most recent comprehensive account is MacMillan, *Nixon and Mao*, which focuses exclusively on the China opening and extensively on the 1972 summit. See also: Robert

policy of normalization of relations with China (Chapter 11). First, the rapprochement was perceived by both sides as a priority. This enabled the beginning of the process that would set aside the problem of Taiwan in order to allow for improved Sino-American relations. Second, and for the purpose of this book most importantly, the potent driving force behind the strategic realignment was the shared common objective of containing the Soviet Union.

Despite the change in the atmospherics of the relationship and the agreement on Kissinger's secret visit, for the US leadership communist China remained a highly mysterious country. Before Kissinger's July 1971 trip, Washington may have had some insight into parallel motivations, but there were very few certainties. In the background briefing book for his secret trip – called Polo I,[55] in homage to Marco Polo, the first Western explorer to venture to the Far East (this in itself reveals the mystique still surrounding the visit) – Kissinger speculated on possible Chinese motivations in moving toward improved relations with Washington. He referred to the possibility of Beijing wanting to humiliate the United States by asking for the withdrawal of the American presence from the Asian continent and the end of defense commitments in the area, while subordinating any progress in relations to these goals. At the same time, however, Kissinger was convinced that such an attitude was unlikely, considering the tone of the messages exchanged. Moreover, while previously referring only to the question of Taiwan, in the last message (of May 1971) the Chinese had accepted the American position on the freedom to discuss, at the upcoming meetings, the issues that each side deemed most important.[56] Consequently, assuming that Beijing wanted to improve relations with the United States because of the Soviet threat along its borders, it seemed plausible that China's scope was to develop a counterweight to the Soviet Union, and certainly not provoke Washington's resentment. Also, the unconditioned withdrawal of the American forces from Asia, called for by Chinese propaganda in the previous years, would appear counterproductive because it would leave a power vacuum which the Soviets could potentially fill.[57]

Dallek, *Partners in Power. Nixon and Kissinger* (New York: HarperCollins, 2007) chapters 10–11; Hanhimäki, *The Flawed Architect*, chapters 3–7 for the events leading to the summit and chapter 9 on the February 1972 summit itself; Bundy, *A Tangled Web*, chapters 3–5; Garthoff, *Détente and Confrontation*, chapter 6.

[55] "Polo I," NA, NPM, NSC files, box 850, folder 3.
[56] "Message from Premier Chou En Lai to President Nixon," May 29, 1971, NA, NPM, NSC files, box 1031, folder 1.
[57] "Scope Paper" in Polo I, NA, NPM, NSC files, box 850, folder 3.

Therefore, Kissinger believed that the Chinese had some concrete objectives. Apart from the recognition of the importance of China's role in international relations, they were likely to search for some form of agreement on nonaggression and peaceful coexistence between the People's Republic and the United States. The reduction and eventual withdrawal of the American forces from Taiwan was still a priority. However, considering that in the exchange of messages there had been no reference to the political relationship between Washington and Taipei, Kissinger concluded that the Chinese leaders were willing, for the moment, to accept a compromise, while postponing the definitive solution to the problem.[58]

Interestingly, Kissinger's considerations were in line with the results of the meeting of the Chinese politburo of May 1971, which established the guidelines for the future evolution of the rapprochement with the United States. The concluding report in fact introduced the distinction between the conditions required for a full normalization of relations and those for the creation of informal ties, which did not demand the definitive solution to the problem of Taiwan.[59] Specifically, the guidelines stated that four conditions had to be met for a complete normalization of relations: 1) the United States would have to withdraw its forces from Taiwan; 2) it would have to recognize that Taiwan was part of China and that its "liberation" was an internal Chinese affair; 3) the People's Republic would liberate Taiwan peacefully; 4) the policies that recognized "two Chinas" or "China and Taiwan" were unacceptable. If the United States would not accept all these conditions, then full normalization would have to wait. However, liaison offices (and other informal ties) could nonetheless be established. Moreover, the report stated that the Chinese would not demand an immediate settlement of the issue of representation at the United Nations Security Council.[60]

The records of the high-level conversations between the American and Chinese leaders confirm their parallel motivations. In fact, the discussions on Taiwan – both during Kissinger's preparatory visits and at the February summit – proceeded along the guidelines established by the Politburo (and in line with Kissinger's intuitions in the Polo I briefing paper).

On July 10, 1971, Zhou Enlai immediately stated that the issue of UN representation was not an obstacle on the way to rapprochement:

---

[58] Polo I, 3–5.
[59] Ross, *Negotiating Cooperation*, 37.
[60] Jian, *Mao's China and the Cold War*, 264.

The Diplomatic Revolution: The China Opening 51

We have gone through this for twenty-one years, and we have lived through it. Even if war should break out again, we will live through it. Therefore, we do not attach any importance to the U.N. question.[61]

But this was just the beginning. The issues of Vietnam, for the United States, and Taiwan, for the People's Republic of China, had to somehow be addressed. Both countries' commitments and security requirements had to be respected but in a way in which they would no longer prevent the future evolution of Sino-American relations.

The difficulties surfaced during Kissinger and Zhou's first conversation in July 1971. The fact that Taiwan was the most significant issue for China, and that Vietnam was the vital matter for the United States, was openly stated by both sides.[62] In addition, Kissinger witnessed a stiffening of the Chinese position when Zhou outlined the controversies still open and the concerns regarding US-Soviet collusion against China.[63] He then provocatively asked whether preparations for the summit between Nixon and Mao made any sense, considering the deep divergences still existing between the two countries. Afterwards, however, the Chinese returned to overall cordiality and cooperativeness. Therefore, the dominant impression was that the rigidity had been expressed more for the official record, and for reasons of prestige and pride vis-à-vis the American "adversary," rather than as a demonstration of authentic intransigence.[64]

---

[61] Memorandum of Conversation, July 10, 1971, NA, NPM, NSC files, box 1032, folder 2. This issue is important, since it has in the past been erroneously considered a powerful incentive for the Chinese search for better relations with the United States. The People's Republic had never obtained the UN seat and the related veto power in the Security Council. In view of the revision of this anachronistic situation, the US Department of State was working on the different options to be presented at the United Nations. The situation was delicate because, while this aspect remained in the domain of the DOS, the evolution of the China policy depended exclusively on Nixon and Kissinger, with the consequent difficulties in trying to avoid contradicting positions. On these matters: Kissinger, *White House Years*, 718–720. It was a peculiar coincidence that the United Nations voted for admission of the PRC and expulsion of Taiwan while Kissinger was in Beijing for his second official visit in October 1971. For the debate at the United Nations and the positions of the DOS: Kissinger, *White House Years*, 770–774, 784; Nixon, *Memoirs*, 557.

[62] Memorandum for the President from Henry Kissinger, "My Talks with Chou En-lai," July 14, 1971, NA, NPM, NSC files, box 1032, folder 3.

[63] The simultaneous evolution of US-Soviet relations, with the significant step forward in the SALT context after the May 20, 1971, agreement aroused preoccupations in Beijing. As will be illustrated, the Chinese leadership searched for assurances that the United States and the USSR were *not* agreeing to a superpower condominium. The United States displayed complete willingness to reassure the Chinese that this was not the case.

[64] Memorandum for the President from Henry Kissinger, "My Talks with Chou En-lai," July 14, 1971, NA, NPM, NSC files, box 1032, folder 3.

During the following discussions, in fact, both sides made significant concessions. Postponing the issue of the formal normalization of diplomatic relations, hinting that Nixon himself would solve the problem during his second term,[65] Kissinger stated that the United States would not support a Taiwanese armed intervention against mainland China. Furthermore, partly contradicting what was still the State Department's official position, he said that the United States neither sustained the "two Chinas," nor the "one China and Taiwan," formulation. On his part, Zhou Enlai cooperated and accepted to defer the solution of the problem. He expressed satisfaction with the short-term American verbal reassurances and the commitment to a gradual withdrawal of the American military forces from the island.

The most significant step forward on Taiwan occurred during Kissinger's second visit, in October 1971. Washington had to recognize China's unity, a point on which Taipei and Beijing both agreed, but without endorsing either side's claims. After several failures, Kissinger was able to find a solution, reformulating a phrase used in a State Department document of the 1950s:

The United States acknowledges that all Chinese on either side of the Taiwan Straits maintain that there is but one China and that Taiwan is part of China. The United States Government does not challenge that position.[66]

With this sentence, the acceptance of which depended on its ambiguity, the United States recognized that both Taipei and Beijing claimed the status of sole legitimate government of China. The United States thus implicitly admitted that the problem would be solved by the two sides alone, but avoided formally sanctioning the position of the People's Republic.

During the meeting between Nixon and Mao in February 1972, the chairman himself definitely removed Taiwan from constituting the major obstacle on the road to Sino-American rapprochement. Mao, in fact, conveyed neither impatience nor the intention of seeking definitive deadlines for the final solution to the problem.[67]

On the American side, the search for an acceptable compromise on Vietnam proved to be more complex. While failing to obtain direct Chinese aid in exercising pressure on Hanoi, the issue continued to feature

---

[65] Kissinger's reference to the presidential election was significant since he took for granted Nixon's upcoming victory.
[66] Kissinger, *White House Years*, 782–783.
[67] Memorandum of Conversation, Monday, February 21, 1972, 2:50–3:55 P.M., Chairman Mao's Residence, Peking, NA, NPM, NSC files, HAK Office files, box 91, folder 4.

prominently in the discussions at the 1972 summit, particularly during the conversations between Nixon and Zhou Enlai.[68] The president stated that the United States could not "abandon" Saigon because the credibility of American commitments toward allied or friendly countries needed to be defended. Hence, the reference to the importance of Washington's reliability as a factor that could, in the future, be important also for the defense of Chinese security interests.[69] On his part, Zhou implicitly acknowledged America's difficult position by stating that Vietnam was not North Korea: Chinese troops would not enter Indochina. Moreover, the Chinese premier stated that he hoped for a rapid solution and for the prompt withdrawal of American forces because only the Soviet Union, with its expansionist ambitions in Southeast Asia, benefited from the continuation of the war.[70]

On the basis of the indications that emerged from these high-level bilateral conversations, Kissinger and the Chinese vice foreign minister, Qiao Guanhua, drafted the Shanghai Communiqué, issued at the end of the February 1972 summit. Despite the complexity of the negotiations, it was evident that the parts would no longer permit divergences on issues, their importance notwithstanding, to interfere with the nascent relationship, firmly grounded on their geopolitical interests. By proposing to link the definitive disengagement from Taiwan to the Chinese renunciation of the use of force, and the gradual withdrawal of American forces from the island to a decrease in the tension in the area, Kissinger managed to break the impasse. The connection between the two issues, introduced in Warsaw from the very beginning of the rapprochement process, was eventually accepted by the Chinese. This enabled Washington to justify its concessions: Taiwan, a former ally, was protected from a possible aggression, and at the same time an incentive for the common search for peace in Vietnam was provided.

The text of the communiqué on these two issues reads as follows:

The United States acknowledges that all Chinese on either side of the Taiwan Straits maintain there is but one China and that Taiwan is part of China. The

---

[68] Kissinger had spent a lot of time discussing Vietnam with Zhou Enlai during the July secret trip *without* obtaining any support from the Chinese to put pressure on Hanoi. The Chinese position was that the United States had to withdraw its troops from Vietnam as soon as possible. In the meantime, China would continue to support North Vietnam; Hanhimäki, *The Flawed Architect*, 138–139. With these premises, it was particularly significant that the Sino-American rapprochement continued.
[69] Kissinger, *White House Years*, 1072–1073.
[70] Mann, *About Face*, 45.

United States Government does not challenge that position. It reaffirms its interest in a peaceful settlement of the Taiwan question by the Chinese themselves. With this prospect in mind, it affirms the ultimate objective of the withdrawal of all US forces and military installations from Taiwan. In the meantime, it will progressively reduce its forces and military installations on Taiwan as the tension in the area diminishes.[71]

In this way, the problem of Taiwan, that for more than twenty years had been at the center of the Sino-American hostility, and the support for opposite factions in Vietnam, which had previously been paramount in deepening the fracture, were set aside in order to allow for the rapprochement to begin. Clearly, these two issues, however important, were no longer considered vital security matters. For both China and the United States the central concern now was the Soviet Union.

"NEITHER SIDE SHOULD SEEK HEGEMONY"

Despite the Chinese leaders having put emphasis on Taiwan in their initial exchange of messages the American leadership had, from the start, been convinced that China's interest in a dialogue with the United States had a much broader scope. According to Kissinger, Zhou Enlai and Mao had to be moved by more general preoccupations than those related to the future of one of China's provinces; they had to be concerned about China's security, which was being threatened by the deteriorating relationship with Moscow.[72]

Based on this assessment, though not yet confirmed by direct statements on the Chinese part, the American overtures, up to the July 1971 visit, had centered on the belief that the fundamental motive for the opening was Beijing's desire to reestablish a wide-ranging relationship with Washington. Consequently, in accepting the invitation to the summit, Nixon moved the emphasis away from Taiwan. He refused to limit the scope of the upcoming conversations, during which "each side would be free to raise the issue of principal concern to it."[73] From the American point of view, this meant that the talks would center on the global balance of power, therefore necessarily entailing a direct exchange of views on the Soviet Union. Significantly, during the high-level discussions of July 1971 and February 1972 – when the essence of the nascent relationship

---

[71] "The Shanghai Communiqué" in Ross, *Negotiating Cooperation*, 268–269.
[72] Kissinger, *White House Years*, 701.
[73] For the complete text of these exchanges, and details on the Pakistani role as intermediary: Kissinger, *White House Years*, 714–725.

was being defined – the Soviet Union was, indeed, the central topic of conversation. This would influence the future evolution of the US-Chinese relationship also during the Ford and Carter administrations.

On July 10, 1971, Zhou underlined the fear of a Soviet invasion of Chinese territory and claimed that the construction of shelters for the protection of the population against aerial bombings had already begun. He pointed to the aggressiveness the Soviets had demonstrated in the border clashes and explained in detail the nature of the conflict with Moscow.[74] On the American side, during the three days of the secret visit in July, Kissinger repeatedly reassured Zhou of Washington's readiness to support China in its dispute with the Soviet Union. In this way, the United States tried to establish the confidence necessary for the development of an authentic Sino-American rapprochement that was to become, according to Nixon and Kissinger's design, a fundamental element in their new strategy of containment of the Soviet Union.

On July 9, 1971, for example, Kissinger referred to the long-term Soviet goal of creating cooperation between states targeted against China. The United States, he stated, not only would never share such objectives, but would also try to dissuade any other country from pursuing them. In addition, Kissinger declared that President Nixon did not consider the People's Republic a threat to American security. As a concrete follow-up to these statements, Kissinger added that the United States was prepared to discuss any initiative that might affect China's interests. In particular, he was authorized to reveal the essence of the agreements being negotiated with China's "neighbors" – a clear reference to the talks with the Soviet Union.[75] The following day, Kissinger directly mentioned the Soviet Union and SALT. Reaffirming that the United States supported China's integrity, he again offered to keep Beijing informed on negotiations with "other countries." He then specified, twice, that in order to eliminate all Chinese concerns he could disclose information regarding the ongoing Strategic Arms Limitation Talks.[76] In the final meeting with Zhou in July, Kissinger further underscored the US openness on SALT and also mentioned the so-called accidental war agreement. This was an agreement under discussion with the Soviet Union (then finalized in September 1971) that focused on means to reduce the outbreak of nuclear war in case of accidental

---

[74] Memorandum of Conversation, July 10, 1971, NA, NPM, NSC files, box 1032, folder 2.
[75] Memorandum of Conversation, July 9, 1971, NA, NPM, NSC files, box 1032, folder 2.
[76] Memorandum of Conversation, July 10, 1971, NA, NPM, NSC files, box 1032, folder 2.

explosions. But because the Soviets had linked this to discussions on one concerning provocative attacks – a proposition widely considered to be aimed against China – Kissinger's frankness in regard was crucial in dispelling any possible misinterpretation on Beijing's part. If this agreement contained provisions that could be interpreted as anti-Chinese, stated Kissinger, the United States would inform China in advance, in order to avoid any type of misunderstanding.[77]

Overall, therefore, the discussions on the Soviet Union were extremely significant. On the one hand, Zhou explicitly described the Chinese fears and concerns regarding a Soviet attack. On the other, Kissinger repeatedly underlined the US willingness to support China's integrity and respect its interests. In this way, both sides clearly identified the common perception of the Soviet threat as the main driving force of the Sino-American rapprochement.

These indications were confirmed at the February 1972 summit, during the conversations between Nixon and the Chinese leadership, and then further, with the inclusion of a particularly significant clause in the text of the Shanghai Communiqué. In his meeting with Chairman Mao, Nixon pointed to their parallel foreign policy interests and underlined that the United States and China did not threaten each other. Mao went a step further, specifying that China neither threatened Japan nor South Korea, thus offering an important reassurance to Washington's allies and an implicit guarantee of noninterference in America's defense of its commitments.[78] To Nixon's long analysis on which of the superpowers represented a major threat for China, Mao responded by underlining that no major issue divided the United States and the People's Republic:

> At the present time, the question of aggression from the United States or aggression from China is relatively small; that is, it could be said that this is not a major issue, because the present situation is one in which a state of war does not exist between our two countries. You want to withdraw some of your troops back on your soil; ours do not go abroad.[79]

---

[77] Memorandum of Conversation, July 11, 1971, NA, NPM, NSC files, box 1032, folder 2.

[78] Memorandum of Conversation, Monday, February 21, 1972, 2:50–3:55 P.M., Chairman Mao's Residence, Peking, NA, NPM, NSC files, HAK Office files, box 91, folder 4.

[79] Ibid. Scholars have pointed to the lack of detailed conversations on the Soviet Union between Nixon and Mao, in particular MacMillan, *Nixon and Mao*, 73. The transcript of the conversation, however, shows that while not too much time was dedicated to the topic, and the references were indirect and implicit, they were nevertheless crucial and unequivocal in conveying US and Chinese parallel objectives.

The Diplomatic Revolution: The China Opening 57

The Soviet Union was the key topic also during Nixon's conversations with Zhou Enlai. The president confirmed America's determination in resisting Soviet expansionism and restated the commitments already made by Kissinger in July: to inform Beijing on the developments in the negotiations with Moscow and to refrain from concluding agreements which could potentially interfere with Chinese interests without previous consultation.

In general, therefore, the American long-term objective of redefining the global balance of power was shared by the Chinese[80] and inserted in the Shanghai Communiqué, at the end of "the week that changed the world."[81] The section of the communiqué, which Nixon himself defined as "the most vitally important"[82] was the one which listed the common US and Chinese goals for the creation of a new international order. Particularly significant was the pledge that "neither side would seek hegemony in the Asia-Pacific region" and both "opposed efforts by any other country or group of countries to establish such hegemony."[83]

With this commitment the United States and the People's Republic agreed to set limits to their actions in Asia and, most importantly, formally agreed to oppose any expansionist and hegemonic ambitions of other countries. The reference to Soviet foreign policy was indisputable. As Kissinger later stated, "alliances have been founded on far less … the enemies of a little more than six months earlier were announcing their opposition to any further expansion of the Soviet sphere. It was a veritable diplomatic revolution, for the next step would be inevitably to discuss a strategy to counter Soviet ambitions."[84] The significance of the anti-hegemonic clause was enhanced further by the following passages of the communiqué, which stated that:

Neither side is prepared to negotiate on behalf of any third party or to enter into agreements or understandings with the other directed at other states.

---

[80] "The Soviet Union," Briefing Papers sent to the President for the February '72 China Trip, NA, NPM, NSC files, HAK Office files, box 91, folder 2.
[81] Nixon defined his week in China in this way in his memoirs: Nixon, *Memoirs*, 580. This expression has then been repeatedly picked up by scholars in the texts on the February 1972 summit, for example Hanhimäki, *The Flawed Architect*, Chapter 9 "The Week that Changed the World," and the title of MacMillan's book, *The Week That Changed the World. Nixon and Mao*.
[82] Nixon, *Memoirs*, 577.
[83] "The Shanghai Communiqué" in Ross, *Negotiating Cooperation*, 265–269.
[84] Kissinger, *On China*, 270.

Both sides are of the view that it would be against the interests of the peoples of the world for any major country to collude with another against other countries, or for major countries to divide up the world into spheres of interest.[85]

Between these lines the meaning of the diplomatic revolution that had just occurred could be easily grasped. The Sino-American rapprochement, apart from constituting one of the most outstanding and enduring events of the history of the Cold War, caused a profound change in the equilibrium of power in favor of the United States. While the Sino-Soviet rivalry had diminished Moscow's maneuvering space, the Sino-American reconciliation greatly strengthened Washington's strategic position vis-à-vis its long-time opponent – the Soviet Union.

The Shanghai Communiqué would remain a guide for the future evolution of Sino-American relations for the following seven years, until the formal normalization of diplomatic relations in 1979. As stated by Kissinger, it neither contained codes, nor secret clauses. Its importance depended less on the words used than on the meanings they concealed. Its objective was not to resolve bilateral issues, but to tackle with the changes taking place on the global scene.[86] It created the basis for a strategic cooperation between two states with opposing ideologies but with shared security interests.

The opening to China was a triumph for Nixon and Kissinger and for their *realpolitik*. They had successfully taken advantage of the rupture within the communist camp and demonstrated that it was possible to create a tacit alliance with a country still proclaiming ideological enmity. For the United States this meant renouncing the objective – at other times considered essential – of seeking to change the internal structure of states non-aligned with the American model. It was the foreign policy and global outlook of a country that mattered, not its internal affairs.

China was crucial in the context of Washington's search for means to more effectively contain the Soviet Union. The US-Soviet nuclear parity imposed the search for policies – other than those related to military deterrence – to exercise pressure on Moscow. And, for this purpose, the realignment with Beijing was obviously a powerful asset. There are little doubts, in fact, that the opening to China was primarily meant to impress and influence the Soviet Union. As historian Jussi Hanhimäki

---

[85] Ibid.
[86] Kissinger, *White House Years*, 1086.

puts it "neither China, nor the United States was, in 1972, interested in the relationship for its own sake; it was a strategic tool to be used in dealing with the Soviet Union, the reluctant third party in triangular diplomacy."[87] Although Kissinger maintained that the rapprochement with Beijing should not be seen as an attempt to play a China card against the Soviet Union, that was, in essence, the opening's main scope.[88] And this dynamic would – a few years later – be the central driving force also behind President Carter's decision to normalize relations with the People's Republic of China (Chapter 11).

The Nixon administration was far less successful in attaining its other primary objective: enlisting Chinese direct support for a solution to Vietnam. However, establishing a relationship with Beijing despite the ongoing conflict in Indochina was, in itself, extremely significant. It was the first step toward isolating the conflict – a process that would reach completion after the Moscow summit in 1972. It demonstrated the fallacy of the so-called domino theory and revolutionized the assumption (that had led to the US involvement) that from Vietnam communism would expand further into the Asian continent. In other words, the opening to China created an entirely new geopolitical framework for working out a US "honorable" exit from Indochina.

With the China opening the United States established the first side of the "triangle," which was then completed by the negotiations with the Soviet Union and the signing of the SALT agreements. By 1972, the architecture of détente reached its climax. But as the scope of Nixon's China policy demonstrated, the US-Soviet superpower rivalry was far from overcome. Its dynamics, however, had drastically changed.

[87] Hanhimäki, *The Flawed Architect*, 197.
[88] Margaret MacMillan, "Nixon, Kissinger and the Opening to China" in Fredrik Logevall and Andrew Preston (eds), *Nixon in the World. American Foreign Relations, 1969–1977* (New York: Oxford University Press, 2008), 112.

3

An "Era of Negotiation" versus the "Supreme Test"

Nixon between SALT I and Vietnam

> After a period of confrontation, we are entering an era of negotiation. Let all nations know that during this administration our lines of communication will be open.
>
> Richard Nixon's Inaugural Address, 1969

> I don't think we've really ever had a situation where so much was on the line, because the credibility of US foreign policy is on the line ... It's really a test as to whether a nation supported by Soviet arms is allowed to get away with naked aggression.[1]
>
> Private conversation between Nixon and Kissinger on Vietnam, April 10, 1972

The year 1972 marked, indisputably, the climax of US-Soviet détente. The call for cooperation and dialogue that President Nixon had set forth in his inaugural address of 1969 had translated into dramatic changes in the policies toward the communist enemies, symbolized by the summits in Beijing and Moscow. This new era not only produced the historic breakthrough in relations with the People's Republic of China but led also to the successful outcome of landmark agreements with the Soviet Union, first and foremost on strategic arms limitation (SALT I). These initiatives provided tangible evidence of the Nixon administration's alleged intention to place cooperation, and not competition and antagonism, at the center of its foreign policy making.

---

[1] Conversation between Nixon and Kissinger, April 10, 1972, National Archives (hereafter NA), Nixon Presidential Materials (hereafter NPM), White House Tapes (hereafter WHT), Conversation No. 705-13. Transcribed in FRUS, Volume XIV, Foreign Relations, 1969–1976, Soviet Union, October 1971–May 1972, 281.

However, in the spring of 1972 the fighting in Vietnam also escalated dramatically. In response to the North Vietnamese Easter offensive, Nixon ordered an intensification of the bombing of areas in the north and, later, the mining of the Haiphong harbor. These decisions were made only a few weeks before the scheduled signing of SALT I at the Moscow summit. While at the White House the president and his aides repeatedly affirmed that it was impossible to go to Moscow, and toast with Soviet leaders while Soviet arms killed American soldiers,[2] in the end, this is precisely what occurred. As effectively stated by Helmut Sonnenfeldt, the "problem of the disparity between the symbolism of US-Soviet cooperation and the reality of proxy war in Vietnam"[3] was clearly present.

The SALT I agreements were, indeed, the central building block in the creation of the new era of US-Soviet cooperation. At the same time, however, the "disparity," or ambivalent path undertaken by Nixon was also emerging – with cooperative and competitive aspects of US-Soviet relations developing together and simultaneously. Did the "era of negotiation" really mark the shift from confrontation to cooperation? Or was détente simply a means of securing American national interests, a key element of a much more complex picture?

SALT: A NECESSITY, MORE THAN A CHOICE

Although the negotiations with the Soviets encompassed other crucial aspects of the superpower relationship (such as trade and the Berlin Agreements), it is undeniable that the Strategic Arms Limitations Talks (SALT) were perceived as the utmost priority, both in Washington and in

---

[2] For example, during a telephone conversation with Kissinger on April 15, Nixon stated: "Good God, we can't go there with Russian tanks and Russian guns killing South Vietnamese and Americans. Hell, no, we're not going to go! We won't go." Transcript of Telephone Conversation between Nixon and Kissinger, April 15, 1972, Library of Congress (hereafter LOC), Manuscript Division, Kissinger Papers, Box 397, Telephone Conversations, Chronological File. Transcribed in FRUS, Volume XIV, Foreign Relations, 1969-1976, Soviet Union, October 1971–May 1972, 341. The same concept was repeated by Nixon during a conversation with Alexander Haig on May 2: "How can you possibly go to the Soviet Union and toast to Brezhnev and Kosygin and sign a SALT agreement in the Great Hall of St. Peter when Russian tanks and guns are kicking the hell out of our allies in Vietnam?" Conversation between Nixon and Haig, May 2, 1972, NA, NPM, WHT, Conversation No. 717-20. Transcribed in FRUS, Volume XIV, Foreign Relations, 1969-1976, Soviet Union, October 1971–May 1972, 689.
[3] Memorandum From Helmut Sonnenfeldt of the National Security Council Staff to the President's Assistant for National Security Affairs (Kissinger), May 4, 1972, FRUS, Volume XIV, Foreign Relations, 1969-1976, Soviet Union, October 1971–May 1972, 732.

Moscow. By the late 1960s, in fact, both sides had come to consider the advantages of arms control – a process that was, consequently, placed at the center of the US-Soviet dialogue.

During the 1960s, and particularly after the Cuban missile crisis, the acquisition programs undertaken in Washington and Moscow had determined the future composition of their arsenals. From the standpoint of a widespread perception strength, the United States had focused on achieving an "assured second strike capability," concentrating on the development of very precise silos-based Inter Continental Ballistic Missiles (ICBMs) and of ballistic missiles to be placed on nuclear submarines (Submarine Launched Ballistic Missiles – SLBMs).[4] When, in 1966, a number of nuclear systems deemed able of guaranteeing such a capability had been achieved, the missile production was halted, and only their progressive technological modernization continued.[5] The Soviet Union, instead, reacted to the Cuban "humiliation" by initiating a program of quantitative growth of its strategic weapons, directing its efforts on the production of land-based, heavy (i.e., with significant throw-weight and payload) ICBMs.[6]

The United States, therefore, had established maximum ceilings of missile production when its strategic forces were conspicuously superior to those of the Soviet Union and did not modify those ceilings, even when it became evident that Moscow had engaged in a significant buildup. Moreover, the Soviets did not halt their missile production, the approaching of numerical parity with the United States notwithstanding. On the contrary, they continued to increase their ICBM force, both in quantity and in throw-weight, coupling it with the development of an antiballistic missile (ABM) system, code-named *Galosh*, for the defense of Moscow from a nuclear attack.[7]

---

[4] The development of these systems was made possible by the progress in the electronic field and in the miniaturization of nuclear warheads, and by the shift from liquid missile fuel to solid boosters. Thus, the second-generation of American ICBMs, the *Minuteman*, was smaller and operationally more capable and effective than the first-generation missiles, the *Atlas* and the *Titan*; Gerard Smith, *Doubletalk: The Story of the First Strategic Arms Limitation Talks* (Garden City, NY: Doubleday, 1980).

[5] The modernization produced the shift from the *Minuteman I* to the *Minuteman II* and *III* ICBMs and from the *Polaris* to the *Poseidon* and *Trident* SLBMs; William Bundy, *A Tangled Web. The Making of Foreign Policy in the Nixon Presidency* (London: IB Tauris, 1998), 84; Henry Kissinger, *White House Years* (London: Phoenix Press, 2000), 196.

[6] The numbers of the Soviet buildup were impressive: In 1965, the Soviets could field 200 ICBMs and little more than 100 SLBMs; in 1968, the ICBMs had increased to 860 and the SLBMs to 120; Kissinger, *White House Years*, 197.

[7] Bundy, *A Tangled Web*, 84.

Consequently, by the second half of the 1960s the Soviet programs started to arouse profound preoccupations in Washington. In 1967 the CIA assessed the Soviet buildup as "being aimed at narrowing the lead that the US has had" in strategic attack forces, mainly through an "extensive intercontinental ballistic missile (ICBM) deployment."[8] The report then projected the Soviet missile development on a ten-year period (thus well into the 1970s). Although the document considered all types of Soviet strategic systems, the most alarming data referred to the numerical increase of ICBMs. The Soviet Union was expected to be able to field between 1,000 and 1,500 ICBMs by the mid-1970s if, at the same time, it tested the Multiple Independently-targeted Re-entry Vehicles (MIRVs) technology. Without this innovation (with which the Soviets had not yet experimented) it was likely that the Soviets would exceed 1,500 ICBMs and, by 1977, have more than 1,700 missiles. A force of about 1,100 ICBMs could only result from a Soviet deliberate decision to maintain a level more or less equal to that of the United States.[9]

If for other categories of weapons, such as the SLBMs and the strategic bombers, the United States was expected to retain its superiority, despite the Soviet buildup, the picture regarding the ICBMs would be one of clear inferiority. While the United States decided not to invest in the numerical increase of its forces, concentrating instead on the development of new technologies (the MIRVs and the ABM), the growing Soviet ICBM force caused constant preoccupations in Washington. This constituted the single major incentive to negotiations with the Soviet Union. The objective was to bring about a political decision in Moscow to halt missile production once parity with the United States had been achieved.

These were the technical motivations behind President Nixon's – himself not a longtime advocate of arms control – support for SALT. Moreover,

---

[8] Memorandum for Recipients of NIE 11-8-67, "Extreme Sensitivity of NIE 11-8-67 – Soviet Capabilities for Strategic Attack," National Security Archive (hereafter NSA), Soviet Estimate Collection, document se0425, 6. It is interesting to note that CIA Director Richard Helms wrote in the memorandum that the dissemination of the Intelligence Estimate had to be "carefully limited because of extreme sensitivity of the information therein." He stressed that there should be "no reproduction of this Estimate, and that no revelation of its existence be made to unauthorized persons." The tone of these statements conveys a certain degree of preoccupation concerning the subject of the study: the pace of the Soviet buildup. On the other hand, the same document stressed that, despite the ICBM buildup, the Soviet Union would remain vulnerable in other categories and, overall, the United States remained in a position of strength.

[9] Ibid, 8.

the particular domestic context which the administration inherited provided further incentives for the pursuit of a strategic dialogue with the Soviet Union. The public widespread criticism of the Vietnam War involved all aspects of American defense policy and extended to the entire military establishment. The pressures for the reorganization of national priorities translated into demands for reducing the defense budget. The military-industrial complex was criticized for having acquired an excessive influence on policy making, while armaments were considered the cause rather than the barometer of tension. To counter these criticisms, the incoming presidency had to conceive a policy aimed at controlling and containing defense requirements.

Therefore, Nixon faced domestic pressures for unilateral American constraint precisely at a time when the Soviet Union's nuclear force had reached unprecedented levels. Consequently, the dialogue with the Soviets seemed to be the only means to avoid the potential tilting of the strategic balance in favor of Moscow. The negotiations would both seek to stop the Soviet buildup and provide the only context in which future acquisition programs, aimed at strengthening the US strategic posture, would be accepted by the American public opinion and Congress.

From Washington's standpoint, the "time had come" to engage in arms limitation talks. But their successful outcome was eventually possible only due to the parallel and converging motivations of the Soviet Union. While in the years preceding the Nixon presidency, Moscow had not responded to the reiterated American efforts to begin SALT, in 1969 the Soviet interest in the talks was explicit. "Past experience indicated the importance of beginning negotiations as soon as possible. Delay could be harmful," stated Ambassador Dobrynin during his first conversation with President Nixon. And, he continued: "(The Soviet) government, of course, would be interested in having a more precise idea as to when the president would be prepared to begin an exchange of views on the missile problem, even if preliminary and at the level of experts."[10]

Also, from Moscow's viewpoint the late 1960s appeared, in fact, to be the appropriate moment to engage in talks, given that the negotiations would be all the more valuable from the position of strength that the Soviets had acquired. Moreover, a SALT agreement represented the opportunity to formally codify the status of superpower and of strategic

---

[10] "Ambassador Dobrynin's Initial Call on the President," Memorandum of Conversation, February 17, 1969, NA, NPM, NSC files, box 489, folder 1.

equality with the United States, a long-sought objective and an essential element of Soviet foreign policy.

Moscow had, also, more technical motivations. The traditional American lead in technological research and development cautioned the Kremlin against a future competition in ABM systems (this represented a significant change of stance since the Glassboro meeting of 1967 between President Johnson and Premier Kosygin, when the Soviet leader had rebuked the possibility to enter talks on defensive systems).[11] For the same reasons, the Soviets were aware of the need to monitor the American MIRV development which, through the multiplication of the warheads, was eventually bound to deprive Moscow of the gains reached through the numerical increase of its missile force. Moreover, and most importantly, the Kremlin realized the necessity of curtailing the potentially destabilizing effect of the combination of the two innovations – a nationwide ABM system coupled with the large-scale deployment of MIRVed missiles.[12]

The Soviet broader political objectives and the military-technical motivations were, at the same time, interrelated with the complex world scene of the late 1960s. The process of improved relations between the Soviet Union and Western Europe, especially with the Federal Republic of Germany, would become complicated with US opposition, and the American position (in the context of the Berlin Agreements) was in large part determined by the prospect of strategic arms control. Furthermore, Moscow had to face the deteriorating relationship with the People's Republic of China. The improvement of relations with the United States

---

[11] During the June 1967 Johnson-Kosygin meeting in Glassboro, McNamara had tried to convince the Soviets of the risks and costs of an ABM systems competition and had proposed to abandon their development. McNamara's arguments on the future destabilizing effects of ABMs did not persuade Kosygin, who stated that asking for the abandonment of *defensive* systems was an absurd proposal. Significantly, the consequent realization that defensive systems could upset the strategic balance, while the offensive ones assured MAD and stability, would lead to the negotiating basis of the SALT I package.

[12] An operationally effective ABM system could encourage its possessor to assess the advantages of a massive first strike aimed at the destruction of the adversary's missile bases, as the system would protect the country from the retaliatory strike. Furthermore, if the country possessed MIRVs, the incentives for a first strike would be even greater, because multiple warheads had a higher possibility of weakening the opponent's retaliation. Therefore, while in the past the strategic arsenals had been conceived to minimize the advantages of a first strike, guaranteeing an overall stability, it would no longer be the case if these developments remained unlimited; William C. Foster, *Prospects for Arms Control*, "Foreign Affairs," April 1969, Vol. 47, n. 3.

was thus in Moscow's broader interest and on that path SALT was the central building block.[13]

Therefore, by the late 1960s both superpowers considered the Strategic Arms Limitation Talks a necessity, and a priority. This enabled the preliminary talks to start in Helsinki in late 1969. The Soviet and American delegations then continued to meet alternatively in Vienna and Helsinki, until the signing of the SALT I agreements at the Moscow summit in May 1972.

THE CONTENT AND SCOPE OF SALT I

Considering the complexity of issues related to nuclear arms control, and the fact that notable participants in the SALT I process have published extensive accounts of the negotiations,[14] it seems superfluous here to provide a comprehensive and detailed description of the talks. The aim, instead, is to outline the main characteristics of the agreements, while interrelating their outcome to the broader definition of Washington and Moscow's Cold War strategic posture.

Since the launching of the nuclear arms race, the deterring capacity of the superpowers' forces constituted the main feature of the bipolar rivalry, while the logic of mutual assured destruction (MAD) guaranteed strategic stability. However, given the pace of the strengthening and modernization of their arsenals, Washington and Moscow realized that the potential for tilting the equilibrium in favor of one or the other was potentially present – a development which, ultimately, neither considered desirable. Consequently, the SALT process was elaborated as a means to maintain and respect the Cold War equilibrium, or the so-called balance of terror.

A reading of the end results of the three-year SALT negotiations enables the affirmation that the sides, to a large extent, succeeded in their task. In fact, by signing the accords the superpowers recognized and accepted that neither could, nor would, strive for a "first strike capability."[15] At the

---

[13] Among other motivations on the Soviet side, Dobrynin cites the enormous burden of military expenditures and Brezhnev's personal incentives, as the improvement of relations with the United States would consolidate his position and prestige within the Soviet Union; Anatoly Dobrynin, *In Confidence. Moscow's Ambassador to America's Six Cold War Presidents* (New York: Random House, 1995), 193.

[14] For the most comprehensive and detailed accounts of SALT I: Gerald Smith, *Doubletalk* and Raymond Garthoff, *Détente and Confrontation. American-Soviet Relations from Nixon to Reagan* (Washington DC: The Brookings Institution, 1994).

[15] This is the capability of a nuclear power to destroy the opponent's nuclear forces, eliminating the possibility of a retaliatory strike.

same time, within the limits of the negotiated agreement, the possibility to continue the strengthening of their respective forces was assured.[16] Therefore, in this first, critical, albeit initial phase of the strategic arms control process "unilateral strength and cooperation measures went hand in hand."[17]

The fact that the two sides had entered the negotiations because of concrete necessities and perceptions of insecurity explains the difficulties in reaching a compromise. The United States and the Soviet Union started negotiating by advancing proposals formulated on the basis of their respective specific security concerns. Each side's search for unilateral advantage, though perhaps initially understandable, led to a prolonged impasse. The negotiations remained stalemated between late 1969 and mid-1971.[18]

The main point of contention revolved around which categories had to be included in the agreement. From Moscow's standpoint, the SALT limitations had to curtail all nuclear weapons capable of striking the territory of the other side, their "strategic" or "tactical" role notwithstanding. This position was determined by deeply rooted concerns regarding American forces dislocated in bases close to Soviet territory – the so-called forward-based systems.[19] However, following the Kremlin's rationale, systems unable to reach the territory of the adversary would be excluded from the agreement. This would leave the 600 Soviet medium-ranged missiles (MRBMs/IRBMs) targeted on Western Europe untouched by the limitations.[20] Such a position was obviously unacceptable for Washington. But despite the firm and predictable US refusal to enter negotiations in this

---

[16] As has been underlined, in fact, the SALT I agreement did little to actually curb the arms race, merely shifting it to other categories of weaponry; Jussi Hanhimäki, *The Flawed Architect. Henry Kissinger and American Foreign Policy* (New York: Oxford University Press, 2004), 221.

[17] Condoleezza Rice, "SALT and the Search for a Security Regime" in Alexander L. George, Philip J. Farley, Alexander Dallin (eds), *U.S.-Soviet Security Cooperation. Achievements, Failures, Lessons* (New York: Oxford University Press, 1988), 296.

[18] For the description of the initial comprehensive SALT I proposals: Smith, *Doubletalk*, 118–119, 121–123, 125–126, 149–150.

[19] The FBS were dual-role fighter bombers, capable of carrying both conventional and nuclear weapons, deployed on European or Asian bases and on board US Navy aircraft carriers. By seeking to limit these, Moscow's scope was to reduce NATO's air forces and their support of Allied ground forces in a potential conventional war against the Warsaw Pact.

[20] Semenov explicitly stated that the Soviet territory could be hit by an American fighter-bomber deployed on a European base or by an ICBM launched from the United States and the practical result would not change; Smith, *Doubletalk*, 90–91.

domain, the Soviet delegation insisted, in the words of the head of the American SALT delegation Gerald Smith, "ad nauseam,"[21] almost jeopardizing the overall outcome of the talks.[22]

Considering the difficulties in moving toward a comprehensive agreement (including both offensive weapons, i.e., missiles, and defensive systems, i.e., ABMs), the Soviet Union, already in mid-1970, started to push for a separate ABM treaty.[23] But from the American point of view, given the goal of limiting the buildup of Soviet ICBMs, it was vital to maintain the link between the two (offensive-defensive) categories of weapons. For this reason, the breakthrough represented by the May 20, 1971, agreement[24] was a twofold success for Washington. It stated that an ABM treaty would be concluded immediately and, while negotiations on offensive systems continued, a temporary freeze of missile production would be enforced. This preserved the incentive to continue negotiations on offensive systems, thus assuring Washington's first goal. Secondly, and most significantly, while a single treaty of unlimited duration would have had the same long-term effects for Washington and Moscow, the interim freeze touched only upon the Soviet programs, since the US missile production had been halted many years before.

On the basis of the May 20, 1971, guidelines, in essence defined from above by Kissinger and Dobrynin, the SALT delegations proceeded to finalize the agreements, which were then signed by Nixon and Brezhnev at the Moscow summit on May 26, 1972. The SALT I package included the ABM Treaty and the Interim Agreement on offensive weapons. The ABM Treaty allowed for two ABM sites, for the defense of the capital and of one ICBM base. With the clear objective of preventing that the systems be expanded to cover the whole national territory, it offered a picture of quantitative and functional symmetry, leaving the credibility

---

[21] Ibid, 187.
[22] The American-Soviet disagreement on the FBS issue, in fact, deeply, and negatively, influenced the course of the negotiations on offensive weapons.
[23] For Kissinger's account of the June 23 meeting, the first in which Dobrynin advanced the idea of a separate ABM treaty: Kissinger, *White House Years*, 547.
[24] This is the text of the agreement: "The Governments of the United States and the Soviet Union, after reviewing the course of their talks on the limitation of strategic armaments, have agreed to concentrate this year on working out an agreement for the limitation of the deployment of antiballistic missile systems (ABMs). They have also agreed that, together with concluding an agreement to limit ABMs, they will agree on certain measures with respect to the limitation of offensive strategic weapons"; Kissinger, *White House Years*, 820.

of MAD untouched.²⁵ Interestingly, the American side was determined to complete the Grand Forks ABM base but had no intention of building a second ABM system to defend Washington. The Soviet Union, instead, had no apparent intention to defend its ICBMs with a second site, aiming only to increase to 100 the number of *Galosh* missiles around Moscow. Therefore, the compromise on ABMs had been reached on the basis of deployment options that neither side intended to adopt – due to the huge economic costs and the still uncertain technologies and, for the United States, because of the opposition in Congress. For the superpowers it had been important not only to find a solution capable of safeguarding their national security requirements but also to preserve future opportunities, however unlikely.

The Interim Agreement simply stated that the number of allowed ICBMs and SLBMs, for the five-year duration of the freeze, had to be equal to the number of those operational or in construction as of May 26, 1972, for the SLBMs, and as of July 1, 1972, for the ICBMs. The modernization and replacement of the missiles was permitted openly, with the only exception being the ban on further deployment of "heavy" missiles.²⁶ In terms of aggregates, the agreement favored the Soviet Union,²⁷ but this was more than compensated for in other aspects of the accord. In fact, the extension of the freeze to the missiles in construction substantially limited the potential Soviet advantage, given the pace of the Soviet buildup.²⁸ And, most importantly, the agreement did not limit in

---

[25] Each ABM site could have 100 missiles each. The areas protected could have a maximum radius of 150 km and be separated by at least 1,300 km. No mobile missiles were permitted and they could carry only one warhead. For the defensive system of Moscow and Washington there were restrictions in the radar deployment, but not in their number or dimension. For the system in defense of the ICBM bases it was just the opposite. There were no provisions limiting the qualitative improvement of the antiballistic missiles, which could be replaced by more technologically advanced systems.

[26] The numbers were all in the protocol, not in the actual agreement.

[27] The Soviet Union had 2,424 offensive missiles, of which 950 were SLBMs. The United States had 1,710 missiles, of which 710 were SLBMs. Another aspect in favor of the USSR was that throw-weight, considered a qualitative aspect, was not limited in any way. In this, the Soviet superiority was evident. Moscow had always privileged the production of heavy missiles with very high yield warheads (up to twenty-five MT for the SS-9), while the biggest American ICBM, the *Titan* 2, carried a 10 MT warhead; *The Military Balance 1972–1973*, London, IISS, September 1972, 85.

[28] The Soviet Union was capable of a yearly production of around 250 ICBMs and 128 SLBMs. In theory, without the *freeze* Moscow could have produced, in five years, over 1,200 SLBMs and around 2,800 ICBMs. The United States, as has been underlined, did not have any program for the production of new missiles and would have remained at 1,054

any way the number of intercontinental bombers and MIRVs, for which the United States clearly maintained superiority.[29]

Contrary to the criticism that gradually emerged around the Interim Agreement and the supposed advantages conceded to the Soviets,[30] its most significant aspect was precisely the fact that it left the United States free to secure its advantage in MIRV development. As the Nixon administration was well aware, the agreement, although codifying a Soviet lead in the number of missiles, did not weaken the American strategic forces in any way. As an internal document assessed:

> We estimate that we will maintain our current substantial lead in strategic warheads for at least the next five years. This lead might even be increased. Since the number of targets we can attack is directly related to the number of warheads in our forces, warheads are a better measure of relative strategic strength than launchers.[31]

In short, Washington was convinced that the agreements protected American security, while leaving open the future possibility to strive for superiority. But, obviously, the signing of the agreements was only possible because the compromise reached satisfied both sides. As Brezhnev put it:

> We are both fully aware, Mr. President, of the immense effort that was required in order to prepare these agreements. I am sure that we are both fully aware of how

---

ICBMs and 656 SLBMs. Therefore, it can be said that the agreement substantially limited the potential Soviet advantage in the total number of offensive systems; *The Military Balance 1972–1973*, London, IISS, September 1972, 84.

[29] Regarding intercontinental bombers: The United States had 455 B-52s (including those held in reserve) versus 140 Tu-95s and Mya-4s (100 were propeller driven) of the Soviet Union. The B-52 could carry a bigger weapons load than the Tu-95 and Mya-4. Theoretically, the American strategic air force could drop on the Soviet territory about 2,000 nuclear weapons versus the 420 of the Soviet bombers. A further consideration: If the United States would equip its bombers with the Short Range Attack Missiles (SRAMs), already in production, in five years, the total American weapons systems would increase to above 7,500. Regarding MIRVs: in 1972, the United States had a very advanced "mirving" program, with 360 operational missiles (200 *Minuteman III*, with three warheads each, and 160 *Poseidon*, with ten warheads). The Soviet Union had begun to deploy multiple, but not independently targeted, warheads on some of its SS-9 and SS-11 ICBMs, but had not yet tested MIRVed warheads. The disparity, in favor of the United States, in terms of number of targets which theoretically could be attacked was therefore evident; *The Military Balance 1972–1973*, London, IISS, September 1972, 85.

[30] On the dissatisfaction with the SALT I agreements: Hanhimäki, *The Flawed Architect*, 220–221.

[31] *The Strategic Arms Limitation Agreements and National Security*, NA, NPM, NSC files, box 79, folder 3.

useful it has been from the standpoint of the direct national interests of our two states and in terms of their influence on the general international climate.³²

"Direct national interests" were therefore the key in a process geared toward maintaining strategic stability. Aside from the complexity of the language and the endless quarrels over the details (throw-weight, payload, tactical and/or strategic), the SALT I agreements ultimately confirmed that nuclear deterrence remained the central vital characteristic of the superpowers' strategic posture. At the time – as noted by historian Robert Schulzinger – Nixon was successful in solidifying his "public position as a masterful statesman who had grown far beyond this early anti-communism to usher a new era of stability and peace and to dampen the tension of the Cold War."³³ In reality, however, through the "era of negotiation" the Nixon administration had simply guaranteed the continued reliance on one of the central aspects of the Cold War.

"THE SUPREME TEST"

The fact that the search for agreement with the Soviets had evolved from a realistic assessment of concrete necessities and that the end result assured the respect of deterrence, one of the main elements of the bipolar Cold War system, are inherent characteristics of the Nixon-Kissinger design. The rhetoric of moving from confrontation to negotiation overshadowed the notion that, overall, the superpower relationship continued to be shaped by antagonism. The rivalry was still there. It was, however, changing in nature.

As the unfolding of the Sino-American relationship demonstrated, the American administration was in search of means outside the military-nuclear domain to exert pressure on Moscow and to implement a different and more effective containment of Soviet expansionism. The assurance of stability in the strategic competition was the first step in shifting the competition away from the nuclear arms race and into a broader, more global geopolitical struggle for supremacy. This dynamic emerged gradually (an important building block will be the main focus of the next chapter), but its main features were present from the beginning. In fact, between 1969

---

³² Memorandum of Conversation, Monday, May 22, 1972, The General Secretary's Office, The Kremlin, Moscow, NA, NPM, NSC files, box 487, folder 3.
³³ Robert D. Schulzinger, "Détente in the Nixon-Ford Years, 1969–1975" in Leffler and Westad (eds), *The Cambridge History of the Cold War, Volume II* (Cambridge: Cambridge University Press, 2010), 382.

and 1972, when SALT I was in progress and considered emblematic of the alleged new cooperation between the superpowers, in other contexts the competition continued, and even escalated.

The making of a comprehensive ambivalent policy for the management of the superpower relationship is evident in the Nixon-Kissinger concept of "linkage." The fact of linking the success of one negotiation to the positive outcome of another was not only an effective diplomatic tool, but it gave the American leadership the opportunity to better focus on what was considered more important, or more urgent, in the process of defending US interests worldwide. This emerges in between the lines of a memorandum written for Nixon after the already cited first meeting with Dobrynin, when Kissinger suggests to "use" the Soviet interest in rapidly beginning SALT in order to concentrate on the other problematic issues at the heart of the US-Soviet relationship:

> In a nutshell, I think that at this moment of uncertainty about our intentions, Moscow wants to engage us. Some would argue that regardless of motive, we should not let this moment of interest pass, lest Moscow swing back to total hostility. My own view is that we should seek to utilize this Soviet interest, stemming as I think it does from anxiety, to induce them to come to grips with the real sources of tension, notably in the Middle East, but also in Vietnam.[34]

The coming "to grips with the real sources of tension" revealed a particular concern for the so-called periphery (i.e., areas of the Third World outside the traditional Cold War spheres of influence), together with the determination not to concede any potential advantage to the Soviets. The paradox was, in fact, quite evident. While at the highest level the superpower dialogue led to ceremonies and benevolent speeches, in various regions of the world Soviet (or Chinese) and American armed soldiers continued to kill each other in "proxy" wars. The most sadly notable one was, of course, still fully waging in Vietnam.

The emergence of this cooperation-competition pattern had already surfaced in April 1970. The Soviet reaction to the Cambodian incursion had, in fact, suggested that continued firmness in the Vietnamese context would not negatively influence the continuation of SALT, albeit harsh, but rhetorical and rather limited protests from Moscow.[35] This dynamic

---

[34] Memorandum for the President from Henry Kissinger, "Analysis of Dobrynin Message," February 18, 1969, NA, NPM, NSC files, box 489, folder 1.

[35] The American forces entered Cambodia to destroy the "sanctuaries" where the Vietnamese soldiers found shelter and logistic support. The enlargement of the conflict could have seriously jeopardized the evolution of SALT. The Soviet reaction was immediate, but limited to

emerged all the more significantly in the months immediately preceding the scheduled signing of SALT I at the May 1972 summit.

On March 30, 1972, the North Vietnamese forces launched a massive military offensive invading, through the demilitarized zone, the territory of South Vietnam. Considering the ties between Moscow and Hanoi, it was obvious that the Easter Offensive[36] would raise distressing questions in Washington on the future conduct of American-Soviet relations. Would it be possible to induce Moscow to put pressure on its ally to bring the war to an end, without compromising the summit? Or, alternatively, did the United States risk being manipulated by the Soviets, precluding the possibility of responding to Hanoi's action?

When studying the Nixon administration's reaction to the North Vietnamese offensive and the heated internal debates revolving around how to deal with the Vietnam-summit interrelationship, three elements emerge with clarity. The first is that the president (and, to a large degree, also Kissinger) assigned utmost importance to the need to respond assertively in Vietnam, regardless of the forthcoming meeting in Moscow. Despite the obvious reluctance in jeopardizing the evolution of the US-Soviet relationship, the defense of American prestige and honor, at stake in Indochina, was clearly a priority.[37] The summit could (if need be) be sacrificed, but Vietnam could not be lost (or, at least, not in this way, i.e., with a humiliating defeat).

During their first meeting after the news of the North Vietnamese offensive had arrived in Washington, Nixon and Kissinger agreed that, while up to that moment "great restraint" had been shown in Vietnam, this attack had to be definitely "knocked off." Otherwise, they would

---

Kosygin's declaration at a press conference on May 4, 1970. The Soviet premier strongly condemned the intervention and stated that it would further complicate the SALT negotiations. At the same time, he hinted that Moscow did not intend to assume a more confrontational position. At the following SALT session, Semenov referred to the Cambodian operation as a proof of Washington's unreliable intentions. However, it was the only time it was mentioned. In his report to the president, Smith wrote that the Soviet reaction had, in fact, been minimal. This demonstrated the relevance the Soviets attributed to SALT; Smith, *Doubletalk*, 136–137.

[36] For a description of the Easter Offensive: Bundy, *A Tangled Web*, 307–309; Hanhimäki, *The Flawed Architect*, 202–203.

[37] Robert Dallek, for example, underlines Nixon and Kissinger's eagerness in preserving the summit; *Nixon and Kissinger. Partners in Power* (New York: HarperCollins, 2007), 373. However, as illustrated in this chapter, Nixon's insistence on the need for an assertive response in Vietnam is underlined in a number of documents – both American and Soviet. Hanhimäki also underlines Nixon's determination in responding to the North Vietnamese offensive, *The Flawed Architect*, 203.

have no other choice than to "bomb them."[38] A few days later, when the news from the battle zone further clarified the dimension of Hanoi's challenge, Nixon and Kissinger commented:

> Kissinger: They (the ARVN) are not going to collapse.
> Nixon: (…) We can't take it.
> Kissinger: I agree. That's why we've got to blast the (…) the living bejeezus out of North Vietnam. We will gain nothing for restraint.
> Nixon: I agree.[39]

This exchange vividly conveys the general attitude that shaped the decisions toward Vietnam in the spring of 1972, from the intensification of the B-52 bombing of areas of the north in early April, to the mining of the Haiphong harbor announced on May 8, 1972. These choices were, in essence, motivated by the generalized belief that, should the North Vietnamese succeed, the United States "would be finished as a world power. It's that bad," stated Nixon.[40] Furthermore, as the South Vietnamese limited capacity to resist the offensive became manifest, the president's determination seemed to progressively increase. In another private conversation with Kissinger, Nixon said:

> I'm going to destroy the goddamn country (Vietnam), believe me, destroy it if necessary. And let me say, even the nuclear weapons if necessary. It isn't necessary. But, you know, what I mean is, that shows you the extent to which I am willing to go. By nuclear weapon, I mean that we will bomb the living bejeezus out of North Vietnam and then if anybody interferes we will threaten the nuclear weapon.[41]

The second important aspect is that by stubbornly "holding on" to South Vietnam the administration confirmed its classic bipolar worldview. The Nixon entourage was in fact convinced that the Soviets had backed Hanoi's offensive, that it was, essentially, "a Russian move."[42] Consequently, the rationale behind the president's firmness resulted

---

[38] Conversation between Nixon and Kissinger, March 30, 1972, NA, NPM, WHT, Conversation No. 697-2. Transcribed in FRUS, Volume XIV, Foreign Relations, 1969–1976, Soviet Union, October 1971–May 1972, 235.

[39] Conversation between Nixon and Kissinger, April 3, 1972, NA, NPM, WHT, Conversation No. 700-2. Transcribed in FRUS, Volume XIV, Foreign Relations, 1969–1976, Soviet Union, October 1971–May 1972, 252.

[40] Conversation between Nixon and Kissinger, April 10, 1972, NA, NPM, WHT, Conversation No. 705-13, Transcribed in FRUS, Volume XIV, Foreign Relations, 1969–1976, Soviet Union, October 1971–May 1972, 281.

[41] Conversation between Nixon and Kissinger, April 19, 1972, NA, NPM, WHT, Conversation No. 713-1. Transcribed in FRUS, Volume XIV, Foreign Relations, 1969–1976, Soviet Union, October 1971–May 1972, 433.

[42] This emerges clearly, for example, in documents No. 89, 115, 149 in FRUS, Volume XIV, Foreign Relations, 1969–1976, Soviet Union, October 1971–May 1972, 276, 364, 569.

from his determination not to yield advantages to communist-backed challenges. "I know," stated Nixon, "that nobody can be president of this country, and have a viable foreign policy, if the United States suffers a defeat fighting this miserable, little communist country, fueled by Soviet arms, and that the world is going to be a very dangerous place to live in. If the Soviets succeed here, they will try the Middle East, they will try everywhere else, and the United States will roll over and play dead. So therefore this is the supreme test."[43] In the end, it was all, and still, about dominoes falling.[44] Undeniably, the decisions on Vietnam were also influenced by domestic political considerations (while this book focuses exclusively on foreign policy, this does not diminish the importance of the interplay between foreign and domestic policy). The president was, in fact, also concerned about the impact of events in Indochina on the forthcoming presidential election.[45]

Thirdly, from an analytical viewpoint, the significance of the events of April–May 1972 lay in the opportunity, which gradually unfolded for the United States, to support a strong military action in Vietnam, while simultaneously not abandoning the search for cooperation with the Soviets in other domains, most notably in SALT. This apparently paradoxical stance confirmed the dual nature of Nixon's détente. Both Kissinger's secret visit to Moscow in April 1972 and the events leading to the May summit, in fact, signaled the development of a complex ambivalence in the management of the US-Soviet relationship.

TOASTING WITH THE SOVIETS, WHILE ESCALATING IN VIETNAM

Evidently, therefore, the US leadership was not willing to yield to Soviet-backed pressure in Vietnam. This is confirmed also by the intention

---

[43] Conversation between Nixon and Connally, April 20, 1972, NA, NPM, WHT, Conversation No. 714-4. Transcribed in FRUS, Volume XIV, Foreign Relations, 1969–1976, Soviet Union, October 1971–May 1972, 455.
[44] "Dominoes" are explicitly mentioned in a conversation between Nixon and Haig, May 2, 1972, NA, MPM, WHT, Conversation No. 717-20. Transcribed in FRUS, Volume XIV, Foreign Relations, 1969–1976, Soviet Union, October 1971–May 1972, 692.
[45] Dallek, *Nixon and Kissinger*, 372. Hanhimäki, *The Flawed Architect*, 201, 211. Interestingly, the Soviets were also well aware that Nixon's response to the North Vietnamese offensive was influenced by domestic political considerations; Memorandum of Conversation (USSR), April 3, 1972, Document No. 279 and Memorandum of Conversation (USSR), April 6, 1972, Document No. 281, *Soviet-American Relations. The Détente Years, 1969–1972* (Washington DC: US Government Printing Office, 2007), 639, 643.

(Kissinger's in particular) to "play this" (i.e., manipulate the situation) in order to bring the war to an end.[46] Because the preparations for the Moscow summit were proceeding, and considering the Soviet interest in its successful outcome, Washington hoped to obtain Moscow's aid in negotiating a settlement with Hanoi. It is mainly with this objective that Nixon approved Kissinger's secret trip to Moscow in mid-April 1972.[47] When instructing Kissinger for his upcoming critical conversations with the Soviet leaders, Nixon insisted that the "primary goal in talking to him [Brezhnev] is solely to get action on Vietnam." While the Soviets would focus on the summit, Kissinger's "primary interest," in fact his "indispensable interest," would be "to get them to talk about Vietnam."[48] Interestingly, Ambassador Dobrynin had grasped the importance that the American president assigned to Vietnam and gave advance warning to the Soviet leadership that this would be the main topic of conversation during Kissinger's forthcoming visit:

> On the President's behalf, Kissinger told us that at the Moscow meetings he would be authorized to discuss all issues relating to the upcoming Soviet-US summit in May.
>
> However, there is absolutely no doubt that as a result of recent events surrounding Vietnam, at the President's instructions Kissinger will put his main emphasis on Vietnam, since this has now become the main issue for Nixon, whose views on his relationship with the Soviet Union are primarily colored by this issue.[49]

On his part, instead, Kissinger underlined both the president's determination in Indochina and the opportunity of holding out the carrot of the summit in order to obtain Soviet help:

---

[46] Conversation between Nixon and Kissinger, April 3, 1972, NA, NPM, WHT, Conversation No. 700-2. Transcribed in FRUS, Volume XIV, *Foreign Relations, 1969–1976, Soviet Union, October 1971–May 1972*, 251.

[47] It is interesting to note that while in his memoirs Kissinger underlines that the Soviets had insisted on the secrecy of his Moscow trip (allegedly because his China trip in July 1971 had been secret), the documents consulted clearly show that it was the US side to insist on secrecy due to the delicate situation in Vietnam. Nixon was in fact worried that disclosing Kissinger's visit to Moscow, in the middle of the Vietnamese offensive, would have a negative domestic impact; Kissinger, *White House Years*, 839 and documents No. 95 and 97, FRUS, Volume XIV, *Foreign Relations, 1969–1976, Soviet Union, October 1971–May 1972*, 302, 309.

[48] Memorandum for Henry Kissinger from the President, April 20, 1972, NA, NPM, NSC files, HAK Office files, box 21, folder 2.

[49] Telegram from Ambassador Dobrynin to the Soviet Foreign Ministry, April 19, 1972, Document No. 301, *Soviet-American Relations. The Détente Years, 1969–72*, 675.

I believe it has become clear to the Soviets that you [the president] intend to do what is necessary militarily to stop the Communist offensive and in that sense are prepared to subordinate your relationship with the USSR to the immediate requirements of the Vietnam situation.

To judge from Soviet behavior – including, of course, their urgent desire to have me come to Moscow – Brezhnev does not wish to sacrifice his "Western" policy to Hanoi's pressures. Consequently, we should have some flexibility in insisting on a constructive Soviet role regarding Vietnam before we turn to the summit-related substantive issues of US-Soviet relations.[50]

Even more specifically, Kissinger stated:

I think we should conduct the summit part of the talks in a very conciliatory and forthcoming manner in such a way that they get a maximum panting after the summit. On the Vietnam thing, on the other hand, we should be tough as nails, because we will not impress these guys with conciliatoriness.... So I think we should do both simultaneously.[51]

The potential for maneuvering to the US advantage was, indeed, there. Only a few days after the initial massive American B-52 bombings of the Haiphong area in Vietnam, Kissinger was greeted in Moscow by a Soviet leadership still clearly committed to a productive summit.[52] Brezhnev only implicitly, and quite sarcastically, referred to Hanoi's actions: "Unfortunately, it so happens effusively that events in the recent period – shortly before this private meeting between us – dampened the atmosphere somewhat," he told Kissinger. To this declaration, which already did not offer much support to an ally subject to daily bombings, the Soviet leader added: "I am not saying that this will reduce the prospects of our meeting."[53]

Accordingly, Kissinger pursued his dual path. During the talks, he proceeded with a "judicious mixture" of pressure and flexibility, in the belief that Washington would have greater benefit from Soviet acquiescence

---

[50] Memorandum for the President from Henry Kissinger, "Issues for My Moscow Trip," NA, NPM, NSC files, HAK Office files, box 21, folder 1.

[51] Conversation between Nixon and Kissinger, April 17, 1972, Conversation No. 709-8. Transcribed in FRUS, Volume XIV, Foreign Relations, 1969–1976, Soviet Union, October 1971–May 1972, 361.

[52] For a detailed description of Kissinger's secret visit: Hanhimäki, *The Flawed Architect*, 204–211.

[53] Memorandum of Conversation, Moscow, April 21, 1972, noon–4:45 P.M., NA, NPM, NSC Files, HAK Office Files, Box 72. Transcribed in FRUS, Volume XIV, Foreign Relations, 1969–1976, Soviet Union, October 1971–May 1972, 477.

to the bombing than from a clear-cut rupture.⁵⁴ On the summit issues (including SALT) the April talks proved crucial in securing the eventual successful outcome of the Nixon-Brezhnev summit.⁵⁵ At the same time, in order to avoid the perception of US weakness, Nixon deliberately intensified the bombings in Vietnam.⁵⁶

On enlisting Soviet aid in ending the war, the April conversations were, instead, far less productive. Following Nixon's instructions, Kissinger did initially place Vietnam at the center of the discussions.⁵⁷ However, while reporting some progress, it was evident that he had not, and could not, "achieve a breakthrough in Vietnam."⁵⁸ The only direct positive outcome was Hanoi's agreement to resume the negotiations with the United States. But the optimistic prospects were soon to prove ephemeral. When the talks with the North Vietnamese resumed in Paris (on May 2, 1972), Kissinger was confronted with an absolute unwillingness to compromise.⁵⁹ In

---

⁵⁴ Message from Kissinger to Haig, April 22, 1972, NA, NPM, NSC Files, HAK Office Files, Box 21. Transcribed in FRUS, Volume XIV, Foreign Relations, 1969–1976, Soviet Union, October 1971–May 1972, 545.

⁵⁵ It is interesting to note that from the documentary evidence Nixon's near paranoia that Kissinger would not abide by his instructions and place the summit agenda before Vietnam emerges with evidence; Documents No. 136–138. FRUS, Volume XIV, Foreign Relations, 1969–1976, Soviet Union, October 1971–May 1972. The tone of Kissinger's cable from Moscow to Washington is unequivocal: "We have reported constantly ... But if the president does not trust me there is not much that can be done," Document No. 140, FRUS, Volume XIV, Foreign Relations, 1969–1976, Soviet Union, October 1971–May 1972, 544. Conversely, in his memoirs, Nixon gives full credit to his national security adviser: "Given Kissinger's achievements on the summit issues, I felt that there was no point in gainsaying his performance after the fact. If he had followed my instructions and insisted on a Vietnam settlement as the first order of business, perhaps Brezhnev would have dug in, called his bluff, and told him to go home – and that might have meant the end of the summit, with everything that it could accomplish, while still producing no progress in Vietnam. That was a risk I had thought worth taking. In any event the summit was held, and undoubtedly it owed a large measure of its success to Kissinger's negotiations during his secret visit to Moscow"; Nixon, *Memoirs*, 592. On the tensions between Nixon and Kissinger during the April visit: Hanhimäki, *The Flawed Architect*, 207–210; Dallek, *Nixon and Kissinger*, 377.

⁵⁶ For example, on the evening of April 21, Nixon told Haig: "Al, on an urgent basis, get Moorer to send a 52 strike in North Vietnam ... 25 or 30 planes tomorrow, while Henry is there," NA, NPM, NSC Files, Box 999, Haig Chronological File, Haig Telecons 1972. Quoted in FRUS, Volume XIV, Foreign Relations, 1969–1976, Soviet Union, October 1971–May 1972, 507.

⁵⁷ See, for example, the record of Kissinger's first discussion in Moscow with Gromyko and his first meeting with Brezhnev; Documents No. 129 and 134, FRUS, Volume XIV, Foreign Relations, 1969–1976, Soviet Union, October 1971–May 1972.

⁵⁸ Memorandum for the President from Henry A. Kissinger, "My Trip to Moscow," April 24, 1972, NA, NPM, NSC files, HAK Office files, box 72, folder 7.

⁵⁹ Hanhimäki, *The Flawed Architect*, 211–213.

short, therefore, only a few weeks before the scheduled Moscow summit, Nixon seemed to have no other option than the military one to prevent "humiliation" in Indochina.[60]

Although the concern of not sinking the entire US foreign policy design was still present within the administration, the consensus was ultimately almost unanimous in deciding that a military escalation in Vietnam was necessary. At this point, even Kissinger, who in precedence had been ready to gamble on Moscow's commitment to the summit, was convinced that the decision on blockading (or mining) North Vietnam might entail Soviet cancellation of the summit.[61] The exchanges between Kissinger and Dobrynin confirm the preoccupations of both sides, with neither willing to take the initiative (Kissinger's search for reassurance on Moscow's continued commitment to the summit is particularly interesting and emerges only from Soviet sources).[62] Nixon, however, was prepared to pay the price.

---

[60] Before Kissinger's departure for Moscow in April, Nixon and Kissinger seemed to outline the path later undertaken: "**Kissinger:** If I come back without anything, we've got to do something wild next week. **Nixon:** That's right ... You see, that's the way the game plan would have to come out. We will have to beat their offensive before we go to Moscow. Let me put it this way. Either out of your trip Moscow begins to help us on the war, or, or we will have to give Hanoi a hell of a shock in terms of beating their offensive so that I don't go there hat in hand"; conversation between Nixon and Kissinger, April 18, 1972, NA, NPM, WHT, Conversation No. 711-3. Transcribed in FRUS, Volume XIV, Foreign Relations, 1969–1976, Soviet Union, October 1971–May 1972, 392.

[61] Kissinger's attitude changed quite dramatically from before his April 1972 trip to Moscow – when he seemed confident that the United States could achieve both objectives: bringing the Vietnamese to a negotiated settlement and securing a successful summit with the Soviets – and after, when the failure of his May 2 meeting with the North Vietnamese had a negative impact on both objectives he had sought to achieve. In early May, Kissinger in fact became convinced that the Soviets would not proceed with the summit because of Nixon's bombing and mining in Vietnam. Kissinger's pursuit of both objectives before his April visit emerges clearly in most of the documents compiled in FRUS, Volume XIV, Foreign Relations, 1969–1976, Soviet Union, October 1971–May 1972, 234–408 (in particular during an April 4, 1972, conversation with Nixon, Kissinger states three times his belief that the Soviets would not cancel the summit; Ibid, 259). His subsequent belief that Nixon's actions in Vietnam would lead to Soviet cancellation of the summit is reported, for example, in documents No. 182, 188, 196; Ibid, 675, 708, 743.

[62] On the preoccupations of both sides: Memorandum of Conversation (USSR), May 1, 1972, Document No. 319, Telegram from Ambassador Dobrynin to the Soviet Foreign Ministry, May 5, 1972, Document No. 322 and Memorandum of Conversation (USSR), May 5, 1972, Document No. 323, *Soviet-American Relations. The Détente Years, 1969–1972*, 789, 794–796. Kissinger's search for Soviet reassurance clearly emerges in Memorandum of Conversation (USSR – typing error in printed version of the book, the memo is a Soviet, not American, source), May 11, 1972, Document No. 334; Ibid, 808.

On May 8, 1972, on national television the president broadcasted his justification for the Haiphong harbor mining and aimed straight at Moscow: The North Vietnamese offensive had been made possible only by the tanks, artillery, and other offensive weapons supplied "by the Soviet Union and other communist nations." However, Nixon also underlined the progress made in US-Soviet relations. As noted by Dobrynin, his speech ended with "a kind of appeal" to Moscow to "put these relations ahead of the events in Vietnam."[63]

Nixon's words, in essence, summed up the dual path undertaken by the administration. While the "era of negotiation" moved toward its high point in Moscow, the traditional Cold War antagonism did not subside. Détente had not revolutionized the bipolar conceptual framework within which its chief architects operated. The Vietnam-summit interconnection demonstrated that while cooperation in certain domains was certainly important, it was considered valuable, in terms of US foreign policy objectives if, and only if, Washington negotiated from a position of strength.

The May 8, 1972, escalation in Vietnam was designed to provide "a hell of a shock." But, at the same time, Nixon did not take action on the summit,[64] counting on the fact that, for Moscow, the potential material and psychological benefits of a successful summit outplayed the need to support its ally in Vietnam. In the end, events proved Nixon right. Despite diverging opinions within the Politburo, the Soviet leadership did not retaliate and decided to proceed with the summit as scheduled.[65] It was to be, as Sonnenfeldt put it, a "cynical summit."[66] And, cynically, in May 1972 the Nixon administration managed to achieve the better of

---

[63] Memorandum of Conversation (USSR), May 8, 1972, Document No. 327, *Soviet-American Relations. The Détente Years, 1969–1972*, 801–802.

[64] Initially, Nixon had been inclined to move toward cancellation or postponement of the summit, in order to preempt a likely Soviet cancellation. Afterwards, he became convinced that, given his demonstration of resolve in Vietnam and the limited Soviet reaction, the possibility of him going to Moscow for the summit was a viable opportunity.

[65] Dobrynin, in his memoirs, describes the Soviet difficulties in wanting to stop the American bombing, while yearning to proceed with a summit meeting with the same president who had ordered the attacks. In spite of the divisions within the Politburo, the choice was eventually made on the basis of the fact that Hanoi had repeatedly avoided informing Moscow about its long-term plans in Southeast Asia. The Soviet leadership could not afford to hand to the North Vietnamese a de facto veto over its relations with America; Dobrynin, *In Confidence*, 247–248. In short, as stated by Hanhimäki, "for the Soviet leadership there was simply too much at stake;" *The Flawed Architect*, 217.

[66] Memorandum From Helmut Sonnenfeldt of the National Security Council Staff to the President's Assistant for National Security Affairs (Kissinger), May 4, 1972, FRUS, Volume XIV, Foreign Relations, 1969–1976, Soviet Union, October 1971–May 1972, 732.

two worlds – firm determination in Vietnam (deemed vital for American national prestige and honor), while simultaneously continuing the strategic dialogue with the same, long-time antagonist: the Soviet Union.

SETTING THE COURSE

The events related to Vietnam confirmed the competitive nature of the superpower relationship, but were all the more significant because they evolved in parallel with the celebrated climax of détente. In the spring of 1972, the summits in Beijing and Moscow enabled Nixon to exploit the "era of negotiation" both internationally and for his domestic political success, with an overwhelming victory in the presidential election of the same year. From the American point of view, triangular diplomacy seemed, indeed, to be working.

The analysis of Nixon's China policy demonstrated that the common objective of containing the Soviet Union was the driving force of the diplomatic revolution, a potent incentive for better relations that enabled the overcoming of years of hostility and the setting aside of crucial issues previously considered as insuperable obstacles between China and the United States. The fact that Washington searched for an authentic rapprochement is testified to by the numerous and repeated offers to keep Beijing informed on the evolution of relations with Moscow. The "triangle" was, from the start, unbalanced in favor of the Chinese. While the discussions in Beijing on the Soviet Union were open and frank, in the talks with the Soviets on the Chinese, the reality was concealed and, in some circumstances, overtly denied.[67]

As has been pointed out by notable scholars, the direct influence of China on the unfolding of the US-Soviet dialogue may have been less dramatic than later asserted by the chief policymakers – first and foremost by

---

[67] For example, during the Kissinger-Dobrynin meeting of July 19, 1971: "He [Dobrynin] asked me [Kissinger] if the Soviet Union had come up [in China]. I replied that realistically it was obvious that we could do nothing to help Communist China against the Soviet Union. (…). Dobrynin asked whether Chou-En-lai had indicated any worry about a Soviet attack. I said there were practically no references to the Soviet Union except an occasional vague allusion, while it seemed to me (Kissinger) that the primary fear of Communist China was Japan"; Memorandum of Conversation, July 19, 1971, 1:00 P.M., The Map Room, The White House, NA, NPM, NSC files, box 492, folder 2. These statements, especially when compared to the transcripts of the conversations in Beijing analyzed in the previous chapter, are significant and reveal the difference between the Sino-American and the Soviet-American dialogue. On this occasion, in fact, Kissinger openly lied to Dobrynin.

Henry Kissinger.[68] It is, however, undeniable that Washington did manage to successfully exploit, to its advantage, the Soviet "near obsession" with China. "No one was more surprised and confused than the Kremlin when it received the news of Nixon's plan to go to China" Dobrynin reveals in his memoirs, conceding also that the Soviets had allowed themselves "to be outplayed by the Americans and the Chinese."[69] And, while the idea of holding a summit had been surfacing between Kissinger and Dobrynin since their first meetings in 1969, the records of the back-channel conversations confirm that the actual preparations accelerated after the July 15, 1971, announcement of Nixon's future trip to China.[70]

Determining the tangible benefits of such diplomatic maneuvering is not crucial in this context. But what is important to underline is the Kremlin's overall uneasiness regarding the nascent relationship between Washington and Beijing. "We cannot, of course, have any objections in principle against a normalization of relations between the United States and the People's Republic of China," Brezhnev wrote to Nixon, commenting on the future summit in China. "The whole question," added the Soviet leader, "is on what basis will this normalization proceed ... I can only add that history has taught us long ago to tell a natural process of establishing normal relations between states from the development of all sorts of combinations of ones against the others."[71]

This inherent and never-denied fear on the Soviet leadership's part was, in itself, an advantage for the United States. This alone enabled the playing of the China card, which, after 1972, remained a crucial asset for Washington in the management of its relationship with the Soviet

---

[68] This point is effectively made in Jussi Hanhimäki's essay "An Elusive Grand Design" in Fredrik Logevall and Andrew Preston (edited by), *Nixon in the World. American Foreign Relations, 1969–1977* (New York: Oxford University Press, 2008), 35–38.

[69] Dobrynin, *In Confidence*, 225, 227.

[70] Record of HAK-Dobrynin meetings, NA, NPM, NSC files, box 73, folder 1. For example, during a back-channel meeting only four days after the announcement of Nixon's trip to China, Kissinger registered a sharp change of attitude on Dobrynin's part, who demonstrated impatience and readiness to finalize a date for the Moscow summit. When Kissinger underlined that Soviet responses to American overtures on the summit had been "grudging and petty," and that despite his insistence Moscow had always been evasive, Dobrynin, in replying, "was almost beside himself with protestations of goodwill." The forthcoming meeting between the American and Soviet leaders was deemed very important, stated Dobrynin, who then asked whether it would be possible for Nixon to go to Moscow before going to Beijing; Memorandum of Conversation, July 19, 1971, 1:00 P.M., The Map Room, The White House, NA, NPM, NSC files, box 492, folder 2.

[71] Brezhnev letter to the president, September 7, 1971, NA, NPM, NSC files, box 486, folder 3.

Union. The Carter administration would, in fact, pick up the same policy when pursuing normalization of relations with China in the second half of 1978 (Chapter 11).

In the establishment of the other side of the "triangle," the realization that the strengthening and modernization of each other's strategic arsenals threatened the stability of MAD pushed Washington and Moscow into assessing the advantages of arms control. The search for the codification of the "balance of terror" confirmed that the Cold War remained the basic characteristic of the international system, while the SALT process evolved around the necessity of limitations and the concomitant strive to allow for unilateral strength. In Dobrynin's words, "America's confidence in its technological superiority played a major role in the whole story of nuclear disarmament. From the MIRV controversy all the way to Ronald Reagan's favorite dream of a Stars Wars defense, it is easy to trace an American desire to acquire some form of ultimate weapon guaranteeing superiority over the Soviet Union, however illusory that might have been."[72]

The safeguarding of future opportunities for superiority notwithstanding, the necessities of the 1970s imposed the recognition of parity, together with a focus on the potentially destabilizing effects of certain innovations. The search for ABM limitations had been a starting point, while the need to curtail the deployment of MIRVs provided the incentive for continued negotiations and eventually became the basic link between SALT I and SALT II (Chapters 7 and 10).

It is important to underline that the American decision to enter the negotiations was an implicit rather than an explicit one.[73] It was the consequence of the realization of the loss of supremacy in the nuclear-strategic domain. It had not been explained to, nor was it understood by, the American public and Congress. Consequently, it would later be subject to doubt and fluctuating opinions, which proved crucial in the years following the signing of SALT I. This aspect, when combined with the specific methods adopted by the Nixon administration – from the creation and use of the back channel, its isolation and secrecy, to the centrality of the White House in all of the most critical decisions – constituted the intrinsic weakness of the Nixon-Kissinger design. The fragility

---

[72] Dobrynin, *In Confidence*, 212.
[73] This basic point is made by Philip J. Farley in "Strategic Arms Control, 1967–87," in Alexander L. George, Philip J. Farley, Alexander Dallin (edited by), *U.S.-Soviet Security Cooperation. Achievements, Failures, Lessons*, 220.

of détente will be the focus of Chapter 5. Suffice it here to anticipate that innovative policies when not supported by a strong domestic constituency are inevitably open to criticism, and all the more so when accompanied by unorthodox and democratically questionable methods. In these elements, and not necessarily in the direction of American foreign policy lines, should the causes of the crisis and eventual fall of détente be traced and defined.

One of the themes around which Nixon was almost immediately criticized was that despite the regulations and limitations of SALT, the Soviet Union continued to pursue the expansion of its sphere of influence to the detriment of the United States. What was overlooked at the time was that Washington also never gave up strengthening its power vis-à-vis its antagonist. In fact, with détente the Nixon administration, either deliberately or not, created an innovative way to conduct relations with Moscow. The competition gradually shifted in focus: from the search for superiority mainly through the nuclear arms race (characteristic of the early Cold War) to the struggle for supremacy on a geopolitical scale. This process reached its climax in the years between 1972 and 1975, and will emerge more clearly in the next few chapters. Initially, the emphasis was put on the cooperative component of détente. However, the competitive aspects were clearly present from the beginning: in the nature and scope of the China policy and in the determination to show resolve in Vietnam.

Significantly, in fact, as early as 1971 internal documents reveal the administration's concern for Soviet activities in "Third Areas":

As regards the Soviets, we will need to be particularly alert to any invigoration of their activities in Latin America and in other regions of strategic interest to us (e.g. West and East Africa). This problem is not fundamentally different from what it has been but may be more intense now ... We should keep the limits clearly where we have previously drawn them; it may be desirable to define them more firmly if the occasion arises.[74]

In the Soviet Union the two apparently contradictory principles of internationalism, entailing full support for national liberation movements throughout the world, and peaceful coexistence with the capitalist world, had shaped foreign policy since de-Stalinization. But in the United States

---

[74] Memorandum for Mr. Kissinger from Helmut Sonnenfeldt, "US-Soviet Relations in Light of President's Visit to China," July 20, 1971, NA, NPM, NSC files, box 715. Particularly interesting is the fact that repercussions in Third Areas are listed as potential consequences of the China opening. Also interesting, when put in relation to the events of 1975, is that Africa is mentioned as a possible area for Soviet activities.

the pragmatism that led to openly embracing the pattern of cooperation and competition only emerged in the 1970s, as a result of Nixon and Kissinger's policies. In restrictive terms, some aspects of détente can be seen as designed to codify and respect the status quo between the superpowers (most notably in the administration's policies on nuclear weapons and toward Europe).[75] However, a more ample vision and a focus on Washington's different management of US-Soviet relations reveals broader transformative intentions, which evolved around a greater emphasis on the superpower rivalry in the Third World and the gradual definition of different parameters to reassert American global power worldwide.

If this "new" struggle for supremacy entailed first and foremost securing dominant influence in key areas of the world, it was only logical that Nixon and Kissinger's attention would focus on assuring the pro-Western orientation of the Middle East. It is in this region that the intrinsically competitive aspect of détente emerged in full – through the strengthening of the alliance with the shah of Iran – though concealed behind the success of the Moscow summit.

- Nixon's dual nature of détente
- The importance of the "China card" to U.S. Soviet relations
- maintain American leadership in the world of geopolitics

---

[75] Dobrynin's account to the Politburo on the administration's vision of Europe is significant: "Kissinger said that in Europe Nixon agreed that it is not appropriate to undertake any sort of attempt to change the situation which developed there as a result of the Second World War. The USA, as is well known, in principle favors the unification of Germany, but this is still a question, taking into account, realistically speaking, of the very very distant future. The current administration does not intend to push or force events in this direction"; Memorandum of Conversation of the Ambassador of the USSR to the United States A. Dobrynin with Kissinger, aide to President Nixon, July 12, 1969. Sent to members of the Politburo, CC CPSU and to candidate members of the Politburo, CC CPSU, Cold War International History Project Bulletin, Issue 3, Woodrow Wilson International Center for Scholars, Washington DC, 63–67.

4

"Protect Me"

Nixon and the Shah of Iran

The irony was that Nixon's critics charged he was letting the Russians lull him into a false sense of security, when that was exactly what he was doing to the Russians.

> Ambrose and Brinkley, *Rise to Globalism*

Détente did not prevent resistance to Soviet expansionism; on the contrary, it fostered the only possible psychological framework for such resistance.

> Henry Kissinger, *White House Years*

Don't look at détente as something that weakens you but as a way for the United States to gain influence.

> Nixon to the shah, May 31, 1972

The 1972 Moscow summit not only marked a turning point in the US-Soviet bilateral relationship but was, at the time, perceived as a truly historic event. "Many of those who watched the week unfold in Moscow," wrote *Time* magazine, "concluded that this summit – the most important since Potsdam in 1945 and probably the most significant Soviet political event since Stalin's death – could change world diplomacy." In addition to the SALT agreements, Nixon and Brezhnev signed a number of other accords – relating to trade, public health, scientific and technological cooperation, environmental issues, and space exploration. All this was "all the more impressive," continued the 1972 article, "because it seemed not so much a single, cataclysmic event but part of a process, part of a world on the move."[1] It seemed, indeed, to witness the beginning of a new era.

---

[1] "What Nixon Brings Home from Moscow," *Time*, Monday, June 5, 1972.

This "spirit" was reflected in what was later labeled as the "charter for détente"[2] – the *Basic Principles of Relations between the United States and the Union of Soviet Socialist Republics* (signed on May 29, 1972, the last day of the summit). Wide-ranging and lacking concrete commitments, the document provided a guide for the future conduct of the superpowers. It emphasized peaceful coexistence, contained a pledge not to seek unilateral advantage, and highlighted security interests while downplaying ideological divergences. Considered by other countries an alarming signal of an emerging "condominium" between Washington and Moscow, the document in essence reaffirmed the predominance on the world scene of only two superpowers.[3]

However, the ceremonies taking place at the Kremlin and the new spirit of US-Soviet cooperation contrasted drastically with the continued tension in Vietnam. Interestingly, in his private conversations, Nixon had repeatedly motivated his assertive actions in Indochina by referring to a revised version of the domino theory: Washington had to avoid a debacle in order to thwart Soviet expansionism in other crucial areas, most notably in the Middle East. The link between Vietnam and the Middle East was, therefore, clearly present. And, significantly, initiatives toward both regions came to be connected to the Moscow summit.

In fact, en route back to the United States from Moscow, the Nixon entourage stopped in Tehran to pay a long-overdue and repeatedly postponed return visit to the shah of Iran. Compared to the Moscow summit and the landmark agreements just signed, the meetings with the Iranian leader barely made the headlines. However, the decisions made by Nixon, and their particular timing, are extremely significant when interrelated with the changing dynamics of the superpower rivalry.

President Nixon's relationship with the shah of Iran, in fact, emerges as particularly important in the context of the administration's definition of its overall foreign policy objectives. The implementation of the Nixon doctrine in the region provided the conceptual framework for the further strengthening of US-Iranian ties. Then, starting in late 1971, the United States decisively shifted its policy in favor of Iran, a process which climaxed in May 1972. By focusing on this, still to date, unexplored

---

[2] Raymond Garthoff, *Détente and Confrontation. American-Soviet Relations from Nixon to Reagan* (Washington, DC: The Brookings Institution, 1994), 290.
[3] Jussi Hanhimäki, *The Flawed Architect. Henry Kissinger and American Foreign Policy* (New York: Oxford University Press, 2004), 222. For the text of the *Basic Principles*: National Archives (hereafter NA), Nixon Presidential Materials (hereafter NPM), National Security Council (hereafter NSC) files, box 484, folder 1.

aspect of the Nixon administration's policies at the height of détente,[4] the competitive nature of the US-Soviet relationship fully surfaces, despite (or maybe precisely because of) the concomitant triumphs of "the era of negotiations."

THE TROUBLED RELATIONSHIP

During the Second World War, Iran had become a strategically important base for the passage of Allied provisions en route to the Soviet Union in support of the common anti-German war effort. Starting in late 1941, US troops had thus entered Iran for the first time, joining the British and Soviet occupation forces. Hence began America's troubled relationship with the young Shah Mohammad Reza who, aged twenty-two, had replaced his father in ruling the country. After the end of the war, the crisis caused by Stalin's delay in withdrawing his forces signaled the importance that the emerging "Western camp" assigned to maintaining a predominant influence over Iran.[5] In fact, as the Cold War gradually came to dominate the international scene, Britain and, increasingly, the United States tightened their relationship with the shah in the context of the general drive to contain the expansion of the Soviet Union.

However, the American decision to "throw its support behind the shah" created, from the start, "a crucial long-term cause of tension."[6] Already in the late 1940s, Iranian nationalists started to criticize the United States for backing monarchical authoritarianism and for intervening in Iranian affairs with renewed forms of imperialism. Furthermore, while the old British imperial power had over time necessarily acquired extensive knowledge of Iran's culture and of its internal dynamics, the new American presence seemed to lack the experience and ability to interact with the complex local reality.[7] These two elements, the unrelenting

---

[4] It is interesting to note that even the most recent accounts of the Nixon administration's policies do not consider the strengthening of the relationship with Iran as an important element in the general implementation of détente. For example, Jussi Hanhimäki only mentions the stop in Tehran, on the way back from the Moscow summit, without discussing the impact of the decisions made; *The Flawed Architect*, 226. Robert Dallek does not mention the Tehran visit in connection with the Moscow summit at all; *Nixon and Kissinger, Partners in Power* (New York: HarperCollins, 2007).

[5] On the Soviet withdrawal crisis see, for example: Kenneth M. Pollack, *The Persian Puzzle. The Conflict between Iran and America* (New York: Random House, 2004), 44–48.

[6] James A. Bill, *The Eagle and the Lion. The Tragedy of American-Iranian Relations* (New Haven, CT: Yale University Press, 1988), 49.

[7] According to James Bill, the "American ignorance of Iran was embarrassingly evident at all levels"; Bill, *The Eagle and the Lion*, 42.

domestic dissatisfaction with the rule of the American-backed shah and Washington's incapacity, or unwillingness, to acutely assess the Iranian internal situation remained constant critical elements of the US-Iranian relationship until the revolution of 1978–1979.[8]

Yet, it is important to underline, that despite some criticism from certain sectors of informed public opinion, until the 1953 CIA-sponsored coup, the image exerted by the United States was still generally positive.[9] America represented the ideals of democracy and modernization in a country struggling to emerge from underdevelopment, dominant external influence, and authoritarian rule. In the immediate postwar years, anger and resentment was commonly directed against the British colonial "exploiters" who maintained their presence in Iran and, most importantly, administered the Anglo-Iranian Oil Company's rich revenues.[10] In the early 1950s, Mohammed Mossadeq's nationalism emerged within this context and strengthened itself under the determination to promote the autonomous development of Iran. The decision to nationalize the oil company was the obvious first step in reducing foreign involvement in Iranian affairs, while enabling the country to benefit from its own natural resources.

However, from the perspective of London and Washington, the economic setback combined with the widespread perception of political instability, potentially open to communist infiltration, triggered plans on possible countermeasures. While initially the British and American leaders had been reluctant to intervene directly, with Churchill's return to power in Great Britain and the election of Eisenhower in the United States, the stage was set for "Operation Ajax" – the CIA covert intervention that ultimately led to the removal of Mossadeq and the consolidation of the shah's openly pro-Western regime.[11]

---

[8] The domestic political situation of Iran under the shah's rule in the years leading to the 1978–1979 revolution and the US choice to overlook these problematic aspects in defense of the alliance with the regime will be discussed at the beginning of Chapter 12.

[9] Ali M. Ansari, *Confronting Iran. The Failure of American Foreign Policy and the Next Great Crisis in the Middle East* (New York: Basic Books, 2006), 24.

[10] On the dispute between Britain and Iran in the years leading to the 1953 coup: Kenneth Pollack, *The Persian Puzzle*, 52–62.

[11] The most comprehensive account of the 1953 coup against Mossadeq is Stephen Kinzer, *All the Shah's Men: An American Coup and the Roots of Middle East Terror* (Hoboken, NJ: Wiley, 2003). See also: Pollack, *The Persian Puzzle*, 63–71; Bill, *The Eagle and the Lion*, 72–97 and the *New York Times* online: http://www.nytimes.com/library/world/mideast/041600iran-cia-index.html. On the importance of 1953 as a defining moment in US-Iranian relations see Ansari, *Confronting Iran*, 36–37.

From that moment onward, the United States was able to secure both the existence of a friendly government, geared toward the containment of Soviet expansionism, and the penetration of the Iranian oil fields. In concrete terms, and from the standpoint of a superpower engaged in an increasingly global Cold War, the 1953 coup (the first "regime change" intervention of the US CIA) was, therefore, a clear-cut success. At the same time, however, the coup inevitably, and irreparably, damaged the US-Iranian relationship. Decades later, the words spoken by an Iranian woman are unequivocal: "Why did you Americans do that terrible thing? We always loved America. To us, America was the great country, the perfect country that helped us while other countries were exploiting us. But after that moment, no one in Iran ever trusted the United States again. I can tell you for sure that if you had not done that thing, you would never have had that problem of the hostages being taken in your embassy in Tehran. All your trouble started in 1953. Why, why did you do it?"[12]

The events of 1953 also deepened the fissure between the Iranian society and the shah's autocratic rule, a rupture that would never be completely recomposed. Nevertheless, Washington progressively strengthened its relationship with Tehran. Starting in the mid-1950s, and especially after the 1958 anti-Western coup in Iraq, the US aid program to Iran focused almost exclusively on reinforcing the country's military and defensive capabilities. After the proclamation of the Eisenhower Doctrine, and as the Middle East entered the Cold War "chessboard," the strategic importance of Iran, from the American viewpoint, became increasingly crucial.[13] Consequently, the US government continued to approve arms sales to Iran, despite the domestic turmoil (and consequent repression) that had deeply shaken the shah's rule in the early 1960s.[14]

---

[12] Kinzer, *All the Shah's Men*, ix.

[13] The Eisenhower Doctrine, proclaimed in a special message to Congress in January 1957, formally extended the United States strategy of containment to the Middle East. To sustain America's role in the region, the United States supported the Baghdad Pact, signed in 1955, which included Turkey, Iran, Iraq, Pakistan, and Great Britain and ended in 1958 following the coup in Iraq. The Baghdad Pact evolved into CENTO, signed in 1959, which included Turkey, Iran, Pakistan, and the United States. These alliances signaled America's increased interest in the region.

[14] In the early 1960s, the Kennedy administration had assessed the shah's regime as unpopular and had strongly supported the programs of internal reform. The shah's so-called White Revolution, however, was received with skepticism domestically. The program included land reform, nationalization of forests, the sale of state-owned enterprises, profit sharing in industry, and electorial rights for women. In 1963, antishah riots and demonstrations were repressed by an increasingly autocratic regime. It is important to note that Ayatollah Khomeini was among the leading protesters and was exiled in 1964.

When the Nixon administration entered office, it therefore inherited a policy toward Iran that had constantly overlooked the regime's problematic management of its internal affairs, while relying on the shah's pro-Western and anticommunist credentials. In essence, by the late 1960s the Iranian leader was considered a trusted ally, "a good friend" stated Kissinger, whose strong ties to the United States went unquestioned.[15]

"NATURAL ALLIES"?

At the same time, however, the relationship between Washington and Tehran had not been unproblematic. The constant requests for additional arms sales, and the general American reluctance in fully satisfying the Iranian demands, had become a blueprint in US-Iranian relations. The shah considered increased economic and military assistance essential for his country's development and security. But during the Kennedy and Johnson administrations, the events in Indochina had overshadowed American policy toward the Middle East, inducing the shah to assert a greater margin of independence. In 1967, for example, Iran signed its first arms agreement with the Soviet Union, even if the loyalty to the 1959 treaty with the United States remained unquestioned. Through these independent moves, the Iranian leader may have simply been cautioning Washington not to take Iran for granted.

Despite the difficulties, at the beginning of the Nixon administration the maintenance of a stable and positive relationship with Iran was assessed in Washington as essential, for a combination of factors. First, Iran's economic progress "under the leadership of an increasingly self-assured shah" was deemed "remarkable." Between 1966 and 1969, the growth rate had proceeded at an annual rate of 10 percent, without incurring inflation or substantial increases in debt. This performance had been made possible by the rapidly increasing oil revenues, which enabled public development programs and imports, with only minor strains on the country's foreign exchange position.[16] In short, notwithstanding the need to modernize its agricultural sector and its narrowly based political regime,

---

On the White Revolution and US-Iranian relations in the 1960s: Bill, *The Eagle and the Lion*, 132–182; Pollack, *The Persian Puzzle*, 80–100.

[15] Memorandum for the President from Henry A. Kissinger, "Military Sales Credit for Iran," April 16, 1970, NA, NPM, NSC files, Country files – Middle East, box 601, folder Iran Vol. I (1 of 3).

[16] National Intelligence Estimate 34–69, Washington, January 10, 1969, FRUS, Foreign Relations, 1969–1972, Volume E-4, Iran and Iraq, Doc. No.1.

Iran was considered a "success story" among developing countries.[17] This conveyed general optimism in Washington for the future of the Iranian development process.

Secondly, close ties with the shah were militarily and strategically important. Iran allowed transit rights for American military aircrafts, thus providing the United States and the Western Alliance with a secure air corridor between European NATO and Southeast Asia. Moreover, the shah's regime offered hospitality for vital communications and intelligence facilities, advantageously located close to the border with the Soviet Union.[18]

Thirdly, throughout the 1960s, oil had emerged as an essential commodity for the development and security of the West. The dependence of Japan and Europe on the largest proven reserves of petroleum in the world made access to the Persian Gulf absolutely vital for the free world. If the flow of oil was interrupted, or if it went under control of unfriendly countries, the repercussions for the industrial economies would be incalculable. From this perspective, the pro-Western orientation of the shah's regime was obviously crucial. Moreover, the British decision to withdraw its presence from the Gulf by 1971 added strategic significance to the region entailing, from Washington's standpoint, a greater commitment to its defense.[19]

The Iranian point of view, conveyed during the numerous contacts between the shah and American officials throughout 1969, signaled the potential future convergence between the policies of the United States

---

[17] For example, the Intelligence Estimate pointed to the fact that the living conditions of the population in the countryside remained critical: "The overall position of the peasant in the countryside has not yet changed very much, and efforts to alter attitudes, to raise living standards, and to increase production present a continuing challenge that seems destined to absorb the government's energies and attention for many years to come." Another problem was that the shah had concentrated the political power in his hands, thus the regime's political base remained narrow: "Over the long term, economic development probably will not provide a satisfactory substitute for greater political participation. Hence, in a few years unrest may again begin to reach significant levels among politically aware elements. In time this could pose serious problems for the regime, particularly if dissent were to find support within the military"; Ibid.

[18] Record of National Security Council Interdepartmental Group for Near East and South Asia Meeting, Washington, April 3, 1969, FRUS, Foreign Relations, 1969–1972, Volume E-4, Iran and Iraq, Doc. No. 10.

[19] The intensified military presence of both superpowers in the Indian Ocean demonstrated the region's increased strategic significance. The United States had, in fact, acquired the capability to target Soviet territory with missiles launched from submarines (the Polaris A-3 missiles were deployed in 1968). On its part, the Soviet Union had steadily increased its naval presence and searched for ports to station or refuel its forces.

and Iran. Focusing on the Soviet threat, the shah pointed to the fact that Moscow was "trying to dominate the Mediterranean by establishing control over a triangle with its points at Suez, Aden and Djibouti." The broader objective was to access the Indian Ocean and, ultimately, the Persian Gulf.[20] Moreover, the indication of rising radicalism in countries neighboring Iran offered opportunities to the Soviets to extend their influence, either directly or by proxy. In particular, the shah was concerned about the situation in Iraq. According to his assessment, the Soviets were supplying Baghdad with offensive armaments, including aircrafts, missiles, and hardware. These shipments were significantly strengthening the Iraqi military capabilities. Furthermore, Moscow was pressuring Baghdad to include Iraqi communists in the composition of its government.[21]

Therefore, the shah was deeply wary of Moscow and aware that the United States remained the only ultimate guarantor against a potential Soviet attack. However, he also believed that Iran could play a crucial role in maintaining radical Arab or Soviet influence at an "innocuous level."[22] In short, because he ruled the only country willing and capable of carrying the burden of regional stability, the shah considered Iran as the logical successor of the British in the Persian Gulf. This would require the further strengthening of his armed forces, with the acquisition of modern and sophisticated weapons. Despite the dangerous consequences that increased military investments could potentially entail – domestically, they would hinder development of other sectors of the society, and internationally, they could alarm neighboring countries – the shah was determined to follow his course.[23] In concrete terms, this meant that the relations with the United States, Iran's chief provider of arms, would have to tighten more than ever before. It is thus not surprising that in early 1969 the shah defined the United States and Iran as "natural allies." Consequently, he told Kissinger, it was vital for Washington and Tehran to coordinate their policies for "the next four, hopefully eight, years."[24]

---

[20] Memorandum of Conversation, Washington, April 1, 1969, 10:00 A.M., FRUS, Foreign Relations, 1969–1972, Volume E-4, Iran and Iraq, Doc. No. 8.
[21] Telegram 4183 From the Embassy in Iran to the Department of State, October 13, 1969, 1300Z, FRUS, Foreign Relations, 1969–1972, Volume E-4, Iran and Iraq, Doc. No. 23.
[22] Intelligence Note, US Department of State to the Secretary from George C. Denney Jr., "Shah's Views of Iranian Defense Needs on the Eve of U.S. Visit," October 17, 1969, NA, NPM, NSC files, Country files – Middle East, box 601, folder Iran Vol. I (1 of 3).
[23] Ibid.
[24] Memorandum of Conversation, Washington, April 1, 1969, 10:00 A.M., FRUS, Foreign Relations, 1969–1972, Volume E-4, Iran and Iraq, Doc. No. 8.

IRAN NEEDS "OVERKILL CAPABILITIES"

During his first visit to the United States since Nixon had been elected president, the Iranian leader outlined the plans to strengthen his country's military forces. In October 1969, he met with the top-level officials of the administration and illustrated his defense requirements.[25] Emphasizing the dangerous threat posed by local instability, by which Soviet expansionism could take hold, the shah told Secretary Rogers that he needed "overkill capabilities," so that "should anyone be tempted to attack Iran they would think twice, or even three times."[26] A few hours later, the Iranian leader outlined the details of his military requirements to Secretary Laird. Because the strengthening of the Iranian air force was the first priority, he wanted to purchase more aircrafts, continue to rely on USAF personnel, and increase the number of Iranian pilots that could be sent to the United States for training. Regarding the other sectors of the military, the objective was to build an "adequate naval force" and a "relatively small but effective land force."[27]

Washington on the one hand acknowledged the strategic importance of Iran but, on the other, emphasized the necessity of limiting the extent of the shah's demands. For example, Kissinger defined the shah as a "man of mission," determined to modernize his country. To this end, he was "subtly pressing the idea of a 'special relationship' with the US," which would give Iran a preferred treatment, both in economic terms[28] and on military credits. However, underlined Kissinger, the shah was not "entirely self-seeking." His commitment to the West was, in fact, assessed as "genuine." From this perspective, Kissinger referred to the shah's definition of his

---

[25] The shah met President Nixon on October 21, the secretaries of state and defense on October 22.

[26] Memorandum of Conversation, Washington, October 22, 1969, 10:00 A.M., FRUS, Foreign Relations, 1969–1972, Volume E-4, Iran and Iraq, Doc. No. 33. The shah refers in particular to Iraq, "those fellows in Iraq are mad" he stated.

[27] Memorandum of Conversation, Washington, October 22, 1969, 11:30 A.M.–12:30 P.M., FRUS, Foreign Relations, 1969–1972, Volume E-4, Iran and Iraq, Doc. No. 36.

[28] The shah had, for example, proposed the so-called oil for arms deal. In essence, he asked the United States to buy more Iranian oil and, in turn, Iran would use the increased revenues to purchase US-produced armaments. For more details: Telegram 4185 From Embassy in Iran to the Department of State, October 13, 1969, 1310Z, FRUS, Foreign Relations, 1969–1972, Volume E-4, Iran and Iraq, Doc. No. 24. It is important to note that this proposal would never be accepted by the US government, which could not grant special quotas to single countries, and neither directly control the import quotas of the American oil companies.

country as an "island of stability" – a phrase that would become infamous in the later part of the 1970s.[29]

The importance of a constructive relationship with Iran was confirmed also by Secretary Laird's commitment to provide Tehran with more extensive intelligence briefings on the developments in the Soviet Union and China. On his part, the shah confirmed that Washington could construct "almost any kind of technical collection equipment,"[30] a pledge that reinforced Iran's position as a crucial and irreplaceable base for US intelligence facilities. More generally, the shah's determination to strengthen his country and to play a dynamic role in the region was seen by the Nixon administration as an asset, in the context of the presidency's new global posture exemplified by the Nixon doctrine.[31]

Consequently, there was no doubt in the United States that Iran was, and needed to be, an important ally. But at the same time the American leadership unequivocally stressed gradualism and moderation. Kissinger in fact recommended that during the first meeting with the shah the president avoid concrete promises, though demonstrating appreciation for Iranian policies. "While this administration is committed to a close relationship with its friends," wrote Kissinger, "translating that commitment into practical policies and programs is a political problem that has to be worked out a step at a time in our political system."[32] Secretary Laird's

[29] Memorandum from the President's Assistant for National Security Affairs (Kissinger) to President Nixon, Washington, October 21, 1969, FRUS, Foreign Relations, 1969–1972, Volume E-4, Iran and Iraq, Doc. No. 29.
[30] Memorandum for the Record, Washington, October 22, 1969, FRUS, Foreign Relations, 1969–1972, Volume E-4, Iran and Iraq, Doc. No. 31.
[31] Originally formulated in relation to Vietnam (see Chapter I), the Nixon doctrine, with its reliance on local powers for the defense of American interests, rapidly assumed a more general connotation, shaping the administration's posture in the Third World. In its earliest formulation toward the Middle East, in National Security Study Memorandum 66, increased sales of weapons to Iran and Saudi Arabia (the "two pillars") were recommended, in order to enable them to deter Soviet advances and to maintain local stability. Saudi Arabia was mentioned and would remain an important, though difficult, ally for the United States. However, for the combination of reasons mentioned above, Iran was to become Washington's regional strongpoint.
[32] Memorandum from the President's Assistant for National Security Affairs (Kissinger) to President Nixon, Washington, October 21, 1969, FRUS, Foreign Relations, 1969–1972, Volume E-4, Iran and Iraq, Doc. No. 29. In terms of military credits, Kissinger's position at this point was that Iran was already receiving enough aid. Accordingly, he recommended that the president not discuss the details directly, but to let the shah discuss them with Secretary Laird (which is what occurred). Moreover, Kissinger recommended the postponement of Nixon's trip to Iran. This was not, at that moment, considered an important issue.

responses to the shah's detailed requests were along the same line. The American government would try to be forthcoming but, the secretary observed, "the Department of Defense has money problems on Capitol Hill regarding foreign military assistance and credit."[33]

Therefore, the first high-level contacts between the Nixon administration and the shah seemed to confirm the pattern – the shah's demands versus American reluctance – that had characterized US-Iranian relations in the recent past. A pattern that was to become all the more problematic during the following two years.

THE "CONTINUING TENSION"

On the surface, between early 1970 and late 1971, the tone of US-Iranian relations remained friendly and cordial. A more in-depth view, however, confirms the existence of a persistently tense relationship. The shah's repeated and pressing demands were ultimately satisfied by Washington but with general reluctance, made worse by the internal divisions of the administration on the position to take toward Iran. Until mid-1971, Nixon himself seemed undecided about the precise role the shah could play, both in regional affairs and for the implementation of US foreign policy objectives.

The shah's insistence in seeking a rapid follow-up to the requests outlined in October 1969 emerged immediately after his visit and, all the more explicitly, during the first months of 1970. In a meeting with the US ambassador in Tehran, Douglas MacArthur, the shah observed "with some feeling" that in the past Washington "had sometimes shown a disposition to tell him that Iran did not need this or that for its own defense." Such "dispositions" might be acceptable if the United States were willing to give "an iron-clad guarantee to come to Iran's assistance." But, clearly, the United States was not in such a position (which, besides, was not deemed "wise," even if feasible). Therefore, Washington should acknowledge Iran's right to "decide what its own defense requirements are since its security and independence are at stake."[34] These comments anticipated

---

[33] Memorandum on Conversation, Washington, October 22, 1969, 11:30 A.M.–12:30 P.M., FRUS, Foreign Relations, 1969–1972, Volume E-4, Iran and Iraq, Doc. No. 36. In particular, Laird refers to the problems related to Vietnam as inhibiting the freedom of maneuver regarding military credit requests.

[34] Telegram 4833 From Embassy in Iran to the Department of State, November 27, 1969, 1435Z, FRUS, Foreign Relations, 1969–1972, Volume E-4, Iran and Iraq, Doc. No. 42.

the stance taken by the Iranian leader a few months later given that, from his point of view, the Nixon administration failed to "respond favorably" to his requests. Four months after the discussions in Washington and with no tangible progress in sight the shah was, in fact, "feeling a sense of deep frustration" and of "deception."[35]

The relatively detached and noncommittal tone, present in both Nixon's letters to the shah and in the administration's overall posture, sharply contrasted with the distressed urgency conveyed by the Iranian leader. In responding to the shah in February 1970, Nixon in principle assured continued cooperation in strengthening Iran's defense capacities. "Your thoughts and mine coincide," wrote the president, referring to the application of the Nixon doctrine in the region. However, on specific requirements, Nixon evidently held back.[36] A clear-cut strategy toward Iran had yet to be conceived.

From the American point of view, some of the shah's demands were inherently complex. They required negotiations with the Western consortium regarding oil,[37] or the revision of the US-Iranian 1968 Memorandum of Understanding, on the basis of which Tehran already regularly received substantial military credit. At the same time, "everyone" agreed that the American relationship with Iran was important, for reasons ranging from the stationing of intelligence facilities, to its potential contribution to

---

[35] Telegram 602 From Embassy in Iran to the Department of State, February 17, 1970, 1425Z, FRUS, Foreign Relations, 1969–1972, Volume E-4, Iran and Iraq, Doc. No. 46. The shah's frustration may have increased due to the changed conditions regarding military sales credit, compared to the previous year. In a letter to the president in March 1970, he in fact pointed to the fact that "the conditions for procuring our requirements from your country have become more and more difficult"; Letter from the shah of Iran to President Nixon, Tehran, March 11, 1970, FRUS, Foreign Relations, 1969–1972, Volume E-4, Iran and Iraq, Doc. No. 52.

[36] Letter from President Nixon to the shah of Iran, Washington, February 23, 1970, FRUS, Foreign Relations, 1969–1972, Volume E-4, Iran and Iraq, Doc. No. 48. Nixon responded favorably to only one of the shah's requests, the increase in the number of US Air Force technicians in Iran. Regarding the problem of pilot training (Iranian pilots sent to the United States to be trained) the president was noncommittal and took time. Furthermore, he made no commitment on increased oil revenues, and did not mention the conditions of the Military Sales Credit.

[37] According to Kissinger, the oil issue was inherently complex: both lifting more oil (which required negotiations with the consortium) and increasing US imports were not considered viable options, at least not in the short term; Memorandum From the President's Assistant for National Security Affairs (Kissinger) to President Nixon, Washington, April 13, 1970, FRUS, Foreign Relations, 1969–1972, Volume E-4, Iran and Iraq, Doc. No. 59.

regional stability.³⁸ This point in particular was repeatedly underlined by Kissinger in his memos to the president:

> The shah's Iran is an island of stability in an otherwise unstable area which includes not only the broader Middle East but also the Persian Gulf from which the British will withdraw next year.³⁹

For this reason, Washington would have to find ways of dealing with the "continuing tension"⁴⁰ caused by the shah's persistent demands. This was, however, a tall order, because the administration was (and remained) divided on the policy choices to make.

The terms of the question were clearly described by Kissinger in April 1970. On the basis of the 1968 Memorandum of Understanding, Tehran received about 30 percent of the Foreign Military Sales Program. This made Iran the largest recipient, even superior to Israel.⁴¹ Satisfying the shah's requests for more credits would either take away from other beneficiaries, or would entail asking Congress for additional funds, with a favorable response unlikely. Furthermore, only by maintaining the current level of credits, the Iranian debt burden would remain within reasonable limits.

More generally, Kissinger shared the shah's concerns on the need to prevent political instability in the area but questioned whether the direct military threat to Iran was growing so rapidly "as to require rates of expenditure even higher than those with which we are now cooperating."⁴² The close and friendly relationship with the shah was not in question. The issue was how to deal with his always increasing demands:

> The question, then, is mainly one of helping a friend as much as possible within restraints posed by resources on both sides. No one argues against helping the shah to the extent we are now. The problem arises as he pushes the limits of his resources and ours. He is understandably a man in a hurry who will press all resources available to their limits. The diplomatic problem here is to explain what

---

³⁸ Ibid.
³⁹ Memorandum for the President from Henry A. Kissinger, "Military Sales Credit Program for Iran," April 16, 1970, NA, NPM, NSC files, Country files – Middle East, box 601, folder Iran Vol. I (1 of 3).
⁴⁰ Memorandum from the President's Assistant for National Security Affairs (Kissinger) to President Nixon, Washington, April 13, 1970, FRUS, Foreign Relations, 1969–1972, Volume E-4, Iran and Iraq, Doc. No. 59.
⁴¹ From the FY 1970 appropriations, Iran was to receive $100 million, Israel $75 million.
⁴² Memorandum for the President from Henry A. Kissinger, "Military Credit Sales Program for Iran," April 16, 1970, NA, NPM, NSC files, Country files – Middle East, box 601, folder Iran Vol. I (1 of 3).

our limits are and to see whether we can be helpful by making adjustments in the program that will not exceed our budgetary limits.⁴³

In line with his characteristically realistic approach, the US national security adviser therefore stressed the acknowledgment of limits and an adequate correspondence between resources and needs. It was, however, precisely on how to tackle this issue that the administration was divided. On one side, the US Embassy in Tehran and the CIA sponsored the shah, on the other, the Department of Defense sought to curtail Iranian demands. In a middle position, the State Department cautiously supported the study of the actual needs of the Iranian military forces before committing to the sale of specific weaponry.

In Tehran, US Ambassador Douglas MacArthur's position was essentially threefold. Washington needed to rely on Iran, particularly after 1971, in order to secure the future stability and security of the Gulf. To attain this objective it was necessary to respond "as favorably as possible" to the shah's requests.⁴⁴ Secondly, the ambassador warned that a prolonged deadlock caused by Iranian insistence and US restraint would eventually lead to a crisis in the "special relationship" with the shah.⁴⁵ This was all the more preoccupying, according to MacArthur's third basic point, because there were indications that if the difficulties in procuring arms in the United States persisted, the shah would turn "elsewhere." In this context, "Soviet pressure and continuing offers of military equipment on increasingly attractive terms" clearly indicated Moscow's intention of diminishing US influence in the region. Washington needed to counter such pressures, demonstrating analogous

---

⁴³ Ibid.
⁴⁴ Telegram 602 From the Embassy in Iran to the Department of State, February 17, 1970, 1425Z, FRUS, Foreign Relations, 1969–1972, Volume E-4, Iran and Iraq, Doc. No. 46.
⁴⁵ Telegram 1247 from the Ambassador in Iran to the Assistant of State for Near East and South Asian Affairs (Sisco), April 1, 1970, 1430Z, FRUS, Foreign Relations, 1969–1972, Volume E-4, Iran and Iraq, Doc. No. 57. Specifically, the deadlock was caused: "(A) On the one hand by shah's absolute conviction – near obsession, that unless he substantially strengthens his military posture, the Arab side of the Gulf will, after British withdrawal, fall before massive radical Arab campaign of subversion encouraged by Soviets with Iran left standing alone. (B) On the other hand, by our [the United States] inability to make either special oil arrangement for Iran or extend more than $100 million per annum of FMS credit during critical years ahead when Iran's financial resources are going to be stretched to limit." In order to break the deadlock and prevent a crisis in the relationship with the shah, the ambassador recommended the revision and extension of the 1968 agreement, in order to allow Iran to benefit from the $100 million for another three to five years.

(if not superior) determination in securing positive and friendly ties with the Iranian leadership.⁴⁶

In outlining his position, CIA Director Richard Helms acknowledged that the shah's demands could easily be rejected by the United States on the grounds of "cost, lack of urgency, limited capability, undesirable precedent and other arguments." Nevertheless, Helms firmly believed that it was in the American interest to support the Iranian concept of a "special relationship." And, as director of intelligence, he felt a "particular responsibility" to point out that close ties between Washington and Tehran were essential in order to ensure the continued receipt of information vital to US national security. Specifically, Helms underlined that the intelligence collection activities in Iran were irreplaceable:

> Ruling out Afghanistan as politically unfeasible, there is no place to which we could transfer these activities were Iran denied us. In time we hope that some of the important coverage now obtained from Iran can be picked up by overhead sensors, but for some years ahead the ground based facilities will remain absolutely essential if we are to keep our knowledge of the Soviet programs up to date.

It was obvious that maintaining these installations in Iran was entirely dependent on the shah's willingness to permit them to operate and to promptly transmit the information they collected. For these reasons, Helms wrote to the National Security Council and to the Departments of Defense and State:

> As we consider both our general policy toward Iran, and also the action to be taken on the shah's requests for assistance, I urge you to accord great importance to our need to continue utilizing Iran as a base for the collection of highest priority intelligence on the USSR.⁴⁷

---

⁴⁶ Telegram 1312 from the Embassy in Iran to the Department of State, April 7, 1970, 1259Z, FRUS, Foreign Relations, 1969–1972, Volume E-4, Iran and Iraq, Doc. No. 58. It must be noted that, the crucial relationship between Washington and Tehran notwithstanding, Iran had purchased armaments, and would continue to do so, also from other countries. After the 1967 agreements, the shah had obtained weapons even from the Soviet Union. Interestingly, when the United States had terminated its economic aid program, which had operated since 1954, the shah had immediately turned to Moscow for the continuation of his plans of rapid industrialization. Soviet participation in the Iranian development program was in fact massive and, consequently, Tehran resulted in being the largest Third World purchaser of Soviet machinery and equipment; Alvin Z. Rubinstein, *Soviet Policy Towards Turkey, Iran and Afghanistan. The Dynamics of Influence* (New York: Praeger Publishers, 1982), 76–77. For these reasons, the implications, from Washington's point of view, of the shah turning "elsewhere" to obtain military equipment were particularly disconcerting.

⁴⁷ Memorandum from Harold Saunders of the National Security Council Staff to the President's Assistant for National Security Affairs (Kissinger), Washington, April 16,

"Protect Me": Nixon and the Shah of Iran 101

The Department of Defense's position was radically different. Though acknowledging the importance of Iran for the application of the Nixon doctrine in the Middle East,⁴⁸ there were serious doubts on Tehran's capability to absorb the equipment it was requesting within the time frame specified – the new five-year acquisition plan. The chairman of the Joint Chiefs of Staff, General Earle Wheeler, stated that the Iranians "would have trouble digesting all the equipment they have in mind."⁴⁹ Furthermore, the Department of Defense urged a study of the actual threats facing Iran before committing to massive sales of sophisticated weaponry (the main point of contention at this time was the sale of C-130 and F-4 aircrafts). On this point in particular, the State Department converged. In fact, in the summer of 1970 State and Defense cabled the US Embassy in Tehran:

[State and Defense] realize that negative decisions would cause grave problems in our relations with Iran. Nevertheless we believe we must examine again the question of whether our military sales to Iran are in our overall interest, whether they may affect area security and stability, and whether there is a military requirement for this equipment. In this connection, DOD has requested a special national intelligence estimate of the threat to Iran.⁵⁰

Such sharp divisions within the administration could only prolong the stalemate on the actual decisions regarding arms sales to Iran. More generally, no overall, coherent posture was outlined. Ultimately, Nixon himself remained undecided. In fact, between the summer and the fall of 1970, the administration initiated a series of studies: on the potential role Iran could play within the regional dynamics of the Persian Gulf,⁵¹

1970, FRUS, Foreign Relations, 1969–1972, Volume E-4, Iran and Iraq, Doc. No. 63. Saunders forwarded Helms's memorandum to Kissinger.

⁴⁸ The connection between the conceptualization behind the Nixon doctrine and Iran's strive to build an adequate strength to enhance its role in the region was evident. For example, General Wheeler himself underlined that: "Iran has the necessary resources, peoples, and determination to provide for her defense and she has the responsibility for carrying out same. Iran must be capable of handling local conflicts and she should not look to the US to become involved except in case of general war," Memorandum for the Record, "Audience with His Imperial Majesty," 1700 Hours, 6 April 1970, General Earle G. Wheeler, Chairman, Joint Chiefs of Staff, and Major General H. A. Twitchell in Attendance (U), 8 April 1970, NA, NPM, NSC files, Country files – Middle East, box 601, folder Iran Vol. I (1 of 3).

⁴⁹ Memorandum of Conversation, Washington, April 14, 1970, FRUS, Foreign Relations, 1969–1972, Volume E-4, Iran and Iraq, Doc. No. 61. This would remain the DOD position for a long time.

⁵⁰ Telegram 115967 from the Department of State to the Embassy in Iran, July 20, 1970, 2106Z, FRUS, Foreign Relations, 1969–1972, Volume E-4, Iran and Iraq, Doc. No. 77.

⁵¹ The reference here is to a memorandum prepared by Assistant Secretary of State Sisco in response to Nixon's query on "how far the U.S. could go in leaving it to Iran to guarantee

on the implications of the British withdrawal[52] and on the composition, and future needs, of the Iranian military forces.[53] These clearly demonstrate that a strategy had not yet been defined. Accordingly, the president wrote to the shah stating that to his "very great regret" the Foreign Military Sales bill (to which decisions on sales to Iran were subordinated) was delayed by Congressional debate, a process in which he could not intervene. In short, while the tone of the exchange remained cordial and friendly, Nixon took his time.[54]

In the end, in late 1970 the decision on the sale of additional squadrons of aircrafts was made. Despite the divisions within the administration, the United States satisfied the shah's requests.[55] However, it is important

stability in the Persian Gulf." Kissinger summarized the conclusions and forwarded them to the president. The main points were that: Iran can deter actual attack (with its "formidable" military forces, which the shah was further strengthening) and foster cooperation with certain Gulf states (most notably with Saudi Arabia). Iran could not, however, prevent internal subversion in its neighbors, nor prevent expansion of Soviet influence via Arab radicalism. Kissinger also referred to further studies on the Gulf and discussions of US strategy within the NSC, which would be later forwarded to the president; Memorandum from the President's Assistant for National Security Affairs (Kissinger) to President Nixon, Washington, June 25, 1970, FRUS, Foreign Relations, 1969–1972, Volume E-4, Iran and Iraq, Doc. No. 75.

[52] The reference here is to a compressive study completed by the NSC Review Group on the implications for the United States of the British withdrawal from the Persian Gulf that Kissinger forwarded to the president. While the potential for future instability in the Gulf was clear, what the United States could do to prevent it was less evident. The proposed strategy – "to promote Saudi-Iranian cooperation as the mainstay of a stable regional system but to recognize that Iran is in fact the preponderant power in the Gulf" – was being defined. As Kissinger stated "no precise decision is required now." He simply asked Nixon to approve the strategy that was being "contemplated" for the near term, while further studies for longer-term decisions were in process. Nixon approved; Memorandum from the President's Assistant for National Security Affairs (Kissinger) to President Nixon, Washington, October 22, 1970, FRUS, Foreign Relations, 1969–1972, Volume E-4, Iran and Iraq, Doc. No. 91.

[53] These studies were sponsored by the Departments of State and Defense. Nixon refers to the assessments of Iranian military forces which were in process in his July 30, 1970, letter to the shah.

[54] Letter from President Nixon to the shah of Iran, Washington, July 30, 1970, FRUS, Foreign Relations, 1969–1972, Volume E-4, Iran and Iraq, Doc. No. 80.

[55] It is interesting to note that on the text of an NSC document written in November 1970, which summarized the different positions toward the sale of F-4s, Kissinger added a handwritten note "the Pres. wants to go ahead"; Memorandum from Harold Saunders of the National Security Council Staff to the President's Assistant for National Security Affairs (Kissinger), Washington, November 20, 1970, FRUS, Foreign Relations, 1969–1972, Volume E-4, Iran and Iraq, Doc. No. 100. Other documents urged the DOD to withdraw its opposition to the sale. Even if the military justification for this particular sale was "extremely weak," the agreement to the sale should be made "on political grounds"; Memorandum from the Assistant Secretary of Defense for International

"Protect Me": Nixon and the Shah of Iran

to underline both the prolonged impasse in Washington caused by such requests and the doubts of the American leadership surrounding the relationship with Iran. In communicating to Tehran that the additional purchase of aircrafts had been in principle approved, MacArthur was told to also emphasize the American concerns. The State and Defense Departments, for example, asked the ambassador to again "specify" why the US government had studied the Iranian demands "so carefully" and to point out the "major reservations" that had been held throughout consideration of the shah's requests.[56]

The American attitude thus sharply contrasted with the Iranian leadership's position. According to the shah, Iran had to defend its western and southern frontier stretching from Turkey to Pakistan, in addition to the northern border with the Soviet Union. While realizing that he would never have the resources necessary to completely secure the totality of his borders, the shah calculated his risks and needs in order to create a credible deterrent against Soviet (or other) aggression. For this reason, he considered his requests "austere in light of the vast area"[57] to be defended. Therefore, while in Washington his demands were assessed as exaggerated and to a large degree superfluous, in Tehran the shah considered them the "absolute and indispensable minimum."[58] This divergence could only lead to persistent tension caused by Iranian requests versus US restraint. Indeed, the pattern continued during the following year, from the beginning to mid-1971.

Only a few months after the decision on the F-4 aircraft sale, which had been so laborious in Washington, the messages from Iran reiterated the same themes: More armaments were necessary for the defense of Iranian and regional stability; no more limits should be imposed on the military acquisitions desired by the shah. On the American side, instead, reservations and limits were again stressed.[59] Significantly, a conversation between Nixon and Ambassador MacArthur reveals that, apart from the problems related to the divisions within the administration and the difficulties in Congress, the central question was that the president himself

---

Security Affairs (Nutter) to Secretary of Defense Laird, Washington, December 7, 1970, FRUS, Foreign Relations, 1969–1972, Volume E-4, Iran and Iraq, Doc. No. 103.

[56] Telegram 202975 from the Department of State to the Embassy in Iran, December 14, 1970, FRUS, Foreign Relations, 1969–1972, Volume E-4, Iran and Iraq, Doc. No. 107.

[57] Telegram 5335 from the Embassy in Iran to the Department of State, December 10, 1970, FRUS, Foreign Relations, 1969–1972, Volume E-4, Iran and Iraq, Doc. No. 106.

[58] Ibid.

[59] Memorandum of Conversation, Washington, March 24, 1971, 11:30 A.M., FRUS, Foreign Relations, 1969–1972, Volume E-4, Iran and Iraq, Doc. No. 120.

was still undecided regarding the political relationship with the Iranian leader. After the British withdrawal, the "vacuum is going to be filled. Iran is going to play the major part in doing it," stated MacArthur. In responding Nixon, however, was not entirely convinced:

Are they capable of it?
If he [the shah] could do it, it'd be wonderful because he is our friend. Right?
Does he need – what he's saying, he says 'Look, we're – if we can have more arms,' in effect, as I understood it, then can play, fill that – the role out there, you know, in the whole darn Gulf area. Well, now maybe he's thinking too big ...[60]

The administration remained hesitant, not only on arms sales but also in avoiding a commitment on a precise date for a presidential visit to Tehran, an issue that had been surfacing since 1969. While in principle Nixon had agreed to return the shah's visit, no actual concrete plans were being made.[61] In October 1971, Vice President Agnew told the Iranian leader that the United States "wished to cooperate with Iran and help in all feasible ways." However, there were problems in Washington and it was "becoming increasingly difficult to get the Congress to support the necessary appropriations for military aid and assistance."[62]

Therefore, between 1969 and 1971 the US-Iranian relationship, though in essence positive, was characterized clearly by tension and, on the American side, uncertainty and conflicting opinions on the concrete posture to adopt. How and why did the course of this problematic relationship shift so rapidly, enabling not only Nixon's 1972 visit to take place but also to provide the setting for the definite strengthening of the bond between Washington and Tehran?

"A VISIT TO IRAN IS A SERIOUS PROPOSITION"

By the end of 1971, in fact, the subsurface continued tension that has been described seemed to subside, while a more clear-cut policy progressively

---

[60] Conversation among President Nixon, Ambassador Douglas MacArthur II, and General Alexander Haig, Washington, April 8, 1971, 3:56–4:21 P.M., FRUS, Foreign Relations, 1969–1972, Volume E-4, Iran and Iraq, Doc. No. 122.

[61] In the cited conversation with MacArthur, for example, Nixon refers to the visit, stating that he "intends" to go but that he can't make a commitment regarding the date (the fall of 1971 is mentioned). The president simply states that he has it "under consideration"; Ibid.

[62] Telegram 16 from the US Delegation to the 25 Centenary in Shiraz, Iran, to the Department of State, October 15, 1971, 2010Z, FRUS, Foreign Relations, 1969–1972, Volume E-4, Iran and Iraq, Doc. No. 149.

emerged. The internal divisions and reservations in Washington remained, but the strategic location of Iran, and the consequent need to secure a tight relationship with the shah, became increasingly important. This was due to both regional developments and, most significantly, to the evolution of America's policy of détente with the Soviet Union. Although the shah had constantly and repeatedly referred to the Soviet threat in the region as a justification for his military spending, Washington only gradually came to share the perception of an increased potential for Moscow's advancement into the Gulf. Interestingly, this change in attitude toward Iran chronologically coincided with the administration's major foreign policy initiatives – the summits in Beijing and Moscow – which, by late 1971, had become a concrete reality.

Since 1969, the shah had pointed to the Soviet long-term design of acquiring warm water ports in the Persian Gulf and the Arabian Sea, with all the related and potentially grave consequences for the West. Almost two years later, the shah continued to underline that his fears were not misplaced. For example, during an audience with Ambassador MacArthur in December 1971, he provided a detailed analysis of the expansion of Soviet influence over the previous "seven months." These developments threatened Iran and other nations friendly to the West:

He [the shah] pointed out that not only had Soviet Union substantially increased its presence and influence in Mid-East-South Asia area as result of Soviet-Egyptian and Soviet-Indian pacts, but that parallel with this disturbing expansion of Soviet influence, Iraq had received visit of East German Defense Minister and most recently Soviet Defense Minister Grechko, who had stated publicly not only that Soviets and Iraq had total identity of views on all subjects but also that Soviets would assist Iraq in further strengthening its armed forces.[63]

In addition, the shah was wary of the situation along the other Iranian borders. "Afghanistan's utter weakness" and Pakistan's disarray created a "very unstable and dangerous situation on Iran's eastern frontier." In general, the indication of rising radicalism in countries neighboring Iran offered opportunities to the Soviet Union to expand its influence, either directly or by proxy. Moreover, due to the weakness of the Royal Family's position and the necessity of internal reforms, the shah

---

[63] Telegram 7283 from the Embassy in Iran to the Department of State, December 22, 1971, 1400Z, FRUS, Foreign Relations, 1969–1972, Volume E-4, Iran and Iraq, Doc. No. 154.

expressed preoccupations also with reference to Saudi Arabia, which for Washington constituted the fundamental second pillar of policy in the region.⁶⁴

Whereas in the past the shah's assessments had been overlooked or deemed excessively alarmist, the recent developments seemed to arouse greater attention in Washington. In December 1971, both Kissinger and Rogers wrote to the president urging, for the first time, to seriously consider a visit to Tehran – notably in connection with the trip to Moscow for the summit meeting with Brezhnev. The shah's invitation had been pending since 1969. Nixon had repeatedly reiterated the intention of visiting Iran but had never expressed a concrete commitment. At this point, both the national security adviser and the secretary of state advised the president to insert Tehran into his travel itinerary. As Kissinger put it, the purpose was twofold:

One, of course, is his [the shah's] special relationship with you and his great sensitivity and pride in not being overlooked, especially in view of the fact that you are meeting with other major leaders in connection with your Peking/Moscow travels.

On the substantive side, he has overriding concerns about long-range Soviet objectives in the area, including the Persian Gulf and Indian subcontinent.

Because the shah had again raised the issue of Nixon's visit, Kissinger concluded his memo stating:

While I had my doubts previously I now believe that with the momentous developments in South Asia and the potential in the Mid East, a visit to Iran is a serious proposition.⁶⁵

---

⁶⁴ It is important to underline that for the United States, Saudi Arabia was of crucial importance in the context of the general policies toward the Middle East. It provided for an alliance with an Arab country, avoiding probable Arab resentment caused by reliance only on a Persian regional proxy; Pollack, *The Persian Puzzle*, 103. In fact, Washington encouraged the ties between Tehran and Riyadh, the shah's views notwithstanding. In the briefing papers for Nixon's May 1972 visit, the Department of State stressed that: "United States policy remains one of close cooperation with Iran and Saudi Arabia and encouragement of their playing a constructive role in furthering the stability of the Peninsula and cooperation among the states;" Department of State Briefing Paper, Conditions on Neighboring Countries, NA, NPM, NSC files, President's Trip files, box 479, folder Briefing Book 1972 Visit.

⁶⁵ Memorandum for the President from Henry A. Kissinger, "Your Foreign Travels – Possibility of Including Iran," December 28, 1971, NA, NPM, NSC files, President's Trip files, box 481, folder Iran Visit (Part 2). It is important and curious to note that the president underlined the phrase "a visit to Tehran is a serious proposition" and handwrote "I agree."

A few weeks earlier, Rogers had outlined the same order of motivations, "strongly recommending" a visit to Tehran, for example, in connection with the Moscow trip.[66]

Predictably, this line of action was supported strongly by Ambassador MacArthur in Tehran. Conveying the Iranian viewpoint, he underlined the sense of "bitterness" regarding the "tendency of the United States to take Iran completely for granted." While the president had publicized his meetings with other great leaders before his trips to Beijing and Moscow, he seemed to ignore completely the shah, who was one of America's "best friends." For this reason, MacArthur cabled:

> If the President does not come, I fear that the basic structure of the relationship of confidence and cooperation which we have built up so painstakingly with Iran and which serves our national interest so well, could begin to erode away.

By early 1972, therefore, prominent members of the administration clearly perceived a greater need of reassuring the Iranian leader.[67] From the American standpoint, the significance of not letting the relationship with the shah "erode away" was intrinsically related to guaranteeing a solid pro-American asset; willing and capable, if need be, of influencing regional dynamics.[68]

In early 1972, the shah once again updated his package of demands, requesting additional squadrons of F-4 aircrafts.[69] The exchange of

---

[66] Memorandum for the President from William P. Rogers, "Visit to Iran Either Just Before or Just After Your Visit to Moscow," attached to Ibid.

[67] Accordingly, in early 1972 Kissinger recommended that Nixon sign the "determination" to allow Iran to continue to benefit from "grant assistance." The Foreign Assistance Act prohibited such assistance in excess of an established amount unless the president signed a determination that such assistance was important to US security. In Iran's case, this related to training programs and maintenance of US military advisers. Since the shah attached "great importance" to these programs, Kissinger recommended Nixon to allow them to continue; Memorandum from the President's Assistant for National Security Affairs (Kissinger) to President Nixon, Washington, January 11, 1972, FRUS, Foreign Relations, 1969–1972, Volume E-4, Iran and Iraq, Doc. No. 158. It is significant that this memo came from Kissinger who, earlier, had instead stressed limitations and restraint in continued aid to Iran.

[68] It is important to note that despite the unquestionably positive ties between the United States and Iran in the early 1970s, not all of Iran's positions coincided with Washington's desires. For example, among the actions that ran counter to US interests: the public and private opposition to the small American military presence in the region, such as the naval base in Bahrain, and the illegal transfer of American weapons to Pakistan during its war with India in 1971; Pollack, *The Persian Puzzle*, 104–105.

[69] Letter from the Deputy Chief of Mission at the Embassy in Iran (Heck) to the Director for Iranian Affairs (Miklos), Tehran, March 1, 1972, FRUS, Foreign Relations, 1969–1972, Volume E-4, Iran and Iraq, Doc. No. 170.

cables to and from Tehran, together with the sale of only eight squadrons as opposed to the sixteen requested originally by the shah,[70] could have produced the analogous pattern of tense complex negotiation which had shaped the first few years of the Nixon administration. However, the shift in attitude that had led Kissinger and Rogers to underscore the importance of a visit to Tehran anticipated a break from the "continued tension" of 1970 and 1971. Indeed, the content, timing, and scope of Nixon's two-day visit to Iran in late May 1972 charted a new course in Washington's relationship with Tehran.

"DECISIONS ON THE ACQUISITION OF MILITARY EQUIPMENT SHOULD BE LEFT PRIMARILY TO THE GOVERNMENT OF IRAN"

President Nixon's May 1972 trip to Tehran was a decisive moment in the strengthening of the US-Iranian bilateral relationship. During the conversations with the shah, Nixon in essence handed to the Iranian government "the keys to the store"[71] and committed the US government to the sale, with no more restraints, of its most recently produced and sophisticated weapons. In this way, Iran entered with full title the circle of America's closest allies. But what were the motivations behind this shift in policy? Why did Nixon finally decide to overrule the conflicting recommendations, breaking away from the pattern of emphasis on limits that he had shared until a few months earlier? What is the significance of the particular timing of these decisions?

As the policy of US-Soviet détente reached its climax with the Moscow summit, the Nixon administration gave greater importance to Iran. It was the common objective of preventing Soviet expansionism that brought Washington and Tehran closer together. In fact, the discussions between Nixon and the shah focused on Iran's role within the framework of the Nixon doctrine and on American support and aid in effectively implementing it. A few days before traveling to Tehran, Nixon returned to the theme of Iran as the only moderate and stable power in the region. He wrote to the shah that Washington was "counting on Iran to play an

---

[70] Telegram 1261 (March 2, 1972, 1124Z) and Telegram 1379 (March 8, 1972, 1345Z) from the Embassy in Iran to the Department of State, FRUS, Foreign Relations, 1969–1972, Volume E-4, Iran and Iraq, Doc. No. 171 and 173.

[71] William Bundy, *A Tangled Web. The Making of Foreign Policy in the Nixon Administration* (London: IB Tauris, 1998), 330.

important part in maintaining the stability of the area." Their upcoming discussions would provide an opportunity "to exchange views" on how best they could cooperate in this task.[72] In responding, the shah underlined that he was looking forward to the president's visit with "greatest pleasure," his people and he would finally have the opportunity to demonstrate their "warm feelings of friendship."[73] Setting the irritants and tensions of the previous months aside, the forthcoming meeting therefore seemed to be, as noted by Kissinger, a meeting with "one of America's best, most important, and most loyal friends in the world."[74]

While the study of the period before the 1972 Tehran trip may cast some doubt on the reliability of Kissinger's statement, the content and scope of Nixon's direct conversations with the shah certainly support the affirmation. In the afternoon of May 30, 1972, during the first of his scheduled meetings with the Iranian leader the president revealed, with surprising frankness, the essence of American policy toward the Soviet Union. To the shah's congratulations for the success of his foreign policy, "it was a masterpiece of strength on one side and dexterity on the other," Nixon responded:

When we arranged this trip, he explained, it all had to come together. Going to China made the Russian trip possible. Taking strong action in Vietnam (the May 8 measures) did not thwart the Moscow Summit. There was no reason for euphoria or for the assumption that the Soviet leaders had changed their long-term goals.[75]

There were no illusions, therefore, about Soviet policies, despite détente and the SALT agreements just signed which, Nixon underlined, were based on the American and Soviet "common interest." The president and the shah then referred to the 1971 India-Pakistan crisis as a confirmation of the unrelenting opportunistic objectives behind Soviet actions.[76] It was "what convinced us" stated Nixon, while the Iranian leader pointed out that the Indians had attacked only two months after signing the treaty

---

[72] Letter from the President to the shah of Iran, May 18, 1972, NA, NPM, NSC files, President's Trip files, box 479, folder Briefing Book 1972 Visit (2 of 2).
[73] Letter to the President from the shah of Iran, May 22, 1972, NA, NPM, NSC files, President's Trip files, box 479, folder Briefing Book 1972 Visit (2 of 2).
[74] Kissinger, *White House Years*, 1262.
[75] Memorandum of Conversation, Tuesday, May 30, 1972, 5:35 P.M.–6:35 P.M., Saadabad Palace, Tehran, Iran, NA, NPM, NSC files, President's Trip files, box 487, folder The President's Conversations (Part 2).
[76] On the India-Pakistan crisis and on the Nixon administration's *realpolitik* in relation to this conflict: Hanhimäki, *The Flawed Architect*, 154–184.

with Moscow. For this reason, he "didn't want to be told that the Soviets were restraining their clients."

The importance of these words is twofold. First, their immediate significance is that they confirm the notion of the Soviet Union as an adversary. Once again, it was evident that détente had not changed Washington's notion of a fundamentally competitive relationship with Moscow. Secondly, they lead to the following question: Why did Nixon feel compelled to outline the complexity of his broader strategy to his Iranian counterpart? In this respect, some of the exchanges circulating within the administration before Nixon's conversations in Tehran are revealing.

In early May 1972, Ambassador MacArthur sent a series of lengthy cables to Washington on the subjects that were likely to emerge during the Nixon-shah exchanges. In one of these messages, the ambassador anticipated that the shah's "primary and overall interest" would be to focus on Soviet activities in the Middle East and, in particular, discuss the American "interest, will and determination" to secure this part of the world from Moscow's influence. To this end, the shah would want to hear about the discussions with the Soviet leaders. "While of course he favors détente," continued the ambassador, he is at the same time concerned that "détente in Europe will release Soviet energies and strength to step up the Soviet campaign to penetrate the Middle East."[77]

In a lengthy memo written to the president in preparation for his talks in Tehran, Kissinger described the shah's concerns in more detail. The danger posed by the instability of countries bordering Iran – Pakistan and Afghanistan in particular – was juxtaposed to the fear that East-West détente would "tempt" the Soviets to expand into the region (South Asia and the Middle East). Hence, the shah was strengthening his country's military forces and promoting regional cooperation with other countries friendly to the West, in an effort to thwart Soviet ambitions. Against this background, Kissinger outlined the "two main purposes" of the president's visit. One, obviously, was to encourage the shah's efforts to "knit" closer regional ties with the countries willing to resist Soviet pressures in the Middle East. Significantly, the other, which was listed as the priority (point A), was to make sure that the shah understood the US global strategy. On this point, Kissinger was unequivocal:

You [Nixon] will be describing to the shah the strategy lying behind your trips to Peking and Moscow and the purpose behind your recent decisions on Southeast

---

[77] Telegram 2642 from Embassy in Iran to the Department of State, May 6, 1972, 1415Z, FRUS, Foreign Relations, 1969–1972, Volume E-4, Iran and Iraq, Doc. No. 187.

Asia. The shah will understand your efforts to establish a framework of relationships between the nuclear powers that will permit regional powers like Iran to play the principal role in contributing to stability in their areas. The shah has long understood the principles of the Nixon Doctrine – the necessity for great-power relationships that will permit countries like Iran, as the world changes, to develop the capacity to do what the US can no longer do around the world in providing the principal ingredients of regional security and stability.

Kissinger then concluded by stating:

Too often, we feel that this has not been clearly understood, and there would be no better platform for restating your views than Tehran.[78]

These words clearly spell out America's complex new strategy toward the Soviet Union – cooperation in negotiations on strategic arms (and in other aspects of mutual interest), while the competition shifted into the geopolitical domain and into the hands of local powers. From this perspective, Nixon's revelations to the shah are all the more meaningful: Precisely because of détente it was more (not less) important than before to demonstrate American determination in resisting Soviet expansion. There were to be absolutely no doubts in the mind of the shah, one of the leaders responsible for carrying the burden of regional defense. Accordingly, Nixon told the shah:

We came to visit Iran because we considered it symbolic of our strong support for our friends. We would not let our friends down.[79]

Nixon had decided that it was in the American interest to reassure firmly the shah and to sustain his role of anti-Soviet regional stronghold. Both the commitments on arms sales and the president's comments unequivocally confirm this. Specifically, Nixon agreed to sell laser-guided bombs and F-14 and F-15 aircrafts,[80] then both considered among the most advanced and sophisticated weaponry of US production. The third concession was the agreement on the assignment to Iran of an increased

---

[78] Memorandum from the Assistant for National Security Affairs (Kissinger) to President Nixon, Washington, May 18, 1972, FRUS, Foreign Relations, 1969–1972, Volume E-4, Iran and Iraq, Doc. No. 196.
[79] Memorandum of Conversation, Tuesday, May 30, 1972, 5:35 P.M.–6:35 P.M., Saadabad Palace, Tehran, Iran, NA, NPM, NSC files, President's Trip files, box 487, folder The President's Conversations (Part 2).
[80] From the documents compiled after the visit it emerges that the only condition imposed on the sale was that the aircrafts had to be operationally effective before being sold. Once the operational effectiveness of the new planes had been tested in the United States, the decisions on the purchases and their timing would be left to the government of Iran.

number of uniformed technicians, the so-called blue suiters, to work with the Iranian military. In this way, Nixon, overcoming the vacillations of the departments and the contradictory recommendations of his advisers,[81] gave weighty substance to the affirmation that he would not "let down" his friends. Most significantly, right after the agreement on arms sales, the president turned to the shah and asked him to understand the purpose of American policy. "Protect me," he said. "Don't look at détente as something that weakens you but as a way for the United States to gain influence."[82]

The change in policy in favor of the shah is all the more evident in the recommendations compiled after the Tehran trip, intended to provide concrete "follow-up" to the president's decisions. In writing to the Departments of State and Defense, Kissinger made clear that in the future there were to be no more hesitations in fulfilling Iranian demands:

The President had also reiterated that, in general, decisions on the acquisition of military equipment should be left primarily to the government of Iran. If the Government of Iran has decided to buy certain equipment, the purchase of US equipment should be encouraged tactfully where appropriate, and technical advice on the capabilities of the equipment in question should be provided.[83]

These words sharply contrast with those used by Kissinger in precedence, when he had repeatedly underlined that limits had to be imposed on the shah's ever-increasing demands. In this, the dimension of the shift in policy is manifest. Before the 1972 visit the shah's insistence was considered an "irritant" in the Iranian-American relationship, as his military requests posed domestic problems to the United States and were not immediately satisfied.[84] But Nixon's May decisions firmly eliminated such

---

[81] It is important to note that the DOD opposed a commitment on the sale of F-14s and F-15s. Also Kissinger recommended not to make a commitment on these aircrafts; Memorandum from the Deputy Secretary of Defense (Rush) to the President's Assistant for National Security Affairs (Kissinger), Washington, May 18, 1972 and Memorandum from the President's Assistant for National Security Affairs (Kissinger) to President Nixon, Washington, May 18, 1972, FRUS, Foreign Relations, 1969–1972, Volume E-4, Iran and Iraq, Doc. No. 195 and 196.
[82] Memorandum of Conversation, Tehran, May 31, 1972, 10:30 A.M.–12:00 P.M., FRUS, Foreign Relations, 1969–1972, Volume E-4, Iran and Iraq, Doc. No. 201.
[83] Memorandum for the Secretary of State and Secretary of Defence, "Follow-up on the President's Talk with the shah of Iran," July 25, 1972, NA, NPM, NSC files, Country files – Middle East, box 602, folder Iran Vol. IV.
[84] Department of State Telegram from AM Embassy Tehran to SecState WashDC, "President's Visit – US/Iran Relations and What They Mean to Shah," May 4, 1972, NA, NPM, NSC files, President's Trip files, box 481, folder Iran Visit (Part 2).

"Protect Me": Nixon and the Shah of Iran

irritations, further and unquestionably strengthening the bond between Washington and Tehran.

In his memoirs, Kissinger explains the motivations of Nixon's decisions and firmly defends them on the basis of their significance in the broader context of American-Soviet relations:

> The real issue in 1972 was that the required balance within an area essential for the security, and even more, prosperity, of all industrial democracies appeared in jeopardy ... Our friends – Saudi Arabia, Jordan, the Emirates – were being encircled.
> It was imperative for our interests and those of the Western world that the regional balance of power be maintained so that moderate forces would not be engulfed nor Europe's and Japan's (and as it later turned out, our) economic lifeline fall into hostile hands ... To have failed to match the influx of Soviet arms into neighboring countries would have accelerated the demoralization of moderate forces in the Middle East and speeded up the radicalization of the area, including Iran's.[85]

Surprisingly, Kissinger covers only the 1972 trip, underlining its importance, but makes no references to the previous hesitations in satisfying the shah and to the significance of the May decisions in terms of adjustment of policy. Therefore, the question that remains unanswered concerns the timing of the visit: Why did Nixon opt to so decisively strengthen the bond with the shah only in 1972 and to make such fundamental policy choices on a one-and-a-half-day trip to Tehran, a stop on the way home from the Moscow summit?

A plausible reason is that by 1972 the indications of Soviet advancement into the region had become more concrete, with the signing of the Soviet-Iraqi treaty only days before Nixon's visit. From the shah's point of view, the treaty entailed the probable modernization and growth of Iraqi armed forces, further exacerbating the existing tensions between Tehran and Baghdad and providing tangible evidence of Moscow's increased presence in the Gulf. In the Department of State briefing papers for Nixon's visit the shah's fears regarding the Soviet-Iraqi Pact are considered "exaggerated."[86] The decisions of May 1972 instead indicate that the president shared the shah's concerns.

---

[85] Kissinger, *White House Years*, 1263–1264.
[86] In fact, in the briefing papers the Iraqi capability to harm Iran is considered minimal and the Soviet intention to instigate Iraq against Iran deemed unlikely. Furthermore, with reference to the expansion and modernization of the Iraqi armed forces as a consequence of the 1972 Pact, the paper reads: "We do not share these assessments." This is interesting, when juxtaposed to the magnitude of the decisions made during the 1972 visit, for which

However, the other evidence of potential for Soviet expansionism, cited in the documents on the shah's preoccupations and quoted by Kissinger in his memoirs – the Soviet presence in Egypt and Syria, the British withdrawal from the Persian Gulf, the radicalization of Arab states – were present even before 1972, when the hesitance in giving the shah freedom to purchase virtually anything still shaped US policy toward Iran.

This suggests that further motives may have been at the basis of Nixon's 1972 decisions. Apart from securing continued reliance on Iran as the anti-Soviet regional stronghold, the timing of the visit was also particularly significant. The fact that it took place immediately after the Moscow summit adds to its relevance, when related to the broader design of US-Soviet relations. In fact, the particular symbolic impact of such resolute strengthening of a de-facto alliance based on the containment and, if necessary, resistance to Soviet expansionism, while practically at the same time signing agreements in Moscow, needs to be underlined. For in this lay, once again, the intrinsically dualistic nature of the Nixon administration's acclaimed policy of US-Soviet détente.

At the Moscow summit, the cooperative aspect of détente had reached its climax, both substantially, with the signing of the SALT agreements, and symbolically, as the improvement of US-Soviet relations became a selling point for both sides domestically.[87] But the stop in Tehran, though opportunistically remaining in the shadows of the triumphs of détente, demonstrated that the determination to resist the geopolitical strengthening of the Soviet Union remained a fundamental and unquestionable priority for Washington.

Compared to the Nixon-Brezhnev summit, the discussions in Tehran received little attention – both at the time and in subsequent historiography.[88] The May 1972 visit was, instead, extremely significant. The

---

these documents were to constitute the briefing book; Department of State Briefing Paper, Iran's Role in Regional Security, NA, NPM, NSC files, President's Trip files, box 479, folder Briefing Book 1972 Visit.

[87] The interrelation between domestic politics and foreign policy will be assessed in the next chapter.

[88] Even the studies on the Nixon administration by such scholars as Jussi Hanhimäki, Jeremi Suri, and Robert Dallek hardly mention the May 1972 Iran trip. The recent biography on the shah by Abbas Milani generally and briefly discusses the shah's ambitions in playing a dominant role in the Persian Gulf, but does not refer to the May 1972 visit; Abbas Milani, *The Shah* (London: Palgrave Macmillan, 2011), 327. An in-depth study of the relationship between the Nixon administration and the shah of Iran is the subject of Roham Alvadi's recent article in *Diplomatic History*. The author, however, comprehensively analyses and reconstructs the origins of Iranian primacy in the Gulf and the

conversations between Nixon and the shah in fact contribute to a better understanding of the administration's policy of détente with the Soviet Union. Nixon's decisions also set a blueprint for the future. America's relationship with the shah – so solidly grounded on the common objective of countering Soviet expansionism – would no longer be seriously questioned by subsequent presidents Gerald Ford and Jimmy Carter.

The notion of détente with its concomitant and simultaneously reinforcing cooperative and competitive aspects may have appeared an interpretative artifact, but the study of the Nixon administration's choices both before and immediately after the 1972 Moscow summit substantiates that interpretation. When focusing only on the high-level summits of 1972, the emphasis is on cooperation and on the "new era" initiated by the US administration in its relationship with the Soviet Union. However, by shifting attention also to other initiatives, inherently related to the summit – the measures against North Vietnam and the trip to Tehran, for example – the resulting picture is, inevitably, more complex.

The alleged inconsistency between America's geopolitical ambitions and its new era of negotiation with the Soviet Union, ultimately leading to the crisis and fall of détente, is generally considered to have surfaced in connection with the 1973 October War in the Middle East (which will be the focus of the next chapter). However, the initiatives analyzed in the period between 1969 and 1972 – the nature of the China policy, the determination in Vietnam and, most significantly, the relationship with Iran – suggest that a different type of competition with Moscow was present all along, from the conception to the implementation of Nixon's US-Soviet détente.

> *Strengthening the relationship with Iran reinforced American strength in the region, and coupled with the China card reinforced the U.S.'s determination to contain Soviet power, influence, & expansion*

role played by Nixon and Kissinger in boosting Iran's policies, but he does not interrelate the evolution of the US-Iranian bilateral relationship to the broader context of US-Soviet relations and of superpower détente (which is instead the focus of this chapter); Roham Alvadi, "Nixon, Kissinger and the Shah: The Origins of Iranian Primacy in the Gulf" in *Diplomatic History*, Vol. 36, No. 2 (April 2012).

5

Détente Questioned

Domestic Challenges and International Crisis

> Clearly, détente had not prevented a crisis, as some of our critics with varying degrees of disingenuousness were claiming it should have – forgetting that détente defined not a friendship but a strategy for a relationship between adversaries.
>
> Henry Kissinger, *Years of Upheaval*

> The Soviet Union will always act in its own self-interest; and so will the United States. Détente cannot change that.
>
> Richard Nixon, *RN: The Memoirs of Richard Nixon*

The foreign policy successes of 1972 definitely contributed to Nixon's overwhelming victory in the November presidential elections, securing what should have been the administration's second term in office. Until the first half of 1973, the US foreign policy lines proceeded along the path outlined during the first term: the SALT II talks started in November 1972; Kissinger visited China in February 1973 and the Soviet Union in May 1973; Nixon and Brezhnev held their second summit in Washington and San Clemente (in California, at the so-called Western White House) in June 1973. Moreover, Kissinger managed to successfully (or so it appeared at the time) negotiate the Paris Accords which, by early 1973, ended the American involvement in Vietnam.[1] However, beneath the

---

[1] For a brief assessment of the accords, Jussi Hanhimäki, *The Flawed Architect. Henry Kissinger and American Foreign Policy* (New York: Oxford University Press, 2004), 257–259. On the continuation of the war after the Paris Accords and for an overall assessment, Robert D. Schulzinger, "The End of the Vietnam War, 1973–1976" in Fredrik Logevall and Andrew Preston (eds), *Nixon in the World. American Foreign Relations, 1969–1977* (New York: Oxford University Press, 2008).

surface of this general continuity, the germs that would eventually lead to Nixon's downfall had already been planted.

Paradoxically, in fact, the lead up to one of the least disputed presidential elections in US history (Nixon won with a landside victory) coincided with what would become the most well-known and publicized break-in of all times: the intrusion into the Democratic Party's National Committee headquarters at the Watergate apartment complex in Washington, DC. While in the summer and fall of 1972 this incident remained marginal and did not influence the unfolding of US policy (domestic and foreign), the scandal was in the making and would, for the following two years, increasingly paralyze the Nixon administration's decision-making process – until the president's resignation in August 1974.[2]

During the same period of time, the administration witnessed, and was incapable of effectively countering, the emergence of strong domestic criticism against its major foreign policy achievement – détente with the Soviet Union. In fact, almost immediately after the climaxes of 1972, the Nixon administration's acclaimed foreign policy started to be critically questioned. Furthermore, in 1973 the domestic difficulties were coupled with the outbreak of a major international crisis: the October War in the Middle East. The combination of all these factors would seriously challenge and ultimately compromise the solidity of the administration's design and the future of US-Soviet détente.

DOMESTIC CHALLENGES: "ESSENTIAL EQUIVALENCE," JEWISH EMIGRATION, AND ... WATERGATE

After Nixon's return from the 1972 Moscow summit, the inherent fragility of détente gradually began to surface. The criticism touched upon the military, economic, and political aspects of the innovative US-Soviet relationship. The beginning of the SALT II talks (in November–December 1972 and March–June 1973) gave continuity to the arms control process, but no progress was made toward a comprehensive treaty on offensive weapons. On the American side, the debate over MIRV limitation, and in general over how to respond to the Soviet buildup while no longer possessing a credible counterforce capability, paralyzed Washington's

---

[2] For a concise but comprehensive account of the Watergate scandal, Keith W. Olson, *Watergate. The Presidential Scandal that Shook America* (Lawrence, KS: The University Press of Kansas, 2003).

negotiating posture.³ Moreover, the SALT I Interim Agreement was criticized because of the apparent advantages it conceded to the Soviets in terms of aggregates (despite the agreement having frozen the situation according to the force structure chosen by the United States in the preceding years and notwithstanding the differences in the composition of the Soviet forces). The SALT process therefore became the central controversial point for the conservative opposition to détente, with the Joint Chiefs of Staff and the Pentagon in particular insisting on numerical equivalence and absolute symmetry (or on "essential equivalence" in technical language) for any future agreement with the Soviets. This issue would create the basis for a powerful political attack on the Nixon-Kissinger design led by Democratic senator Henry Jackson (who would become one of the leaders of the newly formed "neoconservative" movement).⁴

Also, the economic aspects of détente were increasingly criticized. Nixon and Kissinger had considered trade with Moscow an inducement for Soviet restraint in the conduct of international affairs. Economic incentives had been an important element in the pursuit of détente. In September 1972, the settlement of the Lend-Lease issue had cleared the way for the trade agreement with Moscow, of which the granting of the "Most Favored Nation" status was a central element. However, with the introduction of the Jackson amendment in the Senate, and of the Vanik amendment in the House, the granting of Most Favored Nation status was linked to the flow of Jewish emigration from the Soviet Union.⁵ In this way, increased trade considered by the administration as a pillar of its foreign policy was connected to the prospect of bringing desired changes in Moscow's domestic policies. The promotion

---

³ For reference on the debate over MIRV limitations and the divisions within the American administration between the positions of the Department of Defense, of the Department of State, of the Joint Chiefs of Staff, and of the Arms Control and Disarmament Agency: Henry Kissinger, *Years of Upheaval* (London: Phoenix Press, 2000), 262–274; William Bundy, *A Tangled Web. The Making of Foreign Policy in the Nixon Presidency* (London: IB Tauris, 1998), 406–407.
⁴ Other influential critics were Paul Nitze, Richard Pipes, Eugene Rostow, Albert Wohlstetter, and Edward Teller. They attacked the SALT agreements and the strategic concept behind them, claiming that nuclear superiority still mattered, politically and diplomatically. On the rise of the neoconservatives and on their impact on the decline of détente, Mario Del Pero, *The Eccentric Realist. Henry Kissinger and the Shaping of American Foreign Policy* (Ithaca, NY: Cornell University Press, 2010), Chapter 4.
⁵ For reference on the Jackson-Vanik amendment: Kissinger, *Years of Upheaval*, 246–255 and 986–998; Bundy, *A Tangled Web*, 407–409; Raymond Garthoff, *Détente and Confrontation. American-Soviet Relations from Nixon to Reagan* (Washington, DC. The Brookings Institution, 1994), 460–462; Hanhimäki, *The Flawed Architect*, 340–342.

of human rights thus emerged as an issue capable of influencing foreign policy. This provided the tool through which the liberal opposition criticized and attacked the Nixon administration's excessive *realpolitik* in its dealings with the Soviet Union.⁶

Eventually, the conservative and liberal opposition united and coalesced, forming a potent "anti-détente coalition."⁷ Between late 1972 and the end of 1974, it created a serious and irreversible domestic challenge to the implementation of the administration's foreign policy. Because Nixon had described and promoted détente domestically as the creation of a "new structure for peace," Americans were confused and distraught when the competition with the Soviet Union openly resurfaced. The administration's innovative policy described in the first chapters of this book had not been explained to, or understood by, the American public. Moreover, in the face of rising domestic challenges, Nixon's ambitious design would have needed a strong presidency and unquestioned authority for it to be effectively sustained. Both requirements that no longer existed by mid-1973. As a consequence of Watergate, the American public completely lost trust and confidence in the presidency. Although Nixon would later downplay the impact of Watergate in determining the crisis of détente,⁸ it is undisputable that a strong president could have, and would have, faced the challenges differently and more effectively.⁹

In terms of US foreign policy making, the most direct and enduring consequence of the Watergate scandal was the strengthening of Henry Kissinger's position and authority within the administration. By the

---

⁶ For a comprehensive analysis of the emergence of the Jewish emigration issue and its impact on the decline of détente, see Noam Kochavi, "Insights Abandoned, Flexibility Lost: Kissinger, Soviet Jewish Emigration, and the Demise of Détente" in *Diplomatic History*, Vol. 29, No. 3 (June 2005). See also the first part of the article by Julian E. Zelizer "Détente and Domestic Politics" in *Diplomatic History*, Vol. 33, No. 4 (September 2009).

⁷ Nixon uses this expression in his memoirs; Richard M. Nixon, *RN: The Memoirs of Richard Nixon* (New York: Touchstone, 1990), 1036.

⁸ Nixon, *RN: The Memoirs*, 1036. Nixon states that the antidétente coalition and the military opposition to détente would have existed regardless of Watergate.

⁹ In contrast to Nixon, Kissinger in his memoirs emphasizes the impact of Watergate on the administration's inability to continue to sustain its ambitious foreign policy design. "The Gathering Impact of Watergate" is the title of the chapter; Kissinger, *Years of Upheaval*, 76–126. Also Garthoff recognizes the Watergate scandal as having prejudiced the progress of détente; Garthoff, *Détente and Confrontation*, 458–460. Along the same lines is Soviet ambassador Dobrynin's judgment, as he describes Watergate as "by far the most remarkable influence on the developments in the United States"; Anatoly Dobrynin, *In Confidence. Moscow's Ambassador to America's Six Cold War Presidents* (New York: Random House, 1995), 265.

summer of 1973, the unfolding of the Watergate drama – and the related resignation of a number of Nixon's key aides – made it crucial for the president to rely on a strong and widely respected figure whose popularity had been untouched by the downward spiral that had otherwise permeated the public image of the presidency. As noted by historian Jussi Hanhimäki, "Kissinger's nomination as secretary of state was largely a result of Nixon's own political weakness and the strength of the American public's image of Kissinger." When, in September 1973, Kissinger was sworn in as secretary of state, he also maintained (until 1975) his position of National Security Council adviser (the only individual to ever hold these two posts simultaneously). This was "the ultimate confirmation of Kissinger's position as the Nixon administration's foreign policy czar."[10]

THE CONTINUATION OF TRIANGULAR DIPLOMACY

Regardless of the developments on the domestic scene, during the first half of 1973 (i.e., before Kissinger became secretary of state), the administration maintained the momentum of triangular diplomacy and of US-Soviet détente. After Nixon's visit to China, a partnership – or "quasi alliance" as Kissinger later stated – emerged between Beijing and Washington based not on documents or formal agreements but on the understandings reached during the conversations with Mao – in February and November 1973 – and in the long discussions with Zhou. At the summit in 1972, Mao had blessed the general direction of the Sino-American rapprochement but had refused to discuss the details of a tactic or common strategy. This gap was filled during the conversations with Kissinger. During the two-hour meeting in February 1973, the chairman stressed that the Soviet Union represented a global threat and thus needed to be resisted globally. He clearly disapproved of the continuation of US-Soviet détente, advocating a clear-cut policy of confrontation against Moscow.[11]

On his part, Kissinger again emphasized the American and Chinese strategic goal of containing the Soviet Union. He strongly denied any complicity with the Soviets, underlining that the agreements with

---

[10] Hanhimäki, *The Flawed Architect*, 292–293. Kissinger himself in his memoirs concedes that his nomination as secretary of state was directly related to the consequences of Watergate. While in 1969 Nixon has asserted that foreign policy had to be run primarily from the White House (and had largely succeeded in this between 1969 and 1972), Watergate made the preeminent position of the White House untenable, hence Kissinger's designation as head of the State Department; Kissinger, *Years of Upheaval*, 4–8.

[11] Henry Kissinger, *On China*, (New York: Penguin Books, 2011), 275–282.

Moscow served US interests but were not and would not be directed against China. When Kissinger summarized for Nixon the conversations in Beijing with both Mao and Zhou, he stressed that the Soviet Union "was the centerpiece and completely permeated our talks."[12] This confirmed that the common objective of opposing Soviet expansionist ambitions remained at the center of the US-Chinese relationship. In practical terms, Kissinger's February visit produced the agreement on the establishment of liaison offices – permanent representations in each country's capitals that lacked the formal stature of embassies. From the spring of 1973, these offices formalized, and facilitated, the communications with the Chinese, which no longer had to take place through the good offices of third countries or through secret back channels. Despite the continued difficulties that prevented the rapid movement toward full normalization – divergences mainly over Taiwan, but also in the two countries' policy toward Cambodia – the Sino-American rapprochement was clearly moving forward.[13]

At the same time, Washington continued on the path of US-Soviet détente. In May 1973 Kissinger and his aides travelled to the Soviet Union and held high-level talks with the Soviet leadership at the Politburo's hunting reserve in Zavidovo (northeast of Moscow) in preparation for the second summit between Nixon and Brezhnev, which took place in the United States a month later. Due to the Multiple Independently targeted Reentry Vehicle (MIRV) controversy and the domestic challenges that the administration had started to face, during Kissinger's advance trip and at the June summit itself, substantial progress on SALT was impossible. Thus, in the nuclear-strategic field, the major achievements were the commitment to seek agreement in SALT II by the end of 1974 and the signing of the Agreement on the Prevention of Nuclear War (PNW).[14] The Soviets

---

[12] Hanhimäki, *The Flawed Architect*, 270–271.

[13] James Mann, *About Face. A History of America's Curious Relationship with China, from Nixon to Clinton* (New York: Vintage Books, 2000), 53–77.

[14] For an analysis of the articles of the Agreement: Garthoff, *Détente and Confrontation*, 376. For reference on the negotiation and on the difference between the Soviet original proposal and the final document: Kissinger, *Years of Upheaval*, 274–286; Garthoff, *Détente and Confrontation*, 376–386; Bundy, *A Tangled Web*, 409–410. It is significant to note that while the Soviets had assigned particular importance to their proposal, specifically in relation to the preoccupations regarding US-Chinese relations, the Americans had immediately perceived the potentially grave consequences of an agreement along the Soviet lines not only for the development of relations with China but also in the context of the Alliance with Western Europe. The final document, far from constituting the far-reaching proposal sought by Moscow, assumed the form of a general statement of principles, completing the *Basic Principles* of the previous year. It was a political step,

had sought an agreement that would have conveyed the impression of a superpower condominium. They demanded, in fact, a clause (unacceptable for Washington) in which the United States and the Soviet Union pledged not to use nuclear weapons against each other, but left open the possibility of the use against third countries. Washington managed to shift the focus of the agreement and, ultimately, the PNW amounted to a general renunciation of the use of force and of nuclear weapons. At the June summit, Nixon and Brezhnev also signed a series of other documents – ranging from the peaceful uses of nuclear energy to further development of bilateral cultural exchanges.[15] Compared to the breakthroughs of the previous year, the agreements of 1973 appeared to be minor. They were, nonetheless, important in allowing the process of "improved relations" to continue, amid the first difficulties and contradictions.

Interestingly, the most significant discussions which took place at the June 1973 summit focused on China and on the Middle East. On China, Brezhnev again warned that US-Chinese relations would, in the long run, damage continued US-Soviet détente. While acknowledging that he had no right to interfere with agreements that Washington made with other countries, the Soviet leader stated that should Sino-American ties deepen to include military agreements, then Moscow would have to react: "In 1972 we did not raise the issue. But I am worried about the future. There is no need to undermine the agreement we have concluded (the PNW). We do not intend to attack China but it will be different if China has a military agreement with the United States. That would confuse the issue."[16] This exchange once again confirmed the deep and unrelenting Soviet concerns regarding China and, in turn, the continued inherently positive potential for Washington's triangular diplomacy.

On the Middle East, Brezhnev surprised his counterparts with a late-night session on June 23, 1973, during which he insisted on discussing the developments in the region. During the previous conversations, the only reference to the Middle East had been Soviet foreign minister Gromyko's point on including a reference to the different interpretations

---

rather than a technical instrument for crisis prevention and management. For the Soviet view of the PNW agreement: Dobrynin, *In Confidence*, 277–278.
[15] On the June 1973 summit, Bundy, *A Tangled Web*, 409–413; Garthoff, *Détente and Confrontation*, 371–386.
[16] Memorandum for the President's Files, from Henry A. Kissinger, Meeting with Leonid I. Brezhnev, General Secretary of the Central Committee, CPSU, on Saturday, June 23, 1973, at 12:22 P.M., National Archives (hereafter NA), Nixon Presidential Materials (hereafter NPM), National Security Council (hereafter NSC) files, Henry Kissinger (hereafter HAK) Office files, box 75.

Domestic Challenges and International Crisis 123

of UN Security Council Resolution 242 in the final communiqué of the summit.[17] The American leadership was thus not prepared to initiate negotiations on the complex political situation in the Middle East. Brezhnev, instead, wanted to discuss the key issues. It was up to the United States and the Soviet Union, he stated, to try to bring the "warlike situation to an end." The Soviet leader continued:

> We must have a discussion on these principles (i.e. Israeli occupation of Arab territories after 1967). If there is no clarity ... we will have difficulty keeping the situation from flaring up. Everything depends on troop withdrawals and adequate guarantees. I can assure you that nothing will go beyond this room. But if we agree on Israeli withdrawals, then everything will fall into place.

Brezhnev, therefore, raised the central issue. During the 1967 Six Day War the Israeli army (with the support of US arms) had humiliated its Arab neighbors and occupied the Sinai Peninsula, the Golan Heights and the West Bank. Egypt and Syria had not accepted the situation, and were determined to retrieve their lost territories. The Nixon administration had thus inherited a highly complex and volatile situation, for which it was difficult to conceive clear-cut solutions. On the evening of June 23, Nixon responded to the Soviet leader that nothing definitive could be said on the subject at that moment. But despite the president's firmness, Brezhnev insisted. If a general agreement were reached between them, he stated, Kissinger and Dobrynin could then use their special channel to influence the parts into compliance. Even Nixon's resolute "we can't settle this tonight" did not prevent the Soviet leader from continuing:

> I am categorically opposed to a resumption of war. But without agreed principles that will ultimately help the situation in the area, we cannot do this. If there is a settlement, we can renew relations with Israel. Without such agreement our further cooperation will be weakened.[18]

In his memoirs Kissinger goes as far as asserting that Brezhnev was in effect threatening the United States with a Middle East war.[19] While this may not have been the case – we now know that the Soviet leader was

---

[17] According to Kissinger, such insistence was a consequence of Sadat's expulsion of the Soviet advisers from Egypt in 1972, allegedly due to the fact that the communiqué of the May 1972 Nixon-Brezhnev summit had not alluded to the different interpretations of Washington and Moscow on the Middle East; Kissinger, *Years of Upheaval*, 295–296.
[18] Memorandum for the President's Files from Henry A. Kissinger, President's Meeting with Secretary General Leonid Brezhnev on Saturday, June 23, 1973 at 10:30 P.M. at the Western White House, San Clemente, California, NA, NPM, NSC files, HAK Office files, box 75.
[19] Kissinger, *Years of Upheaval*, 298.

indeed searching for US-Soviet cooperation in the region[20] – the dialogue was interpreted in Washington as confirmation of the continued competitive nature of US-Soviet relations. As Nixon put it "this testy midnight session was a reminder of the unchanging and unrelenting Communist motivations beneath the diplomatic veneer of détente."[21] With hindsight, considering the outbreak of war a few months later, Brezhnev's insistence on wanting to discuss the Middle East at the June summit was particularly significant.

A "PROTRACTED DUEL"

The 1973 Middle East war began on October 6, during the Jewish celebration of Yom Kippur, when Egyptian forces crossed the Suez Canal and, simultaneously, Syrian forces attacked across the Golan Heights. Israel was struck by surprise and, initially, suffered enormous losses. From the start of the conflict, the American leadership focused on the potential Soviet foreknowledge of Egyptian intentions. Apart from Brezhnev's "testy midnight session," the Soviets had again tried to warn the Americans on the grave situation in the Middle East. At the annual meeting of the UN General Assembly, only one week before the outbreak of war, Gromyko told Nixon not to exclude the possibility "that we could all wake up one day and find there is a real conflagration in that area."[22] On this basis, Sonnenfeldt speculated that the Soviets had maneuvered behind the scenes to their advantage.[23] Kissinger, in particular, was convinced that the Soviets had advance knowledge of Sadat's decision to attack.[24]

---

[20] Today, in fact, the controversy over Soviet alleged foresight of Egyptian intentions seems resolved and sources have unveiled the Soviet leader's intention to warn the United States that Moscow was not able to restrain its Arab clients. Brezhnev was, indeed, searching for US-Soviet cooperation. Washington, on the other hand, was not willing to accept a Soviet role in the Middle East; Vladislav Zubok, *A Failed Empire. The Soviet Union in the Cold War from Stalin to Gorbachev* (Chapel Hill, NC: The North Carolina University Press, 2009), 238.
[21] Nixon, *RN: The Memoirs*, 885.
[22] Memorandum of Conversation, Friday, September 28, 1973, 10:00 A.M.–12:05 P.M., NA, NPM, NSC files, HAK Office files, box 68. Brezhnev's attitude at the June 1973 summit and Gromyko's warning at the UN General Assembly were interpreted in Washington as an indication that Moscow knew about Sadat's intentions and had maneuvered before the war to its advantage (as explicitly stated by Sonnenfeldt, see footnote 23 below).
[23] Memorandum for Secretary Kissinger from Helmut Sonnenfeldt, "Soviets and the Middle East – Gromyko's talks with the President of September 28, 1973," October 11, 1973, Ibid.
[24] Hanhimäki, *The Flawed Architect*, 307.

Unsurprisingly, therefore, after a few days of fighting, the Soviet conduct was defined in Washington as "increasingly worrisome." This confirmed the tension between the proclamations of détente and the superpowers' determination to respectively maintain, or enhance, their influence in the region. According to Sonnenfeldt, the Soviets, initially surprised by the Arab success, had then started to "smell victory and the credit that comes with it." They could not remain "indifferent to advantages accruing to their power position and image from the humiliation of a US client" (i.e., Israel). The dimensions of the Soviet airlift in support of the Arab war effort, and the implicit encouragement it conveyed to Egypt and Syria to continue fighting, directly challenged the American position. The combination of these elements triggered the review of the broad implications at stake for the United States:

> The prospect of even the most helpful Soviet attitude on these matters (a post-war settlement) at some future time must be weighed against the character of Soviet conduct before and during the war. And that, to me [Sonnenfeldt], suggests a judgment either that the US commitment to détente is such that the Soviets have substantial leeway in the Middle East or that the stakes of actively supporting the Arabs override any losses due to the disruption of relations with us. In either case, the time is approaching that the Soviets should be proven wrong.[25]

The unfolding of events unquestionably confirms not only the intention to counter the Soviets but, most importantly, Washington's determination in seeking to strengthen its own position in the region to the detriment of Moscow's. In other words, according to Kissinger, the outbreak of war marked the beginning of a "protracted duel"[26] in which both sides sought to weaken the other, the continuing proclamations of cooperation notwithstanding.

"WE WERE NOT WILLING TO PAY FOR DÉTENTE IN THE COIN OF OUR GEOPOLITICAL POSITION"[27]

The American attitude throughout the war was heavily influenced by the constant view of the conflict through the prism of US-Soviet relations. The assessments related to the repercussions of the regional conflict on the broader competition with Moscow shaped the administration's choices, both in the immediate response to the crisis and in the

---

[25] Memorandum for Secretary Kissinger from Helmut Sonnenfeldt, "The Soviet Role in the Middle East War," October 10, 1973, NA, NPM, NSC files, HAK Office files, box 68.
[26] Kissinger, *Years of Upheaval*, 459.
[27] Ibid., 299.

long-term political engagement in the region. The firm determination to resist the introduction of a Soviet direct presence into the region was evident in Washington's decision to raise the alert level of its nuclear forces. After the crisis abated, the United States – and Kissinger in particular – developed a strategy aimed at securing the role of sole mediator in the negotiations on a postwar political settlement. The objective was to totally exclude the Soviet Union's presence and influence from the Middle East.

On October 6, 1973, the day the fighting broke out, Kissinger met the Chinese ambassador in Washington and outlined the American objectives. Although there might have been some overemphasis – considering that he was talking with the Chinese – Kissinger's statements were surprisingly explicit in subordinating the regional conflict to the higher precepts dictated by the rivalry with the Soviet Union:

> Our strategic objective is to prevent the Soviet Union from getting a dominant position in the Middle East. That is our basic objective. Israel is a secondary, emotional problem having to do with domestic politics here. Our objective is always, when the Soviet Union appears, to demonstrate that whoever gets help from the Soviet Union cannot achieve his objective, whatever it is.[28]

It was the Soviet context, therefore, which mattered the most. Along the same lines, on October 10, staffer Jon Howe wrote to Kissinger's deputy at the NSC, Brent Scowcroft, and underlined not to underestimate the situation in terms of its potential global repercussions. He recommended increasing the American military capabilities deployable in the area because, while there was no need to develop an "unnecessary confrontation," the possibility of one had to be at least considered.[29]

After the initial Egyptian-Syrian attack, both superpowers came out in support of their respective allies. By October 10, 1973, the Soviet Union was supplying the Arabs and, after UN-sponsored diplomacy failed to produce a cease-fire, Nixon ordered (on October 13) military materials airlifted to Israel. The next day, Israel was already turning around the balance on the battleground with a military victory in the Sinai Peninsula. By October 18, the Israelis were on the offensive (despite, in

---

[28] Memorandum of Conversation, Saturday, October 6, 1973, 9:10–9:30 P.M., Secretary Kissinger's White House Office, NA, RG 59, Records of the Policy Planning Staff, Director's files (Winston Lord), 1969–1977, box 328.

[29] Memorandum for General Scowcroft from Jon Howe, "U.S. Moves in the Crisis," October 10, 1973, NA, NPM, NSC files, Country files – Middle East, box 664.

the meantime, the Arab countries having had decided on imposing an oil embargo that caused many US allies to distance themselves from the conflict). At this point, Kissinger accepted Dobrynin's invitation for an emergency visit to Moscow (that took place on October 20–21) to negotiate a cease-fire, later backed by the UN Security Council. However, the successive evident violations (on Israel's part) of the cease-fire triggered the escalation of the superpowers' involvement and, in parallel, of the level of tension.[30]

On October 24, in a letter to Nixon, Brezhnev protested against Israel's "gross defiance" of the superpowers' understanding and of the UN Security Council's decisions.[31] He also directly charged the United States with not having effectively influenced Israeli behavior. Referring to Tel Aviv's conduct, the Soviet leader stated: "We, naturally, have questions on what is behind all this." Then, he implicitly further doubted American intentions: "We would like to hope that we both will be true to our word and to the understanding we have reached."[32]

At the same time, the White House received a message from the Egyptian ambassador, confirming that Israel had again broken the cease-fire. This was followed by President Sadat's personal message to Nixon in which a proposal assessed in Washington as "bound to lead to decisions of grave consequence" was put forward. The Egyptian leader demanded American intercession in the crisis, with the immediate dispatch of observers or troops to secure the implementation of the cease-fire. And, most importantly, Sadat stated that he was "formally" issuing the same request to the Soviets. Shortly afterwards, the appeal was made public: Cairo was calling for a Security Council meeting to ask that American and Soviet forces be sent to the Middle East.[33]

---

[30] Hanhimäki, *The Flawed Architect*, 307–312.

[31] The substance of the letter had been conveyed by Dobrynin to Kissinger over the telephone, at 10:19 A.M. on October 24, 1973. See the record of Kissinger's "telcons" transcribed in Henry Kissinger, *Crisis. The Anatomy of Two Major Foreign Policy Crises* (New York: Simon & Schuster, 2003), 329–330.

[32] Note from Dobrynin to Kissinger enclosing letter from Brezhnev to Nixon, October 24, 1973, NA, NPM, NSC files, HAK Office files, box 69. As we now know, Brezhnev rightly doubted US intentions. Kissinger, in fact, had openly told the Israelis that the United States would not object against Israeli violations of the cease-fire for a few hours, those required for him to return to Washington; Hanhimäki, *The Flawed Architect*, 313; Asaf Siniver, *Nixon, Kissinger and US Foreign Policy Making. The Machinery of Crisis* (New York: Cambridge University Press, 2008), 207.

[33] Kissinger, *Crisis*, 330–331.

Kissinger's comments on the American reaction to the Egyptian proposal, both in his memoirs and in his more recent book *Crisis*, are explicit:

> We had not worked for years to reduce the Soviet military presence in Egypt only to cooperate in reintroducing it as the result of a U.N. resolution. Nor would we participate in a joint force with the Soviets, which would legitimize their role in the area and strengthen radical elements.

And:

> We were determined to resist, by force if necessary, the introduction of Soviet troops into the Middle East, regardless of the pretext under which they arrived.[34]

The choices made at the height of the crisis (the critical hours between October 24 and 25), unequivocally confirm America's determination.

In the afternoon of October 24, when consulting with the Israeli ambassador on Sadat's proposal, Kissinger stated: "We will totally oppose the introduction of American and Soviet forces." Then, in the evening, Kissinger repeated, twice, to Dobrynin that Washington would exercise its veto against the prospected resolution at the Security Council.[35] Afterwards, in a letter to Sadat, Nixon explained the US stance: Apart from stressing the difficulties in assembling "sufficient outside military power to represent an effective counterweight to the indigenous forces" engaged in the fighting, the president pointed to the "extremely dangerous potential for direct great power rivalry" should Washington and Moscow introduce their forces in the area. Instead, Nixon called for the arrival of UN observers to ensure the effective implementation of the cease-fire. At the end of the letter, the president stated:

> The United States stands ready to move rapidly towards a political solution to the tragic problems that have made peace in the Middle East such a tenuous thing. But we are equally intent upon avoiding an unnecessary confrontation which would but make more difficult and dangerous an already extremely complex situation.[36]

The Soviets, instead, were determined to support Sadat's request. On the evening of October 24, Dobrynin communicated to Kissinger another, all the more critical, message from Brezhnev. Again strongly protesting against Israel's "brazen challenge" the Soviet leader proposed to "urgently

---

[34] Kissinger, *Years of Upheaval*, 579–580; Kissinger, *Crisis*, 331.
[35] Kissinger, *Crisis*, 331–332, 335.
[36] Back-channel message from Nixon through Ismail to Sadat, October 24, 1973, NA, RG 59, SN 70–73, POL 27-14 Arab-Isr.

dispatch to Egypt the Soviet and American military contingents, to assure the implementation of the decision of the Security Council of October 22 and 23 concerning the cessation of fire." Furthermore, with tones which in Washington were interpreted as intimidating, Brezhnev added urgency and firmness to his request:

> It is necessary to adhere without delay. I will say it straight that if you find it impossible to act jointly with us in this matter, we should be faced with the necessity urgently to consider the question of taking appropriate steps unilaterally.[37]

When recalling this message in their memoirs, Nixon and Kissinger are both explicit. According to Nixon the "message represented perhaps the most serious threat to US-Soviet relations since the Cuban missile crisis."[38] Kissinger states that "it was one of the most serious challenges to an American president by a Soviet leader."[39] The debate over the actual Soviet intentions, however, is still unresolved.[40] But whether the message represented an actual threat to intervene unilaterally, or simply an effort to finally obtain joint action, what needs to be underlined is the American overreaction, which confirmed the absolute determination not to yield to Soviet pressure (actual or even just presumed). In order to warn Moscow against any possible attempt at unilateral action, the United States in fact

---

[37] Message from Brezhnev to Nixon, October 24, 1973, NA, NPM, NSC files, HAK Office files, box 69. The message was read to Kissinger over the telephone, therefore significant partitions of the text are published in Kissinger, *Crisis*, 342.

[38] Nixon, *RN: The Memoirs*, 938.

[39] Kissinger, *Years of Upheaval*, 583.

[40] Sources that underline the Soviet threat: Kissinger, *Years of Upheaval*, 584; Garthoff, *Détente and Confrontation*, 424. But Garthoff also states that the Soviet actual intentions may not have been to act unilaterally but only to obtain joint action; Garthoff, *Détente and Confrontation*, 428. Dobrynin, in his memoirs, does not provide any explanation but curiously reveals his unawareness of the phrase on unilateral action: "So after an argumentative meeting they (the Politburo) finally approved a message to Nixon which was strongly worded but did not contain any threat to act unilaterally. However, a stronger phrase about our possible involvement appeared in the text of the message as it reached Washington. It is anybody's guess how and when it was inserted, since the main participants of the meeting are no longer alive"; Dobrynin, *In Confidence*, 295. For further insight into the Soviet motivations, such as the need to respond to Sadat's urgent pleas for aid and the difficulties in the flow of accurate and timely information to Moscow on the actual military developments on the field: The National Security Archive Electronic Briefing Book, edited by William Burr, at www.gwu.edu, 45. Zubok also emphasizes the need for Moscow to "do something" to save Sadat from complete humiliation. However, he states that the moves initiated by the Soviets after issuing the note on unilateral action – two paratrooper divisions in the Caucasus brought to a state of readiness and the movement of Soviet warships in the Mediterranean toward Egypt – were "a mild bluff, carefully designed not to frighten the Americans. Kissinger, however, panicked"; Zubok, *A Failed Empire*, 240.

decided to raise the alert level of its military forces to Defense Condition (DEFCON) III, therefore putting nuclear armed units on the highest level of peacetime alert. In this way, Washington made categorically clear that it would defend its strategic interests in the region.[41]

After the American display of firmness, the crisis abated.

In Brezhnev's next letter the controversy over unilateral action was not mentioned and the reference was to the dispatch of "observers," not troops.[42] Consequently, the United States moved toward the realization of its longer-term strategy, ultimately designed to obtain a central role in postwar Middle East diplomacy.

KISSINGER'S DIPLOMATIC GAME: ELIMINATING SOVIET INFLUENCE FROM THE MIDDLE EAST

The American leadership's broader political objective was, in fact, to secure a mediating role in the future negotiations on a permanent settlement in the Middle East. The key was to balance Arab and Israeli objectives in a way that both would rely on the United States, and not on the Soviet Union, for their security and long-term strategic needs. In other words, as Kissinger himself admits in his memoirs, he was "determined to use the war to start a peace process."[43] And considering the prominent position that the newly nominated secretary of state had acquired as a consequence of Watergate, his intentions had a good chance of becoming actual policy.[44]

---

[41] It is important to underline that the decision on the alert was made in a meeting with the key US officials (including CIA Director William Colby, Secretary of Defense James Schlesinger, White House Chief of Staff Alexander Haig, Kissinger's deputy Brent Scowcroft, and the chairman of the JCS Thomas Moorer) in the absence of the president, who, because of Watergate, was depressed and had been drinking and was in bed; Hanhimäki, *The Flawed Architect*, 316; Siniver, *Nixon, Kissinger and US Foreign Policy Making*, 188, 211–213.

[42] Note from Dobrynin to Kissinger enclosing letter from Brezhnev to Nixon, October 25, 1973, NA, NPM, NSC files, HAK Office files, box 69.

[43] Kissinger, *Years of Upheaval*, 468.

[44] The Yom Kippur War, more than any other crisis during the Nixon administration, was, in fact, heavily conditioned by the impact of domestic politics. The war broke out on October 6. On October 10, Vice President Agnew resigned because of charges of bribery. Two days later, Watergate special prosecutor Archibald Cox ordered Nixon to release the White House tapes. On October 20 (when Kissinger was in Moscow to negotiate the cease-fire), the infamous "Saturday Night Massacre" took place, with the resignations of Attorney General Elliot Richardson and the dismissal of Cox; Siniver, *Nixon, Kissinger and US Foreign Policy Making*, 185–186. These events strengthened Kissinger's position and gave him almost unchallenged authority during the crisis. As stated by Hanhimäki,

Interestingly, the essence of America's future role, and the identification of Egypt as the crucial counterpart, was outlined by Secretary of Defense Melvin Laird exactly one year before the war. In commenting on the Egyptian leader's decision to expel the Soviet advisers,[45] Laird recommended to "discreetly" step up the dialogue with Egypt. Moreover, he suggested that Washington should act in full secrecy as an "intermediary." To the Egyptians, the United States had to stress the importance of reduced dependence on the Soviets while, at the same time, "strongly interceding" with the Israelis to at least be willing to explore Sadat's position should agreement on secret talks be reached.[46] Washington's tactic of offering to the Arabs the capacity to influence Israel was thus at its inception.[47]

Accordingly, in the months preceding the war and during the first days of the conflict, there were many American back-channel communications with Egypt on a possible way to break the deadlock with Israel. These provide insight into Washington's wide-ranging diplomatic purposes. For example, in August 1973, during a meeting with the Iranian ambassador, Kissinger tried to send a message to Sadat on the need to move away from the Arab standard inflexible position, which demanded total

---

"In October 1973, Nixon was in no condition to execute US policy in the Middle East. Depressed, the president reverted to drinking. On October 11, for example, Kissinger told Brent Scowcroft to refuse a call from the British Prime Minister Edward Heath to Nixon because the president was "loaded"; Hanhimäki, *The Flawed Architect*, 303. It is interesting to note that Dobrynin also acknowledges the absolute centrality of Kissinger's role during and immediately after the October War, to the point of affirming: "American policy during the war seemed to be designed almost exclusively by Kissinger, while Nixon was preoccupied with Watergate and its ramifications. In a way, one could say it was Kissinger's war as far as the American side was concerned"; Dobrynin, *In Confidence*, 287.

[45] Sadat's decision on the expulsion of Soviet advisers in July 1972 was defined in Washington as "a blow to Soviet prestige and a favorable development from our point of view, although how far reaching it will be in its long-term effects remains to be seen"; Memorandum for the President from William P. Rogers, "Expulsion of Soviet Advisors from Egypt," July 20, 1972, NA, NPM, NSC files, Country files – Middle East, box 638.

[46] Memorandum for the President from Henry A. Kissinger, "Secretary Laird's Views on the Middle East," October 7, 1972, NA, NPM, NSC files, Country files – Middle East, box 647.

[47] Contacts with Egypt and the consequent making of the US strategy, however, evolved slowly. Washington had received Sadat's decision to expel Soviet advisers with some satisfaction but also with suspicion. Kissinger in particular had little trust in the Egyptian president. Nevertheless, in late 1972, he did open a back channel with Sadat's National Security Adviser, Hafiz Ismail; Siniver, *Nixon, Kissinger, and US Foreign Policy Making*, 191.

Israeli withdrawal from the occupied territories as a precondition for negotiations. The conditions had to be created in order to "get a process started. We are willing to be helpful," stated Kissinger, but "first we have got to have a workable proposition."[48] The contacts between the United States and Egypt continued both before and during the war, in particular through the exchanges between Kissinger and Sadat's security adviser, Hafiz Ismail. In these, despite the continued relationship between Egypt and the Soviet Union, Washington proposed itself as the key mediator in the future and still uncertain peace process. On October 8, 1973, only two days after the war broke out, Kissinger wrote to Ismail:

> I very much appreciate your taking the time amidst your present heavy preoccupations, to share with me your thinking concerning developments in the Middle East.
>
> Even before the outbreak of the current hostilities, I had told Foreign Minister Zayat that I was prepared to explore seriously and intensely with all parties, and especially with Egypt, what the United States might be able to do to assist the parties in bringing peace to the Middle East. This offer still stands.[49]

The American objectives, therefore, went well beyond the search for a cease-fire. As the hostilities continued, the United States maneuvered to maintain equilibrium on the battleground – a precondition for the parties to engage in serious, longer-term negotiations. In fact, in order to set the stage for Washington's mediating role, neither side had to prevail with an overwhelming victory. The aid to Israel was prompt and massive (although delayed for a few, critical days), thus matching the Soviet airlift to Egypt and Syria. But at the same time the United States tried to maintain a low visibility and to avoid the strengthening of Moscow's influence in the Arab world.[50]

While airlifting armaments to Israel, Washington simultaneously stepped up its diplomatic efforts to minimize the potentially adverse political effects of the decision. For example, in explaining the situation to Saudi king Faisal, a close ally of the United States, but also a key figure in the Arab world, Kissinger stressed the anti-Soviet, and not anti-Arab, motivations which had led to the decision on the airlift. Kissinger openly

---

[48] Memorandum of Conversation Zahedi-Kissinger, Monday, August 13, 1973, 3:10–3:40 P.M., Dr. Kissinger's Office, The White House, NA, NPM, NSC files, HAK Office files, box 132.

[49] Letter from Kissinger to Egyptian Foreign Minister Al-Zayyat enclosing Message for Mr. Hafiz Ismail from Dr. Kissinger, October 8, 1973, NA, NPM, NSC files, HAK Office files, box 132.

[50] Siniver, *Nixon, Kissinger and US Foreign Policy Making*, 199–200.

accused Moscow of lack of cooperation and of seeking to exploit the situation to its advantage:

> I want you to know that in the last three days I have made a major diplomatic effort to develop a consensus which would have brought an end to the hostilities on the basis of the present disposition of forces.... In this connection, a significant factor has been the failure of the Soviet Union to cooperate as much as we all would have desired in the effort to terminate the hostilities.
>
> In addition, your majesty, the Soviets have taken the initiative in launching a massive airlift of arms. They are obviously seeking to exploit the situation to their own advantage in the Arab world.... In these circumstances, we had no alternative but to begin our own airlift.

The American airlift to Israel was therefore a response to the Soviet challenge and, considering the proportions of Moscow's intervention, was simply "inevitable." There were no "anti-Arab" sentiments. Moreover, while hinting at the opportunities that could potentially unfold, Kissinger justified the American involvement on the basis of the role he hoped to play in future negotiations: "it became necessary if we are to remain in a position to use our influence to work for a just and lasting peace."[51]

Although it is doubtful that Kissinger succeeded in convincing Faisal – interestingly the note on the side of the document reads "Faisal is angry" – the significance of his intentions is what needs to be underlined. The American strategy was emerging. Kissinger had perceived, and hoped to capitalize upon, Sadat's wider-ranging objectives: the modification, through the war, of the psychological basis for negotiations. This, if effectively utilized, could pave the way for the overcoming of the Egyptian-Israeli diplomatic stalemate.

The behind-the-scenes maneuvering (and quarreling) that took place between the president and Kissinger during the emergency visit to Moscow to negotiate the cease-fire UN resolution (on October 20–21) confirmed the secretary of state's intention to strive for a unilateral advantage. While the president seemed open to cooperation with the Soviets so as to jointly "impose" a settlement on their respective "clients," Kissinger refused this approach and already envisioned the emergence of the United States at the center of the diplomatic process following the war, with the consequent fundamental setback for the Soviets.

---

[51] Department of State Telegram from SecState WashDC to AM Embassy Jidda, "Message to the King from the Secretary," 14 October 1973, NA, NPM, NSC files, box 1174.

Before flying to the Soviet capital, Kissinger had briefed the secretary of defense, the director of the CIA, and the chairman of the Joint Chiefs of Staff on the agenda of the planned trip. Clearly, his objective was to discuss a simple cease-fire. Wider-ranging negotiations on a future peace settlement were excluded. Unequivocally, Kissinger affirmed: "Everyone knows in the Middle East that if they want a peace they have to go through us. Three times they tried through the Soviet Union, and three times they failed."[52] While the United States could not "humiliate the Soviet Union too much," Kissinger underlined the potential centrality of Washington's future role.

At this point, the divergences between the president's attitude and Kissinger's purposes emerged with clarity. In response to Brezhnev's letter of October 19 in which he requested an immediate visit by Kissinger to Moscow to work on a joint cease-fire resolution to propose to the UN,[53] Nixon granted "full authority" to his secretary of state (i.e., Kissinger did not have to consult with him during the negotiations). Moreover, the president stated: "I am confident that if you [Brezhnev] and I work together on this explosive problem, we can find a solution which can bring a lasting peace to the area."[54]

Kissinger's comment in his memoirs is unambiguous: "I was horrified." In granting full authority, Nixon had deprived him of any capacity to stall, making it difficult to delay decisions in Moscow, if only to consult Israel. Most importantly, the letter implied that the United States and the Soviet Union should cooperate in negotiating a comprehensive settlement in the Middle East, authorizing Kissinger to discuss also that subject during his visit. This, as Kissinger clearly states, was "a concession totally contrary to our strategy until now, which sought to separate the cease-fire from a political settlement."[55]

---

[52] Memorandum of Conversation between Kissinger, Schlesinger, Colby and Moorer, Friday, October 19, 1973, 7:17–7:28 P.M., The Secretary's Office, Department of State, NA, NPM, NSC files, box 1027.

[53] Brezhnev invited Kissinger for urgent negotiations and asked that the Soviet Union and the United States act jointly for "prompt and effective political decisions," which would prevent the situation from taking an even "more dangerous turn"; Letter from Brezhnev to Nixon, 19 October 1973, NA, NPM, NSC files, HAK Office files, box 69.

[54] Letter from Nixon to Brezhnev, 20 October 1973, NA, NPM, NSC files, HAK Office files, box 69. Interestingly, Nixon now proposed to Brezhnev what the Soviet leader had proposed at the June summit in San Clemente, then facing the outright American refusal to discuss the Middle East.

[55] Kissinger, *Years of Upheaval*, 547.

The president's cable on the need to pursue "a permanent peace settlement" reached Moscow only after the first conversation with Brezhnev, providing Kissinger with an excuse for not abiding by the president's instructions. In fact, during his first discussion with Brezhnev, Kissinger stated that, despite Nixon's granting of full authority, should understandings be reached he would want to "check" with the president anyway. In this way, he secured the possibility of buying time, if necessary, to allow Israel to reach the desired position before calling the cease-fire. Afterwards, Kissinger told Brezhnev that the two problems, of ending the war and of negotiating a peace settlement, were distinctive and had to be treated separately. He stressed that the urgent and fundamental scope of his visit was simply to bring the fighting to an end.

This attitude sharply contrasted with Nixon's instructions to pursue comprehensive negotiations with the Soviets – a settlement would be "without question one of the brightest stars in which we hope will be a galaxy of peace stemming from the Nixon-Brezhnev relationship"[56] wrote the president. From Moscow, Kissinger communicated, via cable to Scowcroft, his clear-cut refusal to comply:

I was shocked at the tone of the instructions, the poor judgment in the content of the Brezhnev letter, and the failure to let me know in advance that a press statement would be issued.
  ... As a result, my position here is almost insoluble. If I carry out the letter of the President's instructions it will totally wreck what little bargaining leverage I still have. Our first objective must be a cease-fire. That will be tough enough to get the Israelis to accept; it will be impossible as part of a global deal.[57]

Eventually, the Soviets accepted Kissinger's approach, leaving him free to pursue his strategy. In spite of his cooperative attitude in Moscow and his statements against seeking "unilateral advantage" and on avoiding the "exacerbation of tensions," Kissinger in essence worked to eliminate the Soviet Union from the future Middle East peace process.

---

[56] Situation Room Message from Peter Rodman to Kissinger, TOHAK 20 (20 October 1973), transmitting memorandum from Scowcroft to Kissinger, NA, NPM, NSC files, HAK Office files, box 39.
[57] Message from Kissinger to Scowcroft, HAKTO 06 (20 October 1973), NA, NPM, NSC files, HAK Office files, box 39. Kissinger justified the tone of the "rather strident cable" to "the strain of two weeks of too great tension and too little sleep." Moreover, he explained that Nixon's "poor judgement" was probably due to the troubles caused by Watergate; Kissinger, *Years of Upheaval*, 547–552; Garthoff, *Détente and Confrontation*, 416–420.

With hindsight and with the knowledge of the role exercised by Kissinger during his so-called shuttle diplomacy[58] the duplicity of the comments made in Moscow is more than evident:

> The problem of the Middle East is that the opposing parties have very strong convictions about the local rivalry, but they have no responsibility to the peace of the world. Our present responsibility is to the peace of the world and to apply a global perspective to what is going on in the local area.[59]

For Kissinger "applying a global perspective" in concrete terms meant maneuvering to allow the United States to benefit from Moscow's loss of influence in Egypt and, in general, in the Middle East. This would give important political and geostrategic advantages to the United States in the context of the global competition with the Soviet Union.[60] As recognized by Dobrynin, Kissinger "was pursuing the strategic goal of securing American influence and dominance in the Middle East. It was a continuation of his global 'realpolitik' toward the Soviet Union, with détente only as part of this policy."[61]

The later events, from the disengagement agreements to the renewed relationship with Egypt, simply confirm the successful outcome of Kissinger's intentions. In early November 1973, Egyptian president Sadat – who had come to realize that only the United States had the leverage to break the stalemate – accepted the US secretary of state's twofold position (1) to accept the status quo on the ground while negotiations (led by Kissinger himself) would produce agreements on disengagement (2) to rely on the United States (and on no other outside power) to produce long-term agreements beneficial to Egyptian interests. Accordingly, after the first Egyptian-Israeli disengagement agreement was signed in February 1974, the United States and Egypt restored formal diplomatic

---

[58] This was the term used to define Kissinger's extensive shuttle between Washington and the Middle East capitals to execute his personal diplomacy which ultimately led to the agreements between Israel and Egypt and between Israel and Syria. In thirty-four days (in May 1974) he travelled 24,230 miles (and came to be called "Super K"). This was the climax of Kissinger's reputation as a uniquely able negotiator; Hanhimäki, *The Flawed Architect*, 330.

[59] Memorandum of Conversation, Saturday, October 20, 1973, 9:15–11:30 P.M., General Secretary Brezhnev's Office, The Kremlin, Moscow, NA, RG 59, SN 70–73, POL 7 US/Kissinger.

[60] In the second round of negotiations with the Soviet leaders, Kissinger in fact carefully avoided any more references to the peace settlement; Memorandum of Conversation, October 21, 1973, 12:00 noon–4:00 P.M., General Secretary Brezhnev's Office, The Kremlin, Moscow, NA, RG 59, SN 70–73, POL 7 US/Kissinger.

[61] Dobrynin, *In Confidence*, 299.

relations. Hence began the US-led Middle East peace process – a process that, despite the many setbacks, continued for the following three decades, up until the present day.[62]

THE LIMITS OF COOPERATION

The October War and its implications inevitably posed distressing questions about the future of US-Soviet détente. Although the Basic Principles signed in 1972 contained a clause on both sides' recognition that efforts to obtain unilateral advantage at the expanse of the other, directly or indirectly, were inconsistent with the objectives of détente, Washington had clearly demonstrated its determination not to concede benefits to the adversary. The balance between the two contradictory aspects of détente proved to be increasingly difficult to maintain. The reality of bipolar competition undermined the "legalistic"[63] basis of détente. The choices made by Washington during and after the October War confirmed that strengthening America's geopolitical position was the unquestionable priority. As Nixon later acknowledged:

I evaluated Soviet behavior during the Mideast crisis not as an example of the failure of détente but as an illustration of its limitations – limitations of which I had always been keenly aware...

The Soviet Union will always act in its own self-interest; and so will the United States. Détente cannot change that.[64]

Kissinger's comments are along the same lines:

Détente was not a favor we did the Soviets. It was partly a tranquilizer for Moscow as we sought to draw the Middle East into closer relations with us at the Soviets' expense; partly the moral imperative of the nuclear age.[65]

And:

Clearly, détente had not prevented a crisis, as some of our critics with varying degrees of disingenuousness were claiming it should have – forgetting that détente defined not a friendship but a strategy for a relationship between adversaries.

---

[62] Hanhimäki, *The Flawed Architect*, 319. In May 1974 Kissinger also successfully concluded the Israeli-Syrian disengagement agreement; Ibid, 330–331. By the beginning of 1975, however, the difficulties emerged (as the PLO and Arafat were designated as negotiators for the West Bank, rather than Jordan and King Hussein) and the process stalled.
[63] The term is in quotation marks since there is controversy surrounding the exact relevance and significance of the declarations signed by the United States and the Soviet Union.
[64] Nixon, *RN: The Memoirs*, 941.
[65] Kissinger, *Years of Upheaval*, 594.

After all, a principal purpose of our Mideast policy was to reduce the role and influence of the Soviet Union, just as the Soviets sought to reduce ours.⁶⁶

Interestingly, Dobrynin's remarks indicate that the Soviet Union was also aware of the inconsistency between the ideal proclamations on cooperation and the reality of the superpower rivalry. When referring to the Basic Principles in his memoirs, Dobrynin recognizes the document's importance in creating the friendly atmosphere and the necessary basis for the numerous agreements signed in 1972. At the same time, however, he agrees with Kissinger in considering it "a philosophical concept" and not "a guide to concrete situations."⁶⁷

As one of Kissinger's close aides William Hyland explained, the administration's public statements had prompted undue optimism for the future, but actually "no one in the Kissinger or Nixon entourage believed in the rhetoric about transforming the Soviet-American relationship." The achievements of détente had not been attained by better understandings or different objectives but by "a change in the raw balance of power in favor of a new anti-Soviet coalition" that inevitably preoccupied Moscow and provided Washington with new opportunities.⁶⁸

With the coalescing of two opposing fronts – Western Europe and China – against the Soviet Union, Moscow's global power position had suffered a significant blow. After the February 1972 summit, the China factor remained a constant preoccupation for the Soviet Union. Indeed, in all the subsequent conversations with the American leadership, Brezhnev repeatedly referred to China and, in essence, tried to enlist Washington's support against Beijing.

For example, in a private conversation during Kissinger's trip to Moscow in May 1973, Brezhnev asked what the American reaction would be in case of a Soviet attack on China. Moreover, as mentioned earlier, at the June 1973 summit the Soviet leader openly stated that American military aid to the Chinese would lead to the gravest consequences.⁶⁹ This confirmed the depth of Moscow's preoccupations.⁷⁰ Then, at the last Nixon-Brezhnev

---

⁶⁶ Ibid, 600.
⁶⁷ Dobrynin, *In Confidence*, 252.
⁶⁸ William Hyland, *Mortal Rivals. Superpower Relations from Nixon to Reagan* (New York: Random House, 1987), 55.
⁶⁹ Kissinger, *Years of Upheaval*, 233; Hyland, *Mortal Rivals*, 60.
⁷⁰ It is important to note that in the second half of 1972 and in 1973 Sino-Soviet relations continued to deteriorate while the Sino-American relationship evolved with the establishment, in particular, of the Liaison Offices. For reference on this period: Kissinger, *Years of Upheaval*, 46–67; Mann, *About Face*, 60–65; Bundy, *A Tangled Web*, 400–404; Garthoff, *Détente and Confrontation*, 365.

Domestic Challenges and International Crisis 139

summit in 1974, the Soviet leader, in the initial private conversation with the president, went as far as proposing a US-Soviet nonaggression treaty, which implicitly reproposed a superpower condominium to the detriment of China.[71] On all these occasions, Brezhnev's virtual obsession with China confirmed the inherent opportunities for Washington, as the continuation and further evolution of triangular diplomacy could be effectively exploited to the United States' advantage.

From this perspective, the demonstration of an assertive policy in the Middle East aided the deepening of Sino-American relations, already firmly grounded on the common objective of containing Soviet expansionism. During Kissinger's November 1973 trip both Zhou and Mao congratulated Kissinger on the policy implemented in the Middle East and for the success in reducing Soviet influence in the area. At the same time, the Chinese leaders warned that after the expulsion from Egypt, the Soviets would concentrate on Iraq as their pivot in the Middle East. The United States would thus have to prevent a radicalized Iraq from achieving hegemony in the Persian Gulf. For this purpose, Mao and Zhou stressed the importance of Turkey, Iran, and Pakistan as barriers to Soviet expansion.[72]

The significant loss of influence suffered by Moscow as a consequence of the October War appears, indeed, to have triggered the Soviet reaction in the course of the following years. As Kissinger implemented his personal unilateral diplomacy – and as the Geneva conference on the Middle East provided only a façade of multilateral cooperation – the Soviets repeatedly and vocally protested the violation of the "spirit" of détente.[73] Consequently, Moscow responded by strengthening its ties with Iraq, Syria, and South Yemen and by supporting the Palestinian Liberation Organization (thus polarizing the shift between moderate and radical Arab states). Moreover, the Soviets expanded their influence in areas adjacent to the Middle East – such as the Horn of Africa, with the signing of the Soviet-Somali treaty in 1974[74] – and, later, in Angola. The "loss of Egypt" in fact "had a lasting psychological impact on subsequent Politburo decision making with regard to African crises." In 1979, "these

---

[71] Hyland, *Mortal Rivals*, 62–66; Kissinger, *Years of Upheaval*, 1173–1174; Nixon, *RN: The Memoirs*, 1030.
[72] Kissinger, *Years of Upheaval*, 683–690; Kissinger, *On China*, 282–283.
[73] Hanhimäki, *The Flawed Architect*, 320–329.
[74] Charles Kupchan, *The Persian Gulf and the West. The Dilemmas of Security* (Boston, MA: Allen & Unwin, 1987), 48–52; Garthoff, *Détente and Confrontation*, 449–50.

memoirs would play a crucial role in fomenting Soviet suspicions that Hafizullan Amin could 'do a Sadat' to them in Afghanistan."[75]

Therefore, by the mid-1970s various areas of the Third World had acquired increased strategic importance on the international world scene (for some countries a consequence also of the emergence of the "oil weapon"). This confirmed the gradual transformation of the dynamics of the Cold War. The superpower rivalry became an increasingly more global struggle for supremacy in areas previously considered marginal and peripheral.

Despite these developments, the American preoccupations regarding the Soviet nuclear buildup continued to provide the motivation for the cooperative aspect of détente. The SALT II discussions, in fact, continued. By 1973 it became evident that "détente was built on the twin pillars of resistance to Soviet expansionism and a willingness to negotiate on concrete issues." Between 1969 and 1973 Nixon's ambivalent policy toward the Soviet Union had enabled the dynamic opposition to geopolitical challenges, while at the same time allowing for agreements to be concluded. However, as the October War clearly (and publicly) demonstrated, the US-Soviet negotiations did not signify that the rivalry had subsided. As Kissinger put it: "those who made that the test of our policy misconceived its design or misinterpreted its purpose."[76]

While Nixon became engulfed in the crisis that would prematurely bring his presidency to an end, many in the United States and elsewhere both "misconceived" and "misinterpreted" the administration's design, leading to the generally acknowledged decline of détente. The American public, in fact, became increasingly confused about détente. After the June 1973 summit, such headlines as "Nixon and Brezhnev end summit, declare week's talks moved world nearer to a stable peace" and "Nixon, Brezhnev give peace vows" underscored the new era of negotiation and cooperation with the Soviets.[77] But only a few months later, the October War was assessed by the media as striking "a blow to détente,"[78] while Kissinger declared to the *New York Times* that "détente could not survive

---

[75] Zubok, *A Failed Empire*, 240–241. The connection between Sadat's betrayal and Afghanistan is cited in Odd Arne Westad, *The Fall of Détente. Soviet-American Relations during the Carter Years* (Oslo, Norway: Scandinavian University Press, 1997), 132. Westad quotes KGB general Leonid Shebarshin.
[76] Kissinger, *Years of Upheaval*, 982.
[77] Special to the *New York Times*, June 19, 1973 and June 25, 1973.
[78] The *New York Times*, Oct. 16, 1973.

irresponsibility in any area, including the Middle East."[79] Sustaining such an apparently contradictory policy would become more and more difficult for a president under attack. But the question is: Did some aspects of the innovative management of the Cold War relationship with the Soviet Union introduced between 1969 and 1973 survive Nixon's self-inflicted drama?

- Nixon's downfall weakened his presidency and the ability to protect his foreign policy decision from critics
  ⇓
  the rise of Kissinger and his pursuit of unilateral, geopolitical dominance

- The October War publically demonstrated the dualistic nature of détente
  ↳ demonstrated the U.S.'s desire to remove the Soviet Union from the middle east.

---

[79] The *New York Times*, Oct. 11, 1973.

6

The Ford (and Kissinger) Administration

> The Soviets wanted to preserve the option of détente as a counterweight to China; the Chinese needed us as a counterweight to the Soviets; ... the nations of the Middle East had no alternative to the peace process under our aegis. We had built better than we perhaps knew.
>
> Henry Kissinger, *Years of Upheaval*

> They [Nixon and Kissinger] were open-minded about China and trumpeted their ability to discern that nationalist factors outweighed Communist ideology in Sino-Soviet relations. But in Chile, several Middle Eastern countries, South Asia and Africa, any Communist interest meant to them an early Soviet grab for power, at the expense of the United States.
>
> William Bundy, *A Tangled Web*

The American conduct during the October War inevitably impacted on the Soviet view of détente. The setback suffered in the Middle East, especially when combined with the difficulties in the US approval of the Trade Bill (to which MFN status was attached), obviously raised distressing questions in Moscow on whether détente with the United States was serving the Soviet Union's broader aims.[1] In addition, the continued evolution of US-Chinese relations constantly aroused preoccupations in Moscow. Moreover, the Soviet leadership found the unfolding of the Watergate scandal and the grave complications it caused for President Nixon difficult to understand. In Moscow, the American

---

[1] Raymond Garthoff, *Détente and Confrontation. American-Soviet Relations from Nixon to Reagan* (Washington, DC: The Brookings Institution, 1994), 444.

domestic problems were mainly interpreted as "attacks on the president by 'forces' hostile to détente."[2]

Despite these concerns, America's unilateralism in the Middle East did not immediately translate into the Soviet leadership's abandonment of the policy of "improved relations."[3] On the contrary, the statements in the aftermath of the October War stressed the importance of the policy initiated between 1969 and 1972 as having prevented the conflict in the Middle East from escalating into a dangerous superpower confrontation.[4] In sum, it appeared that the basic factors which had induced Moscow's search for better relations with Washington – the economic problems, the risks of the strategic competition, the problematic relationship with China – were all still present. As was Brezhnev's personal commitment to continuing and strengthening US-Soviet détente.[5]

In the United States, instead, Nixon and Kissinger's policy was increasingly criticized. Throughout 1974 the domestic criticism of the administration's design became all the more widespread and difficult to counter. This, when combined with the outcome of the Watergate scandal, paralyzed the Nixon administration's last months in office. Also Kissinger, despite his increased authority and independence, was unable to deliver major breakthroughs. Still, amid the difficulties, the third Nixon-Brezhnev summit did take place in June 1974 and with some important results. Moreover, the incoming Ford administration immediately endorsed continuity in US-Soviet relations. Détente was being severely questioned, but it was not yet completely abandoned.

In the transition from the Nixon to the Ford administration the continued, and in many ways more dominant presence of Henry Kissinger (confirmed as secretary of state), guaranteed symbolic and concrete continuity to the formation and implementation of American foreign policy. In particular, the 1974 Vladivostok summit between Ford and Brezhnev confirmed the unrelenting importance assigned by the superpowers to the arms control process. At the same time, however, the impact of the domestic attack on US-Soviet détente came to be interrelated to the

---

[2] Meeting with Ambassador Dobrynin, Wednesday, August 14, 1974, from Henry A. Kissinger, Gerald R. Ford Library (hereafter GFL), National Security Adviser (hereafter NSA), Presidential Country Files for Europe and Canada, box 16, folder USSR (1).

[3] Vladislav Zubok, *A Failed Empire. The Soviet Union in the Cold War from Stalin to Gorbachev* (Chapel Hill, NC: The University of North Carolina Press, 2007), 240.

[4] Garthoff, *Détente and Confrontation*, 442–446.

[5] Memorandum for the President from Henry A. Kissinger, "Your Meeting with Foreign Minister Gromyko," (September 1974), GFL, NSA, Presidential Country Files for Europe and Canada, box 16, folder USSR (2).

generalized perception of decline of the executive branch in the face of an increasingly assertive Congress.

"IT WAS A NATIONAL TRAGEDY THAT THOSE WHO SHARED A SIMILAR STRATEGIC ANALYSIS SHOULD CONDUCT A CIVIL WAR OVER TACTICS"

In his memoirs Kissinger describes the growing internal divisions within the administration that hindered the positive evolution of the SALT negotiations in the last year of the Nixon administration. His comments unveil important aspects of his (and Nixon's) vision of US-Soviet détente. There were, he states, no "illusions" about Soviet purposes. They shared the assessment on the problematic growth of certain categories of Soviet nuclear weapons (the SS-17, SS-18, and SS-19 ICBMs in particular). In terms of strategic analysis they, therefore, agreed with the conservative opposition. The differences emerged over how to deal with the potential US vulnerability – that is, over the "tactics."[6]

As has emerged in the previous chapters, Nixon and Kissinger's tactic had been to secure, through SALT, that the Soviet Union's nuclear arsenal would be contained while shifting the superpower competition into other domains. This, states Kissinger, "would better prepare us for the long struggle in which we agreed with our conservative critics we were involved."[7] Until 1973, the combination of cooperation and competition unfolded successfully. Later, it became problematic to sustain. In the context of SALT, the insistence on numerical equivalence and absolute symmetry (that was required by the critics of SALT I) made the pursuit of a second agreement increasingly difficult. The problems multiplied when a prominent and influential member of the administration – Secretary of Defense (from July 1973) James Schelsinger – endorsed the critics of détente and proposed a new strategic doctrine.

The National Security Decision Memoranda (NSDM) 242 – titled "Policy for Planning the Employment of Nuclear Weapons" – signed by Nixon in January 1974 stated in its preamble that it "did not constitute a major new departure in US nuclear strategy." In reality, instead, it introduced some revolutionary concepts. It moved away from the notion,

---

[6] Henry Kissinger, *Years of Upheaval* (London: Phoenix Press, 2000), 1011–1030. In the quotation at the beginning of the paragraph, Kissinger referred to the conservative critics of détente and, in particular, to Secretary of Defense Schlesinger, Ibid., 1029.

[7] Kissinger, *Years of Upheaval*, 1029.

until then accepted by successive American administrations, of mutually assured destruction in favor of more flexible options. The principal purpose of what soon came to be labeled the Schlesinger doctrine was to respond to the perceived vulnerability of US forces in the face of the Soviet buildup by multiplying Washington's strategic options – that is, options lying between "surrender" and the launching of a massive second strike which would plunge the superpowers into general war (considered "suicide"). In concrete terms, this meant the development of counterforce capabilities or, in the language of the document, of "limited employment options which enable the United States to conduct selected nuclear operations."[8]

The proponents of NSDM 242 justified it as a more effective way of responding to limited aggression. For the Soviets (and for the advocates of the SALT process), however, it meant that America was moving toward a greater capability to launch a destabilizing first strike. It conveyed a lack of confidence in détente and seemed contrary to the concepts at the basis of the SALT agreements.[9] Secretary of Defense Schlesinger, in fact, had clearly expressed his skepticism of the SALT process. And, as a consequence of Watergate and of Nixon's weakened position, Schlesinger's influence within the administration had grown considerably (and on positions which challenged Kissinger's). Hence, when the secretary of defense openly endorsed Senator Jackson's insistence on "essential equivalence" and proposed options for SALT different from those until then pursued by the administration (and by Kissinger in particular), the divisions within the administration became manifest. These prevented the definition of a unified American position in the negotiations and, in turn, obviously had a negative impact on the possibilities of reaching agreement with the Soviets.

In early 1974, the controversies over SALT became coupled with the continued impasse in the congressional approval of the trade bill, as Jackson insisted on the link between MFN and Jewish emigration (and constantly raised his demands).[10] The combination of these factors made

---

[8] National Security Decision Memorandum 242, January 17, 1974 downloadable at: http://www.fas.org/irp/offdocs/nsdm-nixon/nsdm_242.pdf
[9] Garthoff, *Détente and Confrontation*, 466–467.
[10] On the divergences between Kissinger and Schlesinger and in general on the difficulties of the administration in early 1974: Kissinger, *Years of Upheaval*, 1006–1020 and 1152–1160; Garthoff, *Détente and Confrontation*, 466–475; William Bundy, *A Tangled Web. The Making of Foreign Policy in the Nixon Presidency* (London: IB Tauris, 1998), 465–467; Jussi Hanhimäki, *The Flawed Architect. Henry Kissinger and American Foreign Policy* (New York: Oxford University Press, 2004), 340–342.

Kissinger's negotiating position during his advance trip to Moscow in March 1974 – in preparation for the third Nixon-Brezhnev summit to be held in June – particularly difficult. As Kissinger eloquently told Sonnenfeldt: "the same sons of bitches who drove us out of Vietnam and said it would be immoral for us to tamper with the North Vietnamese internal system now try to destroy détente and assert that its our moral obligation to change internal Soviet policies." The reference was, obviously, to the issue of Jewish emigration. More broadly, and most importantly, Kissinger was aware that he had very little to offer to the Soviets: They "are getting nothing out of détente. We are pushing them everywhere and what can I deliver in Moscow?"[11]

Predictably, therefore, Kissinger's March 1974 trip to Moscow was rather uneventful. Regarding SALT, the key issue discussed with Brezhnev was the limitation of the number of MIRVs for each side. After debating on numbers, it became evident that the prospects for a SALT II agreement during the Nixon-Brezhnev summit were very dim. Moreover, Brezhnev again protested that subordinating MFN status to exit visas from the Soviet Union was a clear interference in Soviet internal affairs.[12]

Despite the difficulties and in a context in which Nixon's authority was evidently compromised by the looming impeachment, the third summit of the détente era – a "summit clouded by Watergate"[13] – did take place in Moscow and Oreanda (on the Crimean Sea) in late June and early July 1974.[14] Considering the circumstances under which it took place, its achievements, while clearly not sensational, were significant. In SALT, the parties agreed to restrict the ABM sites permitted under the 1972 treaty, from two sites to one. Nixon and Brezhnev also signed the

---

[11] Quoted in Hanhimäki, *The Flawed Architect*, 342–343.
[12] Garthoff, *Détente and Confrontation*, 468–470; Kissinger, *Years of Upheaval*, 1021–1025; Hanhimäki, *The Flawed Architect*, 344.
[13] This was the title of the *Washington Post* article on the summit of July 4, 1974. The article clearly points to the internal divisions within the administration (between Kissinger and Schlesinger) and to the difficulties in obtaining the support of the military establishment on limiting certain categories of weapons. At the time, the summit was thus assessed as having "produced a mixed score of modest successes and distinct setbacks to higher hopes, under circumstances without precedent in US foreign policy." Full text article available at: http://www.washingtonpost.com/wp-srv/inatl/longterm/summit/archive/july74.htm
[14] The choice of the resort town Oreanda was a particularly unfortunate one for the United States because it was close to Yalta, where the famous conference had taken place between Roosevelt, Churchill, and Stalin. The critics of the administration therefore made the connection to the alleged appeasement of the Soviet Union's domination of Eastern Europe by Roosevelt in 1945.

Threshold Test Ban Treaty (TTB), banning nuclear tests over 150 kilotons (the treaty was, however, not ratified until 1990 with the addition of a supplementary verification protocol). The Soviets had long sought a comprehensive test ban treaty, but considering US opposition, agreed to the TTB.[15] Apart from these two agreements, the most important element of the discussions on SALT was the oral agreement undertaken by Nixon and Brezhnev to hold a "mini summit" for the conclusion of an offensive arms treaty before the end of 1974. This would be the main legacy related to SALT left to the incoming Ford administration.

Another significant aspect of the last Nixon-era summit was Brezhnev's discussion on China that, once again, confirmed the unrelenting Soviet preoccupation regarding the evolution of US-Chinese relations (the Soviet leader again proposed a US-Soviet nonaggression treaty, which the Americans, for obvious reasons, could not pursue). Numerous other minor agreements were signed at the summit – on economic, industrial, and technical cooperation, and on energy, housing construction, and medical research. These demonstrated that the momentum of "improved relations" continued. In terms of ground-breaking agreements, détente stalled. But, overall, it was not deteriorating either.[16]

THE FORD ADMINISTRATION'S "RENEWAL"

Following Nixon's resignation in August 1974, Gerald Ford became America's thirty-eighth president (the only US president who had never been elected, but only appointed to both the vice presidency and the presidency). The circumstances under which Ford entered the White House were hardly foreseeable. No one in America, least of all the incoming president – who had been loyal to Nixon until the end – was proud to witness the ungracious downfall of Richard Nixon. Ford was known to be a sensible, focused, tenacious, and honest politician, qualities that seemed welcome in the White House at a time of such disarray. But many

---

[15] According to Kissinger, the importance of the TTB was that for the first time the Soviets had allowed the possibility of on-site inspection. Thus, the Carter administration, in abandoning it, lost the only opportunity that the United States could have had for on-site inspection in Soviet territory; Kissinger, *Years of Upheaval*, 1168.

[16] On the third summit between Nixon and Brezhnev: William Hyland, *Mortal Rivals. Superpower Relations from Nixon to Reagan* (New York: Random House, 1987), 62–75; Richard Nixon, *RN: The Memoirs of Richard Nixon* (New York: Touchstone, 1990), 1023–1037; Bundy, *A Tangled Web*, 467–469; Garthoff, *Détente and Confrontation*, 475–479; Kissinger, *Years of Upheaval*, 1151–1178; Hanhimäki, *The Flawed Architect*, 352–356.

in Washington doubted the incoming president's capabilities and credentials for facing the difficult challenges ahead – both domestic and in foreign policy.[17]

Before replacing Spiro Agnew as vice president in 1973, Ford had had a long career as congressman for Michigan, serving also as the Republican minority leader. He had entered politics after World War II, winning the congressional seat in November 1948 (a seat he never lost in thirteen consecutive elections). Unlike Nixon, Ford rested content in Congress and – if the Republicans were to win back the majority – hoped to one day become Speaker of the House (however, during his career, not only would the Republicans fail to gain a majority but would suffer severe setbacks). As a moderate Republican and stalwart anticommunist, he had (like many others) backed the US involvement in Vietnam. During the first Nixon administration, the president knew he could count on Ford's loyalty but, for the most part, the two had little contact (Nixon hardly disguised his contempt for Congress). Considering the disappointing results for the Republicans in the 1972 congressional elections, Ford had thought of stepping down from his seat four years later. But when Spiro Agnew was forced to resign for financial impropriety in October 1973, Nixon for the first time applied the 25th Amendment of the US Constitution and, in December 1973, appointed Gerald Ford as vice president. Less than a year later, as a consequence of America's worst ever constitutional crisis, Ford entered the White House as the new American president.[18]

In August 1974, President Ford faced the daunting task of renewing America and of reestablishing public confidence in the executive branch. In Kissinger's words, "no new president since Harry S. Truman had inherited quite the same gamut of foreign policy challenges in his first few weeks in office and none since Lincoln in so uncongenial a domestic environment."[19]

In order to carry out his task, Ford brought to Washington many of his trusted assistants from his years in Congress – Robert Hartmann, Philip Buchen, and L. William Siedman (labeled as the "Grand Rapids group"). Two future prominent figures of the Republican Party were called on to replace Alexander Haig (Nixon's last chief of staff): Donald Rumsfeld

---

[17] Douglas Brinkley, *Gerald R. Ford* (New York: Times Books, 2007), 53–64.
[18] For more background on the Gerald Ford presidency see also John Greene, *The Presidency of Gerald R. Ford* (Lawrence, KS: University Press of Kansas, 1995) and Thomas M. Defrank, *Write When I am Gone* (New York: Berkley Publishing Group, 2007).
[19] Henry Kissinger, *Years of Renewal* (London: Phoenix Press, 2000), 33.

and Dick Cheney (initially Rumsfeld picked Cheney as his assistant. The latter then became chief of staff after Rumsfeld's nomination as secretary of defense in 1975). However, for the two most prominent foreign policy positions, Ford openly endorsed continuity. James Schlesinger remained as secretary of defense and Henry Kissinger maintained his dual position of secretary of state and NSC adviser. The less than idyllic relationship between Kissinger and Schlesinger was to guarantee moments of tension (which, in fact, surfaced repeatedly). But despite the challenges (from Schlesinger and in general from the entire "antidétente" coalition that continued to strengthen itself notwithstanding the presidential transition), Kissinger's position and dominance of US foreign policy making was further strengthened during the Ford presidency. Moreover, Ford's decision to nominate Nelson Rockefeller as vice president seemed to further highlight Kissinger's prominent role and influence in the administration.[20]

In particular, Kissinger's confirmation as "foreign policy czar" demonstrated the intention to continue implementing the complex strategy for the management of Soviet affairs initiated under Nixon. Both during the first meeting with Dobrynin,[21] and in a letter to Gromyko, Ford and Kissinger explicitly reassured Moscow on continuity. Although the change in presidency would not immediately end the domestic criticism surrounding détente, the new president told the Soviet leadership that he was convinced that attention would once again focus on the issues in order not to lose the momentum of crucial negotiations, such as SALT.[22]

But if on one side (and in particular in the dialogue with the Soviets) the incoming administration stressed conciliation, on the other it was evident that, in line with Nixon's approach, this did not mean diminished determination in resisting Soviet expansionism. During one of his initial exchanges with the president, Kissinger in fact unequivocally stated: "On the Soviets – we are brutal when they step over the line. They will test you and we should keep this in mind ... Our experience is hit them early and hard when they threaten."[23] After Vietnam and Watergate, and considering the congressional attitude on defense budgets, it was impossible for

---

[20] Hanhimäki, *The Flawed Architect*, 361–366.
[21] Anatoly Dobrynin, *In Confidence. Moscow's Ambassador to America's Six Cold War Presidents* (New York: Random House, 1995), 319–320.
[22] Letter from Kissinger to Gromyko, August 9, 1974, GFL, NSA, Presidential Country Files for Europe and Canada, box 16, folder USSR (1).
[23] Memorandum of Conversation Ford, Kissinger, Scowcroft, Thursday, August 15, 1974, 9:00 A.M., The Oval Office, GFL, NSA, box 5, Memoranda of Conversations 1973–1977.

the United States to be openly confrontational toward the Soviets. It was thus crucial to maintain the basic ambivalence that had characterized Nixon's relationship with the Soviet Union. This was to constitute the basis of the Ford administration's approach to détente.

On matters of vital concern for American security, it was better "to err on the side of being too firm" in order to thwart the Soviets' capacity to exploit any perceived American vulnerability. At the same time, Washington had to continue "to convey in tone and words" the intention to seek accommodation with the Soviet Union on issues where mutual interests were at stake, such as in the strategic arms limitation talks.[24] The first step, therefore, was to continue negotiations with Moscow. In fact, Ford upheld the agreement made at the last Nixon-Brezhnev meeting to hold a mini summit to work out an agreement on offensive weapons. This would take place in Vladivostok, in November 1974.

CONTINUITY: THE VLADIVOSTOK AGREEMENT

By the time of Kissinger's October 1974 trip to Moscow, during which he had to pave the way for the future meeting between Brezhnev and Ford, the criticism of détente in the United States had become widespread. It focused on the alleged unilateral concessions made by Washington in the absence of concrete benefits resulting from the policy. Ironically, Kissinger's report on his first session with Brezhnev instead revealed the preoccupations on the poor results of détente from *Moscow's* standpoint. "The Soviet perception of the US is the most negative I had encountered in the last two years," stated Kissinger, mainly because of the failure to live up to the obligations on MFN and what Moscow "believed was a deliberately staged humiliation on the emigration issue." This, together with the cancellation of the grain contracts, the exclusion from Middle Eastern diplomacy, and US "foot-dragging" on the issue of a European Security Conference triggered suspicions in the Kremlin regarding a change of direction of American policy. According to Kissinger it was important not to overlook the negative effect on the Soviets of these recent trends.[25]

---

[24] Talking points for the Secretary to use with the President preparatory to September 20 (1974) Meeting with Gromyko, GFL, NSA, Presidential Country Files for Europe and Canada, box 16, folder USSR (2).

[25] Memorandum for the President from Brent Scowcroft, October 24, 1974, GFL, NSA, Kissinger Reports on USSR, China and Middle East Discussions, box 1, folder October 24–27, 1974 Kissinger/Brezhnev Talks in Moscow (1).

The Ford (and Kissinger) Administration

During the Kissinger-Brezhnev October 1974 discussions, the Soviets, in fact, seemed to be stonewalling on SALT, probably because of the by then more than evident limits posed on the administration's actions by the American Congress. "It is clear we are paying a price for our domestic disarray," Kissinger wrote to the president, referring both to the Jackson Amendment and to the general congressional mood, manifestly unfavorable to increased defense budgets. Nevertheless, Kissinger continued to stress the importance of reaching agreement, "it is a crucial moment" for seeking to curtail the arms race, he repeatedly told the Soviet leader.[26]

Some progress in SALT was made on October 26, 1974, when Brezhnev put forward a proposal clearly designed to overcome the divergent positions. This was an important step toward developing agreed principles on aggregates and MIRVs during the summit in Vladivostok. In his memo to Ford, Kissinger expressed his satisfaction but, at the same time, asked that the content of the proposal not be publicized before his return to Washington. Conveying the depth of the internal divisions within the American administration, Kissinger feared that the opposition of the Department of Defense and of Senator Jackson would once again delay the successful conclusion of the negotiations.[27]

During the last day of the October talks Brezhnev referred to the conversation on China initiated with Nixon at the Moscow summit in June 1973. The Soviet leader was in search of obtaining the American acceptance of what, in essence, was a proposal of nuclear condominium.[28] The United States evidently could not accept such a proposition because of the negative repercussions it would have on the Atlantic Alliance and on the emerging relationship with the People's Republic of China. Brezhnev nevertheless returned to the subject (with Kissinger and then again in Vladivostok), therefore confirming his continued preoccupation regarding the evolution of Washington's triangular diplomacy.

The November 23–24, 1974, "mini-summit" in Vladivostok focused mainly on SALT, although other issues were discussed on the second

---

[26] Memorandum for the President from Brent Scowcroft, October 25, 1974, GFL, NSA, Kissinger Reports on USSR, China and Middle East Discussions, box 1, folder October 24–27, 1974 Kissinger/Brezhnev Talks in Moscow (2).
[27] Memorandum for the President from Brent Scowcroft, October 27, 1974, GFL, NSA, Kissinger Reports on USSR, China and Middle East Discussions, box 1, folder October 24–27, 1974 Kissinger/Brezhnev Talks in Moscow (3).
[28] Ibid; Memorandum of Conversation, Brezhnev's Kremlin's Office, October 26, 1974, 4:30–6:45 P.M., Ibid.

day (such as the European Security Conference and the Middle East).[29] The agreement reached on SALT after two days of "intense and heated but generally businesslike"[30] discussions was based on the principles of equality and of essential equivalence, the fundamental requirements for its acceptance in the United States. On November 23, the basic framework limiting each side to 2,400 launchers and 1,320 MIRVed missiles was agreed upon, while the issue of sublimits on heavy missiles and bombers was postponed. In order to provide an incentive for Brezhnev's acceptance of equal levels, Ford presented the withdrawal from Rota, Spain, as a concession to the Soviets.[31] On his part, Brezhnev renounced the inclusion of a differential which would have taken into account the US advantages related to Forward Based-Systems (FBS) and British and French forces. The general compromise was reached on November 24, 1974. Eventually, this agreement would provide the basis for the future SALT II Treaty negotiated and signed by the Carter administration in 1979 (Chapter 11).[32]

From the American point of view, Vladivostok was important because it maintained the momentum of détente in a period of severe domestic attacks on the administration's management of East-West relations.

---

[29] For reference and details on Kissinger's advance trip to Moscow and on the Vladivostok summit: Kissinger, *Years of Renewal*, 264–298; Bundy, *A Tangled Web*, 476–477; Hyland, *Mortal Rivals*, 78–96; Garthoff, *Détente and Confrontation*, 494–497; Hanhimäki, *The Flawed Architect*, 369–373.

[30] Dobrynin, *In Confidence*, 330.

[31] Memorandum of Conversation, November 23, 1973, 6:15 P.M. Okeanskaya Sanatorium, Near Vladivostok, "SALT II," GFL, NSA, Kissinger Reports on USSR, China and Middle East Discussions, box 1, folder Vladivostok summit (1). In reality, the decision on the withdrawal from the base in Rota, Spain, had been made in the United States independently from SALT, and it was presented as a concession only to obtain leverage in the negotiations; Kissinger, *Years of Renewal*, 291–296; Hyland, *Mortal Rivals*, 85–86.

[32] Memorandum of Conversation, November 24, 1974, 10:10 A.M. Okeanskaya Sanatorium, Near Vladivostok, "SALT II, Cyprus," GFL, NSA, Kissinger Reports on USSR, China and Middle East Discussions, box 1, folder Vladivostok summit (2). The aggregate number of 2,400 was to include ICBMs, SLBMs, and heavy bombers equipped with bombs or air-to-surface missiles with a range not exceeding 600 km (the definition of "heavy," despite Ford's insistence, was not provided). For bombers equipped with missiles with a range over 600 km, each of such missiles would be counted as one delivery vehicle in the aggregate number of 2,400; Aide-memoire handed to Dobrynin by Kissinger, December 10, 1974, GFL, NSA, Kissinger Reports on USSR, China and Middle East Discussions, box 1, folder Vladivostok summit (2). It is important to note that this point was to constitute one of the major points of contention which would provoke the impasse in the negotiation for the SALT II Treaty. The American interpretation of "air-to-surface missiles" referred only to ballistic missiles, whereas the Soviets wanted to extend the accord to all missiles, including cruise missiles.

At the time, the accord generated cautious optimism for the future. The *Washington Post*, while pointing to the continued divisions of the administration, assessed the agreement as going "well beyond what a number of senior US arms experts expected from the first meeting between President Ford and Soviet party leader Leonid Brezhnev ... the Soviets apparently wanted to take some positive steps toward good relations with the new American president and help allay growing suspicions in the United States that détente with the Russians was rapidly eroding."[33] Most importantly, Vladivostok demonstrated that both in Washington and Moscow the intention to limit the arms race persisted. The process started with SALT I, as a first step toward reductions and more sophisticated accords in the future, was not interrupted. In continuity with the summit meetings initiated by the Nixon administration, Brezhnev was invited to the United States for the signing of the treaty, which was expected to be concluded in 1975.[34]

CONTINUITY: TRIANGULAR DIPLOMACY

In line with the previous administration's careful balancing of moves toward Moscow with moves toward Beijing, Kissinger traveled to China in the immediate aftermath of the Vladivostok summit. Apart from being the first visit to China for the Ford administration, the November 1974 trip was different from the previous numerous – and by then almost ritual – visits because of a significant change that had taken place within the Chinese leadership: Deng Xiaoping, and not Zhou Enlai, was Kissinger's primary interlocutor.

A member of the Communist Party since his youth, after the birth of the People's Republic of China, Deng Xiaoping held numerous high-level posts: member of the Central Committee, member of the Politburo, secretary-general of the CCP, and vice-premier of the State Council. In the late 1950s, however, Deng and Mao had clashed over divergent economic policies (Deng disagreed with Mao's Great Leap Forward of 1957–1958). During the Cultural Revolution, he had been a major target. He was purged and sent into exile. But in late 1973 he was rehabilitated and, as a

---

[33] "Accord Exceeds Hopes for Ford's First Summit" in the *Washington Post*, Nov. 25, 1974.
[34] Ford in his memoirs explicitly states that after Vladivostok he was convinced that the SALT II agreement would be signed soon; Gerald R. Ford, *A Time to Heal* (New York, Harper & Row Publishers, 1979), 218.

consequence of Zhou's political downfall and physical illness, had again risen to prominent influence.[35]

In late November 1974, Kissinger met Zhou Enlai at a hospital in Beijing for their last, purely ceremonial meeting (Zhou's physical conditions allegedly did not permit otherwise). From that moment onward, in fact, conversations on the substance of US-Chinese relations would take place with Deng Xiaoping. From Kissinger's account, Deng was no match to Zhou as a negotiating partner. Instead of Mao's "cryptic philosophical allusions" and Zhou's "smooth professionalism," Deng was a man with an "acerbic, no-nonsense style" who had a "disdain of the philosophical in favor of the eminently practical."[36] However, America's master of *realpolitik* seemed to appreciate China's ultimate pragmatist less than his more philosophical predecessor.[37]

In their bilateral conversations, Deng firmly rejected and criticized US-Soviet détente, despite Kissinger's efforts to explain that détente was merely a tactic in the longer-term strategy of countering Soviet expansionism. The Chinese leader also pointed to the issue of normalization of US-Chinese diplomatic relations and stated that if the United States would not break ties with Taiwan, a full normalization of relations was impossible (but at the same he repeated that on this issue China was "not so much in a hurry"). Overall, therefore, there was a cooling of the relationship. Nonetheless, as Kissinger stressed, the basic rationale that had made the China opening possible in 1972 remained in place, that is "the Chinese preoccupation with Soviet hegemony."[38]

In fact, despite the lack of concrete progress and the more difficult personal rapport, the US leadership was able to maintain the impetus of triangular diplomacy. Kissinger had travelled to China and with a large entourage, therefore giving the impression of the first actual state visit since Nixon's summit.[39] Most importantly, at the end of Kissinger's visit President Ford was formally invited for a summit in China in 1975. Amid

---

[35] For more details on Deng's rehabilitation – and in general on the power struggles within the Chinese leadership between 1973 and 1975: Robert Ross, *Negotiating Cooperation. The United States and China, 1969–1989* (Stanford, CA: Stanford University Press, 1995), 60–71. On Zhou's downfall, see also: Henry Kissinger, *On China* (New York: Allen Lane, 2011), 297–303.

[36] Hanhimäki, *The Flawed Architect*, 345.

[37] James Mann, *About Face. A History of America's Curious Relationship with China, from Nixon to Clinton* (New York: Vintage Books, 1998), 56–57.

[38] Hanhimäki, *The Flawed Architect*, 373–378; Kissinger, *Years of Renewal*, 868–874.

[39] Patrick Tyler, *A Great Wall. Six Presidents and China: An Investigative History* (New York: Century Foundation, 1999), 193–200.

no breakthroughs, the triangle that had been built between 1969 and 1972 persisted. This, in itself, was extremely significant.

The Vladivostok agreement and the invitation issued to Ford to visit China created some optimism in Washington in late 1974. The president was convinced that they had "put a cap on the arms race" and that an agreement with the Soviets would be signed the following year. Kissinger, on his part, stressed that Brezhnev had been willing to make concessions, demonstrating the Soviet leadership's eagerness to establish a good relationship with the new US president. On China, there was analogous confidence. Kissinger stated: "We have this triangular game going on again as a result of Vladivostok. The more we talk Soviet strategic superiority, the more it hurts us with China. It is imperative that they don't believe we are inferior militarily to the Soviets."[40] The key – for US-Chinese relations and for US-Soviet relations – therefore, was the successful conclusion of the SALT II Treaty.

The optimism, however, would soon give way to frustration and to an overall sense of disillusion. The SALT II talks would again come to a standstill due to technical controversies and also because the Vladivostok agreement became the target of severe domestic criticism, once again instigated by Henry Jackson. While the senator could not object to the concept of equal ceilings between the United States and the Soviet Union established in Vladivostok (he had been one of the proponents of "essential equivalence"), he adamantly criticized the numbers as too high and as legitimizing an arms buildup rather than fostering a reduction of the nuclear arsenals.[41] More broadly, Jackson led the neoconservative attack on the strategic dimension of détente, and the alleged vulnerability that the United States had accepted with the SALT accords. For Jackson and his allies, the concept of nuclear parity was "an intellectual and moral error" – a form of appeasement of the Soviet Union doomed to endanger the United States in the face of the next, inevitable, act of aggression from Moscow.[42] These arguments clearly ran counter to the positions set forth by Nixon, Kissinger, and Ford. Whether founded or not, they would constitute the basis of the future rise of the moralistic and idealistic anti-Soviet crusade launched by Ronald Reagan in the early 1980s. During the

---

[40] Quoted in Hanhimäki, *The Flawed Architect*, 378.
[41] Ibid, 379.
[42] Mario Del Pero, *The Eccentric Realist. Henry Kissinger and the Shaping of American Foreign Policy* (Ithaca, NY: Cornell University Press, 2010), 133.

Ford administration, Jackson's attacks ultimately resulted in the paralysis of SALT.

At the same time, the MFN-Jewish emigration controversy was used by the antidétente front as a means to flag the moral deficit of détente – that is, the United States' passive acceptance of the constant human rights violations inside the Soviet Union. Whether or not Kissinger had a point in forcefully criticizing Jackson's approach[43] – Jewish emigration from the Soviet Union had increased in the years preceding Jackson's public attacks and was then again drastically reduced after January 1975 – the neoconservatives had identified a crucial vulnerability in the Nixon-Kissinger-Ford foreign policy design. Human rights would, from that moment onward, become a dominant issue in the US foreign policy discourse. They would, in fact, be one of the bases of Jimmy Carter's victory in the presidential election of 1976.[44]

In terms of the evolution of US-Soviet détente, Jackson's insistence on publicly attacking the Soviet Union and on requesting formal assurances on the emigration issue (linking this to the MFN status) eventually led to the Soviet refusal to accept the terms of the 1974 Trade Bill. In January 1975, Moscow rejected the terms of the bill and abrogated the 1972 trade agreement with the United States. Ford and Kissinger were thus deprived of one of their main "carrots" – economic détente – and, in general, US-Soviet relations suffered a serious setback.[45] Clearly, by early 1975 the American Congress's capacity to influence the evolution of US foreign policy had significantly grown.

The difficulties of the Ford administration multiplied in late April 1975 when the United States withdrew from Saigon, leaving the old noncommunist capital to fall to the North Vietnamese. Images of the last Americans fleeing from Vietnam circulated throughout the world

---

[43] Kissinger's frustration emerges in full in his memoirs when discussing the issue: Kissinger, *Years of Renewal*, 255–260 and 304–308.

[44] On the emergence of the issue of human rights and its increased influence on foreign policy during the Ford administration, see: Barbara Keys, "Congress, Kissinger and the Origins of Human Rights Diplomacy" in *Diplomatic History*, Vol. 34, No. 5 (November 2010) and the second part of Julian E. Zelizer's article "Détente and Domestic Politics" in *Diplomatic History*, Vol. 33, No. 4 (September 2009). For a comprehensive appraisal of the issue of human rights during the 1970s, see Michael Cotey Morgan, "The Seventies and the Rebirth of Human Rights" in Ferguson, Maier, Manela, Sargent (eds), *The Shock of the Global. The 1970s in Perspective* (Cambridge, MA: Belknap Press, 2010), 237–250.

[45] For more details on the MFN-Jewish emigration controversy: Hanhimäki, *The Flawed Architect*, 379–380; Del Pero, *The Eccentric Realist*, 140; Garthoff, *Détente and Confrontation*, 505–513; Kissinger, *Years of Renewal*, 255–260 and 304–308.

The Ford (and Kissinger) Administration

and came to symbolize the relative decline of US strength, power, and legitimacy abroad. It was the last, sad chapter in America's longest and darkest war. The outcome was, by then, hardly unexpected. While until 1973 the US leadership had heavily focused on Vietnam, the opening to China and US-Soviet détente had stripped Indochina of its global significance. And, in parallel, it no longer featured as a top priority for US foreign policy. After the Paris Accords, Kissinger's attention (and thus, to a large extent, the US executive's attention) focused on other issues and areas – primarily in the Middle East. This confirmed that regional crises were significant for the United States only if they had potentially global repercussions for the superpower rivalry.

Despite the somber mood and the concrete problems facing the administration, in mid-1975, Ford and Kissinger remained determined to follow their course: defend and try to once again implement the complex twofold path of negotiations in SALT, while at the same time refusing to yield in the face of Soviet geopolitical challenges. This led to engagement (or, at least, to the intention to engage) in a country and a continent that had, until then, been of marginal interest to US foreign policy: Angola. Consequently, the African continent entered the superpower "chessboard."

7

Defending the Dual Track

SALT II, Angola, and the Crisis of Détente

> Kissinger understood that the Soviet leaders were doing what the United States had done in this and other cases – they were pursuing competition in a Third World area where they had local advantages ... He certainly did not regard geopolitical competition as incompatible with détente, and under his guidance the United States, too, had been seeking unilateral advantages elsewhere, and as long as they could in Angola too.
>
> Raymond Garthoff, *Détente and Confrontation*

> In six years I have been on the tough side. But I push détente in order to be able to be tough.
>
> Henry Kissinger to President Ford, July 1975

Already in the early 1960s, as a consequence of the rapid decolonization process, the African continent had become "a battleground of first order" between the superpowers. US National Intelligence Estimates assessed the situation as "potentially unstable" and underlined that communist influence had rapidly grown from "negligible" to "substantial proportions" because of the inexperience of the new governments and the resentment they bore against the West, in their minds clearly associated with the colonial rule.[1] However, despite some attempts by the KGB to bolster the governments of Ghana, Guinea, and Mali during the 1960s and the dramatic crisis that ensued in the Congo (then renamed Zaire),[2]

---

[1] Quoted in Piero Gleijeses, *Conflicting Missions. Havana, Washington and Africa, 1959–1976* (Chapel Hill, NC: The University of North Carolina Press, 2002), 6.

[2] Overall, the efforts during the 1960s proved disappointing for Moscow. The wave of optimism came only later, in the second half of the 1970s; Christopher Andrew and Vasili

it was not until the mid-1970s that the scale of superpower attention and involvement in Africa escalated – first in Angola and, later, in the Horn of Africa.

Angola had been under Portuguese influence since the late sixteenth century when the first settlers established a presence in Luanda (Portuguese explorers had established contacts and trade routes already during the previous century). Given this century-long tradition, the Angolan population initially responded reluctantly to the calls for independence of the first political organizations, which appeared in the 1950s after the establishment of the colony as an Overseas Province of Portugal. However, in the early 1960s, following the example of many other colonies, armed conflict broke out in Angola and various factions demanded independence. Portugal refused to yield control and held on to its colony until 1974 when, itself engulfed in political turmoil – with a coup and countercoup that ended the decades-long authoritarian rule and, after two years of social turmoil, led to the reestablishment of democracy – Lisbon decided to grant independence to its colonies. In Angola, the Portuguese withdrawal exacerbated the civil war between three competing factions – the Popular Movement for the Liberation of Angola (MPLA), the National Liberation Front of Angola (FNLA), and the National Union for the Total Independence of Angola (UNITA).³ Despite the dim prospects for a peaceful transition, in January 1975 the three factions met in Alvor and, while Portugal publicly accepted Angola's right to independence – set for November 11, 1975 – the three principal insurgent groups agreed to tripartite collaboration in a transitional government. This accord notwithstanding, the factions continued to fight and proved unable, or unwilling, to effectively cooperate.⁴

Mitrokhin, *The World Was Going Our Way. The KGB and the Battle for the Third World* (New York: Perseus Books, 2005), 423–449.

³ Odd Arne Westad, *The Global Cold War* (New York: Cambridge University Press, 2005), 218–228. The MPLA had a strong base in Luanda and was externally supported by the Soviet Union, the Eastern bloc, and Cuba; the FNLA had a strong base in the north of the country and was externally supported by the United States, the People's Republic of China, and the Mobotu regime in Zaire; the UNITA had a strong base at the center of the country and was externally supported by South Africa and marginally by the United States.

⁴ For reference on the Alvor meeting and for background information on the three competing groups: Raymond Garthoff, *Détente and Confrontation. American-Soviet Relations from Nixon to Reagan* (Washington, DC: The Brookings Institution, 1994), 557–560; Henry Kissinger, *Years of Renewal* (London: Phoenix Press, 2000), 794–795; Westad, *The Global Cold War*, 220–227. For insight into the administration's review of the situation in Southern Africa, with particular attention devoted to Angola: Memorandum for

The struggle for Angolan independence became intertwined with the competition for dominance and influence of outside powers (mainly the United States, South Africa, the Soviet Union, and Cuba). In the last months of 1975 and in early 1976, this geopolitical struggle was, from Washington's standpoint, in turn interrelated with the continued, albeit increasingly more difficult, search for a SALT II agreement with the Soviet Union. The US leadership in fact continued to search for a nuclear-strategic dialogue with Moscow, while at the same time seeking to firmly counter the Soviet gains in Angola. Though ultimately unsuccessful in its outcome, did the Ford administration's intended policy signal the persistence of the cooperation-competition scheme outlined during the Nixon years?

ANGOLA BECOMES AN ISSUE

The Soviet Union had established some links with the MPLA since the early 1970s, while the United States had sent aid to the main competing faction (the FNLA) since January 1975. But it was not until a few months later that "outside intervention" into African affairs became an issue in Washington.[5] In the spring of 1975, the United States in fact started to receive reports on the Soviet and Cuban active involvement in support of the MPLA (although we now know that the most significant amounts of

---

Lieutenant General Brent Scowcroft, The White House, "Issues Paper on Southern Africa," September 4, 1974, Gerald Ford Library (hereafter GFL), National Security Adviser (hereafter NSA), Presidential Country Files for Africa 1974–1977, box 1, folder Africa general (1). It is interesting to note that the same paper was reviewed and updated in October 1974, December 1974, May 1975, and June 1975, demonstrating that the evolution of the situation was closely studied in the State Department. In the latest version of June 1975, the issue of US involvement in Angola was raised for the first time.

[5] Soviet aid had, however, been limited and the Soviets were disappointed with the MPLA because of its internal divisions; Jussi Hanhimäki, *The Flawed Architect. Henry Kissinger and American Foreign Policy* (New York: Oxford University Press, 2004), 405. Garthoff affirms that the Forty Committee decision to aid the FNLA encouraged further Soviet support for the MPLA; Garthoff, *Détente and Confrontation*, 560–561. Both Kissinger and one of his aides, William Hyland, instead state that it is absurd to assume that the US decision on limited aid in January could have triggered further escalations; Kissinger, *Years of Renewal*, 795; William Hyland, *Mortal Rivals. Superpower Relations from Nixon to Reagan* (New York: Random House, 1987), 137. Evidence on Soviet plans to arm the MPLA and on Cuban training of the Angolans before 1975 seems to confirm Kissinger and Hyland's view; Odd Arne Westad, "Moscow and the Angolan Crisis, 1974–1976: A New Pattern of Intervention," *Cold War International History Project Bulletin*, Issues 8–9, Winter 1996/1997 (Washington, DC: Woodrow Wilson International Center for Scholars).

aid to the MPLA in early 1975 had come from nonaligned Yugoslavia).[6] These reports were confirmed by Zambian president Kenneth Kaunda in a meeting with Ford and Kissinger in April 1975. Kaunda stressed the massive influx of arms from the Soviet Union and underlined the dangers of a potential victory of the MPLA. He therefore asked Washington to intervene.[7]

Meanwhile, Angola was also becoming terrain for the Sino-Soviet rivalry, as China channeled support (though maintaining low visibility) to the factions opposing the MPLA. Clearly, if the Chinese and the Soviets were involved, for the US leadership, and for Kissinger in particular, it was difficult to remain detached. Moreover, after the collapse of Saigon in April 1975, the issue of defending American credibility in the face of Soviet-sponsored expansionism had become increasingly important for Washington.[8]

Consequently, in the first weeks of June, Angola emerged as a topic in the discussions between Kissinger and President Ford. "We have to give attention to Angola," Kissinger stated on June 6, 1975. "My people want to 'let the democratic process' work. That is total nonsense. There is none ... I don't think we want the Communists there."[9] The reference was to the State Department's opposition to intervention, even if limited and covert.

Ten days later, Kissinger raised the topic again:

I want to discuss Angola for a bit. There are three groups there. With the aid of Portugal and the Soviet Union, the MPLA is on the offensive and may take Luanda. We have been diddling around. We have given Roberto [FNLA] a bit, but he needs weapons and discipline ...

---

[6] Garthoff, *Détente and Confrontation*, 561–562; Hanhimäki, *The Flawed Architect*, 407.
[7] Kissinger, *Years of Renewal*, 791.
[8] Hanhimäki, *The Flawed Architect*, 406–407.
[9] Memorandum of Conversation, Friday, June 6, 1975, 9:40–10:21 A.M., The Oval Office, The White House, GFL, NSA, Memoranda of Conversations, 1973–1977, box 12. In his memoirs, Kissinger discusses at length the different view of the State Department's Africa Bureau. The problem, according to Kissinger, was that until then Africa had only been marginally involved in the logic of the Cold War and in the balance of power considerations. Therefore, the bureau's view tended to reflect traditional American idealism and to defend local African dynamics; Kissinger, *Years of Renewal*, 800. The divergent views between Kissinger and "his" State Department became manifest after the Task Force presided by Nathaniel Davis, ex-ambassador to Chile and assistant secretary for Africa, compiled a report against intervention, recommending, instead, to redirect factional competition toward a political solution. The report also opposed covert action because of the risks of committing US prestige in a doubtful course of action; Garthoff, *Détente and Confrontation*, 563.

We don't want to see a Communist government in Angola.... I think we should have a meeting over the next two weeks to discuss it.[10]

The meeting of the National Security Council took place on June 27, 1975. The talking points for its preparation reveal the administration's initial indecision on a course of action. Both the implications of neutrality and of active support for the FNLA and UNITA were analyzed. American interests in Angola were defined as "important but not vital" when referring to the country's richness in minerals and to its location along the lines of communication between the United States and the Indian Ocean. But, unmistakably, the main focus was on the repercussions of a "Soviet dominated Angola" as a "definite threat to its neighbors" and, in general, as a setback for US policy.

Initially, the discussion centered on promoting a peaceful solution through diplomatic measures in order to reduce the flow of foreign arms to the MPLA, encourage Portugal to exert authority in Angola firmly and impartially, and enlist the cooperation of other African states. However, a general and wide-ranging motivation was cited in support of active intervention:

> In addition to our substantive interest in the outcome, playing an active role would demonstrate that events in Southeast Asia have not lessened our determination to protect our interests. In sum, we face an opportunity – albeit with substantial risks – to preempt the probable loss to Communism of a key developing country at a time of great uncertainty over our will and determination to remain the preeminent leader and defender of freedom in the West.[11]

Therefore, the fundamental question was the credibility of America's commitment to the defense of the West. And the context was, yet again, the global struggle against communism. All of the classic Cold War issues – credibility, containment, potential spill over or domino effect – seemed to be at stake and intertwined with the dispute over Angola's future government.

During the meeting, Kissinger was particularly vocal in stressing the impact of Soviet arms shipments on the balance of the forces on the ground. While admitting that neutrality would avoid a costly involvement in a situation potentially beyond American control, he warned that in case of US nonintervention, the Soviet-sponsored MPLA would establish

---

[10] Memorandum of Conversation, Monday, June 16, 1975, 9:22–10:24 A.M., Oval Office, GFL, NSA, Memoranda of Conversations, 1973–1977, box 12.

[11] Meeting of the National Security Council (Talking points), Friday, June 27, 1975, GFL, NSA, NSC Meeting File, 1974–1977, box 2.

a dominant position. On the "diplomatic offensive" option, Kissinger was clearly skeptical: Appealing to the Soviets not to be active would be interpreted as a sign of weakness and, considering the American domestic scene, US leverage was very limited. The practical outcome would be to "be bound to do nothing."[12] Secretary of Defense Schlesinger challenged Kissinger's position by stating "if we do something we must have some confidence that we can win, or we should stay neutral." But President Ford's comments unequivocally supported Kissinger's argument: "It seems to me that doing nothing is unacceptable. As for diplomatic efforts, it is naïve to think that's going to happen."[13]

Considering the need to maintain low visibility – in order not to further compromise the already strained path of détente with the Soviets and the domestic political scene in the United States, which rendered American direct involvement in a distant Third World country impossible in the immediate aftermath of the fall of Saigon – the only logical and pursuable course of action seemed to be the channeling of covert assistance to the anti-Soviet factions (primarily the FNLA).[14]

In a few weeks, the decision was made. On July 14, 1975, the Forty Committee – the organism that examined and approved covert operations during the Nixon and Ford administrations[15] – met and asked the CIA to provide a covert action plan within forty-eight hours. On the same day that the committee was to consider the plan, Kissinger told Ford:

> On Angola, I favor action ... I think reluctantly we must do something. But you must know that we have massive problems within the State Department. They are passionately opposed and will leak.[16]

The State Department's Africa Bureau, in fact, saw few benefits and many dangers in any kind of US involvement in Angola.[17] But despite

---

[12] Minutes of the National Security Council Meeting, Friday, June 27, 1975, 2:30 P.M. to 3:20 P.M., Cabinet Room, The White House, "Angola," GFL, NSA, NSC Meeting File, 1974–1977, box 2.
[13] Ibid.
[14] Hanhimäki, *The Flawed Architect*, 408.
[15] The Forty Committee examined and approved covert activities during the Nixon and Ford administrations. It was chaired by the NSC adviser, and it was composed of representatives of the Departments of State and Defense, of the JCS and CIA.
[16] Memorandum of Conversation, Thursday, July 17, 1975, 9:55–10:40 A.M., The Oval Office, The White House, GFL, NSA, Memoranda of Conversations, 1973–1977, box 13.
[17] In particular, the Africa Bureau stressed that supporting one faction would have a negative impact on the development of relations with the other factions and this was dangerous considering that the balance on the ground was still uncertain. Moreover, covert

the bureau's opinion, the president was inclined to intervene. "I have decided on Angola," stated Ford, "I think we should go." Kissinger did not hide the risks: Luanda was lost and unless it was won back the situation would be hopeless. Moreover, the approval of covert action would provoke the resignation of Nathaniel Davis as head of the Africa Bureau and, in general, cause a major rupture in the State Department. These problems notwithstanding, Ford defended the decision to intervene:

> If we do nothing, we will lose Southern Africa. I think we have an understandable position. I think we can defend it to the public. I won't let someone from Foggy Bottom deter me.

Kissinger agreed, with a statement that gives broad insight into his notion of détente and, considering his central role in American foreign policy making, into the comprehensive motivations of the policies pursued by the United States throughout his tenure in office:

> In six years I have been on the tough side. But I push détente in order to be able to be tough. If we were publicly tough, the Soviet Union would have no incentive. Now, so long as they think we are pushing détente, they will keep their heads down.[18]

On July 18, 1975, President Ford approved the covert action plan prepared by the CIA. By the end of July, American weapons were being channeled to the FNLA. In his memoirs, Kissinger justifies the decision on the basis of American responsibilities in the context of a classical Cold War approach to world affairs:

> If the Soviet Union could prevail so far from its borders in the face of such logistical difficulties and our command of the seas, to what measures might it be tempted in areas closer to Russian historical interests – such as the Middle East?
> The issue, in short, was not the intrinsic importance of Angola but the implications for Soviet foreign policy and long-term East-West relations.[19]

Interestingly, and ironically, the approval for action in Angola, so solidly based on the Cold War logic of avoiding the expansion of the opponent's sphere of influence, took place only a few weeks before the summit in Helsinki where the signing of the Final Act of the European Security

---

involvement would eventually become known and this would damage US interests throughout Africa and the Third World in general; Hanhimäki, *The Flawed Architect*, 408–409.

[18] Memorandum of Conversation, July 18, 1975, 9:07–10:12 A.M., The Oval Office, The White House, GFL, NSA, Memoranda of Conversations, 1973–1977, box 13.

[19] Kissinger, *Years of Renewal*, 810.

Conference took place. This moment came to symbolize the high point of East-West détente, after which its decline became general and inexorable. But from a different, more global perspective, the battle for supremacy between the superpowers in areas previously considered peripheral was ongoing. The American-Soviet relationship was, indeed, increasingly characterized by the competition for geopolitical influence worldwide.

THE DIFFICULTIES IN SALT II

In parallel with the discussions and the decision to intervene in Angola, the Ford administration continued in its pursuit of a SALT II agreement. The framework agreed upon in Vladivostok should have been a turning point, paving the way for the rapid conclusion of the treaty. Instead, in the United States the Vladivostok accord was attacked by the same "anti-détente coalition" that had denounced Nixon's policies. This, together with the technical difficulties delaying SALT II, created the impression of a generalized decline of the US executive's assertiveness and strength in defending American interests and prestige worldwide. The planned summit between Ford and Brezhnev was postponed (to the second half of 1975) and the American media increasingly pointed to the strains in the US-Soviet relationship, while questioning whether détente had been a "total illusion."[20]

In addition to the collapse of the trade bill and the impact of the events in Indochina, which had already created a widespread sense of decline of US authority, new criticism on the alleged "softness" of the administration's dealings with communism emerged around Ford's attendance of the CSCE (with the polemic on Soviet domination of Eastern Europe later constituting a major setback in Ford's presidential campaign).[21] This general tendency notwithstanding, or perhaps in

---

[20] See, for example, "Ford-Brezhnev Summit" in *New York Times*, May 5, 1975 and "Detente: Past and Future" in *New York Times*, May 20, 1975.

[21] The positive aspects and wide-ranging implications of the CSCE, related to the Third Basket on human rights, emerged only later, at the end of the 1970s and early 1980s, with its impact on the dissident movements in Eastern Europe. At the time of Ford's attendance, the CSCE was regarded as conceding to the Soviets the Western acceptance of the status quo in Europe, and was therefore broadly criticized. This issue constituted an important element of the Ford-Carter presidential campaign; Hanhimäki, *The Flawed Architect*, 433–438. For general reference on the period of uncertainty following Vladivostok and on the first signs of the decline of détente: Garthoff, *Détente and Confrontation*, 501–523; Hyland, *Mortal Rivals*, 98–114; Kissinger, *Years of Renewal*, 299–308.

order to counter it, Ford and Kissinger remained determined to secure the conclusion and signing of the offensive arms treaty along the outline traced in Vladivostok.

During the cited conversation of July 18, 1975, in which Ford communicated his decision on Angola, Kissinger affirmed that a SALT agreement had to be signed "this year – before the election year."[22] A few days later, Ford underlined that the "maximum effort" had to be made in order to conclude the agreement as soon as possible.[23] The insistence on searching for a rapid positive outcome to SALT did not depend only on domestic political opportunism linked to the approaching election. In sharp contrast with the growing mood in the United States, Kissinger, in fact, was aware that a broader view of US-Soviet relations conveyed a picture still clearly favorable to Washington. Therefore, steps had to be taken not to definitely compromise the Soviet commitment to "improved relations." As he effectively summarized for Ford:

> With the Soviets, we are on the ragged edge on détente. They are getting nothing out of détente. The Middle East is a humiliation, but they would have probably kept it quiet if grain was being shipped. The only thing left is SALT. Since you became President, all the concessions have been theirs. If we don't give way or something, it may all be over.[24]

The necessity of regulating the arms race had been at the basis of the American search for détente with the Soviet Union from the beginning. Between 1969 and 1972 it had shaped the complex strategy through which Washington sought to manage, differently and more effectively, its relationship with Moscow. While elements of that strategy were gradually dismantled by the American domestic opposition, the Ford administration's continued commitment to SALT was increasingly important for two intrinsically related reasons: first, because a treaty remained a vital strategic necessity for the United States in the face of the unrelenting Soviet nuclear buildup; second, because it would provide tangible evidence that the main pillar of détente remained in the interest of both superpowers, thus allowing for arms control negotiations to become a permanent feature of US-Soviet relations.

---

[22] Memorandum of Conversation, July 18, 1975, 9:07–10:12 A.M., The Oval Office, The White House, GFL, NSA, Memoranda of Conversations, 1973–1977, box 13.

[23] Memorandum of Conversation, Monday, July 21, 1975, 9:30 A.M., The Oval Office, The White House, GFL, NSA, Memoranda of Conversations, 1973–1977, box 14.

[24] Memorandum of Conversation, Monday, September 8, 1975, 1:15 P.M., The Oval Office, GFL, NSA, Memoranda of Conversations, 1973–1977, box 15.

However, the path toward a treaty proved to be more and more complicated. After Vladivostok, the main points of contention emerged around the limitation of cruise missiles and the definition of the new Soviet bomber, code-named "Backfire" by NATO. The problems in drafting the Vladivostok aide-mémoire, that was to record the specific terms of the accord but that was not completed until December 10, 1974, anticipated the later impasse.

The first major issue related to air-launched cruise missiles. The American position was that the limitations had to apply only to air-to-surface ballistic missiles, and not to air-to-surface cruise missiles, while the Soviets insisted that all missiles with a range over 600 km be counted in the aggregate of 2,400. The omission of the word "ballistic" from the aide-mémoire permitted its conclusion but did not signify a change in the American position.[25] The Pentagon and the JCS were firmly against banning long-range air-launched cruise missiles. This would remain their position until 1977.

The second issue was whether the "Backfire" had to be considered a theater medium-range bomber, therefore not a "heavy bomber," or an intercontinental strategic bomber that had to be counted in the accord. While the American side, again the Pentagon and the JCS in particular, insisted on its inclusion,[26] the Soviets repeatedly denied that the bomber had intercontinental capability and refused to consider it as part of the limitations of SALT II. This question would constitute the other main obstacle in the negotiations for the treaty and would, in 1979, provoke major objections against SALT II ratification.[27]

The difficulties over these technical issues and the growing divisions within the administration made it impossible to define a univocal American SALT position acceptable to the Soviets. These obstacles notwithstanding, it is important to underline that from the beginning to the fall of 1975 the dialogue with the Soviets on SALT was never interrupted.

---

[25] The text simply refers to "air-to-surface missiles"; Aide-mémoire handed to Dobrynin by Kissinger, December 10, 1974, GFL, NSA, Kissinger Reports on USSR, China and Middle East Discussions, box 1, folder Vladivostok summit (2).

[26] It is important to note that the administration was profoundly divided on this issue. Although the difference of views was known, it seems that Kissinger had conceded that the Backfire would not be included in the accord; Garthoff, *Détente and Confrontation*, 499. The author cites reference, released pursuant to a Freedom of Information Act request, in which Kissinger had stated, during a background briefing with selected American reporters, that the accord would exclude Backfires.

[27] For further reference on the cruise missiles and Backfire issues: Garthoff, *Détente and Confrontation*, 498–503; Hyland, *Mortal Rivals*, 101–104.

The reactivation of the White House back channel and the conversations on SALT at the highest level – between Kissinger and Gromyko in Vienna and Geneva (in May and July 1975)[28] and between the president and Brezhnev in Helsinki at the CSCE[29] – confirm the importance Ford and Kissinger assigned to SALT and their determination to overcome the difficulties in order to secure the successful conclusion of the treaty.

"NO ONE WILL EVER BELIEVE US AGAIN IF WE CAN'T DO THIS"

The last months of 1975 illustrate the intrinsically ambivalent nature of America's policy toward the Soviet Union. The search for a way to face the deterioration, from the US standpoint, of the situation in Angola, did not result in diminished importance assigned to SALT. Indeed, the determination to reach an agreement with the Soviets endured, despite the growing rivalry in Africa.

As the date fixed for the declaration of Angolan independence, November 11, 1975, approached, a combination of elements complicated the implementation of an effective American strategy. First, Cuban forces committed to actual combat arrived in Angola, definitely tilting the balance in favor of the MPLA. Second, the Soviet Union multiplied and intensified its airlifts to aid the Cubans. Third, South African contingents, openly opposed to the MPLA, entered the battleground, giving the Soviet Union and Cuba a justification for their intervention. Finally, the congressional vote of December 19, 1975, cut off further American aid for Angola, compromising all prospects of success for the Ford administration.

Information on the increased Soviet-Cuban presence started to reach the United States by mid-October. A "reliable source" had witnessed the

---

[28] For these conversations, see in particular: Memorandum of Conversation, Tuesday, May 20, 1975, 10:20 A.M.–3:03 P.M., Soviet Embassy, Vienna, GFL, NSA, Kissinger Reports on USSR, China and Middle East Discussions, box 1, folder May 19–20, 1975 Kissinger/Gromyko Meetings in Vienna (2); Memorandum of Conversation, July 10, 1975, 6:55 P.M.–9.30 P.M., Soviet Mission, Geneva, GFL, NSA, Kissinger Reports on USSR, China and Middle East Discussions, box 1, folder July 10–11, 1975 Kissinger/Gromyko Meetings in Geneva (1).

[29] On these conversations, see in particular: Memorandum of Conversation, August 2, 1975, 9:05 A.M., Soviet Embassy, Helsinki, GFL, NSA, Kissinger Reports on USSR, China and Middle East Discussions, box 1, folder July 30–August 2, 1975 Ford/Brezhnev Meetings in Helsinki (Conference on Security and Cooperation in Europe).

SALT II, Angola, and the Crisis of Détente

arrival of ships which offloaded arms and "large numbers" of troops. This "source," after having talked with the soldiers, reported, in a cable to Washington, that they were Cuban volunteers that had come to fight for the MPLA.[30] Between October and November, Cuba had in fact escalated its presence with the large-scale arrival of troops, which were then directly aided by the Soviet Union.[31]

Consequently, the situation on the ground rapidly deteriorated for the United States. "I think we should appeal for a cease-fire to the OAU and the Soviet Union,"[32] Kissinger suggested to Ford in November 1975, thus anticipating the diplomatic "countermeasures" adopted by Washington. In fact, starting in mid-November the administration reacted to the changed circumstances on the battleground by initiating a campaign against the recognition of the MPLA and by calling for the withdrawal of all outside forces. At the same time, additional funds were requested for the CIA to support the anti-MPLA factions. Moreover, the issue of Angola was raised directly in the conversations with the Soviets.[33]

In a meeting with Dobrynin on December 9, 1975, for example, Kissinger appealed directly to the Soviet ambassador, asking for the withdrawal of the Cuban troops. But Dobrynin refused to reveal information on the Soviet-Cuban relationship and on the dynamics that had led to intervention in Angola. Provocatively, he told Kissinger: "Why don't you talk to the Cubans?" The US secretary of state responded:

> We have almost no contact [with Cuba]. But if you could withdraw them we would get other outside forces withdrawn. If you stop the airlift we will do likewise, and we could turn into a coalition.

Dobrynin remained evasive. He underlined that a political settlement was necessary before calling for withdrawal. The Soviet Union was not

---

[30] Department of State Telegram from AM Consul Luanda to SecState WashDC, October 10, 1975, "Cuban Troops in Angola," GFL, NSA, Presidential Country Files for Africa, 1974–1977, box 2, folder Angola – State Department Telegrams.

[31] Recent accounts on the Angolan civil war underline that the initiative in support of the MPLA had come from Cuba, and that the USSR decided only later to support Havana, after the acknowledgment of the South African intervention in anti-MPLA operations in what was seen in Moscow as a joint US-South African effort to defeat the Cuban-aided MPLA; Westad, *The Global Cold War*, 228–241. For an account of the Cuban role in Africa, based on Cuban sources: Piero Gleijeses, *Conflicting Missions: Havana, Washington and Africa* (Chapel Hill: University of North Carolina Press, 2002).

[32] Memorandum of Conversation, Wednesday, November 19, 1975, 9:15 A.M., The Oval Office, GFL, NSA, Memoranda of Conversations, 1973–1977, box 16.

[33] Kissinger, *Years of Renewal*, 818–822; Hanhimäki, *The Flawed Architect*, 418.

directly interested in Angola, he affirmed, "it was the process of decolonization." In reply, Kissinger stated:

We can't defend to our people your massive airlift and the Cuban troops. It can't go without raising serious questions here. We will have to find ways either to insulate it or match it.

President Ford then stepped in, supporting his secretary of state: "I am for détente, but this is difficult for me to explain."[34] Dobrynin did not provide a concrete response, but promised to report the conversation to Moscow. At this point, it seemed that the American objectives could still be achieved: by "moderately" increasing the American military support to the Angolan factions and with the logistical assistance of the French, discussed between President Giscard d'Estaing and Kissinger in Paris, the United States hoped to prevent a Soviet-Cuban victory and to create the basis for negotiations that would return the conflict to its local dimension.[35]

One central piece of the puzzle was, however, still missing. Increased American aid, in proportions that would permit the execution of the French proposal and, in general, allow for a significant delivery of material in order to reintroduce a balance between the Angolan factions, had to necessarily be approved by Congress. This task proved to be all the more problematic. After the Africa Bureau's opposition on intervention in Angola had become public (with Davis's resignation), members of Congress that had acquiesced previously refused to openly take a stance.[36] Overall, Congress was increasingly hostile to interventions abroad, especially if covert and in developing countries.

Nevertheless, Kissinger was determined to obtain approval for new funds. He explained the scope and the motivations of the request to the Senate's leadership, the day before the "crucial vote." Referring to the covert nature of the operation, he stated:

We wanted to keep our visibility to the minimum. We wanted the greatest possible opportunity for an African solution. We felt that overt assistance would elaborate a formal doctrine justifying great power intervention.

---

[34] Memorandum of Conversation, Tuesday, December 9, 1975, 4:15–4:49 P.M., The Oval Office, The White House, GFL, NSA, Memoranda of Conversations, 1973–1977, box 17.
[35] Kissinger gives a punctual reconstruction of his discussions with Giscard d'Estaing, explaining the French motivations in wanting to support the US; Kissinger, *Years of Renewal*, 822–825.
[36] More details on the making of decisions regarding Angola and Nathaniel Davis's opposition to the course chosen by the administration, see Nathaniel Davis, "The Angola Decision of 1975: A Personal Memoir" in *Foreign Affairs*, Vol. 57, No. 1, Fall 1978.

He then justified the action on the basis of America's determination to resist and challenge Soviet expansionist ambitions worldwide:

Do we want our potential adversaries to conclude that in the event of future challenges America's internal divisions are likely to deprive us of even minimal leverage over developments of global significance?

... And what conclusion will an unopposed superpower draw when the next opportunity for intervention beckons?[37]

For Kissinger, therefore, Angola's significance was global. Its civil war and decolonization process were part of the US-Soviet broad geopolitical struggle. This explains the obstinate determination with which Ford and Kissinger defended their course, refusing to concede failure even after the negative outcome of the Senate vote that, with the introduction of the Tunney Amendment to the Defense Appropriations Bill, banned further use of funds for Angola.

During a meeting with Ford and Scowcroft on December 18, 1975, evidently aware of the unfavorable vote in the Senate (that took place the following day), Kissinger commented on the domestic divisions: "We are living in a nihilistic nightmare. It proves that Vietnam is not an aberration but our normal attitude." Then, in broader terms, he expressed his anxiety on the increased difficulties in the implementation of American policy:

We have to manage the emergence of the Soviets to a superpower status without a war. We are being deprived of both the carrot and the stick. We will lose Angola and then they [the domestic opposition] will want us to cut off grain to the Soviet Union. We are losing all flexibility and we will soon be in a position of nuclear war or nothing.

... No one will ever believe us again if we can't do this.[38]

A few days later, during the NSC meeting of December 22, 1975, Ford expressed agreement with Kissinger:

The vote in the Senate on Angola was, to say the least, mildly deplorable. I cannot believe it represents a good policy for the US and it is not fundamentally the way the American people think.

---

[37] Kissinger, *Years of Renewal*, 832. The quotations are from Kissinger's intervention before the Senate Foreign Relations Committee which took place over a month later: Hearing on Angola before the Senate Foreign Relations Subcommittee on African Affairs, January 29, 1976. But Kissinger states that in essence his remarks during the meeting with the Senate leadership on December 18, 1975, were the same.

[38] Memorandum of Conversation, Thursday, December 18, 1975, The Oval Office, GFL, NSA, Memoranda of Conversations, 1973–1977, box 17.

… We should spend every dime legally that we decided upon. We should spend every nickel and do everything we can…

If we become chicken because of the Senate vote, prospects will be bad. Every department should spend all it can legally – do all we can in that area.[39]

As the discussion continued – between Ford, the chairman of the JCS General George S. Brown, the newly nominated secretary of defense Donald Rumsfeld, and Kissinger – it was more than evident that the debate on Angola, and on the possible actions to be taken, focused almost exclusively on the Soviet Union. Even the possibility of sending military ships to the area surfaced during the conversation. While Rumsfeld pointed out that there was no military motivation for deploying them, the president underlined that moving naval vessels into the Atlantic would convey a signal to the Soviets, and "perceptions are sometimes more important" than tangible military requirements. Brown backed Rumsfeld, affirming that there was no military justification to deploy ships and, after the congressional vote, public opinion would oppose US involvement. But Kissinger sided with the president:

Our concern is that if the Soviets make substantial military efforts and taste a local advantage, it would be a dangerous situation … There is no military need, but there is a psychological benefit. We can send them a message doing this.[40]

During the meeting no actual decision was made on the deployment of vessels. Yet, the intrinsic significance of the conversation lies in Ford and Kissinger's reasoning around two basic concepts: the importance of perceptions and the dangerous consequences of conceding local advantages to the Soviets. In underlining the value and meaning of signals and perceptions, Ford and Kissinger confirmed that their way of thinking was shaped by a classic Cold War logic. Throughout the history of the bipolar conflict, in fact, "psychological benefits" had often been as decisive as concrete gains. The special attention devoted to local advantages instead demonstrated that, though still within the same basic conceptual framework, the Cold War had evolved and regional conflicts had gradually acquired a truly global significance.

As stated by Kissinger, local conflicts had to be put into the context of the Soviet Union's increased nuclear capabilities. In this situation,

---

[39] Minutes National Security Council Meeting, Monday, December 22, 1975, 9:30 A.M.–11:30 A.M., Cabinet Room, "SALT (and Angola)," GFL, NSA, NSC Meeting File, 1974–1977, box 2.
[40] Ibid.

SALT II, Angola, and the Crisis of Détente

regional crises had a deeper impact on the general evolution of US–Soviet relations:

> Our most glaring deficiency will be in dealing with regional conflicts. No President has had to manage a crisis in such a situation where we were not overwhelmingly superior in strategic forces. During the Berlin crisis, the Soviets had no strategic capability. In 1962, they had 70 long-range missiles which took seven hours to fuel.
> The situation is changed, and this will present a real strategic problem, not only in a crisis, but in the way the Soviets throw their weight around. This is one reason why Angola is so important; we don't want to whet the Soviet appetite.[41]

In line with the complex policy initiated in 1969, America had to acknowledge its rival's nuclear capabilities, and consequently negotiate in the interest of both sides. But precisely because of the opponent's increased nuclear strength, even apparently marginal geopolitical gains – such as the one in Angola – had to be countered with firm determination.

On the basis of this reasoning, Ford and Kissinger tried to respond to the Soviet-Cuban challenge in Angola, while at the same time tenaciously seeking to conclude a SALT treaty as soon as possible. In fact, the most significant conversations thus far cited on Angola (the December 18 discussion between Ford and Kissinger, and the December 22 NSC meeting) had also dealt with the search for a unified SALT position which Kissinger had to present to the Soviets during his forthcoming trip to Moscow. Contrary to Ford's assertion in his memoirs, that the trip had been postponed because of the deterioration of the situation in Angola,[42] these conversations suggest that the delay had been caused mainly by the incapacity to overcome the internal divisions within the administration.

Despite the domestic difficulties – negotiations in Moscow would certainly provoke more criticism given the "uproar on Angola"[43] – Ford was convinced that Kissinger's conversations with the Soviet leaders were critically important. On January 8, 1976, he told Kissinger: "You have negotiated under adverse criticism before. I think you should go. If you don't, SALT II is probably down the drain and we may lose attempts at solving Angola."[44]

---

[41] Ibid.
[42] Gerald Ford, *A Time to Heal* (New York: Harper and Row Publishers, 1979), 345–346.
[43] Kissinger uses this expression during his discussions with Ford and Rumsfeld; Memorandum of Conversation, Thursday, January 8, 1976, 9:23–10:30 A.M., The Oval Office, The White House, GFL, NSA, Memoranda of Conversations, 1973–1977, box 17.
[44] Ibid.

Therefore, in early January 1976 Kissinger prepared to leave for yet another seemingly crucial visit to Moscow. His mission was to obtain progress on SALT, while not disregarding the implications of the confrontation unfolding in an apparently distant, but by then generally well-known, regional conflict. Indeed, conditions under which high-level negotiations on strategic arms had taken place before.

THE DUAL TRACK AND THE LEGACY OF THE NIXON-FORD-KISSINGER YEARS

In January 1976, during his first conversation with Brezhnev in Moscow, Kissinger himself referred to the recent past:

> Mr. General Secretary, I first came to Moscow in April of 1972 at a very critical period in our relations. At that time, there was a sharp increase in tensions in the world. The talks on strategic arms were stalemated. Conflicts in other parts of the world, especially South-east Asia, threatened our relationship. Nevertheless, both our countries, conscious of our responsibility, worked with dedication to overcome all obstacles ...
>
> In some respects this present meeting occurs in similar circumstances.

Angola, obviously, was not Vietnam. But the fact that Kissinger was in Moscow to negotiate on SALT while, simultaneously, in a regional conflict the United States and the Soviet Union were struggling to secure a geopolitical advantage provided for a significant analogy.

Interestingly, Brezhnev picked up Kissinger's parallel in order to underline the Soviet dedication to "improved relations:"

> You mentioned your first visit in 1972 and the situation and atmosphere at that time. You are quite right, it was complicated then ... The bombs were falling on Vietnam; Communist parties all over the world were berating the United States. We had to face the dilemma of whether to receive Dr. Kissinger and President Nixon in Moscow or not. We gave proof to that.[45]

As the discussion continued, it clearly emerged that moving forward on SALT was the priority for both sides (as had been the case in April 1972). Kissinger stated that progress on strategic arms was the "first task" of his trip and emphasized the importance President Ford attached to bringing

---

[45] Memorandum of Conversation, Wednesday, January 21, 1976, 11:00 A.M.–1:50 P.M., Brezhnev's Office, The Kremlin, Moscow, "SALT; Angola," GFL, NSA, Kissinger Reports on USSR, China and Middle East Discussions, box 1, folder January 21–23, 1976 – Kissinger Moscow Trip (1).

the negotiations to a successful conclusion. On his part, Brezhnev pointed out that the Soviet willingness and determination to move on in SALT was demonstrated by the fact that the most significant concessions had been made by Moscow.

It was inevitable, however, that Kissinger, more than his Soviet counterpart, was eager to also discuss Angola. He stated that from the American standpoint it was "intolerable" that Cuba would launch a "virtual invasion" of Africa. The Soviet support of this effort created a precedent that the United States had to resist, continued Kissinger, lest the introduction of a "chain of action and reaction with the potential for disastrous results." In responding, Brezhnev diminished the importance of the Soviet role in the Angolan crisis but at the same time warned that if Washington spoke of "catastrophic consequences" for the Soviet Union because of Angola, Moscow would talk analogously about the Middle East. However, added the Soviet leader, this was the "wrong way to talk."[46] While Brezhnev only hinted at the potential link between the two conflicts, the parallel traced between the Middle East and Angola is very significant. In the context of the superpower rivalry both sides strived to secure advantages and, clearly, local conflicts merely constituted the background for their competition.

Concerning the discussions on SALT, Kissinger's last official trip to Moscow ended in a paradox, with "success regarding the provisions of a possible agreement" and "paralysis in actually consummating it."[47] The two-day conversations in fact demonstrated that, ironically, the difficulties in securing agreement were caused by the sharp disagreements hindering the US decision-making process, and not by Soviet intransigence.

After the first session with Brezhnev, Kissinger reported that despite the tough stance on the Backfire, he had been positively surprised by the Soviet leader's determination in wanting the conversation to focus on the substance of SALT.[48] Thus, considering the constructive attitude displayed by Brezhnev and the priority assigned to arms control, in the following session Kissinger put forward the latest American proposal agreed upon before his departure. It sought to limit the Backfire in exchange for limits on cruise missile platforms placed on surface ships.[49] However,

---

[46] Ibid.
[47] Kissinger, *Years of Renewal*, 859.
[48] Memorandum for the President from Brent Scowcroft, January 21, 1976, GFL, NSA, Kissinger Reports on USSR, China and Middle East Discussions, box 1, folder January 21–23, 1976 – Kissinger Moscow Trip (1).
[49] Specifically, option III, which Kissinger put forward according to the decisions of the NSC before his departure, was to balance 300 Backfires against 375 cruise missiles on

after consulting Washington, Kissinger discovered that the JCS no longer backed this option. In this way, he was deprived of the possibility of further pursuing the Backfire-cruise missile tradeoff. In general, the American incapacity to adopt and maintain a unified position resulted in unworkable conditions for Kissinger (which he eloquently describes in his memoirs).⁵⁰

In spite of this American self-provoked setback, on January 22, 1976, significant progress was made in particular on MIRV counting rules, on throw-weight and on the definition of heavy missiles. Most importantly, Brezhnev agreed on further reductions, even below the aggregate level of 2,300. "I could have probably wrapped up the agreement under normal conditions," reported Kissinger. Instead, he simply told Brezhnev that the Soviet approach was constructive, that he would have to report it to Washington and reply within two or three weeks. Kissinger concluded his memo to the president with a degree of regret and frustration since he had "no choice but to let the opportunity to exploit this breakthrough go by."⁵¹

Before leaving Moscow Kissinger again raised the subject of Angola with Brezhnev and stressed that the United States would not tolerate the Cuban presence.⁵² During a lengthy discussion with Gromyko on the last day of his trip, Kissinger went a step further, seeking to obtain the commitment of Cuban troop withdrawal in exchange for South African disengagement.⁵³ But Kissinger was constantly faced with the Soviet rebuff

---

25 surface ships in a five-year interim agreement starting in 1977; Kissinger, *Years of Renewal*, 856.

⁵⁰ Kissinger conveys his frustration and anger in the pages of his memoirs, citing the cables to and from Washington and defining the meeting with Brezhnev, following the cable on the reversal of position of the JCS, as "one of the most difficult of my service in government"; Kissinger, *Years of Renewal*, 858. On the difficulties in Kissinger's negotiating position during the January 1976 trip: Hanhimäki, *The Flawed Architect*, 441–442.

⁵¹ Memorandum for the President from Brent Scowcroft, January 22, 1976, GFL, NSA, Kissinger Reports on USSR, China and Middle East Discussions, box 1, folder January 21–23, 1976 – Kissinger Moscow Trip (2).

⁵² Memorandum of Conversation, Thursday, January 22, 1976, 6:04–9:42 P.M., Brezhnev's Office, The Kremlin, "SALT; Angola; MBFR," GFL, NSA, Kissinger Reports on USSR, China and Middle East Discussions, box 1, folder January 21–23, 1976 – Kissinger Moscow Trip (2).

⁵³ Memorandum of Conversation, Friday, January 23, 1976, 9:34–11.45 A.M., Tolstoi House (Foreign Ministry), Moscow, "Middle East; Angola; Japan; China; Limitation of New Weapons of Mass Destruction; PNE Negotiation; MBFR," GFL, NSA, Kissinger Reports on USSR, China and Middle East Discussions, box 1, folder January 21–23, 1976 – Kissinger Moscow Trip (3).

and simply had no leverage to push further. Brezhnev continued to state that the Soviet role in Africa was minimal and Gromyko refused to talk about Cuba: "I have no intention of discussing whatever actions Cuba is taking, we have not been authorized by the Cuban government to speak on its behalf" was his uncompromising position. Although Kissinger continued to underline the gravity of the situation from Washington's standpoint, it was obvious that he could not obtain any concrete results.

After the congressional vote of December 1975, which banned additional funds for covert actions, Kissinger was no longer in the position of linking Angola to SALT from a position of strength. As he later stated, by creating "such a moment of geopolitical weakness" the Tunney Amendment destroyed the "psychological environment for a negotiation with the Kremlin."[54] Furthermore, the discussions were paralyzed by the American incapacity to put forward a unified position on SALT. Indisputably, therefore, "neither the international nor the domestic circumstances could have been much worse."[55]

An increasingly assertive Congress, which influenced and in some cases vetoed the implementation of American foreign policy, contributed to creating the image of a divided and ineffective America that suffered setbacks both domestically and internationally. Even the image of the previously acclaimed American foreign policy czar, super K (Henry Kissinger), started to suffer from the attacks on the moral deficiency of his policies, which constantly overlooked the promotion of human rights and of democratic values.

In November 1975, President Ford had tried to counter these criticisms by making some major changes in his cabinet, in what later became known as the "Halloween Massacre": Donald Rumsfeld replaced James Schlesinger as secretary of defense; Dick Cheney stepped up to become White House chief of staff; George Bush returned from China and replaced William Colby as director of the CIA; Henry Kissinger, while remaining secretary of state, was no longer also the national security adviser, a post taken up by his deputy, Brent Scowcroft. These changes signaled the administration's intention of distancing itself from past policies. In sum, détente – and its principal architect, Henry Kissinger – far from constituting an asset, had become a political liability in Gerald Ford's pursuit of reelection. In fact, Ford's campaign staff advised the president that détente was a "particularly unpopular idea with most Republican voters

---

[54] Kissinger, *Years of Renewal*, 851.
[55] Ibid, 853.

and the word is even worse."⁵⁶ Accordingly, Ford – challenged by Ronald Reagan during the Republican primaries – stopped referring to "détente" during the campaign (throughout 1976 the word was no longer used in public).⁵⁷

Despite the impact of the US domestic divisions, the clear-cut failure in Angola, and the generally perceived crisis of the entire Nixon-Ford-Kissinger foreign policy design, it is important to underline the Ford administration's intention of continuing a dual-track policy in its dealings with Moscow. Between late 1975 and early 1976, the exchanges with the Soviets and the discussions during Kissinger's trip to Moscow demonstrated the willingness to proceed with SALT, while also searching for ways to respond to the Soviet challenge in Angola. This was a policy of "simultaneous confrontation and cooperation,"⁵⁸ in obvious continuity with the strategy theorized and implemented during the Nixon years.

Hence, the analogy between Kissinger's first trip to Moscow in April 1972 and his last trip to the Soviet capital as secretary of state in January 1976. The differences were many, and substantial. During the mining and bombing of Haiphong, the United States was identified as the aggressor, while in Angola the Soviet-Cuban presence put Washington on the defensive. The relative impact of Vietnam and Angola was obviously different, domestically in the United States and, in general, both in regional and global affairs. And the outcome of the two situations was clearly opposite. In 1972 the United States secured the signing of SALT I and displayed its determination in Vietnam. In 1975/1976 Washington neither succeeded in Angola, nor reached the conclusion of SALT II. These crucial differences notwithstanding, Ford and Kissinger's intentions and purposes in late 1975/early 1976 were clearly similar to those of the Nixon administration in 1972. Does this analogy suggest that the basic

---

⁵⁶ Quoted in Jussi Hanhimäki, *The Flawed Architect*, 428.
⁵⁷ Ronald Reagan rallied the right wing of the Republican Party around criticism of Ford and Kissinger for having appeased the Soviet Union through détente. Reagan stated that "during the years of détente momentum has shifted to the Soviet Union. Détente has been a one-way street," "Criticism of Foreign Policy" in the *New York Times*, April 29, 1976. In general, Nixon, Ford, and Kissinger were blamed for an "immoral" foreign policy (the same arguments which would then be taken up by Jimmy Carter against Gerald Ford); Hanhimäki, *The Flawed Architect*, 443–447. The rejection of the word "détente" raised questions in Moscow on the direction of US policy, thus contributing to the image of disarray of the presidency. But in the Soviet Union, the media reported that rejection of the word "was not the same as rejecting the policy," "Moscow Assesses Ford's Rejection of Word Détente" in the *New York Times*, March 11, 1976.
⁵⁸ Kissinger, *Years of Renewal*, 845.

framework for the management of the Cold War relationship conceived during the Nixon administration remained, amid the generally acknowledged decline of détente, an important reference point for the shaping of American policy toward the Soviet Union?

In other words, looking beyond the sense of crisis and perceived US vulnerability that indisputably characterized the mid-1970s, what aspects of the Nixon-Ford years remained of crucial significance for American *foreign* policy, despite the *domestic* crisis of détente? From this standpoint, the legacy of the Nixon-Ford years seems to rotate around three main points: the necessity of SALT, the importance of a constructive relationship with China, and the determination to resist Soviet expansionism.

THE NECESSITY OF SALT

The Ford administration's firm intention to continue the process initiated in 1969 despite the growing domestic problems confirms that SALT was perceived as a necessity and a priority. After Kissinger's return from Moscow in January 1976, the internal divisions that had complicated his negotiations multiplied and the prospects of concluding the agreement before the presidential election progressively diminished. As a consequence, Brezhnev's planned visit to the United States was also indefinitely postponed.

The accounts on this phase of SALT consider the February–March 1976 exchanges between Ford and Brezhnev as the end of the arms control negotiations for the Ford administration, with the Soviet leader's predictable rejection of the last American proposal as representing a step back.[59] From the transcripts of the conversations between Kissinger and Ford, it seems, however, that the president did not want to give in. In February, he stated "I am completely dedicated to a SALT agreement" and then, referring to the domestic debate, "they haven't figured out what a mess we will be in without an agreement."[60] Part of the motivation in wanting to conclude a treaty was undoubtedly linked to the possibility of exploiting the success in order to positively influence the election, but

---

[59] For reference on this phase of SALT II: Raymond Garthoff, *Détente and Confrontation. American-Soviet Relations from Nixon to Reagan* (Washington, DC: The Brookings Institution, 1994), 599–600; William Hyland, *Mortal Rivals. Superpower Relations from Nixon to Reagan* (New York: Random House, 1987), 162; Henry Kissinger; *Years of Renewal* (London: Phoenix Press, 2000), 860.

[60] Memorandum of Conversation, Friday, February 6, 1976, 9:25–10:16 A.M., The Oval Office, Gerald Ford Library (hereafter GFL), National Security Adviser (hereafter NSA), Memoranda of Conversations, 1973–1977, box 17.

Ford also affirmed: "it is in the national interest to have an agreement."[61] Surprisingly, the president's insistence on SALT can be traced until July 1976, as he decisively responded "I want a SALT agreement"[62] when confronted with the possibility of delay until after the election.[63]

President Ford, in the end, did not accomplish his goal. But his rigid determination and, in general, the administration's repeated attempts to secure a treaty confirm the intrinsic necessity of continuing the arms control process and of regulating the strategic competition in the interest of both superpowers. The Carter administration therefore inherited not only a process that was, by then, no longer in its initial and explorative phase but also, and most importantly, the framework established in Vladivostok, which, together with some of the additional understandings negotiated by Kissinger, constituted a basic guideline for the continuation of SALT II. The reports on the Soviet military balance confirmed Moscow's continuous qualitative improvement of its nuclear arsenal (at the end of 1975 the fear was that Soviet ICBM modernization would render the US ICBMs increasingly vulnerable in the coming decade and, by 1976, attention was placed on the potential deployment of Soviet SS-20s in Europe).[64] Consequently, negotiations on strategic arms limitation were to remain at the center of the future evolution of the US-Soviet relationship.

THE RELATIONSHIP WITH CHINA

Between 1974 and 1976 the evolution of the US-Chinese relationship was hindered by a combination of factors. First, US-Chinese relations were heavily influenced by domestic developments in the United States and, to a lesser degree, in China. President Ford shared the strategic calculus that had shaped Nixon's China opening – that is, that improved relations with

---

[61] Memorandum of Conversation, Wednesday, February 25, 1976, 9:21–10:10 A.M., The Oval Office, GFL, NSA, Memoranda of Conversations, 1973–1977, box 17.
[62] Memorandum of Conversation, Wednesday, July 7, 1976, GFL, NSA, Memoranda of Conversations, 1973–1977, box 19.
[63] It is curious to note that Kissinger, and not Ford, repeatedly raised the issue of postponing SALT until after the election because of the difficulties in defining a unified position with a strong domestic constituency in support of it. Surprisingly, even in September 1976, Kissinger suggested postponing SALT, implicitly revealing that Ford had not yet made the final decision; Memorandum of Conversation, Thursday, September 2, 1976, 5:40–6:46 P.M., The Oval Office, GFL, NSA, Memoranda of Conversations, 1973–1977, box 21.
[64] DOD Annual Reports FY 1975 and 1977; Garthoff, *Détente and Confrontation*, 856.

China enhanced Washington's position vis-à-vis Moscow. And, considering the decline of US-Soviet détente, China became all the more strategically important. However, as the presidential primaries exacerbated the divisions within the Republican Party, with Ronald Reagan increasingly criticizing the relationship with "Red China" at the expense of the links with Taiwan, it became progressively evident that the domestic price for normalization of relations would simply be too high. During this same period of time, domestic divisions also surfaced in China, where the battle for the succession of Chairman Mao (whose physical condition continued to worsen) resulted in a clear-cut division between the moderates (led by Zhou Enlai first and Deng Xiaoping later) and the radicals (led by Jiang Qing). But, unlike in the United States, these divisions did not yet seriously influence the making of foreign policy (the radical faction still had insufficient political authority and no responsibility in foreign policy). Until 1976, Mao (despite his deteriorating health) still guided China's policy choices. And the chairman was firmly in favor of the continued relationship with the United States.[65]

Secondly, in spite of the decision not to change the course of the opening with the United States, the perception of American weakness did cause a chilling of the relationship on Beijing's part. The fall of Saigon, the incapacity to move on in SALT, the increasing domestic divisions that clearly thwarted the Ford administration's policies and the failure to effectively resist the Soviets in Angola negatively impacted on the Chinese, who shared the generalized perception of decline of American power and prestige.

Finally, the inherent difficulties of the relationship started to emerge. The Shanghai Communiqué provided the basic framework of relations and did not require adjustments. The next step necessarily entailed the formal diplomatic normalization of relations – a step that the United States was not yet ready to take.

The growing complexity of the Sino-American relationship was evident during Kissinger's October 1975 trip, which preceded Ford's visit to China in December 1975.[66] During the discussions, the Chinese doubted America's continued determination in opposing Soviet expansionism and their innate hostility toward US-Soviet détente clearly resurfaced.

---

[65] Robert S. Ross, *Negotiating Cooperation. The United States and China 1969–1989* (Stanford: Stanford University Press, 1995), 55–67.
[66] Kissinger describes the chilled climate of the October and December conversations in China also in his recent book *On China* (New York: Allen Lane, 2011), 306–320.

Kissinger reported that, already during the first evening banquet, the Chinese foreign minister, Ch'iao Kuan-hua, had sharply attacked the relationship between Washington and Moscow. Though welcoming Ford's forthcoming trip, Ch'iao stated that "hegemony" had to be resisted by all means and that all other strategies were "substituting wish for reality."[67]

Kissinger tried to soften the criticism by explaining the meaning and purpose of the American pursuit of détente with the Soviets. When discussing global issues with Deng Xiaoping, he again underlined the difference between strategy and tactics. The strategic necessity of both the United States and China was to confront the Soviet threat. But the United States had different tactical needs, because it was impossible for Washington to assume an openly confrontational attitude. Deng, however, did not appreciate the difference and continued to state that, from the Chinese standpoint, détente was unacceptable and that the Soviet Union had to be challenged openly.[68]

The difficulties in the Sino-American relationship surfaced also during Kissinger's October conversation with Mao. The meeting was described as "friendly and wide-ranging" but "frankly" also as "disturbing." The chairman expressed the same criticisms as Deng, "only with more pungent emphasis." Moreover, according to Kissinger, Mao evidently questioned the United States' capacity to maintain its role in the world:

Clearly he sees our domestic problems as emasculating our staying power in the world, thinks we are floundering largely as a result of domestic weaknesses, and believes China must rely on itself.[69]

Despite the difficulties and the Chinese criticism of US policies, President Ford was received in China in December 1975 with "impeccable courtesy."[70] During the summit, the American objective was to ensure the continuation of a positive relationship without having to pay the political price for normalization. The Chinese, instead, expected the fulfillment of Nixon's 1972 promise to normalize relations during his second term. These divergent objectives inevitably caused some tension. The

---

[67] Memorandum for the President from General Scowcroft, October 19, 1975, GFL, NSA, Kissinger Reports on USSR, China and Middle East Discussions, box 2, folder October 19–23, 1975 – Kissinger's trip (1).

[68] Kissinger, *Years of Renewal*, 877–879.

[69] Memorandum for the President from General Scowcroft, October 21, 1975, GFL, NSA, Kissinger Reports on USSR, China and Middle East Discussions, box 2, folder October 19–23, 1975 – Kissinger's trip (3); Memorandum of Conversation, Tuesday, October 21, 1975, 6:25–8:05 P.M., Chairman Mao's Residence, Peking, Ibid.

[70] Kissinger, *Years of Renewal*, 887.

Ford summit, in fact, ended without a formal communiqué.[71] Ultimately, however, security considerations on both sides dictated the need to defend the relationship. The objective of curbing Soviet expansionism – that had shaped Nixon's opening to China – continued to be at the center of the evolution of Sino-American relations, notwithstanding the differing contingent needs.

During the meeting with Ford in December 1975, Mao expressed his concerns on the Chinese internal divisions over his succession, which could negatively influence the policy of rapprochement with the United States. Indeed, after the chairman's death in September 1976, Sino-American relations ambiguously stalled (also because of the momentary dismissal of Deng from power – see Chapter 10). However, as China was emerging on the world scene, with the announcement of the peace treaty with Japan, the development of relations with Europe, and the cooperation initiated with Egypt, Sino-Soviet relations remained fundamentally hostile.[72] In contrast, despite the complexity of the relationship and the adjustments to policy choices made under different domestic circumstances, the dialogue between Washington and Beijing remained open. This constituted the second fundamental legacy left by the Nixon and Ford presidencies to the incoming Carter administration.

RESISTING SOVIET GEOPOLITICAL EXPANSION

The dynamic opposition to Soviet expansionism even during the era of détente clearly emerged when assessing the American response to the North Vietnamese spring offensive in 1972 (Chapter 3), the relationship between Nixon and the shah of Iran (Chapter 4), and the determination demonstrated by Washington during the 1973 October War in the Middle East (Chapter 5). In these contexts, the American choices were made on the basis of a potential Soviet threat – whether factual, supposed, or only perceived. The main scope of America's policy was always to counter its global rival.

While not successful in its outcome, the Ford administration had based its intervention in Angola on analogous motivations. From the beginning, Washington had focused on outside intervention capable of influencing

---

[71] The US side sought a significant communiqué to emerge from the summit in order to tangibly demonstrate improved relations. But the Chinese were not willing to have a "public relations summit" in the absence of normalization, Ross, *Negotiating Cooperation*, 83–85, 91.
[72] Garthoff, *Détente and Confrontation*, 617–620.

the local conflict. As Kissinger states in his memoirs: "our red line was intervention from outside the continent and domination from Moscow."[73] It was not the intrinsic importance of Angola but the prospect that it be subjugated by the Soviets and, broadly, of "losing Southern Africa" to cause alarm and to demand Washington's reaction.

In the post-Vietnam era and with the uncertainties surrounding the US determination to face effectively Soviet challenges, the Angolan dilemma evolved around the necessity to demonstrate the credibility of American willpower and strength to continue exerting leadership of the free world. The fall of Saigon, with its consequences in terms of concrete losses and of perceived vulnerability, was intrinsically linked to Angola, as a test case of Soviet adventurism that had to be resisted. Moreover, on this geopolitical chessboard, Angola was related to the Middle East because, as clearly outlined by Kissinger, if the Soviet Union prevailed in the African conflict it would be tempted to seek expansionism in "areas more vital for its national interests." Brezhnev, on his part, made the same connection, implying that the loss of influence in the Middle East had triggered, even if indirectly, Soviet dynamism and activism in other areas. Statements that are, after all, not unexpected, as both sides were consciously engaged in a global competition with the objective of securing advantages at the expense of their rival.

Ford and Kissinger's obstinate determination in seeking to demonstrate the US capacity to respond in Angola can therefore be explained on the basis of their Soviet-centric mind-set. During both the Nixon and Ford administrations, in fact, all aspects of American foreign policy were directly or indirectly related to the overriding US-Soviet relationship. Within this framework, local conflicts became relevant only when, and if, they affected the broader picture.

With the Angolan crisis, the African continent entered the mainstream of the Cold War and increasingly became the battleground for superpower competition. After the failure in Angola, it became clear to the United States that the further radicalization of Africa had to be prevented and that the Cuban and Soviet interference in African affairs had to be firmly opposed.[74] The Carter administration inherited this situation, together with the mind-set and Cold War framework which had created it.

---

[73] Kissinger, *Years of Renewal*, 795.
[74] Memorandum of Conversation, Sunday, May 9, 1976, 2:45–4:03 P.M., The Oval Office, GFL, NSA, Memoranda of Conversations, 1973–1977, box 19. In this context, Kissinger justified his African trip of 1976 precisely on the basis of avoiding the future radicalization of Africa and of preventing the expansion of the Soviet-Cuban presence.

From the Soviet point of view, the success of the MPLA encouraged other interventions,[75] such as the one in the Horn of Africa in 1977/1978 (Chapter 9). The support for national liberation movements was a traditional strongpoint of Moscow's policy in the Third World and became all the more important under conditions of détente with the United States. For Moscow it was essential to demonstrate, domestically and to its communist allies, that "détente, warding off the threat of nuclear war for mankind" was "also creating the favorable conditions for the struggle for national liberation and social progress."[76] The strategic dialogue with the United States was a necessity but the competition remained, even if it had shifted to other domains. The dualistic notion, it seems, was also part of the Soviet approach to superpower détente.

At the end of the Ford administration, the policy of US-Soviet détente was severely criticized domestically and became associated increasingly with a generalized weakness of American strength and determination. President Ford tried to distance himself from "détente," avoiding direct references to the word in his public speeches and campaigning, instead, for a "policy of peace through strength." However, despite the generally perceived downfall of détente and the domestic debate in the United States, these three elements – the necessity of continuing the arms control process, the Sino-American relationship with a distinct anti-Soviet connotation, and the determination to resist Soviet expansionism in areas outside the traditional sphere of influence of the Cold War – were an important legacy left to the incoming Carter administration.

Although expressing a commitment to diminished tensions and better relations with Moscow, President Carter entered the White House promising radical changes in American foreign policy and in the priorities placed at the center of policy making. But did his administration, with the shift to the Democratic Party after eight years of Republican presidencies, actually introduce revolutionary changes in US policy toward the Soviet Union? Or did Carter, the different rhetoric and style notwithstanding, in essence connect to the policy lines outlined by Nixon and followed by Ford?

---

[75] According to Andrew and Mitrokhin, "success in Angola was later to make Moscow much more willing than it would otherwise have been to intervene in Ethiopia"; Christopher Andrew and Vasili Mitrokhin, *The World Was Going Our Way. The KGB and the Battle for the Third World* (Cambridge: Basic Books, 2005), 453.
[76] Speech of Comrade A. P. Kirilenko, *Pravda*, December 6, 1977 cited in Garthoff, *Détente and Confrontation*, 588.

The Legacy of Nixon-Ford-Kissinger
- necessity of SALT
- importance of U.S.-China relations
- prevention of Soviet expansion

divisions among the administration and with Congress hindered policy making, diminished Kissinger's power which contributed to the stall/postponement/stalemate of the relationship evolution but did not diminish/prevent continued dialogue and efforts

PART TWO

RETHINKING THE FALL OF DÉTENTE,
1977–1980

8

The Carter Administration's Ambitious Agenda

> All through the 1960s and early 1970s, new forces and actors appeared in areas of the world that had been on the periphery. It required a broader American conception of US security interests and of the scope of our foreign policy than merely the US-Soviet or East-West geopolitical competition.
> Cyrus Vance, *Hard Choices*

> I argued that we should move away from what I considered our excessive preoccupation with the US-Soviet relationship ... Instead, I felt that the United States should address itself to a variety of Third World problems, either on its own or through trilateral cooperation with Western Europe and Japan. The Soviet Union should be included in that cooperation whenever it was willing, but should not be made the focal point of American interest to the detriment of the rest of the global agenda.
> Zbigniew Brzezinski, *Power and Principle*

The traumas of Vietnam and Watergate, the generalized sense of decline of US power, and the resulting widespread lack of confidence in American government institutions contributed to the election of an "outsider"– Jimmy Carter – to the presidency. His relative inexperience, particularly in the area of foreign policy, had become an asset during the 1976 presidential campaign. Seeking to distance himself from the corruption and deception of the Republican years, Carter had rallied support around the need for a more competent, efficient, and compassionate government.[1]

---

[1] John Dumbrell, *The Carter Presidency. A Re-evaluation* (Manchester, England, and New York: Manchester University Press, 1993), Chapter 1. Gaddis Smith, *Morality, Reason and Power. American Diplomacy in the Carter Years* (New York: Hill and Wang, 1986), 3–7.

Jimmy Carter's call for an open, value-based administration was rooted in the incoming president's personal and political background. The son of a peanut farmer from the small rural town of Plains, Georgia, James Earl Carter Jr. (nicknamed Jimmy) left his hometown in 1943 when, at age eighteen, he entered the US Naval Academy in Annapolis. He served on battleships in the Atlantic and Pacific fleets and, in 1952, applied for service in the navy's nuclear submarine program (where, as a young officer, he worked on the development of America's first nuclear-powered submarines). Judged by his colleagues as intelligent, a perfectionist, and self-confident, Carter had planned a career in the navy. However, after the unexpected death of his father, he instead decided to return to Plains and take over the family peanut farm, which he would turn into a modern and successful business. Carter's political career started with a bid for the Georgia State Senate seat, which he initially lost amid widespread electoral fraud (at the time still endemic in rural Georgia). The future president contested the outcome and, despite threats to his life and property, eventually demonstrated the illegality of the election and took his legitimate place in the local senate. A few years later, Carter raised his ambitions and entered the race for governor of Georgia – first in 1966, when he lost to the segregationist Lester Maddox, and then in 1970, when he won with a populist platform of government reorganization, tax reform, racial harmony, and civil rights. Inspired by his firm evangelical Christian beliefs, Carter successfully governed the state of Georgia, which came to be labeled as the "New South," and made the end of racial discrimination the defining issue of his term.[2]

Reacting with aversion to the Watergate disgrace, Carter made the renewal of America his personal mission. He decided to run for president in 1976. Aided by Ted Kennedy's decision to withdraw from the race, the virtually unknown Carter towered over his rivals and secured the Democratic nomination. Boasting a promising career in the navy, a successful business, and an outstanding performance as governor, Carter seemed to be the ideal candidate for revitalizing a still traumatized nation. During the presidential campaign, Carter wisely targeted Nixon (and not Ford), as his election slogan became "I will never lie." Time and time again he reinforced the pledge, "if I ever lie, if I ever mislead you, if I ever

---

[2] Bruce Mazlish and Erwin Diamond, *Jimmy Carter: A Character Portrait* (New York: Simon and Schuster, 1980), 100–194; Peter G. Bourne, *Jimmy Carter: A Comprehensive Biography from Plains to Post-Presidency* (New York: Scribner, 1997), 80–131; Betty Glad, *Jimmy Carter. In Search of the Great White House* (New York: Norton, 1980), 23–229.

betray you, I want you to come and take me out of the White House."[3] Once elected, President Carter made the restoration of consensus and of the nation's moral purpose the central themes of his inaugural address. Repeatedly referring to the "American dream" and to the rebirth of the American "spirit," he promised to lead the country in a new direction, with an open and less secretive government, which would give absolute priority to the values that had made America "the first society openly to define itself in terms of both spirituality and of human liberty."[4]

On Inauguration Day (January 20, 1977) Carter became the first president in modern times to get out of the armored limousine and, accompanied by his wife, walk from the Capitol to the White House. This then unprecedented gesture was symbolic of the incoming president's intention to exercise power in close connection and proximity to the American people. As Carter later stated:

> I thought it would be a good demonstration of confidence by the new president in the people of our country as far as security was concerned, and also would be a tangible indication of some reduction in the imperial status of the president and his family. We were gratified at the response. Many people along the parade route, when they saw we were walking, began to weep, and it was an emotional experience for us as well.[5]

The contrast with the inauguration of President Nixon could not have been greater. Carter had succeeded in embodying the needs and desires of the American people in the critical post-Vietnam and Watergate years. As a commentator of the time stated, the election of Jimmy Carter represented a "landmark in the history of American politics, an act of faith on the part of the American voter, and an indication that the electorate is looking to an activist future instead of to a stagnant past.... With the departure from the White House of President Ford ... the chapter will at last be closed on one of the saddest eras in the history of the presidency, the Nixon era. As the Bicentennial Year comes to its close,

---

[3] Peter Meyer, *James Earl Carter: The Man and the Myth* (Kansas City, KS: Sheed, Andrews and McMeel, 1978), 3.

[4] Jimmy Carter's Inaugural Address, January 20, 1977, available online at: http://www.britannica.com/bps/additionalcontent/8/116860/Document-Jimmy-Carter-Inaugural-Address. See also Jimmy Carter, *Keeping Faith. Memoirs of a President* (Fayetteville, AR: The University of Arkansas Press, 1995), 21–24. In particular, Carter stresses the need for an open government to cast away the "ghosts of Watergate," still clearly present when he entered the White House in 1977, Ibid, 29.

[5] Jimmy Carter, *White House Diary* (New York: Farrar, Straus and Giroux, 2010), 9–10. Carter explains the motivations behind this decision also in his memoirs, Jimmy Carter, *Keeping Faith: Memoirs of a President* (Fayetteville: The University of Arkansas Press, 1995).

Americans now can look forward with hope to the new leadership of a new generation."[6]

But how did Jimmy Carter plan to concretely rechart the foreign policy of the nation? In particular, how would he reconcile the sorely needed idealism that he brought back to the White House with the necessity of reasserting US power and strength? "We are a purely idealistic Nation," stated the president in his inaugural address, "but let no one confuse our idealism with weakness." Avoiding this confusion would, indeed, become the central challenge of his administration.

THE CARTER ADMINISTRATION'S INITIAL AGENDA

The former Georgia governor's approach to foreign policy was very different from that of his predecessors. Instead of incremental, step-by-step, cautious diplomacy he favored an audacious, high-risk policy that would redefine US foreign policy objectives on the basis of the traditional American values of liberty and democracy. Carter not only sharply criticized the Nixon administration's secretiveness and trickery, but also condemned Kissinger's *realpolitik* for its emphasis on the dynamics of power rather than on morality. Invoking a return to Wilsonian idealism, Carter stressed the importance of negotiations and dialogue as the primary means of solving international disputes. American leaders, stated Carter, had too often "ignored those moral values" that characterized the United States, with the result of weakening Washington's image and stature abroad. These views shaped most of the ambitious initiatives pursued by Carter during his first year in office, such as the defense of human rights; the nonproliferation of nuclear and conventional weapons to Third World countries; and the pursuit of actual reductions in the nuclear arsenals of the superpowers.[7]

An engineer by training, Carter approached policy making in a highly rational and mechanical way, often seeking to master the technical details of complex international issues but lacking an overarching or unifying concept.[8] Most of the scholarship on the Carter years in fact stresses the inconsistency of his policies or, alternatively, points to the absence, from the very beginning, of a clear-cut, long-term vision. Carter's lack of

---

[6] "The Carter Victory" in the *New York Times*, Nov. 3, 1976.
[7] Scott Kaufman, *Plans Unraveled. The Foreign Policy of the Carter Administration* (DeKalb, IL: Northern Illinois University Press, 2008), 11–15. In his memoirs, Carter stresses the need to return to promoting Wilson's ideals, *Keeping Faith*, 21.
[8] Glad, *Jimmy Carter*, 485–486.

political experience – particularly in the field of foreign policy – and his genuine naiveté, combined with the disagreement of his key advisers on important issues, resulted in vacillation and fragmented policies.[9] This has led to particularly polarized assessments of Carter's performance in office. On the one hand, those who stress the achievements – such as the Camp David Accords, the Panama Canal Treaties, the normalization of relations with China, and the emphasis on human rights – flag him as the quintessential post-Vietnam president with a vision and mind-set that predated his times.[10] On the other, those who underline his shortcomings – the fall of the shah, the Soviet invasion of Afghanistan, the second oil crisis, and the hostage crisis in Iran – charge him as a weak, ineffective, and naïve president who, instead of rebuilding a renewed idealistic America, accelerated its decline.[11]

Undeniably – as will clearly emerge in the following chapters – the Carter presidency underwent a comprehensive, gradual, albeit continuous, transformation during its four years in office. While unveiling the motivations of the administration's "return to militarism"[12] is one of the scopes of this book, it is all the more significant to interrelate the unfolding of Carter's policies to the overall evolution of American foreign policy throughout the 1970s. Therefore, avoiding the temptation to assess policies as inherently positive or negative, the aim is to juxtapose the intended policies – that were initiated throughout 1977 – to the actual policies pursued by the president after 1978.

As historian Gaddis Smith puts it, the Carter administration's initial ambitious design has the merit of having triggered a "fundamental debate

[9] This is the conclusion made in the latest comprehensive assessment of the Carter administration's foreign policy by Scott Kaufman in *Plans Unraveled*. In his memoirs Soviet ambassador Anatoly Dobrynin also assesses the Carter foreign policy as contradictory and lacking a clear priority, *In Confidence. Moscow's Ambassador to America's Six Cold War Presidents* (New York: Times Books, 1995), 375, 387.

[10] Positive assessments of the Carter presidency include: Robert A. Strong, *Working in the World: Jimmy Carter and the Making of American Foreign Policy*, (Baton Rouge, LA: Louisiana State University Press, 2000); John Dumbrell, *The Carter Presidency. A Re-evaluation* (Manchester, England: Manchester University Press, 1993); Erwin Hargrove, *Jimmy Carter as President: Leadership and the Politics of the Public Good* (Baton Rouge, LA: Louisiana State University Press, 1988).

[11] Accounts on the Carter administration which, though praising the intentions, are generally negative include: Gaddis Smith, *Morality, Reason and Power. American Diplomacy in the Carter Years* (New York: Hill and Wang, 1986); Burton I. Kaufman, *The Presidency of James Earl Carter, Jr.* (Lawrence, KS: University Press of Kansas, 1993).

[12] This is the eloquent phrase used by Gaddis Smith to describe the more assertive policies undertaken by the Carter administration from 1979 onward; Smith, *Morality, Reason and Power*, 9.

about how the United States should behave in international affairs."[13] According to Carter, the US position in the world had to become more "humane and moral." By rediscovering what America stood for, instead of remaining principally preoccupied with what it opposed, Washington would align its policies to the evolving historical trends, ultimately compensating for reduced power and strength with reinvigorated principles and values. This, in essence, translated into an effort to diminish the importance of the Soviet Union in the shaping of American foreign policy, while focusing instead on issues – such as energy, resources, and nonproliferation – of truly global concern. As President Carter stated in his address at the commencement exercises of Notre Dame University in May 1977:

Being confident of our future, we are now free of that inordinate fear of communism which has led us to embrace any dictator who joined us in that fear. I'm glad that that's being changed.

For too many years, we've been willing to adopt the flawed and erroneous principles and tactics of our adversaries, sometimes abandoning our own values for theirs. We've fought fire with fire, never thinking that fire is better quenched with water. This approach failed, with Vietnam the best example of its intellectual and moral poverty. But through failure we have now found our way back to our own principles and values, and we have regained our lost confidence.[14]

Therefore, compared to the Nixon and Ford years the Carter administration initially assigned a lower profile to US-Soviet relations (except for the priority of arms control) and promised not to view the complexity of world affairs exclusively through the restricting prism of the Soviet-American rivalry.[15] Acknowledging that the international system had changed and, consequently, that American power was receding in the face of increased multipolarity, Carter also intended to focus on trilateral cooperation between the three centers of democratic, economic, and technological power – the United States, Western Europe, and Japan.[16] At the same time, more attention had to be dedicated to the emergence

[13] Smith, *Morality, Reason and Power*, 3.
[14] *Public Papers on the Presidents of the United States: Jimmy Carter, 1977* (Washington, DC: Government Printing Office, 1977), Book I, 955–56.
[15] Raymond Garthoff, *Détente and Confrontation. American-Soviet Relations from Nixon to Reagan* (Washington, DC: The Brookings Institution, 1994), 625–626.
[16] In the early phases Carter's foreign policy reflected the general views of the Trilateral Commission, which were based on a post-Vietnam analysis of America's place in the world. The key concept was "complex interdependence," which meant that the United States needed to engage in new collaborative internationalism with the economic dimension being emphasized over the military one; Dumbrell, *The Carter Presidency*, 111.

The Carter Administration's Ambitious Agenda

of North-South issues or, in other words, to the relationship between the United States and the developing world.[17]

During his first year in office – while neither coherently, nor always successfully – Carter tried to demonstrate his commitment to these proclaimed intentions by initiating ambitious policies, which would take months or years to bear fruit, in at least four domains: (1) high-level diplomatic negotiations on crucial issues; (2) the promotion of human rights; (3) the development of the Third World; (4) and the pursuit of deep cuts in the nuclear arsenals of the superpowers.

According to Carter, high-level negotiations were particularly important in areas where he believed US policies had fostered anti-American sentiments or charges of imperialism. Relying on the fact that American prestige was dependent on more than its power, Carter wanted to make progress on the Arab-Israeli conflict, place the United States on the side of majority rule in Africa, and settle the Panama Canal dispute in a manner which demonstrated US respect for Panama's territorial sovereignty. In these initiatives, the president took enormous political risks and was rewarded with some major achievements. In the Middle East, Carter committed his personal prestige and – continuing the mediating role initiated by Henry Kissinger – brought Egyptian president Anwar al Sadat and Israeli prime minister Menachem Begin to Camp David in September 1978. The Camp David accords, in turn, led to the Egyptian-Israeli Peace Treaty signed the following year. In Africa, President Carter devoted more attention to the issue of majority rule than any of his predecessors. On the grounds that white minority rule violated the human rights of black Africans, the United States cooperated with the British in achieving majority rule in Zimbabwe (the fact that this would eventually lead dictator Robert Mugabe to power was an unintended consequence of the accords sponsored by Carter). The negotiations on the Panama Canal led to the signing of two treaties. One on the neutrality of the canal – which guaranteed continued navigation rights to all ships, a right that the United States would continue to defend – and a second treaty which transferred to Panama full control of canal operations and the responsibility for its defense at the end of the year 1999. These treaties ended the control of the canal, which Washington had maintained since 1903, solving a decade-long source of controversy and tension in US-Latin American relations. The treaties were ratified by the US Congress in 1978 despite a fierce political battle (many American conservatives considered

---

[17] Kaufman, *Plans Unraveled*, 15.

them a surrender of an American strategic asset). While the Panama Canal Treaties were an undeniable accomplishment for the administration, Carter would pay the political price of success when many of the senators who had supported the treaties lost their seat in the congressional elections of 1978. This would have repercussions on the ratification process of the SALT II Treaty a few years later.[18]

The second distinctive feature of the Carter administration's policies was the priority assigned to supporting human rights worldwide. Impelled by his own convictions and aided by a Congress fresh from its battles with Kissinger, Carter immediately began to speak out against human rights violations in the Soviet Union and in a number of other countries, for example Brazil, Argentina, Chile, Nicaragua, South Korea, the Philippines, Thailand, and Indonesia. When exhortation alone failed, Carter implemented tougher measures such as suspending arms transfers to violators and voting against economic loans from international financial institutions to these countries. In his campaign against the Soviet Union, Carter expressed vocal support for prominent dissidents sending, for example, a highly publicized letter to Andrei Sakharov in February 1977. Carter also put emphasis on the implementation of the so-called third basket of the Helsinki Accords (on human rights) in the follow-up conferences of the Conference on Security and Cooperation in Europe. Soon, however, the administration's human rights policy would face problems. It was difficult to reconcile vocal denunciations of human rights in the Soviet Union with the negotiations on arms control. Consequently, in September 1977 the *New York Times* already warned of the dangers of Carter's "evangelical crusade" and called "to put détente back on the rails." Despite the importance of having "rehabilitated the tarnished American image of the Vietnam and Watergate years," stated former State Department adviser Samuel Pisar, "in pursuing a venture in morality whose chances of success are questionable, to say the least, the president may be jeopardizing other, more vital objectives – above all the hope of defusing the perilous military rivalry between the superpowers."[19] In fact, as Ambassador Dobrynin repeatedly underlines in his memoirs, Carter's human rights policy greatly damaged the relationship with the Soviet Union, thus making agreements more difficult to reach:

---

[18] Kaufman, *Plans Unraveled*, 59–86; Smith, *Morality, Reason and Power*, 109–133 and 157–180; A. J. DeRoche, "Standing Firm for Principles: Jimmy Carter and Zimbabwe" in *Diplomatic History*, vol 23, no 4 (1999).

[19] Samuel Pisar, "Let's Put Détente Back on the Rails" in the *New York Times*, Sep. 25, 1977.

Moscow believed Carter was deliberately interfering in the Soviet Union's internal affairs in order to undermine the existing regimes in the Soviet Union and Eastern Europe. Carter proved incapable of seeing that, and his insensitivity to our concerns was responsible for the disagreements that followed. Whether or not Carter meant it, his policy was based on linking détente to the domestic situation in the Soviet Union. This represented an abrupt departure from the policy of preceding administrations, thus inevitably making his relations with Moscow tense.[20]

Moreover, the flaws of the human rights campaign initiated by the president – which appeared to be a selected case by case list of violations rather than a real, coherent policy – surfaced almost immediately. The administration was charged with inconsistency and double standards. In fact, while the Soviet abuses were flagged and publicized, Carter remained silent on the situation in China and in Iran, for example. Nevertheless, it is important to acknowledge the merits of Carter's efforts. Thanks to his administration's insistence on human rights, the issue came to the forefront of international debates, setting the stage for more value-based policies pursued in the post–Cold War era.[21]

The third characteristic of the administration's initial approach to world affairs was the belief that the complex impact of global interdependence had to be assessed as one of the main elements threatening the US global power position. By the time Carter entered the White House, it had become evident that American well-being and prosperity was linked to the political and economic conditions of foreign countries and to the fluctuating dynamics of global markets. And Carter realized that these were increasingly influenced by the developments in the Third World. As Secretary of State Vance stated, global interdependence made it crucial for the United States to "assess a wide range of problems that affected the well-being and development of the Third World." Therefore, the United States had to be more accommodating toward the demands of these countries for greater access to the world's resources and a larger role in the global economic system. Consequently, rather than concentrating on providing military aid to developing countries, the Carter administration hoped to support national development and forge multifaceted

---

[20] Dobrynin, *In Confidence*, 388.
[21] For a comprehensive assessment of Carter's human rights policy: David F. Schmitz and Vanessa Walker, "Jimmy Carter and the Foreign Policy of Human Rights: The Development of a Post-Cold War Foreign Policy"in *Diplomatic History*, vol 28, no 1 (2004). On Carter's human rights Soviet policy: Dumbrell, *The Carter Presidency*, 116–130. For a general assessment of the human rights policy, Ibid, 185–194; Kaufman, *Plans Unraveled*, 28–46; Joshua Muravchik, *The Uncertain Crusade: Jimmy Carter and the Dilemmas of Human Rights Policy* (Lanham, MD: Hamilton Press, 1986).

relationships with emerging "regional influentials." To illustrate this Third World focus, Carter traveled much more frequently than his predecessors to less-industrialized countries and became the first US president to visit sub-Saharan Africa.[22]

In line with this innovative approach, the fourth element of Carter's initial ambitious agenda was a clear-cut, strong stance against the militarization of the international system, making nuclear nonproliferation, superpower arms control, and reduction in conventional arms sales priorities in his foreign policy. Carter made curbing the transfer of US weapons to third countries a defining characteristic of the presidency (amid, however, widespread inconsistency, as Iran was soon to become an exception, see Chapter 11). In the arms control negotiations with the Soviet Union, Carter wanted to negotiate more comprehensive reductions than his predecessors. Abandoning the scheme negotiated by Kissinger and Ford in Vladivostok, in March 1977 (i.e., only two months after the administration took office) Carter proposed – and the Soviets rejected – deep cuts on the nuclear arsenals of the superpowers (the offer presented to the Soviets by Secretary Vance was a 20 to 25 percent cut in existing offensive forces). This initiative – which will be analyzed in Chapter 10 – complicated the path toward the SALT II Treaty, but it nevertheless provided at least theoretical evidence of Carter's intention of raising the stakes in the actual reduction of nuclear weapons.

Throughout 1977 Carter pursued these initiatives with a comprehensive and idealistic approach, aided also by the absence of challenges that directly or indirectly involved the Soviet Union. Potential complications were, however, already looming. The president's message was, in itself, ambiguous. While he proclaimed his intention of promoting human rights, curtailing arms transfers, and advocating nonproliferation, he never provided a specific plan on how to achieve these noble goals. How, for example, would the administration counter the resentment of allies, recipients of nuclear technology or conventional arms sales? And, even more importantly, would Carter actually curb the transfer of arms to countries vital to American national security if those countries had repressive, antidemocratic regimes? Ultimately, it would be in the dichotomy between human rights and national security that the Carter administration's actual policy would – perhaps inevitably – distance itself from its initial, ambitious intentions.

[22] Terry L. Diebel, *Presidents, Public Opinion and Power. The Nixon, Carter and Reagan Years*, Headline Series, Foreign Policy Association, No. 280, 1987, 37–38.

THE CARTER WHITE HOUSE

In order to implement his ambitious policies, President Carter initially underlined collegiality and joint decision making. Once again in sharp contrast with the recent past – when the prominence of Henry Kissinger had dominated US decision making – Carter sought to reconcile the different viewpoints of his advisers in order to foster a more balanced foreign policy. The president encouraged frank, wide-ranging discussions and did not want to be shielded from unpleasant facts. His style of leadership was unpretentious and open-minded. According to Secretary of State Cyrus Vance, the president's "use of his nickname 'Jimmy' rather than the more formal 'James' as his official signature epitomized his idea of himself and his presidency. He could not abide pomposity and inflated egos. He emphasized his desire for a 'team spirit' among his advisers."[23]

Generally, the views of Carter's top two advisers on foreign policy, Cyrus Vance and National Security Adviser Zbigniew Brzezinski, have been portrayed as opposite and contradictory, ultimately leading to undermining the authority of the administration and skewing the popular perception of it.[24] Coming from different backgrounds, Vance and Brzezinski had, indeed, diverging worldviews. Vance was a lawyer who had gained significant experience in the Kennedy and Johnson administrations (as undersecretary for the army and deputy secretary of defense, in addition to serving as a delegate to the peace talks with the North Vietnamese in Paris). Brzezinski was a Polish-born Harvard academic who had also served as an adviser to Kennedy and Johnson (as well as for Hubert Humphrey's bid for the presidency in 1968). While Vance emphasized diplomacy and negotiations, particularly on arms control, Brzezinski stressed the primacy of power and had, in general, a more hawkish approach to negotiations, which he thought could only be pursued from a position of strength.[25]

However, at the beginning of the administration these views were seen as complementary and as mutually reinforcing. Most importantly, both the secretary of state and the national security adviser initially agreed

---

[23] Cyrus Vance, *Hard Choices. Critical Years in America's Foreign Policy* (New York: Simon and Schuster, 1983), 34.
[24] Nancy Mitchell, "The Cold War and Jimmy Carter" in Leffler and Westad (eds), *The Cambridge History of the Cold War, Volume III, Endings* (Cambridge: Cambridge University Press, 2010), 68–69.
[25] Kaufman, *Plans Unraveled*, 18–21; Smith, *Morality, Reason and Power*, 35–43; Carter, *Keeping Faith*, 52–54.

on the need to modify America's "hysterical preoccupations" with Soviet communism. Cyrus Vance not only shared Carter's principled approach to foreign policy but was convinced that it was essential in order to reestablish domestic support for the administration's initiatives. Vance underlined that in recent years the major flaw in America's foreign policy was "that it was too narrowly rooted in the concept of an overarching US-Soviet 'geopolitical' struggle. Obviously, such a conflict did exist and it was of major dimensions," he admitted, but American "national interests encompassed more than US-Soviet relations." In a rapidly changing world order, many developments did not neatly fit into the context of the East-West struggle.[26]

Brzezinski's deemphasis on Soviet affairs had different motivations. In order to adjust to the changed dynamics of the international system, America had to strengthen the cooperation with Western Europe and Japan and concentrate on economic interrelationships (he therefore advocated the need to give more attention to the European-Japanese-American "triangle" rather than to the Soviet-Chinese-American one). In harshly criticizing Nixon and Kissinger's approach to relations with the Soviet Union, Brzezinski stressed that détente was desirable but had to be both "more comprehensive and more reciprocal." This meant avoiding excessive euphoria surrounding the "era of negotiation," while making clear to the Soviets that détente also entailed restraint in fundamental global issues (i.e., responsible behavior in Third World crises). Furthermore, in the management of an increasingly polycentric world, Brzezinski believed that the United States had to seek rapid normalization of relations with China.[27]

Although Carter's own initial notion of détente is difficult to decipher, there definitely was common ground within the administration that US-Soviet relations involved both cooperation and competition (thus, in continuity with the bitterly criticized Nixon and Kissinger-inspired détente). In the course of the Carter presidency, the differences would emerge over when and how to emphasize one aspect over the other.[28] While Vance agreed that the priority was competition with the Soviets, he criticized Brzezinski's excessive emphasis on geopolitics and often saw more possibilities for cooperation, particularly in arms control.[29] By mid-

---

[26] Vance, *Hard Choices*, 26–34.
[27] Zbigniew Brzezinski, *Power and Principle. Memoirs of the National Security Adviser, 1977–1981* (New York: Farrar, Straus and Giroux, 1983), 147–150.
[28] Garthoff, *Détente and Confrontation*, 624–625.
[29] Vance, *Hard Choices*, 27.

1978, as the administration started to face critical challenges – of a typically geopolitical nature, such as in the Horn of Africa and in Iran – the divergent viewpoints of the national security adviser and of the secretary of state inevitably surfaced and deeply affected major policy decisions. Far from constituting merely a personal rivalry, the differences between the two were a manifestation of a deeper unresolved conflict over how the United States should exercise its power worldwide.

As Brzezinski's approach gradually emerged as the more influential in shaping Carter's decisions, the NSC adviser could rely on the support of another prominent member of the administration, Secretary of Defense Harold Brown. Director of research and engineering of the Defense Department during the Kennedy administration and secretary of the air force under the Johnson administration, Brown was considered an expert on cost-effectiveness and military efficiency. He had also been a member of the US delegation that had negotiated the SALT agreements in 1972. While committed to continuing the arms control process, Brown – like Brzezinski – stressed the importance of avoiding any semblance of military inferiority toward the Soviet Union.[30] Moreover, by mid-1978 he became an exponent of the need to build up US power and to project it assertively (though always maintaining a cost-effective approach on the acquisition of new weaponry). As Brzezinski later acknowledged, "without Brown I would have been much more isolated on the critical issues during the more difficult phases of the Carter presidency."[31]

The rise of Brzezinski's influence, evident by mid-1978, was aided by a combination of factors. First, his proximity and more direct access to the president compared to that of the secretary of state (the same dynamic that had facilitated Kissinger's close rapport with Nixon). Carter's frankness regarding his lack of knowledge of foreign affairs, and his assiduous willingness to acquire information, gave Brzezinski the opportunity to "stand in" on national security matters. Their extensive and wide-ranging discussions would, inevitably, influence Carter's outlook and worldview.

Secondly, the national security adviser's more assertive approach would – from the second year of the presidency onward – be supported by other influential members of the administration. In addition to Brown's backing, Brzezinski had a positive relationship with the First Lady, Rosalynn Carter (who was, perhaps more than any of her predecessors,

---

[30] Kaufman, *Plans Unraveled*, 23–24.
[31] Brzezinski, *Power and Principle*, 47. Carter underscores the overall importance and influence of Secretary Brown within the administration, Carter, *Keeping Faith*, 57–58.

capable of influencing the president's opinions).[32] Also Vice President Walter Mondale, who played a significant role within the administration (particularly during the discussions at the Friday mornings' foreign policy breakfasts), would, on certain issues, sponsor Brzezinski's policies. In short, as historian Scott Kaufman maintains, "with Brown and Mrs. Carter on his side, and with Mondale sometimes joining them, Brzezinski stood a good chance of influencing the direction of the Carter administration's diplomacy."[33]

Last, while the structure created for the decision-making process reflected the collegiality endorsed by the president, Brzezinski's position within the system was, from the beginning, a relatively privileged one.[34] In January 1977, Carter approved a more simplified NSC structure (compared to the one under Nixon and Ford) with only two committees: the Policy Review Committee (PRC) – chaired by the secretary of state – and the Special Coordination Committee (SCC) – chaired by the national security adviser. In theory these provided for a division of labor to which no one objected.[35] However, Vance's preoccupations concerned the procedure for recording the views and recommendations emerging from the PRC and SCC. Brzezinski would either draft a summary – if no specific conclusion had been reached – or submit a presidential directive (PD) – if the committee had agreed on a recommendation. In neither case would these documents be circulated among the committee members for review before reaching the president. Vance opposed this decision from the beginning, but Carter defended it in order to avoid potential leaks of sensitive documents. However, this "meant that the national security adviser

[32] In his memoirs, Carter repeatedly refers to the discussions with the First Lady, and sums up her importance by stating "we had been married for thirty-one years and were full partners in every sense of the word"; Carter, *Keeping Faith*, 20. Brzezinski acknowledges the importance of his relationship with Mrs. Carter, Brzezinski, *Power and Principle*, 31-32. See also Kaufman, *Plans Unraveled*, 24-26.
[33] Kaufman, *Plans Unraveled*, 27.
[34] In his memoirs, Carter describes all of his advisers in very positive terms, especially Vance, Brzezinski, and Brown. But the "special" position occupied by Brzezinski emerges implicitly in between the lines, for example: "To me Zbigniew Brzezinski was interesting. He would probe constantly on new ways to accomplish a goal, sometimes wanting to pursue a path that might be ill-advised – but always thinking. We had many arguments about history, politics, international events and foreign policy – often disagreeing strongly and fundamentally – but still got along well. Next to members of my family, Zbig would be my favorite seatmate on a long-distance trip; we might argue, but I would never be bored"; Carter, *Keeping Faith*, 57.
[35] The SCC focused on matters of intelligence policy, arms control, and crisis management. The PRC oversaw foreign policy, defense, and international economic issues; Kaufman, *Plans Unraveled*, 22.

had the power to interpret the trust of discussion or frame the policy recommendations of department principles."[36] Ultimately, this mechanism would allow Brzezinski to deeply influence the making of Carter's foreign policy on many of the most important issues that touched upon the US-Soviet relationship.

Initially, the differences between Carter's chief advisers were considered by the president as a strength and potential asset for the future of his presidency. As he later stated:

> The different strengths of Zbig and Cy matched the roles they played, and also permitted the natural competition between two organizations (the NSC and the State Department) to stay alive. I appreciated those differences. In making the final decisions on foreign policy, I needed to weigh as many points of view as possible.[37]

In general, the ambiguity of the president's message at first remained in the background, while the new administration tentatively tried to implement its ambitious policies. The motivations that triggered the shift in Carter's course of action, starting with the reaction to the crisis in the Horn of Africa, will be assessed in the next chapter. Indeed, one of the main thrusts of this book is to point to the ultimate centrality of the Soviet Union in the making of US policy *also* during the Carter years. In this respect, was there more continuity with the previous administrations – both in form and in substance – than one could have anticipated at the beginning? Why did Carter shift away from his proclaimed intentions? And what are the broader implications of the rise of Brzezinski's influence?

---

[36] Vance, *Hard Choices*, 37
[37] Carter, *Keeping Faith*, 57.

9

Initial Shift

The Horn of Africa

> In my view, the situation between the Ethiopians and the Somalis was more than a border conflict. Coupled with the expansion of Soviet influence and military presence to South Yemen, it posed a potentially grave threat to our position in the Middle East, notably in the Arabian Peninsula. [...] the Soviets had earlier succeeded in sustaining, through the Cubans, their preferred solution in Angola, and they now seemed embarked on a repetition in a region in close proximity to our most sensitive interests.
>
> Zbigniew Brzezinski, *Power and Principle*

> I did not believe Soviet actions in Africa were part of a grand Soviet plan, but rather attempts to exploit targets of opportunity. It was not that Soviet actions were unimportant, but I felt realism required us to deal with those problems in the local context in which they had their roots.
>
> Cyrus Vance, *Hard Choices*

In line with the general imprint given to the presidency, the Carter administration came into office with the intention of respecting regional dynamics and determined to treat local issues on local terms, and not as elements to be manipulated in the confrontation with the Soviet Union. This was the approach also toward African issues, despite the preoccupations regarding the increase of the Soviet-Cuban presence, which had expanded from Angola to other countries. Carter's commitment to respect and promote human rights, while implementing a more moral foreign policy compared to the one of his predecessors, motivated his relatively detached attitude.

The African continent, with the emergence of the issue of majority rule and with its inherent regional complexities, was in fact an ideal arena for demonstrating a rupture from the past and the different priorities on which the Carter administration based its policies. The appointment of Andrew Young as US ambassador to the United Nations, the first African American to hold such a high diplomatic position and a firm advocate of the need to focus on African realities rather than on outside intervention was, in this respect, a signal both domestically and internationally. Young was convinced that the white repressive regimes in Africa were Moscow's major asset. By ending those regimes, the Africans would have no motive to turn to Soviet or Cuban arms. Secretary Vance had a similar vision: "Our best course is to help resolve the problems which create the opportunities for external aggression."[1]

While never completely agreeing with this approach, Brzezinski's recommendations initially did not contradict the line of nonintervention in African affairs. His assessment of the international situation at the beginning of 1977 was cautiously optimistic. The Soviets remained strategically vulnerable in two critical areas, China and the Middle East. Brezhnev had personally committed himself to the reestablishment of détente based on an early SALT agreement.[2] Such a context created no reason for alarmism in Africa. Accordingly, in one of the first weekly reports written to the president, Brzezinski, although firm in wanting to counter Soviet influence in Africa, acknowledged the local causes of the upheavals and warned against direct American involvement:

Africa. It is a morass. Current African events can be seen in terms of two broad interpretations, both of them probably right but each yielding a contradictory conclusion. The first is that Africa is in the midst of a social-political upheaval, with postcolonial structures simply collapsing. In that case, it is clearly inadvisable for the US to become involved. On the other hand, events in Africa can also be seen as part of a broad East-West struggle, with pro-Western regimes being challenged by pro-Soviet regimes. This dictates resistance to Soviet efforts. Both interpretations are probably right, and they point to the conclusion (in my mind) that we should press the Soviets to desist, but to do so outside of Africa, through diplomatic leverage, trade denial, etc., but not through direct involvement in Africa per se.[3]

Despite this general attitude, the events unfolding in the Horn of Africa were bound to attract Washington's attention. The Horn was

---

[1] Gaddis Smith, *Morality, Reason and Power. American Diplomacy in the Carter Years* (New York: Hill and Wang, 1986), 133–135.
[2] Memorandum for the President from Zbigniew Brzezinski, "NSC Weekly Report #2," February 26, 1977, Jimmy Carter Library (hereafter JCL), Donated Historical Material – Brzezinski Collection (hereafter DHM-BC), box 41.
[3] Memorandum for the President from Zbigniew Brzezinski, "Weekly Report #7," April 1, 1977, JCL, DHM-BC, box 41.

strategically located along East-West communication and transportation routes that enabled it to serve as a vantage point to command or interdict oil shipments from the Middle East. Moreover, the developments in the area were seen as part of a broader and generalized postcolonial trend in which African states had become targets of Marxist-Leninist ideological expansion.[4]

Indeed, from the mid-1970s, the Soviet Union had increasingly focused on the Third World and on the battle in the so-called periphery as one of its primary assets in seeking to prevail in the global competition with the United States. Historian Christopher Andrew effectively conveyed Moscow's optimism during those years by titling his book *The World Was Going Our [the Soviets'] Way*.[5] Though cautiously relying on the evidence on which the book is based, because the dynamics of the Soviet system possibly necessitated overtly optimistic assessments on the part of the KGB, it is important to underline that the gains, from the Soviet point of view, had been many and in rapid succession: Laos, Vietnam, Angola, Mozambique, Nicaragua, and Ethiopia, only to cite a few examples.[6]

The Soviet support for national liberation movements in the Third World was viewed in Moscow as a continuation of the "natural" ideological struggle between imperialism and socialism. Conceived and implemented by the International Department of the Party and, mainly, by Mikhail Suslov, who for many years was in charge of the party's ideological work, the making of Moscow's Third World policy was kept separate from the evolution of US-Soviet relations. Under the slogan of solidarity, Suslov and his followers involved the Politburo in many Third World conflicts. Engagement in these countries was supported by the KGB – which handled the contacts in the areas through its agents – and the military – which was prepared to dispatch arms and advisers to tilt the balance on the battleground to Moscow's favor. The Soviet Foreign Ministry believed – as it turned out wrongly – that events in the Third World would not influence the relationship with the United States. Thus, "having suffered no major international complications because of its

---

[4] Ermias Abebe, "The Horn, The Cold War, and Documents From The Former East-Bloc: An Ethiopian View," *Cold War International History Project Bulletin*, Issues 8–9, Winter 1996/1997, 40.

[5] Vasili Mitrokhin was responsible for transferring the KGB's foreign intelligence archives to new headquarters in 1972. For over a decade, he made notes and transcripts of those classified documents and smuggled them out of the archive; Christopher Andrews and Vasili Mitrokhin, *The World Was Going Our Way. The KGB and the Battle for the Third World* (New York: Basic Books, 2005). See Foreword, "Vasili Mitrokhin and His Archive."

[6] Ibid, 17.

interference in Angola, Moscow had no scruples about escalating its activities in other countries, first Ethiopia, then Yemen, a number of African and Middle Eastern states, and, to crown it all, in Afghanistan."[7]

Therefore, when Carter entered the White House, he had to reconcile the reality of Soviet assertiveness in the Third World with the stated intention of avoiding decisions based on the restricting prism of the US-Soviet rivalry. As the crisis erupted in the Horn of Africa, this would prove to be an increasingly challenging task. The 1977–1978 war between Somalia and Ethiopia, in fact, had a deep impact on the Carter administration's overall approach toward the superpower relationship. The conflict triggered the shift toward a renewed focus on the traditional objective of containing the Soviet Union. The subsequent internal adjustments within the administration, with the emerging preeminence of Brzezinski, signaled the changing priorities.

ETHIOPIA OR SOMALIA?

The United States and the Soviet Union had established close links with the two major states of the Horn of Africa well before President Carter entered office. However, during the first few months of the administration, the regional dynamics shifted significantly. The internal developments in Ethiopia, and the Soviet Union's decision to align itself with the new Ethiopian regime to the detriment of its previous relationship with Somalia, posed distressing questions in Washington on how to react to the potential loss of influence over the entire region.

Washington had a long-standing military relationship with Ethiopia since the Mutual Defense Assistance Agreement of 1953. But after the fall of Emperor Haile Selassie's rule in 1974, and due to the Marxist inclinations of the revolutionary movement, the American position had started to vacillate. Between 1975 and 1976, the head of the Ethiopian military junta Mengistu Haile Mariam emerged as the leading figure and started to seek closer relations with the Soviet Union.[8] Despite these developments, the Ford administration had decided not to break the ties with the new regime. Considering Moscow's relations with Somalia, Ethiopia's regional antagonist, and the necessity to ensure an American presence

---

[7] Anatoly Dobrynin, *In Confidence. Moscow's Ambassador to America's Six Cold War Presidents* (New York: Times Books, 1995), 403–404.

[8] Jeffrey Lefebvre, *Arms for the Horn. US Security Policy in Ethiopia and Somalia 1953–1991* (Pittsburgh, PA: University of Pittsburgh Press, 1991), 160–166.

in Africa after the Angolan debacle, the United States wanted to maintain a flow of aid to Ethiopia in order to prevent the further expansion of Soviet and Cuban influence.[9] Moreover, according to the American embassy in Addis Ababa, the future course of the Ethiopian revolution was still uncertain. The embassy thus recommended:

> To continue all of our assistance programs at full strength in the belief that this would help to strengthen the position of those who will struggle for a continuation of close and friendly relations with us.[10]

Accordingly, in January 1975 the Ford administration decided to continue economic and military assistance to Ethiopia, provided that the Provisional Government would take no action contrary to US interests.[11] Throughout 1976, the US arms transfers to Ethiopia reached an all time high.[12]

The Soviet Union had instead provided training and weaponry to Somalia since the early 1960s. Through these contacts, General Muhammad Said Barre, the leader of the Somali army, grew closer to Moscow and, after taking power in 1969, established a communist regime in Mogadishu. The Somali-Soviet ties climaxed in 1974, with the signing of a treaty of friendship, under which Moscow supplied military aid to Somalia in return for access to the strategically located port of Berbera.[13]

The Carter administration therefore inherited a situation in which the US-Ethiopian relationship continued, although strained, while the relationship with Somalia was practically nonexistent. In fact, the Soviet presence in Somalia was judged as dominant and as having profoundly penetrated the civil society. Brzezinski summarized the opinion of the US ambassador in Somalia:

---

[9] Odd Arne Westad, *The Global Cold War. Third World Interventions and the Making of Our Times* (New York: Cambridge University Press), 260.

[10] Department of State Telegram from American Embassy Addis Ababa to SecState Washington, November 1974, Gerald Ford Library (hereafter GFL), National Security Adviser (hereafter NSA), Presidential Country Files for Africa, box 2, folder Ethiopia.

[11] Memorandum for Brent Scowcroft from Hal Horan, "US Policy Towards Ethiopia – Economic and Military Assistance," January 2, 1975, GFL, NSA, Presidential Country Files for Africa, box 2, folder Ethiopia. For details on the entity of the military and economic assistance provided to Ethiopia: Department of State Action Memorandum to the Secretary from Donald Easum, December 24, 1974, Ibid.

[12] Lefebvre, *Arms for the Horn*, 152.

[13] Andrews and Mitrokhin, *The World Was Going Our Way*, 447–449; Anatoly Dobrynin, *In Confidence. Moscow's Ambassador to America's Six Cold War Presidents* (New York: Random House, 1995), 402–403.

Initial Shift: The Horn of Africa

He described the present state of our Embassy in Mogadishu. He said they lead a life just about as isolated and circumscribed as if they were in Bulgaria – much more so than in Communist countries such as Poland and Hungary. He gave a vivid account of how you find a Soviet behind every Somali.[14]

Despite this reality, in early 1977 the Carter administration began to consider balancing the deterioration of relations with Ethiopia with improved relations with Somalia. In February 1977, African policy expert at the NSC Paul Henze suggested that the Somali concern about Soviet arms supplies to Ethiopia could and should be exploited by the United States to draw Somalia away from the Soviets. This had to be America's longer-term objective, together with rendering Mogadishu less intractable on its ambitions on Ethiopian territory, Ogaden in particular. At the same time, Henze stated that American-Somali relations were too strained to act directly. An American move could be erroneously interpreted as supportive of Somali irredentism. Instead, the United States had to act indirectly, encouraging, for example, the Saudis to start playing a role in Somalia: "They have the money to buy Somalia away from the Soviets if they really wanted to."[15]

In a memo to the vice president, Brzezinski outlined the US position in more detail. According to his assessment, Somalia was searching for ways to lessen its dependence on the Soviets. At the same time, the United States had, through diplomatic contacts, repeatedly signaled the intention of improving relations. In the meantime, the Saudis had offered Somalia up to $300 million to break with the Soviet Union. Therefore, in the future the problem would not be economic but military, because the Somalis were completely Soviet equipped. From Washington's point of view, the situation was evolving but Brzezinski still emphasized caution: It was not yet time to give up Ethiopia in exchange for Somalia.[16]

In the meantime, Mogadishu's search for contacts with the United States continued to capture the White House's attention. In April 1977, the president reportedly asked Vance and Brzezinski to further explore the possibilities of improved relations with Somalia.[17] At this point, the main

---

[14] Memorandum for the President from Zbigniew Brzezinski, "NSC Weekly Report #9," April 16, 1977, JCL, DHM-BC, box 41.
[15] Note for David Aaron from Paul B. Henze, "Your note re Somali concern about Soviet arms for Ethiopia," February 22, 1977, JCL, NSA files, Staff Material Horn/Special, box 1, folder 2/77.
[16] Memorandum for the Vice President from Zbigniew Brzezinski, "Somalia," March 1977, JCL, NSA files, Staff Material Horn/Special, box 1, folder 3/77.
[17] Lefebvre, *Arms for the Horn*, 175.

concern in Washington was that the Soviets and Cubans might succeed in consolidating their relations with Ethiopia, while retaining their position in Somalia. Carter's chief advisers thus recommended taking time, while avoiding a clear-cut choice between the two regional rivals.[18]

The administration remained ambivalent even as the relationship with Ethiopia continued to deteriorate. In early 1977, Carter had decided to cut military aid to Addis Ababa because of the manifest violations of human rights of the new regime. Mengistu had struck back by closing American installations and drastically reducing the US embassy personnel.[19] Washington, however, hesitated in totally abandoning Ethiopia. The country's strategic location and the need to determine whether Mengistu had definitely opted to rely solely on the Soviet Union motivated the US stance.[20] In May 1977, Brzezinski in fact proposed to wait until after Mengistu's visit to Moscow (scheduled for the same day the memo was written) before making basic policy decisions:

The Soviets may not be as eager as he [Mengistu] thinks to take over full responsibility for re-equipping and supplying Ethiopia militarily when it is far from clear that Mengistu's government can hold the country together.[21]

These words suggest that the United States had not grasped that the Kremlin could have, instead, already made its basic choice. According to historian Odd Arne Westad, the reservations in satisfying the long-standing Ethiopian requests for massive military support, which dated from 1975, had been overcome by February 1977. Mengistu's coup and "Red Terror" had reinforced Moscow's confidence in the regime and swept away the previous hesitations and doubts regarding the "authenticity" of the Ethiopian dedication to Marxism.[22] Moreover, after meeting both

---

[18] Memorandum for the President from Zbigniew Brzezinski, "NSC Weekly Report #15," June 3, 1977, JCL, DHM-BC, box 41; Memorandum for Zbigniew Brzezinski from Paul Henze, "Military Aid for Somalia," May 14, 1977, JCL, NSA files, Staff Material Horn/Special, box 1, folder 4–5/77. In this memorandum, Henze also alludes to the possibility that Mengistu's regime would not remain in power because of the lack of domestic consensus and inherent instability. The United States, therefore, according to Henze, should not openly back Somalia because it would complicate relations with Djibouti, Kenya, and a future different regime in Ethiopia.

[19] Scott Kaufman, *Plans Unraveled. The Foreign Policy of the Carter Administration* (DeKalb, IL: Northern Illinois University Press, 2008), 121.

[20] Memorandum for Zbigniew Brzezinski from Paul Henze, "Ethiopia – What Next?" April 25, 1977, JCL, NSA files, Staff Material Horn/Special, box 1, folder 4–5/77.

[21] Memorandum for the President from Zbigniew Brzezinski, "Ethiopia – Where Do We Go Next?" May 3, 1977, JCL, NSA files, Staff Material Horn/Special, box 1, folder 4–5/77.

[22] Westad, *The Global Cold War*, 271.

Mengistu and the Somalian leader Said Barre, Cuban leader Fidel Castro had decided to support and send his advisers to Ethiopia.[23] During an extended trip to Africa in early 1977, Castro had been positively impressed by the Ethiopian revolution and by Mengistu, whom he described as an "honest and convinced revolutionary leader." In contrast, the Cuban leader had been utterly unimpressed by Said Barre, defined as "above all a chauvinist."[24] Castro's assessments and decision to help Ethiopia contributed to further convince the Soviets to fully support Addis Ababa.[25]

While Ethiopia moved closer to the Soviet Union, Somalia tried to engage the United States. By May 1977, Said Barre was explicitly asking for US military aid, promising in exchange to end the ties with the Soviet Union. The memorandum of a meeting between the US vice president and the Somali ambassador reads:

> According to Addou [the Somali ambassador], the Soviets have as their objective the creation of a cluster of states including Ethiopia, Somalia, Aden and Djibouti, under Moscow's influence. Addou stated that Somalian national interests dictate otherwise: Somalia seeks self-determination for the Somali people throughout the Horn. Because of this divergence, Somalia is turning to us for economic and military assistance. Addou cautioned that only he and President Said know of this initiative, which is being pursued at Said's request.[26]

The ambassador expressed appreciation for US availability to aid economically but was, at the same time, concerned about the State Department's vagueness on military assistance. While understanding the difficulty of sending large-scale military aid immediately, Addou stressed the material and symbolic importance of receiving some American military assistance, even at a low level and on a limited basis: "Only the US can help Somalia in dealing with the Soviet Union." In return, he stated, the Somalis would reconsider their ties with Moscow: "Military assistance from the US would lead Somalia to reduce Soviet presence. Somalia would end its military arrangements with the Soviet Union," alluding also

---

[23] Memorandum for Paul Henze from Zbigniew Brzezinski, "Somalia," March 24, 1977, JCL, NSA files, Staff Material Horn/Special, box 1, folder 3/77. For a detailed analysis of the Horn of Africa crisis (including the Soviet and Cuban role): Raymond Garthoff, *Détente and Confrontation. American-Soviet Relations from Nixon to Reagan* (Washington DC: The Brookings Institution, 1994), 695–719.
[24] Piero Gleijeses, "Moscow's Proxy? Cuba and Africa 1975–1988" in *Journal of Cold War Studies*, Vol. 8, No. 4, Fall 2006, 109–110.
[25] Westad, *The Global Cold War*, 274.
[26] Memorandum for the President from the Vice President, "My Meeting with Somali Ambassador Addou, May 11, 1977," May 12, 1977, JCL, NSA files, Staff Material Horn/Special, box 1, folder 4–5/77.

to the port and airfields at Berbera. In addition, Addou pointed out that while the Soviets had targeted Ethiopia as a model for communist revolution, Moscow had never been as certain about Somalia because of its religious traditions and strong nationalistic aspirations.²⁷

Despite the clear-cut requests of the Somali leadership, the United States continued to remain undecided. Even the more hawkish Brzezinski recommended relative detachment: "I am very skeptical about our getting involved in providing even token direct military assistance to the Somalis, as much as we want to encourage them to disengage further from the Soviets."²⁸ It was better for Washington to work behind the scenes. Relying on Saudi money, with which the Somalis could buy equipment from Western Europe and America, and eventually engaging Iran, Washington could achieve the goal of reducing Soviet influence in Mogadishu, while not becoming openly involved.²⁹

Therefore, between June and July 1977, Washington signaled that, while not supplying direct military aid, it would encourage its allies (Saudi Arabia and Iran) to help Somalia build up its military strength.³⁰ Evidently, through diplomatic means the United States was seeking to establish a foothold in Somalia in order to counter the strengthening of the Soviet position in Ethiopia. The outbreak of the Ogaden War complicated the scenario and limited Washington's options, but ultimately did not alter the US line of action: relative detachment and reliance on regional allies to defend American interests.

The US position was motivated by a combination of factors. Throughout 1977, the Carter administration's human rights policies still influenced decisions, making it difficult for the United States to intervene directly in support of either of the regional rivals. In fact, both Mohamed Said Barre, the military autocrat ruling Somalia, and Mengistu

---

²⁷ Ibid.
²⁸ Memorandum for the President from Zbigniew Brzezinski, "Military Aid for Somalia," May 1977, JCL, NSA files, Staff Material Horn/Special, box 1, folder 4–5/77.
²⁹ Ibid; Memorandum for Zbigniew Brzezinski from Paul Henze, "Iranian Interest in Somalia," May 21, 1977, JCL, NSA files, Staff Material Horn/Special, box 1, folder 4–5/77.
³⁰ After Ethiopia signed a second arms agreement with the Soviet Union in May, a private back channel was established between Carter and Somali president Said Barre. The link apparently was Dr. Kevin Cahill, a US citizen and Barre's personal physician; David Korn, *Ethiopia, the United States and the Soviet Union* (Carbondale and Edwardsville, IL: Southern Illinois University Press, 1986), 36; Lefebvre, *Arms for the Horn*, 175–176; Cyrus Vance, *Hard Choices. Critical Years in America's Foreign Policy* (New York: Simon and Schuster, 1983), 73–75.

Haile Mariam, the head of the communist military junta that had come to power in Ethiopia in 1974, were ruthless despotic leaders. Secondly, until the breakout of the Ogaden War and the consequent massive Soviet airlift in support of Ethiopia, Brzezinski and the NSC were also recommending that the United States not become directly involved (therefore not fundamentally contradicting the State Department's position). Lastly, the hesitation in openly embracing Somalia reflected a clear bias at the State Department in favor of Ethiopia. The Africa Bureau continued to consider Ethiopia as the key to the Horn and that "the best policy lay in mending old fences with Addis Ababa rather than in constructing new ones with Mogadishu." In order to leave the option of "mending old fences" open, the United States had to avoid public support for Somali irredentist claims.[31]

From a broader perspective, it is important to underline two points. First, Washington followed closely the developments in the region, even before the outbreak of the Ogaden War, in order to conceive policies that would reduce the expansion of Moscow's influence. The exclusively regional dynamics of the conflict were hardly discussed at the highest level of the administration. Although still publicly rebuked, a Soviet-centric view was thus clearly resurfacing in the shaping of American foreign policy. Secondly, to counter Soviet expansionism – an objective on which there was overall convergence within the administration[32] – Carter chose to rely mainly on two countries: Saudi Arabia and Iran; the "two pillars" that had shaped Washington's regional policy since the Nixon

---

[31] Lefebvre, *Arms for the Horn*, 192.
[32] Vance and Brzezinski converged on the overall objective of seeking to counter Soviet expansionism in the Horn, but differed on how to achieve this objective. According to Vance, the United States had to retain as much influence as possible in Ethiopia, while strengthening relations with Somalia *without* getting involved directly. He and the State Department in general were convinced that in the long run the Soviets would lose influence over Ethiopia, as had been the case in Egypt and Sudan. In the meantime, the United States would have to work to achieve negotiated solutions to regional problems; Vance, *Hard Choices*, 73–75. Brzezinski on the other hand was convinced that the implications of the Soviet assertive expansion in the Horn of Africa went far beyond the regional context and thus required a strong and more global American response; Zbigniew Brzezinski, *Power and Principle. Memoirs of the National Security Adviser, 1977–1981* (New York: Farrar, Straus and Giroux, 1983), 178–190. However, it was over the issue of linkage that their disagreements grew stronger and later became public. Brzezinski declared that Soviet adventurism in Africa would have a negative repercussion on SALT, while Vance adamantly opposed linking Soviet behavior in Africa to the evolution of arms control negotiations. Carter seemed to side with the NSC adviser at times and with the secretary of state on other occasions. This contributed to conveying the image of a divided and indecisive administration, Kaufman, *Plans Unraveled*, 118–128.

years. This revealed both the inherent inconsistency of Carter's human rights policy (the "twin pillars" were not regimes with an exceptionally good human rights record) and, most significantly, an evident continuity with the regional policy of his so bitterly criticized predecessor. This basic approach – seeking to counter Soviet expansionism by relying on regional allies – shaped the Carter administration's stance toward the Ethiopian-Somali conflict even after the acknowledgment of the Soviet Union's direct and massive involvement in favor of Ethiopia.[33]

THE OGADEN WAR

Ogaden is the southeastern part of Ethiopian territory, bordering Djibouti, Kenya, and Somalia, which was (and is) predominantly inhabited by ethnic Somali Muslims. The region had been conquered in the late nineteenth century by Ethiopian king Menlik II but then became part of Italian Somaliland in 1936 after Italy's occupation of Ethiopia. Following the British takeover of the Italian territories, the Ogaden was unified with the former British and Italian Somaliland to form Greater Somalia. After successive appeals to the Allies, and thanks to American support, in 1948 the restored Kingdom of Ethiopia regained control of the Ogaden. But since then, the Ethiopian rule over this territory has been disputed by Somali irredentists.

In July 1977, Somali leader Said Barre decided to invade Ethiopia in order to "liberate" the oppressed Somalis (according to Barre, Ethiopia had implemented laws that directly or indirectly discriminated against the Somali population, in addition to preventing it from moving freely across the border between the two countries).[34] The decision to intervene was based on the erroneous assumption that the Ethiopian internal instability resulting from the revolutionary process, combined with the ongoing conflict in Eritrea, which diverted Ethiopian forces, provided a unique opportunity for Somalia to annex the Ogaden. Furthermore, Barre was convinced that the Soviet Union – that up to that point had supplied both countries – would not openly intervene to upset the scenario. The conflict would thus remain a local one and the Somali leader deemed he had a good chance to emerge on the winning side.[35]

---

[33] The Soviet intervention in the Horn of Africa was particularly significant because of its proportions and because the region was outside the traditional sphere of influence of the Warsaw Pact; Westad, *The Global Cold War*, 277.

[34] Lefebvre, *Arms for the Horn*, 190

[35] Ibid, 178–179.

Unfortunately for Somalia, however, Moscow did decide to intervene in support of Ethiopia. Despite efforts – reported by Ambassador Dobrynin – to convince the Soviet leadership that engagement in the conflict would damage relations with Washington, the Kremlin supported intervention, rebuking the American protests. Why did the United States raise complaints about Moscow's policies in the region when they were themselves so active around the globe?[36] On these grounds, the Soviet Union stepped in to tilt the Ogaden conflict to Ethiopia's favor. During the winter of 1977–1978, the critical phase of the war, the Soviet arms deliveries to Ethiopia were, in fact, massive: For a period of three months, Soviet military transport aircrafts reportedly landed every twenty minutes; an estimated 225 planes were involved in operations coordinated via a Soviet military reconnaissance satellite; and, at the same time, 17,000 Cuban troops were airlifted from Angola to join the 1,000 Soviet military advisers and the 400 East Germans who were already training intelligence and internal security units.[37] In addition, a Soviet army general, Vasilii I. Petrov, was in charge of the Ethiopian military planning. This signified that, unlike in Angola, the Soviet military had planned and coordinated the operations, making use of Cuban forces massively airlifted to the war zone. This meant, in Westad's words, "that the Soviet Union had become the arbiter and, ultimately, the decider of the relationship between sovereign states in a faraway conflict; it had taken for itself the position that Britain and then the United States had had in international relations. It had, in other words, become a complete superpower – a global alternative to the United States."[38]

Despite the realization in Washington of the dimension and implications of the Soviet airlift,[39] without which the Somali invasion would never have been pushed back, there was still no intention of intervening directly to openly counter the Soviet challenge. In December 1977, Brzezinski wrote:

No matter what the Soviets say to us, the evidence seems to indicate that they are involved in a major escalation of their involvement in Ethiopia and that they

---

[36] Dobrynin, *In Confidence*, 405.
[37] Andrew and Mitrokhin, *The World Was Going Our Way*, 458–459.
[38] Westad, *The Global Cold War*, 279.
[39] The Americans had, however, underestimated the Soviet-Cuban presence. In fact, Brzezinski mentions an expected presence of about 1,000 Soviet advisers and up to 2,000 Cubans; Memorandum for the President from Zbigniew Brzezinski, "NSC Weekly Report #40," December 16, 1977, JCL, DHM-BC, box 41. The evidence cited by Andrews and Mitrokhin instead refers to the same number of Soviets, but up to 17,000 Cubans; Andrews and Mitrokhin, *The World Was Going Our Way*, 458.

are using the Cubans in much the same fashion as they used them two years ago in Angola.... We are going to have to consider much sharper approaches to the Soviets in the Horn than we have made up to date.[40]

But the "sharper approaches" never developed into a coherent and immediate response. The January 1978 assessment of the administration's foreign policy after the first year in office still referred to "superpower interference in Africa" as "inappropriate."[41] Moreover, the transcripts of the Special Coordination Committee (SCC) and NSC meetings of early 1978 confirm that the administration still had neither developed a clear-cut strategy, nor was prepared to act directly.

The fact that David Aaron, deputy assistant to the president for National Security Affairs, had conducted a mission to Ethiopia demonstrates the continued ambivalence of the American attitude, still seeking not to completely lose all contacts with Ethiopia, despite the massive Soviet involvement. In his report to the SCC, Aaron stated that Mengistu's tactical objective was to keep the United States from supporting Somalia in the Ogaden, while his strategic objective was to work with both superpowers. His meeting with the Ethiopian leader had led Aaron to conclude that Mengistu was not ideologically committed to Moscow and that if Washington helped settle the Ogaden issue, then the Soviet influence in Ethiopia would diminish.[42] It is interesting to note that the KGB instead deemed Mengistu's loyalty to the Soviet Union as total and absolute.[43] These opposite views disclose both the inherent danger of misperceptions in the assessment of such complex regional realities and the ability of Third World leaders to play the superpower rivalry to their country's advantage.

In January 1978, the SCC discussed the future line of action toward the Somali-Ethiopian war. Involving the United Nations or the Organization of African Unity, the main American objective was to demand Ethiopian restraint in not crossing the border with Somalia in exchange for Somali withdrawal from the Ogaden. Apart from the usual divergences between Vance and Brzezinski (which would later leak to the press), the transcripts of the conversations reveal a generalized lack of determination

---

[40] Memorandum for the President from Zbigniew Brzezinski, "NSC Weekly Report #40," December 16, 1977, JCL, DHM-BC, box 41.
[41] Memorandum for the President from Zbigniew Brzezinski, "NSC Weekly Report #42," January 13, 1978, JCL, DHM-BC, box 41.
[42] Special Coordination Committee Minutes, February 22, 1978, JCL, DHM-BC, box 11, folder Ethiopia-Somalia – 4/77–2/22/78.
[43] Andrews and Mitrokhin, *The World Was Going Our Way*, 459.

Initial Shift: The Horn of Africa

in developing an assertive US posture. Attention focused on prohibiting the transfer of arms of US origin from Saudi Arabia to Somalia because the support for a country engaged in an offensive war was clearly contrary to all moral and legal obligations (in fact Vance proposed not to aid Somalia at all, not even with non-US-origin weapons). This is important, especially when juxtaposed to the concomitant commitment of the Soviets to Ethiopia. Although Brzezinski raised the possibility of sending an American task force to the region, the idea was rejected from both a strictly military point of view and because of the negative implications in case of failure. In general, the members of the SCC opted for appealing to regional allies, notably Iran and Saudi Arabia, but also Egypt, rather than engaging directly.[44]

In the NSC meeting the following day, the president endorsed the basic SCC approach. A more assertive line of action was not deemed necessary, considering also the shah of Iran's commitment to intervene should the Soviets-Cubans-Ethiopians cross the Somali border. Moreover, intelligence reports pointed to Soviet restraint in keeping Ethiopian forces from crossing into Somalia. Hence, Carter decided that America had to simply denounce the Soviet role in Ethiopia, condemn the intervention from outside forces, and develop initiatives within the Organization of African Unity. No other actions were considered.[45]

The United States would later compensate for the loss of Ethiopia (and the parallel gain of the Soviet Union) with renewed ties with Somalia and access to the strategic Somali base of Berbera (Chapter 12). However, in retrospect, the United States and the Soviet involvement in the area and the respective successes or failures would prove rather ephemeral. As Dobrynin later stated:

I cannot help being surprised at the amount of energy and effort spent almost entirely in vain by Moscow and Washington on these so-called African affairs. Twenty years later no one (except historians) could as much as remember them. Even when American marines were sent to Somalia in 1992 by George Bush to join the United Nations forces to help feed the starving there, no one in the US government and only a very few in the press remarked that the seeds of the anarchy then prevailing in Somalia had most probably been planted by the great powers' engagement there fifteen years before. Somalia was only one of a number of countries whose local quarrels became enmeshed in the Cold War – Angola,

---

[44] Special Coordination Committee Minutes, February 22, 1978, JCL, DHM-BC, box 11, folder Ethiopia-Somalia – 4/77–2/22/78.
[45] National Security Council Meeting Minutes, February 23, 1978, JCL, DHM-BC, box 11, folder Ethiopia-Somalia – 2/23/78–3/78.

Ethiopia, Afghanistan, among them, and all of them worse off for their involvement with the two superpowers.⁴⁶

In early 1978, instead, the events in the Horn and the Soviet "success" created an image of weakness and ineptitude of the Carter administration. The presidency was depicted by the American press as increasingly paralyzed by the contradictory positions of Vance and Brzezinski.⁴⁷ As noted by historian Nancy Mitchell, at the time "Americans believed that the United States had lost something of great value in the Horn: prestige. Their country had looked weak, and looking weak during the Cold War was tantamount to being weak."⁴⁸

The general impression of an inadequate and contradictory response by the Carter administration to Moscow's display of force in the Horn was made worse by the belief – which was becoming widespread in Congress and the American media – that the Soviet presence in the region endangered the safety of the oil routes between the Middle East and Western Europe. The idea of a Soviet master plan for domination of the entire area thus started to surface, together with the perception of an increased threat posed by Moscow to the vital interests of the United States and of the Western world.⁴⁹

In 1977 and 1978 the American position toward the Horn of Africa, unlike that of the Soviet Union, therefore remained relatively detached. The administration avoided direct involvement and human rights restraints still partly shaped basic policy formulations. Nevertheless, the objective of containing further Soviet expansionism in Africa had been the priority throughout the crisis. While on the surface Carter's response to the unfolding of events in the Horn seemed weak and ineffective, these events initiated the shift in the administration's approach toward an overall refocus on the Soviet Union. The president did react, but in the framework of already established diplomatic options. On a local level, this meant

---

⁴⁶ Dobrynin, *In Confidence*, 407.
⁴⁷ For example, the special to the *New York Times* of March 3, 1978 by Bernard Gwertzman was titled: "Top Carter Aides Seen in Discord On How to React to Soviet Actions" and the article described the different views of Vance (softer) and Brzezinki (tougher).
⁴⁸ Nancy Mitchell, "The Cold War and Jimmy Carter" in Leffler and Westad (eds), *The Cambridge History of the Cold War, Volume III, Endings* (Cambridge: Cambridge University Press, 2010), 80.
⁴⁹ Such views were conveyed by Brzezinski to Dobrynin in early 1978. Despite the Soviet ambassador's insistence on the absurdity of these views – how could the Soviet Union actually cut the oil routes without attacking and sinking American tankers, which would be an act of war, stated Dobrynin – the American concern regarding Soviet activities in the area was more than evident; Dobrynin, *In Confidence*, 407.

relying on long-standing regional allies. More globally, Carter's perception of a more vigorous Soviet challenge triggered the need to conceive broader and wider-ranging means to counter it.

In the pages of his memoirs, Brzezinski does not conceal his disappointment on the administration's management of the Horn of Africa crisis: "Had we conveyed our determination sooner, perhaps the Soviets would have desisted, and we might have avoided the later chain of events which ended with the Soviet invasion of Afghanistan and the suspension of SALT." However, there was "one important beneficial outcome from these troublesome months. We started reviewing more systematically the advisability of developing strategic consultations with the Chinese in order to balance the Soviets."[50]

As Carter picked up this geopolitical linkage and would hand over the management of the administration's China policy to Brzezinski, he indirectly but inexorably moved away from Vance's insistence on understanding the complexity of African dimensions. "By posing the issues in terms of an East-West controversy, we would be avoiding the underlying causes that produced these local conflicts," stated Vance.[51] Ultimately, this is precisely what occurred.

By mid 1978, the overall state of US-Soviet relations seemed to have reached a preoccupying low point.[52] The crisis in the Horn of Africa exacerbated the tension between Moscow and Washington, which had been caused by Carter's stubborn decision to propose deeper cuts in the superpowers' nuclear arsenals, thus delaying the prospects for a SALT agreement (see the next chapter). But from Moscow's standpoint, it was Carter's insistence on human rights that caused the greatest irritants. With his public campaign and support for dissidents, the Soviet leadership believed that the American president was deliberately interfering in Moscow's internal affairs. What was for Moscow an exclusively domestic issue, was instead internationalized. This was an abrupt change in America's dealings with the Soviet Union compared to the policy followed by the Nixon and Ford administrations and, therefore, inevitably created tension and suspicion in the bilateral US-Soviet relationship.[53]

---

[50] Brzezinski, *Power and Principle*, 186, 189.
[51] Vance, *Hard Choices*, 92.
[52] For an assessment of the US-Soviet relationship at the time, and the bad state of the bilateral relationship see Adam Ulam, "US-Soviet Relations: Unhappy Coexistence" in *Foreign Affairs*, Vol. 57, No. 3, 1978.
[53] Dobrynin, *In Confidence*, 388–390.

While this aspect undeniably differentiated the Carter administration from the preceding ones, the foreign policy lines pursued from 1978 onward revealed not only a remarkable shift from Carter's previously stated intentions, but also a return to the priority of geopolitics, in line with the approach initiated by Nixon and Kissinger. Reacting to the perception of Soviet increased strength and assertiveness by turning to China and by refocusing on more realistic SALT limitations, President Carter (perhaps unintentionally) embraced continuity.

> °detachment and division over action in the horn of Africa lead to a perception of a further weakening U.S.
> ↳ instigated the shift back towards a U.S.-Soviet division of the geopolitical sphere

10

Re-Creating the Strategic Triangle

Normalization with China and SALT II

> We consider that the true hotbed of war is the Soviet Union, not the US ... The first characteristic of the Soviet Union is that it always adopts the attitude of bullying the soft and fearing the strong. The second characteristic of the Soviet Union is that it will go in and grab at every opportunity.... If we really want to be able to place curbs on the polar bear, the only realistic thing for us is to unite.
>
> Deng Xiaoping, *Time*, February 1979

> There was a great deal of continuity with the previous administrations. For example, in early 1970, at the very outset of the SALT negotiations, the United States proposed a limit of 1,900 missiles and bombers, and settled for 2,400 at Vladivostok; in March 1977 in the abortive Vance mission to Moscow the proposal was for reductions to a ceiling in the range 1,800 to 2,000, but Carter settled for 2,400, to be reduced to 2,250 later; many years later in the Reagan period, the United States proposed reductions that would have meant a ceiling of about 1,800; and the Soviets eventually countered with a similar plan for a limit of about 1,600.
>
> William Hyland, *Mortal Rivals*

The normalization of relations with the People's Republic of China was not one of the initial declared priorities of the Carter administration. However, as the president reassessed the US-Soviet relationship, China became an important strategic choice. The policy of normalization was clearly linked to the broader Cold War dynamics. In order to improve America's geopolitical position in face of a more assertive Soviet Union, Carter decided to definitely strengthen the relationship with the People's Republic of China, formally recognized on January 1, 1979.

Throughout 1978, as the normalization with China evolved with a distinct anti-Soviet connotation, the Carter administration was at the same time committed to reaching an agreement with the Soviets on SALT. This had been a priority for Carter from the start and, despite the setbacks of 1977, the president remained determined to conclude the SALT II Treaty, which was eventually signed on June 19, 1979.

Therefore, President Carter on the one hand reacted to the perceived increased assertiveness of the Soviet Union through the revitalization of the "China card" while, on the other, he pursued the conclusion of SALT II. This resulted in a renewed dual-track policy in Washington's relationship with Moscow, especially in the second half of 1978. The intention was to re-create the "strategic triangle" – in evident continuity with the Nixon-Kissinger approach – which in 1972 had produced major breakthroughs in America's relationship with both Moscow and Beijing.

THE US-CHINESE RELATIONSHIP "WAS PUT IN THE BACK BURNER"

During the first few months of the administration, Carter had not revealed particular eagerness in moving rapidly toward normalization of relations with the People's Republic of China. At the first meeting of the National Security Council, convened in January 1977 to study the most relevant foreign policy issues, the US-China relationship was not on the list of priorities. The first Policy Review Memorandum (PRM) on Sino-American relations was number twenty-four, launched in April 1977 and not completed until the summer.[1]

The People's Republic of China had set forth the conditions for full normalization of relations since the Shanghai Communiqué of 1972: "The Taiwan question is the crucial question obstructing the normalization of relations between China and the United States; the Government of the People's Republic of China is the sole legal government of China; ... all US forces and military installations must be withdrawn from Taiwan."[2] In Washington, however, the issue of breaking ties with Taiwan had both domestic and international repercussions that Carter was not immediately ready to face. An agreement on normalization would anger the supporters

---

[1] Robert Ross, *Negotiating Cooperation. The United States and China 1969–1989* (Stanford, CA: Stanford University Press, 1995), 104; Scott Kaufman, *Plans Unraveled. The Foreign Policy of the Carter Administration* (DeKalb, IL: Northern Illinois University Press, 2008), 131.

[2] "The Shanghai Communiqué" in Ross, *Negotiating Cooperation*, 268.

of Taiwan in Congress and complicate the ratification of the Panama Canal treaties, one of the priorities of the administration during the first half of 1977 (the treaties were signed in September). Internationally, it was difficult for the United States to justify the abrogation of the Mutual Defense Treaty with the Republic of China (Taiwan), a de-facto abandonment of a trusted ally. In short, while engaged in a number of other important initiatives – SALT, the Middle East negotiations and, domestically, the comprehensive energy programs – President Carter did not want to tackle another highly controversial issue.[3]

Moreover, throughout 1977 the administration's China policy remained in the hands of the State Department and of Secretary Vance, who was cautious in pushing toward normalization. In principle, Vance shared the view that more positive relations with China would serve US interests, but not necessarily, and certainly not exclusively, as a bargaining chip against the Soviets. As he later put it:

> I believed that China constituted a political, economic, and cultural weight in the world that the United States could not ignore. Better relations would help our foreign policy across the board – by producing increased regional stability and, in the long run, a more stable global order. As I saw it, China was a great country that had an important role to play in the final quarter of the twentieth century, not simply one that might be a useful counterweight to the Soviet Union.[4]

On the issue of normalization (as in most other issues), Brzezinski's view greatly differed. While not minimizing the "long-term historical significance" of a new relationship between the United States and China, for him the central aspect was the "Soviet dimension":

> Normalization of relations with China was a key strategic goal of the new administration. We were convinced that a genuinely cooperative relationship between Washington and Beijing would greatly enhance the stability of the Far East and that, more generally, it would be to US advantage in the global competition with the Soviet Union.[5]

Therefore, while Vance's stance on normalization was dominated "by a concern for maintaining US-Soviet stability"[6] in order not to jeopardize

---

[3] Kaufman, *Plans Unraveled*, 133; Vance, *Hard Choices. Critical Years in America's Foreign Policy* (New York: Simon and Schuster, 1983), 79; James Mann, *About Face. A History of America's Curious Relationship with China, from Nixon to Clinton* (New York: Vintage Books, 1998), 82.
[4] Vance, *Hard Choices*, 79.
[5] Zbigniew Brzezinski, *Power and Principle. Memoirs of the National Security Adviser, 1977–1981* (New York: Farrar, Straus and Giroux, 1983), 196.
[6] Ross, *Negotiating Cooperation*, 98.

the evolution of SALT II, Brzezinski was convinced that, because Moscow's concern with China was so profound, the strengthening of Sino-American relations would greatly enhance America's strategic position. This would influence Moscow, inducing restraint in Third World crises and a more cooperative attitude in SALT.[7] Initially, President Carter seemed to be in agreement with Vance and, consequently, did not immediately seek a breakthrough in the relationship with Beijing.

Since early 1977, the Chinese had sent signals of their willingness to move toward normalization but had also clearly stated that any new initiative, "however welcome, had to come from the United States." Only Washington had the key to breaking the impasse.[8] Domestically, China was undergoing a period of uncertainty following the battle for the succession of Chairman Mao. After the death of Zhou Enlai, Mao had appointed Premier Hua Guofeng, who did not belong to either of the principal contending factions (the radical Gang of Four versus the moderate faction led by Zhou first and later by Deng). After the death of Mao in September 1976, Hua also inherited the position of chairman and for a brief period rose through the ranks of the Chinese leadership. Lacking a constituency of his own, Hua fully endorsed continuity with the policy directions traced by Mao before his death. Failing to reconcile the opposite tendencies of the radical and moderate factions, and increasingly outmaneuvered by Deng Xiaoping (who in 1977 reemerged as a central figure), Hua gradually lost influence in the making of Chinese policy despite still formally holding the primary leadership posts of the country.[9]

In order to maintain the momentum of the US-China dialogue, in August 1977 Carter approved Vance's trip to China. However, it was evident that Washington was not ready to seriously compromise on Taiwan. Despite high-level exploratory discussions with the Chinese, Vance's mission predictably did not result in any tangible step forward.[10] As Carter later acknowledged, the administration was concentrated on other initiatives and, after the Vance visit, the prospect of US-China normalization was put "in the back burner in Washington."[11]

[7] Gaddis Smith, *Morality, Reason and Power. American Diplomacy in the Carter Years* (New York: Hill and Wang, 1986, 87; Kaufman, *Plans Unraveled*, 131.
[8] Memorandum for the President from Zbigniew Brzezinski, "Information Items," February 8, 1977, NLC-1-1-8-38-0, Jimmy Carter Library (hereafter JCL).
[9] Henry Kissinger, *On China* (New York: Penguin Books, 2011), 328-329.
[10] In his memoirs, Vance clearly states that he did not expect any real move toward normalization to occur during his August 1977 trip; Vance, *Hard Choices*, 81-82.
[11] Jimmy Carter, *Keeping Faith. Memoirs of a President* (Fayetteville, AK: The University of Arkansas Press, 1995), 196.

In September 1977, the Chinese again signaled their interest in proceeding toward normalization. During a meeting with Vance, the Chinese foreign minister stated:

> Sino-US relations are not a diplomatic question but a political question. It is necessary to consider this issue with long-term strategic interests in mind. I hope Sino-US relations will develop on the basis of the Shanghai Communiqué.

Nevertheless, while publicly stating that normalization was an important objective, in reality the Carter administration decided to "sustain the relationship at its present level for at least the next few months."[12] Therefore, until the end of 1977 Washington's China policy remained stalled.[13]

The shift in Carter's approach toward China which led, with remarkable rapidity, to the agreement on normalization, reflected the change in the president's worldview. The proclaimed effort to abandon an excessively Soviet-centric vision and place different priorities at the center of US foreign policy gradually, albeit promptly, eroded as a consequence of Moscow's activities in the Third World. After the crisis in the Horn of Africa, Carter reassessed his approach toward the superpower relationship and, consequently, his reliance on Secretary Vance as his principal foreign policy adviser.

THE RISE OF BRZEZINSKI'S INFLUENCE

Despite the stalemate in US-China relations during the administration's first year in office, Brzezinski could hardly conceal his opinions on the advantages of further developing the relationship. As he stated later:

> The Soviet dimension was one of those considerations of which it is sometimes said 'think of it all the times but speak of it never.' I, for one, thought of it a great deal, even though I knew that publicly one had to make pious noises to the effect that US-Chinese normalization had nothing to do with the US-Soviet rivalry.[14]

---

[12] Memorandum for the President from Zbigniew Brzezinski, "Vance's Meeting with Foreign Minister Huang Hua on September 28, 1977, JCL, NSC files, Country files – China, box 8, folder China (PRC) 7–9/77.

[13] Memorandum for the President from Zbigniew Brzezinski, "NSC Weekly Report #39," December 9, 1977, JCL, Donated Historical Material – Brzezinski Collection (hereafter DHM-BC), box 41.

[14] Brzezinski, *Power and Principle*, 196.

During the first half of 1977, Brzezinski had encouraged NSC specialist Michel Oksenberg to strengthen the links with the Chinese officials in Washington. In this way, he tried to obtain more leverage in the definition of the administration's China policy.[15] In response to the signals sent by Oksenberg, in early November 1977 Brzezinski received an invitation to visit China. At this point, the president was confronted with a dilemma. Deciding on sending Vance (for a second visit) or Brzezinski (for the first time) to China meant choosing between two different visions and approaches that had by then clearly surfaced.

In early 1978, Brzezinski pushed to obtain presidential approval of his trip by linking the evolution of Washington's China policy to the developments in the Horn of Africa:

A couple of weeks ago, you said that you felt that a consultative visit by me to China would be useful.... Considering the importance of the US maintaining a better relationship with both China and the USSR than either of them have with each other, and bearing in mind developments on the Horn and the related need to send a sensitive signal to the Soviets, the time is ripe for your decision on this subject.[16]

Brzezinski stressed the importance of maintaining the structure of the "strategic triangle" of Washington-Beijing-Moscow, and introduced the possibility of responding to the Soviet actions in Africa by revitalizing the ties with China. The scope of his visit, in fact, would be to give "the Soviets some food for thought."

In March 1978, Brzezinski again pointed to China as a means to convey a signal to the Soviet Union regarding its activities in the Horn. In analyzing the various possibilities for an American reaction, he underlined that "the area of greatest Soviet sensitivity is China. We have neglected this dimension entirely."[17] Despite noting "we mustn't overact" in his response, only days later President Carter decided to send Brzezinski to Beijing for important "consultations" with the Chinese leaders. In mid-March, in fact, the president sent a handwritten note to Vice President Mondale and Secretary Vance stating that he had decided that "it would

---

[15] Ross, *Negotiating Cooperation*, 113; Brzezinski, *Power and Principle*, 196–202.
[16] Memorandum for the President from Zbigniew Brzezinski, "Trip to the Far East," February 27, 1978, JCL, DHM-BC, Geographic file, box 9, folder China (People's Republic of) – Brzezinski's Trip: (11/19/77–5/14/78).
[17] Memorandum for the President from Zbigniew Brzezinski, "The Soviet Union and Ethiopia: Implications for U.S.-Soviet Relations," March 3, 1978, JCL, DHM-BC, Subject file, box 28, folder Meetings – SCC 61: 3/2/78.

be best for Zbig to go to China – perhaps as early as next month, if it is mutually satisfactory with the Chinese."[18]

In making this decision, Carter sent a precise message to both Beijing and Moscow. The national security adviser's reputation as an undisputable anti-Soviet "hawk" would strengthen the ties with the Chinese, who sought to further develop the relationship with the United States on the basis of the common perception of the Soviet threat. At the same time, this would deepen Moscow's concerns on the prospected definitive rapprochement between the United States and China. Carter thus shared the assessment that in the previous months Washington had almost "entirely failed to take advantage of the opportunity inherent in the Sino-Soviet hostility, while concentrating heavily on enlarging the scope of US-Soviet relations."[19] The correction of the administration's line of action had therefore begun.[20]

Carter's decision was encouraged by the parallel views of the People's Republic regarding Soviet activities in Africa. In the spring of 1978, Chinese propagandists repeatedly pointed out that the domination of the Horn of Africa would put the Soviets in a strategically strong position near the oil routes from the Persian Gulf to Western Europe, Japan, and the United States. Consequently, the Chinese expressed the utmost concern.[21] The United States and China thus once again shared the need to counter Moscow's expansionism. This provided the incentive to further improve and strengthen their bilateral relationship.

Moreover, Chinese leader Deng Xiaoping wanted a more comprehensive relationship with the United States for domestic, and not only

---

[18] Handwritten note from Carter to the Vice President and to Secretary Vance, March 16, 1978, JCL, DHM-BC, Geographic file, box 9, folder China (People's Republic of) – Brzezinski's Trip: (11/19/77–5/14/78).
[19] Memorandum for the President from Zbigniew Brzezinski, "NSC Weekly Report #46," February 9, 1978, JCL, DHM-BC, box 41.
[20] The link between the events in the Horn and the Carter administration's move toward normalization is not only present in the documents thus far cited but is also advanced by Raymond Garthoff in *Détente and Confrontation. American Soviet Relations from Nixon to Reagan* (Washington, DC: The Brookings Institution, 2001), 611. The same parallel is made by James G. Hershberg in the introduction to "Anatomy of a Third World Cold War Crisis: New East-Bloc Evidence on the Horn of Africa, 1977–1978," in *Cold War International History Project Bulletin*, Issues 8–9, Woodrow Wilson International Center for Scholars, Washington, DC, Winter 1996/1997, 38–39. See also Ross, *Negotiating Cooperation*, 120–128.
[21] CIA Intelligence Memorandum, "China and the Horn of Africa," May 12, 1978, JCL, NLC-4-38-7-3-6.

foreign policy reasons (in fact while Deng and Hua's views on foreign policy were relatively parallel, they had strikingly different visions on the future of China and on its economic reform programs. Deng's opening to the West ultimately prevailed over Hua's more traditional Soviet-inspired methods).[22] A key element of Deng's vision was the need to modernize China's economy. Beijing had to increase its production of steel, iron, coal, natural gas, and hydroelectricity, but lacked both the capital and know-how to move rapidly. Technological exchanges and joint development programs with the United States and with the West in general would be essential in aiding China to restructure its economy.[23] This would in turn restore unity and faith to the Chinese people after the shock and divisions of the Cultural Revolution. Deng's position was eventually supported by the party and, in the summer of 1977, he was appointed vice premier. Consequently, he was given control over the People's Republic's foreign policy.[24] This paved the way for the normalization of relations with the United States.

"THE UNITED STATES HAS MADE UP ITS MIND"

Brzezinski's May 1978 visit to China definitely marked a turning point in the evolution of Sino-American relations. The firm commitment to normalization that Carter asked his national security adviser to convey to the leadership in Beijing sharply contrasted with the hesitance of the previous months and demonstrated a renewed determination on America's part to strengthening the relationship with China. The president, in fact, told Brzezinski to tell the Chinese "that the United States has made up its mind." The Sino-American dialogue had to proceed along the lines traced by the Shanghai Communiqué. Underlining that relations with China were a central element in America's global policy, Brzezinski had to state that:

The United States and China share certain common interests and we have parallel, long-term strategic concerns. The most important of these is our common opposition to global or regional hegemony by any single power.[25]

---

[22] Kissinger, *On China*, 330.
[23] Department of State Briefing Memorandum to the Secretary from INR – David E. Mark, "Events in China: Implications for Stability and for Sino-US Relations," December 1, 1978, JCL, NSC files – Country file China, box 9, folder China (PRC), 12/78.
[24] Ross, *Negotiating Cooperation*, 98.
[25] President Carter's Instructions to Zbigniew Brzezinski for His Mission to China, May 17, 1978 in Brzezinski, *Power and Principle*, Annex I.

The commitment to resisting "hegemony" was an explicit reference to the common objective of countering Soviet expansionism. On this point, Carter asked Brzezinski to explain his views on the nature of the Soviet threat:

> The combination of increasing Soviet military power and political short-sightedness, fed by big-power ambitions, might tempt the Soviet Union both to exploit local turbulence (especially in the Third World) and to intimidate our friends in order to seek political advantage and eventually even political preponderance.[26]

Washington was concerned about Soviet actions in Africa and considered them part of a more general Soviet expansionist trend pointing to the Indian Ocean. Brzezinski had to thus also discuss such "areas of common concern" with the Chinese. In this way, Carter hoped to foster a genuine and wide-ranging dialogue with Beijing on these issues and, more specifically, to exchange views on how to concretely aid Somalia.

During his visit, Brzezinski found a receptive audience. The Chinese leadership – and Deng in particular – were eager to proceed with normalization and to enlist Washington more firmly in a coalition to oppose Soviet advances in every part of the world.[27] Brzezinski's conversations in Beijing in fact confirmed the centrality of the Soviet Union in the dialogue between Washington and Beijing, in obvious continuity with the approach toward China that had characterized the Nixon-Kissinger years. Continuity was explicitly called for by Brzezinski:

> I have been reading the record of our conversations with you [the Chinese leadership] over the past five years. I am impressed by the candor of our conversations. We have conversations with you that are as candid as with any country in the world. And I hope our conversations about the Soviet Union would proceed in that same spirit.[28]

On the issue of Taiwan, Washington decided to issue a unilateral statement calling for the peaceful settlement of the question by the Chinese themselves, while at the same time searching for ways to maintain a nondiplomatic relationship with Taipei to safeguard, at least in part, the trustworthiness of America's commitments.

---

[26] Ibid.
[27] Kissinger, *On China*, 351.
[28] Memorandum for Zbigniew Brzezinski from Michel Oksenberg, "Talking Points for Your Meeting with Ambassador Han Hsu at 2:30 P.M. Today," May 8, 1978, JCL, NSC files – Country files China, box 8, folder China (PRC), 2–5/78.

Brzezinski's May 1978 visit was "very successful." The Chinese realized that he was in a position to both engage in "a broad strategic review" in order to increase collaboration between the two countries, and to seriously discuss the issue of normalization.[29] The focus on the long-term strategic nature of the relationship between Washington and Beijing had a firm anti-Soviet connotation which, while not explicitly mentioned, was evidently placed at the center of the normalization process. This led to the strengthening of Brzezinski's role within the Carter administration. Moreover, the timing of the decision to push for normalization was particularly significant, a decision "definitely influenced by the Soviet dimension."[30] In other words, Moscow had to be reminded that the United States, too, could effectively compete geopolitically.[31]

The discussions on how to proceed toward normalization began soon after Brzezinski's return to Washington. By the end of June 1978 the decision on the timing of the breakthrough had been made in Washington and communicated to the head of the Liaison Office in Beijing, Leonard Woodcock:

This message contains instructions which have been reviewed by the President for use in your opening negotiating meeting with Foreign Minister Huang Hua on normalization of relations. The main purpose of this meeting is to secure agreement from the Chinese to the negotiating process we envision over the coming months.
The process we have in mind includes: meeting between you and Huang at intervals of approximately two weeks during the course of the summer aiming at final agreement around mid-December.[32]

The negotiations took place precisely along these lines. Over the following six months, Woodcock in Beijing and Brzezinski (together with Assistant Secretary for East Asian and Pacific Affairs Richard Holbrooke) in Washington conducted the negotiations in utmost secrecy. Only "a handful of administration officials" knew about Woodcock's talks. On December 15, 1978, the two governments agreed

---

[29] Brzezinski, *Power and Principle*, 219.
[30] Brzezinski, *Power and Principle*, 197.
[31] Garthoff, *Détente and Confrontation*, 661.
[32] Cable to Ambassador Woodcock from Secretary Vance, June 28, 1978, JCL, DHM-BC, Geographic file, box 9, folder China (People's Republic of) – Alpha Channel: (2/78–11/78).

to a simultaneous announcement, with the date for normalization to begin on January 1, 1979.[33]

The joint communiqué reaffirmed the principles agreed upon in 1972 and "emphasized once again" the commitment to oppose efforts to establish hegemony in the Asia-Pacific region, or in any other region of the world. The "antihegemonic clause" that had been the focal point of the Shanghai Communiqué was restated in its totality, therefore formally placing the same principle at the basis of the normalization of relations between the People's Republic and the United States.

In relation to Taiwan, the United States formally stated that cultural, commercial, and other "non official relations" with the people of Taiwan would be maintained, despite the declaration that recognized the People's Republic as the sole legal government of China.[34] Unofficially, Brzezinski had agreed with the Chinese that the United States would give one year's notice of termination of the Mutual Defense Treaty with Taiwan (rather than abrogate it immediately) and then withdraw all American troops from the island. Washington would also continue to sell defensive military weapons to Taiwan. The People's Republic would not contradict the American expectation that in the future the issue had to be handled peacefully, but would not give an explicit formal pledge not to use force.[35]

In practice, therefore, the issue of the reunification of all Chinese territories was not resolved and, as had been the case in 1972, was set aside in order to allow for the next step of the Sino-American rapprochement to take place. The necessity of definitely confirming the redefinition of the balance of power initiated in 1972 was, clearly, the priority. Turning to

---

[33] Mann, *About Face*, 89–90; Kaufman, *Plans Unraveled*, 135–136. In the pages of his memoirs, Cyrus Vance clearly states that he was surprised by the announcement on normalization; Vance, *Hard Choices*, 109, 119.

[34] "Joint Communiqué on the Establishment of Diplomatic Relations Between the United States of America and the People's Republic of China" in Ross, *Negotiating Cooperation*, 269.

[35] Smith, *Morality, Reason and Power*, 89. Interestingly, in a letter to Carter commenting on the normalization of relations with China, former president Nixon expressed his preoccupations on the inadequacy of the guarantees for Taiwan. According to Nixon, a large part of the American public was still pro-Taiwan, therefore Carter had to make clear that the United States was against Beijing's use of force against Taiwan. In this context, the United States had to reserve its right to continue to sell arms to Taiwan. Nixon's principal concern was, in effect, the credibility of American commitments to other allies as a consequence of the "betrayal" of Taiwan; Letter from Nixon to Carter, December 20, 1978, JCL, DHM-BC, Geographic file, box 9, folder China (People's Republic of) – Alpha Channel: (12/78–1/80).

China as a response to the perceived increased threat coming from the Soviet Union was Washington's strategic choice.

The Soviets realized that the US-China normalization process was a signal directed against them. A few days after the joint communiqué on normalization, Dobrynin gave Brzezinski the text of Brezhnev's formal reaction. While acknowledging that the "establishment of normal relations between two sovereign states is of course a natural thing," the Soviet leader at the same time noted that "another question is on what basis the normalization is taking place" and "what aims are being set by both sides." The US president had personally reassured Brezhnev that the development of Sino-American relations was not directed against the Soviet Union, and that it had no other purpose than to promote the cause of world peace. Nevertheless, the Soviet leader stated:

> We cannot disregard the fact that the joint US-Chinese communiqué allows expressions whose tendency with regard to the Soviet Union taking into account the usual lexicon of the Chinese leaders is beyond doubt.
>
> Evidently the Soviet Union will follow most closely what will be the practical results of the development of US-Chinese relations, and it will draw appropriate conclusions for its policy.[36]

However, despite the understanding that the "China card" had been used to put pressure on the Soviet Union,[37] it is important to underline that Brezhnev concluded his letter to President Carter by restating his commitment to SALT:

> As for the hope you [the president] expressed for achieving at the forthcoming meeting of Gromyko and Secretary Vance an important progress in completing

---

[36] Oral message from Brezhnev to Carter read by Dobrynin to Brzezinski, Memorandum of Conversation, Tuesday, December 19, 1978, 2:59–3:12 P.M., JCL, NSC files, Subject file, box 33, folder Memcons: Brzezinski, 9/78–2/79. According to Vance, the timing of the announcement on normalization had a negative impact on the Soviets, Vance, *Hard Choices*, 111–112.

[37] It is interesting to note that in the summer of 1981, Henry Trofimenko, the head of the department for the study of US foreign policy at the Institute of US and Canadian Studies of the Academy of Sciences of the Soviet Union, wrote an article in *Foreign Affairs* on the motivations of Soviet policy in the Third World. He describes Soviet assertiveness as a response to the Carter administration's actions negatively perceived in Moscow, with particular reference to the moves made by the United States and China; Henry Trofimenko, "The Third World and the U.S.-Soviet Competition: A Soviet View," in *Foreign Affairs*, Summer 1981.

the preparation of the Strategic Arms Limitation Agreement, we would also like to share this hope.³⁸

In fact, notwithstanding the sharpening of the geopolitical competition in the Third World and the Sino-American normalization, the US-Soviet dialogue on strategic arms limitation had _never_ been interrupted. And, amid the difficulties, in the last months of 1978 the US and Soviet delegations gradually proceeded toward the finalization of the SALT II Treaty.

"IT IS IN THE ARMS CONTROL FIELD THAT I FEEL WE SHOULD PLACE THE GREATEST EMPHASIS"

In contrast to China – which had not been an immediate priority – President Carter had placed strategic arms control at the center of the US-Soviet dialogue from the beginning of his administration. In his first letter to Brezhnev in January 1977, Carter had stressed the importance of curbing the nuclear arms race. Referring to a Soviet statement on the intention not to strive for superiority and on maintaining a defense sufficient to deter any potential adversary, the president stated: "The United States seeks nothing more or less for itself." While underscoring the long-term goal of eliminating "all nuclear weapons," the "critical first step" was the conclusion of a SALT II agreement "without delay."³⁹ A month later, Carter told the Soviet leader that it was "in the arms control field that I feel we should place the greatest emphasis."⁴⁰

On his part, Brezhnev endorsed the view that SALT II was a fundamental priority and underlined that the negotiations on arms control were the central element of the US-Soviet dialogue:

> Indeed, the cooperation of our two countries to end the arms race and to achieve disarmament is, due to objective reasons, the central area of relations between the US and the USSR at the present time.⁴¹

---

[38] Oral message from Brezhnev to Carter read by Dobrynin to Brzezinski, Memorandum of Conversation, Tuesday, December 19, 1978, 2:59–3:12 P.M., JCL, NSC files, Subject file, box 33, folder Memcons: Brzezinski, 9/78–2/79.
[39] Letter from Carter to Brezhnev, January 26, 1977, JCL, DHM-BC, Geographic file, box 18, folder USSR – Carter/Brezhnev Correspondence (1/77–5/77).
[40] Letter from Carter to Brezhnev, February 14, 1977, JCL, DHM-BC, Geographic file, box 18, folder USSR – Carter/Brezhnev Correspondence (1/77–5/77).
[41] Brezhnev letter to Carter, February 4, 1977, JCL, DHM-BC, Geographic file, box 18, folder USSR – Carter/Brezhnev Correspondence (1/77–5/77).

Therefore, both leaders considered SALT a necessity and a priority. However, while Brezhnev considered the task "quite attainable," proceeding on the basis of the parameters agreed upon in Vladivostok, Carter wanted to break from the previous understanding and introduce more far-reaching limitations. Although the ultimate objective of completely eliminating nuclear weapons was not achievable in the foreseeable future, the president wanted an agreement that would begin the process of "deep cuts" within the existing arsenals.

Carter had been a critic of SALT I and of the Vladivostok framework because it established excessively high force levels, while not addressing the issue of the vulnerability of the American ICBM force. After his inauguration, Carter had nevertheless repeatedly stated his intention of proceeding along the path outlined by his predecessors. More far-reaching reductions would be pursued in SALT III. But then the president's position changed. The idea of simply "picking up" where Kissinger and Ford had left off was not appealing to Carter, or to his advisers. Brzezinski, in particular, believed that Kissinger had not been strong enough in his negotiations with the Soviet leaders. By proposing reductions, and not only limitations, Carter wanted to provide a tangible demonstration of his administration's different approach toward arms control, compared to that of Nixon and Ford.[42]

In early 1977, Carter thus set forth the idea that while negotiating SALT II, the United States and the Soviet Union could also include in the agreement some "substantial force level reductions." Moreover, if they agreed in principle that the current negotiations were but a first step in a process leading to much greater reductions, the controversial points causing the impasse in the talks could be postponed to a later phase. The reference was, of course, to the Backfire and cruise missiles. Carter stated:

If our objectives are sufficiently ambitious, and particularly if our desire is to achieve real disarmament within minimum forces left which are adequate to assure security to both parties, we may be able to deal more easily later with what appear now to be significant and difficult technical issues.[43]

Brezhnev, however, categorically opposed Carter's approach. The negotiations had to proceed within the framework agreed upon in

---

[42] Smith, *Morality, Reason and Power*, 69–74; Garthoff, *Détente and Confrontation*, 883–886. For a comprehensive account on SALT II; Strobe Talbott, *Endgame. The Inside Story of SALT II* (New York: Harper Colophon, 1980).

[43] Letter from Carter to Brezhnev, February 14, 1977, JCL, DHM-BC, Geographic file, box 18, folder USSR – Carter/Brezhnev Correspondence (1/77–5/77).

Vladivostok. All aspects were interconnected and the Soviet leader was not willing to put aside what was already negotiated with Ford and Kissinger. More comprehensive reductions were important, but at a later stage and within a different framework. From the Soviet point of view, it was impossible to move toward the reduction of existing levels without taking into account the elements which gave the United States a clear-cut advantage, such as the Forward Base Systems and the nuclear forces of NATO allies.[44]

Brezhnev's position did not allow any possibility for compromise. Yet, Carter instructed Secretary Vance to proceed with the "deep cuts" approach during his visit to Moscow in March 1977. The basic elements of the proposal were to reduce the aggregate level of strategic systems from 2,400 agreed upon in Vladivostok to between 1,800 and 2,000, and the number of launchers for MIRVed missiles from 1,320 to 1,100 or 1,200. In addition, the United States wanted to reduce the number of modern ICBMs to 150, the number of launchers for ICBMs with MIRVs to 550 and, in general, to put severe limits on development, testing, and deployment of new types of ICBMs.[45]

Predictably, the Soviet reaction was "total, absolute rejection, and a charge of insincerity."[46] Moscow considered the proposal one-sided, because the reductions focused almost entirely on land-based ICBMs on which Moscow heavily relied (and that from the beginning of the SALT process had constituted the major American preoccupation). The categories in which the United States had superiority – submarine and air-launched weapons – were not mentioned. The only American concession, in case of Soviet acceptance, would be the abandonment of the MX intercontinental missile, then in its research stage. Moreover, the Soviets refused Carter's new approach because they regarded the Vladivostok accord as binding, notwithstanding the change of administration. Brezhnev had personally committed himself to the agreement, and had made significant concessions (especially related to FBS) that Washington was now bypassing. The Soviet reaction to Vance's proposal was summarized in *Izvestia*: "Trust in politics is, at the very least,

---

[44] Letter from Brezhnev to Carter, February 25, 1977, JCL, DHM-BC, Geographic file, box 18, folder USSR – Carter/Brezhnev Correspondence (1/77–5/77). Brezhnev reiterated his position in a second letter to Carter, which immediately preceded Vance's March 1977 trip to Moscow: Letter from Brezhnev to Carter, March 15, 1977, JCL, DHM-BC, Geographic file, box 18, folder USSR – Carter/Brezhnev Correspondence (1/77–5/77).
[45] Garthoff, *Détente and Confrontation*, 889.
[46] Smith, *Morality, Reason and Power*, 76.

firm confidence that your negotiating partner will not repudiate this morning what was agreed to last night.... One cannot talk frivolously with the Soviet Union. The Soviet Union cannot be outplayed."[47]

Vance's March 1977 trip was therefore a clear-cut failure.[48] Consequently, the prospect of concluding the SALT II Treaty before October 1977, the expiration date of SALT I, was dim. Afterwards, Carter returned to the more conventional approach and to the formulation of positions closer to the Vladivostok framework.[49] But the failed attempt to put SALT II on a different track, and the decline in mutual confidence that had resulted rendered the negotiations more difficult.[50] Furthermore, the developments on the global scene influenced the evolution of SALT. However, even after the decision to respond to the Soviet actions in the Horn through the revitalization of the relationship with China, the Carter administration never abandoned its determination to successfully conclude SALT II.

"OUR OBJECTIVE SHOULD BE TO RECREATE THE PHENOMENA OF 1971–1972"

During the first half of 1978, US-Soviet relations stalled. No breakthrough seemed imminent in the SALT talks and, according to Washington, the Soviets were steadily increasing their presence by proxy in areas near the strategically vital Arabian Peninsula (in Ethiopia and South Yemen especially). Publicly, the Carter administration was criticized for mishandling the US-Soviet relationship and for being unable either to accommodate, or to effectively compete with Moscow.[51]

---

[47] Cited in Smith, *Morality, Reason and Power*, 77.
[48] There were, nevertheless, some positive aspects: Vance and Gromyko agreed to meet again in May in Geneva and to establish joint working groups on a wide range of topics – on a comprehensive test ban, on chemical weapons, on the demilitarization of the Indian Ocean, and on the proliferation of nuclear technology.
[49] After Vance's Moscow trip in March 1977, the SALT delegations continued to work on the details of the prospected agreement in Geneva. The most important issues were, however, dealt with at a higher level. Until the signing of SALT II, more than two years later, Vance and Gromyko met nine times, Carter and Gromyko conferred three times, and the contact with Dobrynin was continuous. A procedure that, in essence, was not different from the one adopted by the Nixon and Ford administrations.
[50] On the damage done to the evolution of the US-Soviet relationship by the "deep cuts" proposal set forth during Vance's March 1977 mission, Anatoly Dobrynin, *In Confidence. Moscow's Ambassador to America's Six Cold War Presidents* (New York: Times Books, 1995), 383–386, 388–397.
[51] Brzezinski, *Power and Principle*, 316.

The inside picture was, however, more complex. The Carter administration was, in fact, gradually interrelating the developments in the Horn of Africa to both the normalization of relations with China and the evolution of SALT. Clearly, the intention was to pursue both cooperation and competition in order to reestablish the dynamic of détente. Interestingly, in February 1978 – i.e., at the height of the Soviet involvement in Ethiopia – NSC staffer Mike Armacost forwarded a document to Brzezinski entitled "Saving SALT in Angola" dated December 15, 1975. The memo called for a link between the end of Soviet involvement in Angola and the SALT proposals, which Kissinger had to set forth in his January 1976 trip to Moscow. "I think you might find the attached memo interesting, and/or amusing given the parallels with the current situation," wrote Armacost. "The details may differ, but I think the central premise of the argument remains valid." "Plus ça change, plus c'est la même chose!" was Brzezinksi's response.[52] In the administration there was, therefore, an open acknowledgment of continuity with the past, especially in the basic ambivalence of America's policy toward the Soviet Union: the continued pursuit of SALT notwithstanding the escalating geopolitical competition.

During an NSC discussion of April 1978 the interrelationship between the cooperative aspect of the US-Soviet relationship (progress in SALT) and the competitive aspect (in this case the normalization with China) surfaced clearly. While analyzing the different options for the development of the administration's China policy, Secretary Vance raised the question of the timing between the future (and still only potential) signing of SALT II and the parallel movement toward China. Part of the discussion centered on the domestic "benefits" of pursuing one issue before the other, but the main arguments focused on the Soviet Union. For example, when discussing other means to improve relations with China short of normalization, Michel Oksenberg stated:

It may be possible to expand our relations with China independent of normalization, but if one is worried about SALT and about playing upon Moscow's deepest fears, then those are the measures that would do the trick.

Deputy Assistant Secretary of State for East Asia and Pacific Affairs Richard Holbrooke went a step further:

In talking about the Soviet Union and China, the president has two objectives: to reach a SALT agreement and to normalize relations with the PRC. Our objective

---

[52] Memorandum for Zbigniew Brzezinski from Mike Armacost, "Africa and SALT," February 17, 1978, JCL, NSC files, Country files Africa, box 2, folder Africa, 1–3/78.

should be to recreate the phenomena of 1971–1972, when moves toward both the Soviet Union and China were seen as reinforcing and were seen as politically helpful pursued together.

Secretary of Defense Harold Brown's comments confirmed the need to revive triangular diplomacy. As in 1971–1972, it was important for the United States to simultaneously move forward on both fronts:

> The key here is that we must remain less at odds with China and the Soviet Union than they are with each other.... Put it this way, if we sign SALT and there is not movement on China, then our posture toward the two will be out of kilter.[53]

Accordingly, in the following months, Carter tried to reestablish the strategic triangle by simultaneously pushing both the China normalization process and the conclusion of SALT II. As illustrated above, in May 1978 the president approved Brzezinski's trip to Beijing and, thereafter, followed the unfolding of the negotiations which led to recognizing the People's Republic of China. At the same time, the president searched for agreement in SALT. Despite a series of letters focusing on the Horn of Africa crisis, and an interruption in the personal correspondence between the two leaders, in September 1978 Carter wrote to Brezhnev and expressed his "distress" that bilateral relations had not "developed well." He avoided repeating the causes of tension, or restating their divergent positions. Instead, the president refocused on SALT:

> I do not believe either of us can afford to forget how much responsibility is in our hands for issues vital to the peace and well-being of hundreds of millions of our fellow human beings. I am sure we both agree that our first and most important objective should be to seek to bring these SALT negotiations to a successful conclusion – one that will strengthen the security of both our countries, and of all countries.[54]

The renewed emphasis on SALT yielded results. In November– December 1978, the SALT II negotiations made concrete progress and the two sides made tentative plans for a summit meeting in mid-January 1979, during which the new treaty would be signed.[55] The joint American-Chinese communiqué of December 15, 1978, on normalization was thus issued at a moment when the long-sought first summit meeting between

---

[53] Memorandum of Conversation, Summary Minutes of the April 11, 1978 Meeting on Korea and China, JCL, DHM-BC, Subject file, box 36, folder Serial Xs – (8/77–8/78).

[54] Letter from Carter to Brezhnev, September 2, 1978, JCL, DHM-BC, Geographic file, box 18, folder USSR – Carter/Brezhnev Correspondence (1/78–12/78).

[55] Garthoff, *Détente and Confrontation*, 683, 903; Brzezinski, *Power and Principle*, 325–331.

Carter and Brezhnev seemed to be imminent. Therefore, as long-time US diplomat and writer Raymond Garthoff put it, while "China card I" – the May 1978 Brzezinski trip – was developed in response to the Soviet actions in Ethiopia, "China card II" – the announcement of normalization – was played in close connection to the final stages of SALT II. Carter intended to maintain pressure on Moscow, in the belief that he could simultaneously pursue, and successfully conclude, both SALT II and the normalization with China. According to Brzezinski, "an agreement with the Soviets to limit strategic weapons, undertaken in the context of a decade-long Soviet effort to gain parity" had to be accompanied by "parallel efforts to improve the US geopolitical and strategic position."[56] This was, in essence, the same rationale that had shaped Nixon and Kissinger's triangular diplomacy in 1971–1972.

In reality, the path toward the signing of SALT II proved to be still more complex. The two sides failed to agree on means to verify the compliance with the limits of SALT. This was a crucial issue for Washington in the context of the future ratification process of the treaty by the US Senate. Moreover, the December 15, 1978, announcement on US-China normalization surprised the Soviets and the summit with Deng Xiaoping in January 1979[57] (followed by the Chinese invasion of Vietnam)[58] inevitably complicated the prospect of Brezhnev's visit to the United States.[59] During his week-long tour of the United States, Deng visited Washington, Atlanta, Houston, and Seattle producing scenes that until a few years earlier were unimaginable for a Chinese leader. He dined with the leaders of Coca Cola, PepsiCo, and General Motors, shook hands with a basketball team and attended a rodeo in Texas. Throughout the visit, Deng stressed China's need to acquire modern technology and develop its economy. The Chinese purpose of further and unequivocally distancing itself from

---

[56] Brzezinski, *Power and Principle*, 330.
[57] The Chinese vice-premier and his wife paid the first official Chinese visit to the United States from January 28 to February 5, 1979.
[58] After months of increased tension, due to reciprocal accusations of illegal occupation of frontier territories, the Chinese troops entered Vietnam on February 17, 1979.
[59] Interestingly, the various accounts on the impact of the announcement on normalization greatly differ. Vance underlines that the announcement had a negative impact on the Soviets and thus on the evolution of SALT, Vance, *Hard Choices*, 111–112. Dobrynin instead pointed out that it was the dispute over telemetry encryption, and not the announcement on normalization, that prevented the signing of SALT II in late 1978. Both assistant secretary of state for political and military affairs Leslie Gelb and member of the CIA Robert Gates agreed; Kaufman, *Plans Unraveled*, 139.

the Soviet Union by underscoring the realignment with the United States could hardly be concealed.[60]

For the United States the events unfolding in Iran (assessed in the next chapter) were directly related to SALT, because the overthrow of the shah deprived Washington of technical intelligence collection stations in Iran that constituted an important national means of verification (thus further stressing the need to include verification measures in the text of the treaty). However, despite the difficulties and the generally perceived increased tension in the US-Soviet bilateral relationship, the Carter-Brezhnev summit eventually did take place in Vienna.[61] The SALT II Treaty, and the various protocols and statements connected to the agreement, were signed on June 18, 1979.

The agreement provided for an equal aggregate limit on the number of strategic nuclear delivery vehicles – ICBM and SLBM launchers, heavy bombers, and air-to-surface ballistic missiles. Initially, this ceiling would be 2,400, as agreed at Vladivostok. It would then be lowered to 2,250 at the end of 1981. The number of land-based ICBMs could not exceed 820, the total of land- and submarine-based MIRVs could not exceed 1,200, and the total of land-based missiles, submarine-launched missiles, and heavy bombers equipped with MIRVs could not exceed 1,320.

While there were additional sub-limits, the aggregate numbers (2,400 and 1,320) and the provisions on the heavy bombers were based on the Vladivostok framework. Additional limits included a maximum of ten warheads on any new type of ICBM and ceilings on launch weight and the throw weight of strategic ballistic missiles.

The treaty was accompanied by various additional documents. The protocol covered the cruise missile issue, banning, until December 31, 1981, the deployment of land- or sea-based cruise missiles with a range over 600 km. There was also the Soviet statement on the Backfire in

---

[60] Kissinger, *On China*, 360–367.
[61] It is interesting to note that in outlining for the president the various agreements and decisions to be made in Vienna, Brzezinski pointed to the necessity of "making clear" that the United States had vital interests at stake in the Persian Gulf and Arabian Peninsula and "will act firmly and expeditiously to protect them." According to Brzezinski, Carter had to underline that Soviet, or Soviet-supported attempts, to destabilize the region would be firmly countered by Washington. The president approved; Memorandum for the President from Zhigniew Brzezinski, "Decisions on Summit Objectives," May 24, 1979, JCL, DHM-BC, Subject file, box 20, folder Alpha Channel (Miscellaneous) – (5/79–8/79). Even at the summit, the United States therefore intended to make clear that the signing of SALT did not signify a diminished determination to resist actual or perceived challenges in regions considered vital to American security and to the stability of the West.

which Moscow declared that it was of medium range, that there was no intention of upgrading it to long-range capability, and that its production rate would not exceed thirty per year. Lastly, there was the joint statement on the importance of proceeding with further negotiations, i.e. SALT III.[62]

By the time of the Vienna summit in mid-1979 the Carter administration had definitely taken a different line of action compared to the one proclaimed when entering office, completing the change initiated in 1978 with the Horn of Africa and China normalization policies. By Carter's mid-term, there were no more doubts in Washington that US-Soviet relations were dominated by geopolitical competition. At the same time, the priority given to the signing of SALT II confirmed that continued cooperation in the limitation of nuclear arms was still a vital necessity. Once again, competition and cooperation characterized America's complex Soviet policy.

The climate of 1979 sharply contrasted with the euphoria of 1972, when SALT I had been signed at the Moscow summit. Domestically, President Carter had to overcome the opposition not only to the SALT II Treaty but to the fact of having agreed to meet Brezhnev, a gesture dubbed as appeasement to Soviet aggressiveness and expansionism.[63] Some media comments of the time on the Vienna summit were cautiously optimistic, underlining the importance of the renewed "realistic approach" and future prospects of cooperation.[64] Others, instead, stressed that unlike in the previous US-Soviet summits, Carter and Brezhnev had only signed agreements on arms control (while more general documents on cooperation in various fields were only discussed).[65]

---

[62] The account here is only a summary of the provisions considered more important. For the complete text of the Treaty, of the Protocol, and of the various understandings and joint statements: Strobe Talbott, *Endgame*, 295–326 (Appendix). For a summary of the SALT II package: www.state.gov/www/global/arms/treaties/salt2-1.html.
[63] William Safire, "Stumbling at the Summit" in the *New York Times*, June 18, 1979. Dobrynin also describes the US domestic opposition to the Carter-Brezhnev summit, which Senator Jackson had compared to Chamberlain's meeting in Munich in 1938 to appease Hitler; Dobrynin, *In Confidence*, 422.
[64] See, for example, Flora Lewis's Special to the *New York Times* of June 19, 1979, titled "Beyond the Vienna Meeting. Mood of the Talks was Mature and the Prospect for Cooperation Appears Good on Several Points."
[65] Bernard Gwertzman, "US Abandons Hopes of Signing More Accords at the Vienna Meeting" in Special to the *New York Times*, June 9, 1979.

The Soviet advances in Africa, the absence of high-level summit meetings (prior to Vienna), and the disputes over human rights in the Soviet Union in fact gave the impression that arms control was the only surviving pillar of US-Soviet détente. This was, to a large extent, true. However, the reading of US-Soviet détente set forth in the first part of this book unveiled that even at the height of détente the geopolitical competition had, in reality, never subsided. The different atmosphere notwithstanding, the central feature of US-Soviet cooperation had always been strategic arms limitation. When the signing of SALT I was juxtaposed to the timing and scope of Nixon's Iran visit in 1972 (Chapter 4), the cooperation/competition dynamic, in fact, surfaced fully. Curiously, SALT II also came to be intertwined with the developments taking place in Iran. Indeed, when Carter and Brezhnev signed the SALT II Treaty in Vienna, the United States was in the midst of a serious, and under various aspects unprecedented, geopolitical challenge: revolution in Iran.

11

The Loss of Iran

> All bilateral relationships have a history, some good, some bad. Certain relationships have too much history, mostly bad, and, unfortunately, I think the US-Iranian relationship may well fall into that category.
>
> William L. Nash, April 16, 2009

> Turkestan, Afghanistan, Transcaspia, Persia – to many these names breathe only a sense of utter remoteness or a memory of strange vicissitudes and of moribund romance. To me I confess, they are pieces of a chessboard upon which is being played out a game for the dominion of the world.
>
> G. N. Curzon, *Persia and the Persian Question*, 1892

Although America's conventional long-range strike capabilities in the Persian Gulf had always been limited, until the late 1970s, Washington did not perceive this vulnerability as a constraint to policy making, nor as thwarting the protection of American interests in the region broadly defined as Southwest Asia. In fact, until the late 1960s, the British presence had ensured preponderant Western influence and, later, American allies had guaranteed US security interests on the basis of the Nixon doctrine. Moreover, after the 1973 October War, the American position in the Middle East was strengthened, while Soviet influence was reduced. Anwar El Sadat's initiative for peace further diminished Moscow's presence and role in the region, as Egypt clearly moved toward the West.

As illustrated in Chapter 9, Soviet advances in Ethiopia had aroused deep concerns in Washington and had contributed to triggering the shift in President Carter's approach to the management of the relationship with the Soviet Union (which then led to the rapid normalization of relations with the People's Republic of China). However, American confidence had not been shaken to the point of considering a basic reformulation of policy toward the Persian Gulf. A direct US presence and the enunciation of a firm commitment to the defense of the pro-Western orientation of the region had not been deemed necessary.

A fundamental element of America's strategy, which contributed to maintaining cautiously optimistic assessments despite the escalation of Soviet activities, was the reliance on the shah of Iran as the cornerstone of regional stability. The framework of close US-Iranian ties built by President Nixon and described in Chapter 4 had, in fact, remained the central element in the making and implementation of American policy. Consequently, Washington felt compelled to adjust its posture only after the main pillar upon which the United States had founded its entire strategy started to crumble.

"THE ISLAND OF STABILITY": US-IRANIAN RELATIONS, 1972–1978

Despite the inauguration of three different American administrations, between 1972 and 1978 Washington's relations with Iran continued to evolve on the basis of the framework outlined by President Nixon during his May 1972 trip to Tehran. Concrete follow-up was given to the commitment to the closest possible relationship with the shah and the policy of almost unrestrained arms sales gradually became an established course of action. When Ford succeeded Nixon as president in 1974, the main foreign policy lines of his predecessor were maintained. And, significantly, the election of Jimmy Carter in 1976 did not bring about major changes in Washington's relationship with Iran.

At the beginning of the second Nixon administration, the policy charted in May 1972 was underscored. In early 1973 the president briefed the future US ambassador to Tehran, Richard Helms, by stressing the crucial importance of having the "best possible understanding" with the shah and of a "strong Iran."[1] Accordingly, when the Iranian leader visited the United States in July 1973, the commitments on arms sales made the previous year were restated and enlarged.[2] In general, the importance of

---

[1] Memorandum for the President from Henry Kissinger, "Meeting with Richard Helms Oval Office," February 13, 1973, National Archives (hereafter NA), Nixon Presidential Materials (hereafter NPM), National Security Council (NSC) files, Country Files – Middle East, box 602, folder Iran Vol IV, Sept 71–Apr 73.

[2] James Bill, *The Eagle and the Lion. The Tragedy of American-Iranian relations* (New Haven, CT: Yale Univesity Press, 1988), 204.

Iran for US foreign policy was confirmed by the American leadership's continued openness in disclosing elements of its broader strategy toward the Soviet Union. During the July conversations with the shah, Nixon and Kissinger again stressed the importance of understanding the rationale behind America's policy and underlined that détente with Moscow did not entail a diminished determination in defending the US position in the Middle East.³ Moreover, following the commitment of the previous year, by the summer of 1973 American "blue suiters" were arriving in Iran in significant numbers, thus expanding the US presence in the country. While on his part the shah constantly updated his package of requests for the additional acquisition of weapons, in Washington this, as stated by an NSC official, was no longer considered "an issue."⁴

Therefore, by 1973 the massive investment in the modernization and unprecedented numerical increase of the Iranian military forces proceeded at full speed and was no longer seriously challenged by the American leadership. Furthermore, with the rapid increases in the price of oil following the October War, this policy became all the more sustainable for Iran. With considerably inflated revenues, in fact, the shah seemed to be able to afford all the purchases he desired. And, in the midst of widespread concern regarding the hemorrhage of dollars exiting the United States to pay for Middle Eastern oil, few in Washington resented the return of those dollars as payments for US-produced weaponry.⁵

When Gerald Ford entered the White House in 1974, he immediately embraced continuity. Only a few days after Nixon's resignation, Ford and Kissinger met with the Iranian ambassador and reaffirmed the "warm friendship and close cooperation with Iran." The incoming president stressed that a strong and stable Iran was the "key to the stability of the oil-rich Persian Gulf region" and a fundamental element of American foreign policy. Despite successive disagreements on the determination of the price of oil, the US-Iranian relationship remained absolutely crucial.⁶ Consequently,

---

³ Memorandum for Kissinger from Harold Saunders, "Your meeting with Ambassador Helms," July 23, 1973, National Archives NA, NPM, NSC files, Country Files – Middle East, box 603, folder Iran vol V, May 73–Dec 73.
⁴ Memorandum for Kissinger from Harold Saunders, "Your meeting with Iranian Ambassador Zahedi," July 16, 1973, NA, NPM, NSC files, Country Files – Middle East, box 603, folder Iran vol V, May 73–Dec 73.
⁵ Kenneth M. Pollack, *The Persian Puzzle. The Conflict between Iran and America* (New York: Random House, 2004), 109.
⁶ Memorandum of meeting with Iranian Ambassador Zahedi, August 21, 1974; Briefing material for President, August 17, 1974, Gerald Ford Library (hereafter GFL), NSC files, Presidential Country Files for the Middle East and South Asia, box 12, folder Iran (1).

American arms sales continued to contribute to the unparalleled expansion of the Iranian military forces. According to historian James Bill, between 1972 and 1978, the "transfer of arms from America to Iran took place at levels never before known in international political history." The Iranian defense budget increased from 1.4 billion dollars in 1972 to 9.4 billion in 1977 (an increase of 680 percent).[7] By 1977, half of the total American arms sales were destined for Iran.[8]

The Nixon and Ford administrations implemented this line of action in order to defend US vital national interests in the context of America's global Cold War posture. However, these policies did not always receive unanimous consensus in the United States. In 1973, for example, Secretary of Defense James Schlesinger insisted that the shah needed more trained personnel to help him maintain and absorb his arsenal, while definitely not requiring additional weaponry. Unwilling to simply accept the "avalanche of military sales" he had inherited, Schlesinger sought (however unsuccessfully) to introduce some caution and initiated a (never to be completed) review of the overall US military supply relationship with Iran.[9] Moreover, by late 1974 the arms sales policy toward Iran started to encounter increasing criticism and resistance from members of Congress. In early 1975, Senator Fulbright and Congressman Long requested copies of the memorandums of Nixon's May 1972 conversations with the shah, but were not granted access to the documents (considered to still have sensitive information that was likely to be misinterpreted).[10] A year later, in February 1976, the concern about the intensity of America's military cooperation with Iran prompted the initiation of a study memorandum to assess the situation, a study never completed during the Ford administration and that was passed on to the Carter presidency.[11] Specifically, the advocates of restraint cited Iran's difficulty in absorbing the equipment

---

[7] Bill, *The Eagle and the Lion*, 202.
[8] Pollack, *The Persian Puzzle*, 108.
[9] Gary Sick, *All Fall Down. America's Tragic Encounter with Iran* (New York: Penguin Books, 1986), 18.
[10] Memorandum for Kissinger from Richard T. Kennedy and Robert B. Oakley "Congressional requests for 1972 memorandums on arms sales to Iran," December 13, 1974, GFL, NSC files, Presidential Country Files for the Middle East and South Asia, box 12, folder Iran (2).
[11] This was NSSM 238, reviewed by the incoming Carter administration in January 1977; Memorandum, State Department, Stephen Palmer to various addresses at State "NSSM 238" (US Security toward the Persian Gulf), January 25, 1977; Cold War International History Project (hereafter CWIHP), "The Carter Administration and the 'Arc of Crisis' 1977–1981," Declassified Documents prepared for A Critical Oral History Conference, The Woodrow Wilson Center July 25–26, 2005.

as a major problem (in fact, it was on the basis of this reservation that sales had been limited before 1972). Most importantly, the critics of the Iran policy pointed to the proliferation of DOD units in Iran and to America's remarkably high visibility, which could have potentially negative repercussions.[12]

Despite these dissenting voices, Washington's policy toward Iran did not change. The fact that Henry Kissinger briefed the shah on a regular basis on almost all the most sensitive issues concerning American foreign policy – the evolution of the relations with China, the discussions with the Soviet leaders, the developments in Ethiopia and Angola – confirms the exceptionally close ties between the US secretary of state and the Iranian leader.[13] Overall, American interests in Iran remained vital. The country's stabilizing role in the region, its oil production, its willingness to host intelligence facilities and the market it provided for US equipment were all elements that recommended a continuation of the policy outlined in 1972.[14] Therefore, the American leadership avoided the cancellation or delay of arms deliveries in order not to damage the relationship with the shah.

This was the well-established policy inherited by Jimmy Carter in 1976. And, contrary to the promise of leading the country in a "new direction" and the declared "absolute commitment" to the promotion of

[12] Memorandum for Brent Scowcroft from Clinton E. Granger, "Your meeting with Eric VonMarbod," January 21, 1976, GFL, NSC files, Presidential Country Files for the Middle East and South Asia, box 13, folder Iran (8); Memorandum to the Secretary from Alfred L. Atherton, Jr. "Sale to Iran of 150 F-16s," July 29, 1976, Ibid, folder Iran (11).

[13] Department of State Telegram from SecState to Embassy Tehran, "Information for Shah on Iraq and Ethiopia," November 1974, GFL, NSC files, Presidential Country Files for the Middle East and South Asia, box 13, folder Iran – State Department Telegrams from SecState Nodis (1); Department of State Telegram from SecState to Embassy Tehran, "Message to Shah on Peking Talks," December 1974, Ibid, box 13, folder Iran – State Department Telegrams from SecState Nodis (2); Department of State Telegram from SecState to Embassy Tehran, "Message to Shah on Moscow Talks," January 1975, Ibid, box 14, folder Iran – State Department Telegrams from SecState Nodis (4). Exchanges of letters between President Ford and the shah reveal potential cooperation also on the peaceful use of nuclear energy; Letter from the Shah to President Ford, March 4, 1976, GFL, NSC files, Presidential Country Files for the Middle East and South Asia, box 13, folder Iran (9). In 1974, the United States had in fact signed a ten-year agreement to supply Iran with enriched uranium (Iran cooperated on nuclear issues also with France, Canada, and Britain), Ali M. Ansari, *Confronting Iran. The Failure of American Foreign Policy and the Next Great Crisis in the Middle East* (New York: Basic Books, 2006), 64.

[14] Briefing material for President, August 17, 1974, GFL, NSC files, Presidential Country Files for the Middle East and South Asia, box 12, folder Iran (1).

human rights worldwide,[15] Carter's Iran policy was remarkably similar to the one of his so-bitterly criticized predecessors.[16] Also Carter demonstrated that he assigned more importance to American national security interests than to the values and principles posed at the center of his electoral platform: In fact, neither the declared objective of opposing human rights abuses, nor the stated intention to focus on the local causes and dynamics of upheavals in the Third World, thwarted the development of US-Iranian ties. Despite the growing instability of the shah's regime, which faced inflation, unemployment, and increasing criticism from many sectors of the civil society, during the first year of the Carter presidency the close ties between Washington and the Iranian leader were repeatedly underscored. As a result, the shah's preoccupations that Carter's human rights campaign would negatively impact on the development of the US-Iranian relationship rapidly subsided.[17]

Instead of pressing on Iran's poor human rights record, American officials emphasized the tentatively more liberal path recently undertaken by the Iranian leader. Seeking to ensure the continuation of the Pahlavi dynasty (his son was only sixteen years old) and in part responding to growing international criticism that created embarrassment to the regime, the shah had in fact introduced a series of policies geared toward a gradual liberalization. These included the selected release of political prisoners, the loosening of censorship, and the invitation to major international human rights groups to enter Iran (the International Red Cross, Amnesty International, and the International Commission of Jurists). Although these measures were initiated before Jimmy Carter's election and were motivated by increased domestic pressure, the incoming US president's rhetoric may have reinforced the shah's commitment to reform.[18]

---

[15] Gaddis Smith, *Morality, Reason and Power. American Diplomacy in the Carter Years* (New York: Hill and Wang, 1986), 6–7.
[16] On continuity and change during the Carter administration: Scott Kaufman, *Plans Unraveled. The Foreign Policy of the Carter Administration* (DeKalb, IL: Northern Illinois University Press, 2008), 5–27.
[17] President Carter's human rights rhetoric had put the shah on the defensive, inducing him to show some signs of reform. In mid-1976, during the US presidential campaign, the shah took tentative steps to loosen his repressive regime, freeing some political prisoners. However, the pressure that the Iranian leader resented never came. After assuming office, the new administration did not make human rights an issue in its policy toward Iran; Patrick Tyler, *A World of Trouble: The White House and the Middle East from the Cold War to the War on Terror* (New York: Farrar, Straus and Giroux, 2009), 219.
[18] Bill, *The Eagle and the Lion*, 219–226; Pollack, *The Persian Puzzle*, 121; Sick, *All Fall Down*, 26–27.

The Loss of Iran

These encouraging signs from Iran allegedly justified the Carter administration's choice not to press on human rights issues. In reality, however, the American policy line was determined by other, more tangible, concerns. According to the president's chief adviser on Iran, Gary Sick, "the overriding consideration for US policy was to ensure that the cooperative relationship that had been developed over nearly four decades would be preserved and that Iran would remain a strong, reliable and friendly ally in the vital region of the Persian Gulf. The importance of the security relationship was paramount – even if that relationship should require some accommodation in the areas of human rights or arms limitations."[19] In essence, therefore, the Carter administration shared the notion of Iran as a major force for stability and chose not to let the question of human rights take precedence over vital security interests. Moreover, Tehran's moderating role on establishing the price of oil added another factor to its strategic importance, an element that had become all the more important in the second half of the 1970s.[20] Hence, the Carter presidency embraced continuity. Simply put, the defense of American national security did not allow other courses of action.

Consequently, during his first year in office, President Carter signaled his intention of maintaining a constructive relationship with Iran. When Cyrus Vance visited Tehran in May 1977, he emphasized the "strong desire to continue very close ties." In order to reassure the shah that there would be no significant change in the US-Iranian relationship, Vance specified that the president's announcement of a "new policy of restraint" designed to reduce the transfer of arms was a long-term objective and was not directed against any one country. On human rights, the secretary of state simply "noted" that this issue was important for the United States and referred to the encouraging steps taken by Iran. In concrete terms, Vance stressed that the United State intended to honor its commitments toward friends and allies. There were no illusions in Washington regarding the "basically antagonistic policies of the USSR."[21] Specifically, the secretary of state informed the shah of the decision to proceed with the sale of F-16 aircrafts and of the president's intention to seek approval for the sale of sophisticated airborne warning and control systems (the AWACS).[22]

---

[19] Sick, *All Fall Down*, 28.
[20] Bill, *The Eagle and the Lion*, 226.
[21] Briefing Paper, State Department, "The Secretary's Meeting with the Shah of Iran," May 13, 1977, CWIHP, "The Carter Administration and the 'Arc of Crisis' 1977–1981," Declassified Documents prepared for A Critical Oral History Conference, The Woodrow Wilson Center July 25–26, 2005.
[22] Bill, *The Eagle and the Lion*, 227; Sick, *All Fall Down*, 28.

In the summer and fall of 1977, Carter continued to convey signs of support for the shah, especially concerning arms sales. Although the administration's publicly stated objective was to seek the reduction of the transfer of US weapons, it soon became evident that Iran was an exception. The president's energetic backing of the AWACS sale, amid the opposition in Congress and charges of inconsistency, together with the approval of an additional package of F-16s, demonstrated the importance he assigned to guaranteeing a "strong Iran." Therefore, the Carter administration was also careful in not alienating the shah who, on his part, continued to employ the tactic of threatening to turn "elsewhere" should his requests for arms be denied.[23] While on the one hand Carter tried to advocate that the "days of the blank checks were over," on the other, he personally approved billions of dollars of additional arms sales. As the *New York Times* reported, "Jimmy Carter, like his predecessors, cannot say no."[24] This sent an unmistakable message that the administration "intended no dramatic shift away from the security relationship with Iran."[25]

During the shah's visit to Washington in November 1977, the president again acknowledged the special relationship with Tehran and outlined an understanding on the need to continue to satisfy Iranian defense needs. It is interesting to note that while the shah and his wife were being welcomed at the ceremony taking place on the White House lawn, thousands of Iranian students loudly demonstrated in the areas surrounding the White House. The police used tear gas to dispel the protests causing

---

[23] Bill, *The Eagle and the Lion*, 231; Sick, *All Fall Down*, 29. It is interesting to note that when William Sullivan arrived in Iran as the new US ambassador in June 1977, the message conveyed to the shah was along the same lines: he underlined the importance of Iran for US interests in the Gulf, the continued importance of US access to intelligence facilities, and that there was no objection in Washington to the selling of nuclear plants to Iran for the peaceful use of nuclear energy.

[24] Richard Burt, "Curb on Arms Exports Runs into Obstacles and May Not Survive Beyond 1978" in Special to the *New York Times*, Feb. 13, 1978.

[25] Sick, *All Fall Down*, 31. It is important to note that with PD-13 Carter decided that, after May 1977, all arms sales cases would be reviewed personally by the president. Therefore, there can be no doubts about the president's knowledge of the arms sales policy toward Iran. Gregory F. Treverton illustrates the apparent contradiction in Carter's posture by on the one hand stating that "campaign promises – to reduce arms sales and to emphasize human rights – dominated Washington's relations with Tehran during the first year of the Carter administration" while on the other stressing that "the human rights issue lay dormant" in the first year of the administration; Gregory F. Treverton, "Iran, 1978–1979: Coping with the Unthinkable" in Ernest R. May and Philip D. Zelikow (eds), *Dealing with Dictators: Dilemmas of U.S. Diplomacy and Intelligence Analysis, 1945–1990* (Cambridge: The MIT Press, 2006), 113–114.

The Loss of Iran 251

embarrassment to the Carters and the Pahlavis, who had to hurriedly retreat inside. This incident notwithstanding, the shah's visit proceeded as planned and was considered a diplomatic success by both sides.[26] In essence, it reinforced the administration's pro-shah posture. President Carter then paid a return visit to Tehran in late December 1977.[27]

The timing of what would be the last visit to Iran by an American president dramatically revealed the flawed perceptions, within the United States, on the Iranian domestic turmoil and on the capacity of the shah to maintain control over the internal opposition. Carter flew to Tehran and praised the shah right when his leadership was confronted with increasing antagonism. On December 31, 1977, the US president toasted to the coming of the New Year by stating:

> Iran under the great leadership of the Shah is an island of stability in one of the more troubled areas of the world. This is a great tribute to you, Your Majesty, and to your leadership, and to the respect, admiration and love which your people give to you.[28]

A week later, protests in the city of Qum were crushed by the shah's police, killing dozens of people. After this event, the antiregime demonstrations multiplied in all major Iranian cities and the violence escalated, without interruption, until early 1979.

"THE SHAH WAS IRAN AND IRAN WAS THE SHAH"

With hindsight, the misjudgments of the Carter administration on the internal dynamics of the Iranian regime are particularly evident. While some intelligence reports did point out that the violence in Iran was the "most serious of its kind in a decade,"[29] the briefing materials for Carter's

---

[26] Cyrus Vance, *Hard Choices. Critical Years in America's Foreign Policy* (New York: Simon and Schuster, 1983), 321–322. On the events that took place during the shah's visit to the White House, Vance stated: "these demonstrations ... perhaps foreshadowed the resurgent opposition to the shah that was to dominate the following year in Iran. In hindsight, some analysts of the revolution were to call attention to these demonstrations as one of the early signs of the ferment that was to produce the revolution." Clearly, however, at the time the events unfolded, the American leadership decided not to investigate into their motivations and implications.

[27] Bill, *The Eagle and the Lion*, 227–233.

[28] Cited in Bill, *The Eagle and the Lion*, 233.

[29] Analysis, State Department Bureau of Intelligence and Research, January, 29, 1978, CWIHP, "The Carter Administration and the 'Arc of Crisis' 1977–1981," Declassified Documents prepared for A Critical Oral History Conference, The Woodrow Wilson Center July 25–26, 2005.

last visit to Tehran in no way suggested the potentially imminent collapse of the shah's regime. On the contrary, the majority of the comments and analyses received throughout 1977 simply reflected the by then established view on the stability of Iran – a view that the Carter foreign policy team chose not to question. This acceptance at "face value" was to leave the administration "singularly unprepared as the façade of Iranian 'stability' crumbled with astonishing speed over the following twelve months."[30]

Yet, it is important to underline that the almost unanimous view in the United States that identified the stability of Iran with the continuation of the shah's rule was by no means characteristic only of the Carter administration.[31] It had, in fact, been a distinctive feature of US policy toward Tehran for decades. This, in turn, had led to the constant and repeated overlooking of the Iranian leader's problematic management of his domestic affairs. From the mid-1950s onward, the concern with the Soviet Union and the increased importance of oil had gradually outweighed all other considerations.

In fact, during the Eisenhower administration the aid programs to Iran had primarily focused on military assistance,[32] despite assessments that stressed the need for social and economic reform lest the potential overthrowing of the shah (who had only just returned to power).[33] Between 1953 and 1961, the Iranian military forces expanded substantially and, concurrently, the American military presence in Iran became increasingly visible.[34] In particular, the ties between Washington and Tehran were strengthened after the 1958 coup in Iraq, which led to the overthrow of the monarchy and to the end of the close association between Baghdad and the United States. The notion of Iran as an anti-Soviet strategic ally took hold in Washington and, in March 1959, the United States and Iran signed a bilateral defense agreement.[35]

---

[30] Sick, *All Fall Down*, 35.
[31] Gary Sick in fact uses the expression "The shah was Iran and Iran was the shah" to convey the sense that Washington saw no alternatives to the shah's rule in Iran; Sick, *All Fall Down*, 35.
[32] Ansari, *Confronting Iran*, 41; Pollack, *The Persian Puzzle*, 79.
[33] In 1958, for example, a CIA study assessed that the shah would be overthrown if he did not initiate a process of internal reform. In 1961, the assessments made for the incoming Kennedy administration viewed a revolution as "imminent"; Bill, *The Eagle and the Lion*, 125–126, 135–136.
[34] By 1956, in fact, Iran hosted the largest US military mission in the world; Pollack, *The Persian Puzzle*, 76–77.
[35] Pollack, *The Persian Puzzle*, 79–80; Bill, *The Eagle and the Lion*, 119.

The Loss of Iran

The emphasis on security was not, however, unanimously viewed with favor in Iran. American aid programs were seen as incrementing the corruption of the regime. And, while the military forces expanded, the social and economic conditions of the majority of the Iranian people did not improve.[36] In the early 1960s, the Kennedy administration sought to introduce a different policy toward Iran, advocating internal development, social and economic reform over outright military assistance. The United States thus cautiously favored the so-called White Revolution initiated by the shah – a broad, wide-ranging program intended to transform and modernize the Iranian society and economic structure.[37]

But the shah's reform programs did not have a positive domestic impact. Raising the expectations of the population while not producing the intended results, these policies only provoked further protests and deepened the fissure between the regime and the society. Moreover, the United States, viewed in Iran as intrinsically related to the monarchy and to its failed promises, increasingly emerged as a target of the antiregime demonstrations.[38] With the Johnson administration entangled in Vietnam and less concerned about the shah's management of his internal affairs, the Iranian leader tightened his repressive measures. This, in turn, inevitably produced louder protests and demonstrations (and, giving voice to the religious opposition, Ayatollah Khomeini emerged as a leading figure). In January 1965, Prime Minister Hassan Ali Mansur was killed and later that year the shah himself survived an assassination attempt (the investigation later pointed to the left-wing middle class intellectual opposition to the regime).

---

[36] Bill, *The Eagle and the Lion*, 115. The focus on military aid and the expansion of the American presence in Iran gave rise to increasing anti-American sentiments; Ansari, *Confronting Iran*, 43–45.

[37] The program included land reform, nationalization of forests, the sale of state-owned enterprises, profit sharing in industry, and electoral rights for women. In 1963, anti-shah riots and demonstrations were repressed by an increasingly autocratic regime. It is important to note that Ayatollah Khomeini was among the leading protesters and was exiled in 1964; Bill, *The Eagle and the Lion*, 132–182; Pollack, *The Persian Puzzle*, 80–100. For more details on the White Revolution: Rouhollah K. Ramanzani, "Iran's White Revolution: A Study in Political Development," *International Journal of Middle East Studies*, Vol. 5, No.2 (Apr. 1974). On the Kennedy administration and the White Revolution: Roland Popp, "Benign Intervention? The Kennedy Administration's Push for Reform in Iran" in Manfred Berg and Andreas Etges (eds), *John F. Kennedy and the 'Thousand Days.' New Perspectives on the Foreign and Domestic Policies of the Kennedy Administration* (Heidelberg: Universitätsverlag Winter, 2007).

[38] Ansari, *Confronting Iran*, 47–48.

These events, which evidently revealed the increase of the Iranian domestic unrest, could have – and should have – been warning signs for the United States. But they were not. In the early 1970s, the Nixon administration not only continued to develop the relationship with Iran but, as illustrated in Chapter 4, decisively and irrevocably strengthened the partnership with the shah. There is ample evidence that between 1969 and 1972 some reports on the instability in Iran had reached the US leadership. They were, however, repeatedly disregarded.

In February 1970, for example, American ambassador to Tehran Douglas MacArthur cabled Washington on riots and clashes of protesters against the government but, at the same time, claimed that these did not affect the shah's popularity.[39] Later that year, the ambassador himself was the target of an attack. The incident, deliberately kept secret, revealed the by then tangible anti-Americanism present within Iranian society.[40] Significantly, the shah pointed to communist infiltrations among students as responsible for the abduction attempt on the US ambassador.[41] In May 1971, MacArthur again reported student demonstrations against the shah and the "White Revolution" and stated that these protests were becoming more frequent and increasingly radical. While outside interference may have contributed to instigate them, according to the ambassador the complaints centered on the inequality of the regime and emerged, for the most part, from within the country.[42] Conversely, a month earlier, in a private conversation with President Nixon, MacArthur had praised the shah's rule as "strong" and "sound" and optimistically assessed the results of his "great social revolution."[43] The disparity between the optimistic though at times ambiguous assessments on the American part and the evolution of the local instability is, therefore, evident.

Numerous reports on popular discontent in Iran continuously arrived, up until a few weeks before Nixon's decisive visit of May 1972.

---

[39] Telegram 668 From Embassy in Tehran to the Department of State, February 24, 1970, Foreign Relations of the United States (hereafter FRUS), Foreign Relations, 1969–1972, Volume E-4, Iran and Iraq, Doc. No. 49.

[40] Telegram 5142 From Embassy in Iran to the Department of State, December 1, 1970, FRUS, Foreign Relations, 1969–1972, Volume E-4, Iran and Iraq, Doc. No. 102.

[41] Ibid.

[42] Airgram 136 From the Embassy in Iran to the Department of State, May 10, 1971, FRUS, Foreign Relations, 1969–1972, Volume E-4, Iran and Iraq, Doc. No. 126.

[43] Conversation Among President Nixon, Ambassador Douglas MacArthur II and General Alexander Haig, Washington, April 8, 1971, FRUS, Foreign Relations, 1969–1972, Volume E-4, Iran and Iraq, Doc. No. 122.

In January 1972, bombs exploded outside the US mission in Tehran.⁴⁴ A month later, a situation report described more protests and dissatisfaction with the Iranian government. Complaints focused on the cost of food, the conviction and execution of protesters, and the corruption of the regime.⁴⁵ In addition, Washington received assessments that stressed the increased separation between the shah and his population.⁴⁶ Nonetheless, the American leadership continued to consider Iran an "island of stability in an otherwise unstable area."⁴⁷ On this basis, Nixon proceeded to further and decisively strengthen the special link with Tehran.

Washington's apparent disconnection from reality can be partially explained by the particular nature of the US-Iranian relationship which, though tight and positive, was for the shah never considered as entirely reliable. If on the one side the Iranian leader was indebted to the United States/CIA for restoring him to power in 1953, on the other he remained suspicious that, should the domestic situation appear uncontrollable, Washington might decide to intervene also against him. Thus, the shah not only wanted to strengthen his country's military, which would allow as much margin of independence as possible, but also maneuvered to isolate American officials from the Iranian population and civil society. Consequently, the volume of CIA political reporting on internal developments in Iran during the early 1970s dropped below that of the late 1940s. The US embassy in Tehran had few officials who could speak Farsi, or who had had previous experience in Iran.⁴⁸ In late 1976 a CIA human resources committee report pointed to the need for "additional information and field analysis as to how decisions are formed in Iran"

---

⁴⁴ Telegram 331 From the Embassy in Iran to the Department of State, January 17, 1972, FRUS, Foreign Relations, 1969–1972, Volume E-4, Iran and Iraq, Doc. No. 161. Moreover, up until Nixon's visit, the administration was receiving assessments which increasingly pointed to the separation between the shah's leadership and his population; Memorandum From the Director of Central Intelligence (Helms) to the President's Assistant for National Security Affairs (Kissinger), Washington, May 8, 1972, FRUS, Foreign Relations, 1969–1972, Volume E-4, Iran and Iraq, Doc. No. 190.

⁴⁵ Telegram 1218 From the Embassy in Iran to the Department of State, February, 29, 1972, FRUS, Foreign Relations, 1969–1972, Volume E-4, Iran and Iraq, Doc. No. 168.

⁴⁶ Memorandum From the Director of Central Intelligence (Helms) to the President's Assistant for National Security Affairs (Kissinger), Washington, May 8, 1972, FRUS, Foreign Relations, 1969–1972, Volume E-4, Iran and Iraq, Doc. No. 190.

⁴⁷ Memorandum for the President from Henry A. Kissinger, "Military Sales Credit for Iran," April 16, 1970, NA, NPM, NSC files, Country files – Middle East, box 601, folder Iran Vol. I (1 of 3).

⁴⁸ Pollack, *The Persian Puzzle*, 106.

and, in general, on the Iranian domestic situation.[49] In short, as later admitted by Secretary of State Cyrus Vance, the American knowledge of the opposition to the shah was "sketchy."[50]

The misperceptions and erroneous judgments of the Iranian internal turmoil became all the more manifest in the late 1970s. At the beginning of the Carter administration, the State Department Bureau of Intelligence and Research assessed the Iranian domestic situation as follows:

> Iran is likely to remain stable under the shah's leadership over the next several years, and committed to its relationship with the US as long as the shah rules. The prospects are good that Iran will have relatively clear sailing until at least the mid-1980s, when oil production will probably slow and when the shah says he will step aside in favor of the crown prince.

Despite the fact that "small extremist groups" were likely to continue their attacks on the regime, including assassination attempts against Americans, in general the opposition was considered "more a state of mind than a readiness to act."[51] Along the same lines, in August 1977 the CIA concluded a sixty-page study with the statement that "the shah will be an active participant in Iranian life well into the 1980s" and that "there will be no radical change in Iranian political behavior in the near future."[52] Exactly a year later, a fire broke out at the Cinema Rex in the Iranian city of Abadan, killing hundreds of people. This episode marked the escalation of the popular protest against the regime. In response, the shah tightened his fist and in early September 1978 declared martial law, cracking down on the demonstrators. Hundreds were killed on what became known as "black Friday," today considered a turning point in the unfolding of the Iranian revolution.[53]

In a study compiled immediately after the violence of "black Friday" the American Defense Intelligence Agency (DIA) stated:

---

[49] Report, CIA Human Resources Committee, "FOCUS Iran: An Intelligence Community Review of Reporting by Human Resources from the United States Mission in Iran," November 4, 1976, CWIHP, "The Carter Administration and the 'Arc of Crisis' 1977–1981," Declassified Documents prepared for A Critical Oral History Conference, The Woodrow Wilson Center July 25–26, 2005.

[50] Vance, Hard Choices, 316.

[51] Report, State Department Bureau of Intelligence and Research, "The Future of Iran: Implications for the U.S.," January 28, 1977, CWIHP, "The Carter Administration and the 'Arc of Crisis' 1977–1981," Declassified Documents prepared for A Critical Oral History Conference, The Woodrow Wilson Center July 25–26, 2005.

[52] Quoted in Bill, The Eagle and the Lion, 258.

[53] Tyler, A World of Trouble, 220–221.

Despite the clear danger to the shah's position posed by continuing unrest, we believe that since he has the support of Iran's military leaders and of much of Iran's educated elite that his regime will survive.

According to the Defense Intelligence analysts, the imposition of martial law had restored a degree of order. The shah was taking steps to "come to terms with the religious leaders" and was encouraging more participation by the educated and moderate forces in the political life of the country. For these reasons, they confirmed that "the regime has a better than ever chance of surviving the present difficulties and the shah will probably be able to maintain his position through the early 1980s."[54] This was the general assessment of the intelligence community. Accordingly, in November 1978, Brzezinski wrote in his weekly report to the president: "Good news! According to a CIA assessment ... Iran is not in a revolutionary or even a pre-revolutionary situation."[55]

It is thus not surprising that President Carter's public statements were along the same lines. On December 12, 1978, he stated: "I fully expect the shah to maintain power in Iran and for the present problems in Iran to be resolved."[56] A month later, on January 16, 1979, the shah left Iran, never to return. From the American standpoint, the "island of stability" had suddenly and unexpectedly crumbled.

FAILING TO "THINK THE UNTHINKABLE"

The existing accounts of US policy during the Iranian turmoil, while differing in attributing greater responsibilities to one or the other component of the administration,[57] unequivocally unveil Washington's inability to conceive alternatives to the shah's rule. The American stance during

---

[54] Report, Defense Intelligence Agency, "Assessment of the Political Situation in Iran," September 1978, CWIHP, "The Carter Administration and the 'Arc of Crisis' 1977–1981," Declassified Documents prepared for A Critical Oral History Conference, The Woodrow Wilson Center July 25–26, 2005.

[55] Memorandum for the President from Zbigniew Brzezinski, "NSC Weekly Report #78," November 3, 1978, Jimmy Carter Presidential Library (hereafter JCL), Donated Historical Material – Brzezinski Collection (hereafter DHM-BC), Subject file, box 42.

[56] Quoted in Bill, *The Eagle and the Lion*, 259.

[57] For example, Sick justifies the NSC's shortcomings by stressing that the pattern of US-Iranian relations was so well established that it was difficult to outline alternatives; Bill stresses the fact the opinions of mid-level specialists at the State Department, who had foreseen the instability of the shah's rule, were disregarded; Treverton accuses Sullivan of inconsistency and attributes the administration's difficulties in outlining a coherent posture to his changing assessments.

the crisis, up until a few days before the shah's departure from the country, remained one of support for the Iranian leader. Yet, even this position was not unambiguous. When forced to chose between sponsoring a repression or accepting the transition to a new government (initially intended as provisional), the divisions within the administration became manifest and, in essence, paralyzed the presidency's promptness to respond. Consequently, the United States failed to envision specific countermeasures during the Iranian upheaval and simply reacted afterwards, to the unanimously perceived loss of a crucially important strategic ally.

There were, however, individuals close to the administration that, stressing the intricate complexity of Iranian internal dynamics, cautiously suggested a gradual shift in US policy. These unorthodox voices principally came from Ambassador William Sullivan in Tehran, long-time US diplomatic adviser George W. Ball, and country director for Iran at the State Department Henry Precht. In February 1978, for example, Ambassador Sullivan sent a cable to Washington entitled "Iran: Understanding the Shi'ite Islamic Movement." Although stating that the assessment was based on "incomplete evidence," the cable underlined that the Islamic movement dominated by Ayatollah Khomeini was "far better organized, enlightened and able to resist communism" than its detractors led the United States (and the West) to believe. In fact, it was "rooted in the Iranian people more than any Western ideology, including communism."[58] The cable therefore indirectly warned against taking the potential penetration of Soviet influence for granted. In August 1978, Sullivan again wrote to Washington and advocated support for the shah's decision to "transform his authoritarian regime into a genuine democracy." According to Sullivan, the Iranian leader had come to realize that the only way to preserve the integrity of his country was to change its political system, even if this would put the monarchy at risk. At the same time, the ambassador pointed to the intricate Iranian political scene and to the uncertain reaction of the opposition. In fact, stated Sullivan, should the fabric of the society disintegrate, the shah may return to impose strict political controls. This had happened in the past and the United States had assisted in the reestablishment of "internal security." If this time Washington wanted the shah to maintain his "democratic decision"

---

[58] Cable, American Embassy Tehran to State Department, "Iran: Understanding the Shi'ite Islamic Movement, " February 3, 1978, CWIHP, "The Carter Administration and the 'Arc of Crisis' 1977–1981," Declassified Documents prepared for A Critical Oral History Conference, The Woodrow Wilson Center July 25–26, 2005.

then ways to sustain his efforts had to be found.[59] As we now know, a month after this cable was sent the Iranian leader ordered a forceful reaction against the antiregime demonstrations. In sum, as historian James Bill puts it, after having slightly opened the political door, the shah then "slammed it shut again."[60] And the United States simply watched.

In November 1978, as the violence and disorder in Iran escalated, Sullivan sent another cable to Washington which was later labeled as "one of the most important US policy documents to be produced in the course of the revolution."[61] In the telegram emblematically titled "Thinking the Unthinkable" Sullivan once again, and more explicitly, called for "some fundamental examinations of the situation in Iran" and of the future of US-Iranian relations. In doing so, the ambassador suggested that it would be "healthy" for the American leadership to examine some options never before considered feasible. The confidence in the shah (together with the military establishment's ability) to face down the Khomeini threat was still regarded as "obviously the only safe course to pursue." However, should this line of action fall short, Washington needed to "think the unthinkable" and respond with a coherent policy that would protect vital US interests. In particular, the ambassador stated that a future Iranian government composed by moderate (noncommunist, non-Islamic) political figures could be considered an essentially "satisfactory one," especially if the military would preserve its integrity and status as one of the "pillars" of the country. Significantly, in his considerations, Sullivan stressed that both the Iranian armed forces and the Khomeini Muslims were strongly anticommunist and anti-Soviet – "we say this despite reports of alleged communist infiltration of Khomeini's circle of advisers," he then added.[62]

During the same months a more systematic proposal on a new policy toward Iran came from George W. Ball. Responding to President Carter's request for analysis on the Iranian situation, in December 1978 Ball submitted an eighteen-page study called "Issues and Implications of the Iranian Crisis" in which he argued that the shah's authoritarian

---

[59] Telegram, William Sullivan to Cyrus Vance and Zbigniew Brzezinski, "Recommendation for President to Shah Letter," August 29, 1978, CWIHP, Ibid.
[60] Bill, *The Eagle and the Lion*, 226.
[61] Sick, *All Fall Down*, 94.
[62] Cable, William Sullivan to State Department, "Thinking the Unthinkable," November 9, 1978, CWIHP, "The Carter Administration and the 'Arc of Crisis' 1977–1981," Declassified Documents prepared for A Critical Oral History Conference, The Woodrow Wilson Center July 25–26, 2005.

rule had no chance of being restored. Therefore, Ball recommended that the United States aid Iran in the formation of a broad coalition government. Washington had to propose the creation of a so-called Council of Notables composed of members not associated with the regime that the United States would "suggest" to the Iranian leader. In the process, Washington had to continue to publicly emphasize the importance of the shah's role as a symbol of unity and continuity, but in private the Iranian leader had to be pressured to transfer his power and, at a minimum, create a constitutional monarchy. At the same time, Ball proposed to open a channel of communication with the opposition led by Ayatollah Khomeini.[63]

The recommendations compiled by Henry Precht at the State Department went a step further. According to his assessment, the shah had "only a marginal chance of survival even as a constitutional monarch. No one," he stated, "believes he can return to the exercise of full power, the shah himself has acknowledged this privately." For this reason, Washington had to begin taking concrete measures toward a "post-shah future in Iran," which included contacting the opposition. Precht in fact challenged the generalized assumption that only the shah assured stability vis-à-vis the Soviet Union and that all other alternatives would be destabilizing for the region and for the United States. Therefore, he urged Washington to move rapidly to regain its influential position in Iran, a position seriously weakened because of the "delayed perceptions, hesitancy to make hard choices" and the "unwavering support for the shah."[64]

Ultimately, however, these recommendations, themselves written with tardiness, were not taken into serious consideration by the administration. With a series of high-level initiatives climaxing at approximately the same moment – the finalization of the SALT II Treaty and the normalization of relations with China, but also the Camp David negotiations – the crisis in Iran did not receive high-level attention until late 1978 (it is important to note that Ambassador Sullivan had left Iran for a prolonged period of time during the summer of 1978. This was indicative of the pervasive feeling of no imminent crisis). Moreover, and most significantly, the American position was shaped by the generalized and deeply rooted

---

[63] Report, George Ball to President Carter (with cover memo "Summary Memorandum for the President"), "Issues and Implications of the Iranian Crisis," December 12, 1978, CWIHP, Ibid.
[64] Letter, Henry Precht to Harold Saunders, "Seeking Stability in Iran," December 19, 1978, CWIHP, Ibid.

assumption that for the United States there were no other options than the support for the Iranian monarch. As stated by Gary Sick: "The US relationship with the shah was so deeply ingrained in the minds and policies of everyone responsible that even a carefully reasoned expression of doubt was regarded as a heresy that could destroy a career – hence the immense reluctance to 'make the call' by proclaiming the shah irreparably wounded."[65]

The position of almost one-sided support for the shah was ardently advocated by the National Security Council in general, and by Zbigniew Brzezinski in particular. Like the other members of the administration, Brzezinski had only gradually come to realize the gravity of the Iranian situation. However, he remained convinced throughout the crisis that with a hard-line approach and a tough response from the shah the opposition to the regime would eventually be scattered. Furthermore, despite the reports that indicated that there was no evidence of communist penetration in the religious opposition to the regime, the NSC adviser continued to assess the Iranian upheaval almost exclusively in terms of the potential Soviet-sponsored leftist threat. And considering that by mid-1978 Brzezinski's position within the administration had become dominant, it is not surprising that his views overwhelmingly shaped Carter's stance throughout the Iranian crisis.

In a letter to the shah in late September 1978 (i.e., after the Jaleh Square Massacre), Carter wrote:

Again, let me extend my best wishes to you as you continue your successful effort for the beneficial social and political reforms in Iran. All of us recognize the great benefits to our own nation and to the world of a strong and progressive Iran.

In the second part of the letter, Carter mentioned the importance of the shah's support for the Camp David accords, suggesting that the president's attention focused more on this initiative than on the developments taking place inside Iran.[66] When in November 1978 the White House finally convened an SCC meeting on the Iranian crisis, the president endorsed support for the shah "without reservation."[67] Provoking Ambassador Sullivan's distressed reaction, no serious effort was made

---

[65] Sick, *All Fall Down*, 142.
[66] Letter, President Carter to the Shah, "Personal Note to the Shah," September 28, 1978, CWIHP, "The Carter Administration and the 'Arc of Crisis' 1977–1981," Declassified Documents prepared for A Critical Oral History Conference, The Woodrow Wilson Center July 25–26, 2005.
[67] Sick, *All Fall Down*, 79–80.

to contact the opposition, or to chart a future course which excluded the shah.⁶⁸

At the same time, however, the American leadership hesitated in "going all the way," that is, in sponsoring the restoration of order with a violent repression. When, in late December 1978, the shah asked Washington if it would support the creation of a new military government that would initiate a policy of "brutal repression," the US leadership ambiguously replied that it "could not make such a decision for Iran."⁶⁹ Therefore, despite Brzezinski's insistence, in the end Carter did not totally embrace the hard-line approach. The president failed to provide clarity, thus contributing to the overall confusion and paralysis that characterized the last few weeks of the Pahlavi rule.⁷⁰

Ultimately, the American posture throughout the Iranian crisis was hesitant and ineffective. Despite the questionable wisdom of the unwavering support for the shah, if this was the chosen policy line (and ample evidence points to the fact that it was), then Washington was incapable of sustaining it because no credible attempt was made to bolster the shah's capacity to resist (although it is seriously debatable whether outside intervention could have made any significant impact on the unfolding of the revolution). If, instead, the choice of non-intervening to "save" the shah was deliberate, then the policy failure is all the more palpable since no efforts were made to conceive alternatives that would protect America's vital interests in Iran after the departure of the shah. Moreover, and most significantly, these shortcomings are all the more evident when the policy maintained during the crisis is juxtaposed with

---

⁶⁸ Sullivan cabled Vance in January 1979 and did not conceal his resentment: "You should know that the President has made gross and perhaps irretrievable mistake by failing to send emissary to Paris to see Khomeini as previously agreed – I can not RPT not understand the rationale for this unfortunate decision"; Telegram, William Sullivan Eyes Only for Cyrus Vance, "USG Policy Guidance," January 10, 1979, CWIHP, "The Carter Administration and the 'Arc of Crisis' 1977–1981," Declassified Documents prepared for A Critical Oral History Conference, The Woodrow Wilson Center July 25–26, 2005. Sullivan's attitude in turn provoked Carter's angry reaction. The president reportedly told Vance to "get Sullivan out of Iran," but the secretary persuaded him that it would be a mistake to put in a new ambassador at such a critical mement. Sullivan thus remained in Tehran, but Carter's confidence in him was greatly reduced; Sick, *All Fall Down*, 161.
⁶⁹ Memorandum, Cyrus Vance to President Carter, excerpt from "Evening Reading," December 26, 1978, CWIHP, "The Carter Administration and the 'Arc of Crisis' 1977–1981," Declassified Documents prepared for A Critical Oral History Conference, The Woodrow Wilson Center July 25–26, 2005.
⁷⁰ Tyler, *A World of Trouble*, 225–226.

the stance taken in its immediate aftermath. In fact, once the potentially global consequences of the loss of Iran became manifest, America promptly and forcefully reacted.

THE LOSS OF IRAN

According to Brzezinski, "Iran was the Carter administration's greatest setback. The fall of the shah was a disaster for the United States strategically and politically for Carter himself." The US national security adviser then softened the tone by adding: "Perhaps that disaster was historically inevitable, the Islamic fundamentalist wave too overpowering."[71] Setting aside the task of determining the "inevitability" of the revolution[72] – a questionable exercise in itself after the course of events – in this context it is important to underline that, as the instability of the regime finally became manifest, Washington viewed the Iranian upheaval almost exclusively within the framework of the Cold War. Notwithstanding Brzezinski's reference to the "Islamic fundamentalist wave," the analysis of the administration's policies confirms that the focus of attention was on the global repercussions of the "setback" (i.e., on the Soviet Union) and not on the evolution of internal dynamics (which, with hindsight, proved to have much more far-reaching implications than the Soviet threat). In other words, President Carter, in line with his predecessors, considered Iran a key cornerstone of regional stability. His predetermined priority was set on defending a solid anti-Soviet strategic ally. Consequently, when this proved to be impossible, the administration adjusted its posture with a process that eventually led to the proclamation of the Carter doctrine in 1980.

Between 1978 and 1979 it is unquestionable that the NSC's, and to a large degree Brzezinski's, views swayed US-Iranian policy. But these were far more successful in charting America's comprehensive response to the perceived setback than in designing a coherent policy toward Iran. The global picture evidently dominated and overshadowed the local reality. On this point, some of the NSC's internal assessments are revealing. In December 1978, Brzezinski pointed to an area that he defined as "the arc

---

[71] Zbigniew Brzezinski, *Power and Principle. Memoirs of the National Security Adviser, 1977–1981* (New York: Farrar, Straus and Giroux, 1983), 354.
[72] For a comprehensive study of the internal causes of the Iranian Revolution: *Charles Kurzman, The Unthinkable Revolution in Iran* (Cambridge, MA: Harvard University Press, 2004).

of crisis"⁷³ and referred to the situation in Iran with extreme concern, drawing a parallel with the late 1940s:

> There is no question in my mind that we are confronting the beginning of a major crisis, in some ways similar to the one in Europe in the late 40's. Fragile social and political structures in a region of vital importance to us are threatened with fragmentation. The resulting political vacuum might well be filled by elements more sympathetic to the Soviet Union.... If the above analysis is correct, the West as a whole may be faced with a challenge of historical proportions.⁷⁴

According to Brzezinski, such momentous developments required a major adjustment of policy, entailing long-term solutions as well as more direct security commitments. At the end of 1978, he associated the events in Iran with those in Afghanistan (where the Communist Party – the PDPA – had established a democratic republic with explicit close links to the Soviet Union), and called for a comprehensive American response:

> With regards to the arc of instability along the Indian Ocean, we need to respond collectively.... The disintegration of Iran, with Iran repeating the experience of Afghanistan, would be the most massive American defeat since the beginning of the Cold War, overshadowing in its real consequences the setback in Vietnam.⁷⁵

Evidently, the Soviet-centric view of world affairs, initially criticized and repudiated, came to dominate Carter's policy choices. Consequently, while wavering in the face of the Iranian internal turmoil, the administration promptly formulated wide-ranging countermeasures in the broader context of US-Soviet relations. From Washington's standpoint, the fall of the shah not only deprived the United States of its main strategic "pillar" in the Persian Gulf but also signified the impossibility of maintaining intelligence surveillance stations to monitor military developments in Soviet territory, sites that had been considered irreplaceable by the American intelligence community.⁷⁶ No other country could replace Iran

---

⁷³ Brzezinski used this expression to define the area of concern: "If you draw an arc on the globe, stretching from Chittagong [Bangladesh] through Islamabad to Aden, you will be pointing to the area of currently our greatest vulnerability," Memorandum for the President from Zbigniew Brzezinski, "NSC Weekly Report #81," December 2, 1978, JCL, DHM-BC, Subject file, box 42.
⁷⁴ Ibid.
⁷⁵ Memorandum for the President from Zbigniew Brzezinski, "NSC Weekly Report #83," December 28, 1978, JCL, DHM-BC, Subject files, box 42.
⁷⁶ For example, director of the CIA Richard Helms stated in the early 1970s: "Ruling out Afghanistan as politically unfeasible, there is no place to which we could transfer these activities were Iran denied us. In time we hope that some of the important coverage now obtained from Iran can be picked up by overhead sensors, but for some years

The Loss of Iran

in guaranteeing Western influence in the region.[77] Therefore, the United States needed to broadly rethink its role. With the prospect of no longer being able to rely on Iran, Washington had to enhance its own direct presence and military capabilities in the Gulf, assuming directly the responsibility previously devolved to the shah.

In February 1979, only a few weeks after the departure of the Iranian leader and with the future of US-Iranian relations still to be defined, Secretary of Defense Brown's statements disclosed the shift in America's policy:

> We have made a policy decision about a more active role in the area. We told these countries things that they have not heard for a long time – namely, that the United States is deeply interested in the Middle East, we are very worried about what the Soviets are doing, we intend to be involved. That's a line no American administration has taken with them since Vietnam.[78]

A few days later, Brown announced on television that the United States would be prepared to defend its vital interests in the Middle East with whatever means appropriate, including military force.[79]

In his March 1979 report to the president, Brzezinski again outlined the unfavorable (from the American point of view) developments in the so-called arc of crisis:

> The coup in Afghanistan, the Soviet-Cuban presence in Ethiopia, and improved communist party position in South Yemen open up the possibility of new Soviet threats not only to Iran but also to smaller Persian Gulf States, Saudi Arabia, and North Yemen. As the surprisingly rapid disintegration of the Pahlavi regime in Iran indicates, all of these states are likely subjects for political instability, which could offer the Soviets various opportunities to expand their influence.

---

ahead the ground based facilities will remain absolutely essential if we are to keep our knowledge of the Soviet programs up to date"; Memorandum From Harold Saunders of the National Security Council Staff to the President's Assistant for National Security Affairs (Kissinger) Washington, April 16, 1970, FRUS, Foreign Relations, 1969–1972, Volume E-4, Iran and Iraq, Doc. No. 63. Saunders forwarded Helms's memorandum to Kissinger.

[77] The other regional "pillar," Saudi Arabia, was not deemed capable of exercising the role played by Iran because it lacked the military infrastructure and technical expertise and had a ruling family fearful of building a strong military that could endanger the authority of the regime; Charles A. Kupchan, *The Persian Gulf and the West. The Dilemmas of Security* (Boston, MA: Allen and Unwin, 1987), 70–71.

[78] *International Herald Tribune*, February 20, 1979.

[79] Secretary Brown on CBS News, *Face the Nation*, February 25, 1979, cited in Kupchan, *The Persian Gulf and the West*, 85.

And, most significantly, Carter's national security adviser spelled out a comprehensive US strategy to prevent Moscow's potential advancement into the region, which included:

1. continued efforts to maintain as much access as possible to current regimes in Ethiopia and Afghanistan (as well as Iraq and South Yemen);
2. clarification of US interest in the stability of the area and of the seriousness with which we could view any Soviet efforts to expand their influence in pro-Western countries;
3. technological assistance and political support designed to strengthen current pro-Western regimes in the area;
4. rapid implementation of the PD-18[80] provisions concerning a quick reaction force;
5. increasing US military presence in the Persian Gulf area;
6. reconstitution of CIA covert action capabilities in the area.[81]

Reflecting on Brown's and Brzezinski's words, two elements emerge with clarity. First, the repeated references to Vietnam confirm the almost exclusive focus on preventing another major US foreign policy setback, exclusively assessed in terms of the bipolar competition. The Soviet Union took center stage in the remaking of American policy. Secondly, both the commitment to a greater involvement in the region, potentially entailing a military presence, and the strategy outlined by Brzezinski in the six points illustrated, anticipated the definite shift of policy made public in early 1980 with the Carter doctrine. Therefore, America's basic reformulation of policy was triggered by the realization of the loss of the partnership with Iran, while the Soviet invasion of Afghanistan simply confirmed Washington's perception of geostrategic vulnerability.[82]

In the administration's internal assessments (and in its public pronouncements) no reference was made to the long-term implications of the birth of the Islamic Republic, despite the fact that the unfolding of events should

---

[80] This refers to Presidential Directive 18 on the necessity of greater deployment capabilities for distant military intervention which dated back to August 1977, but was never implemented; Raymond Garthoff, *Détente and Confrontation. American-Soviet Relations from Nixon to Reagan* (Washington, DC: The Brookings Institution, 1994), 733.

[81] Memorandum for the President from Zbigniew Brzezinski, "NSC Weekly Report #92," March 30, 1979, JCL, DHM-BC, Subject file, box 42.

[82] This argument will emerge in full in the next chapter, which traces the evolution of the Carter doctrine. See also Olav Njolstad, "Shifting Priorities: The Persian Gulf in US Strategic Planning in the Carter Years" in *Cold War History*, Vol. 4, No.3 (April 2004), 21–55.

have imposed a reflection on the deeply rooted anti-Americanism of the new regime. Although Khomeini was an outspoken anticommunist (as well as antiimperialist), the American leadership continued to disregard the local component and remained predominantly focused on Moscow's potential advancement into the Persian Gulf. The anti-Soviet dimension clearly shaped America's shift in policy, while specific countermeasures toward the emergence of Islamic fundamentalism were not conceived.[83]

The words later written by Cyrus Vance confirm the almost unanimous bias of American foreign policymakers. Despite having led the State Department, the one institution which had tried to educate the American leadership on the intricate complexity of Iranian affairs, and having distinguished himself as one of the members of the administration most sensitive to considering issues in their own right and not as elements to be manipulated in the confrontation with the Soviets, Vance stated:

> At this writing [in 1983], an evaluation of the long-term consequences of the Shah's fall cannot be made. That will depend on what happens in the power struggle that is likely to follow the death of Khomeini. If a durable, non-Communist regime emerges, it is probable there will be an improvement in US-Iranian relations based on our common interests in a secure, united and prosperous Iran. If, however, Iran slides into a civil war, the temptation will exist for the Soviet Union to fish in the troubled waters ... If this should happen there would be grave danger of a US-Soviet confrontation.[84]

As we now know, a durable noncommunist regime did consolidate itself in Iran and there (happily) never was a US-Soviet confrontation. However, after more than three decades, American-Iranian relations have yet to concretely improve.

Reflecting on the inglorious US policies toward Iran is, still today, a particularly difficult task. To a certain degree it is understandable that the accounts of this troubled period would seek to justify the policy failures of 1979 by attributing greater responsibilities to one or the other of the

---

[83] It is interesting to note that even in the commentary of the time on the Iranian crisis there was little or no emphasis on the potentially grave repercussions of the Islamic anti-Americanism that was taking hold in Iran. In assessing the "Struggle in Iran" for example, one article points to the preoccupation that massive amounts of US weaponry sold to Iran not end up in Soviet hands as a consequence of the revolution: James Reston, "The Struggle in Iran" in the *New York Times*, Dec. 15, 1978. Also in an article which questions "Who Lost Iran" – and that criticizes US one-sided support for the shah – no reference is made to the strong religious forces which toppled the shah: Anthony Lewis, "Who Lost the Shah" in the *New York Times*, Jan. 1, 1979.

[84] Vance, *Hard Choices*, 348.

protagonists. This, however, risks precluding the possibility of a deeper understanding of America's shortcomings. Perhaps, one should try to look beyond the responsibilities of the NSC and/or the merits of the State Department (or vice-versa) in order to disclose the broader significance of the American incapacity to effectively deal with the Iranian turmoil. The divisions within the administration and a general indecisiveness clearly thwarted the making of a coherent Iranian policy throughout the crisis. However, these did not hinder the subsequent decisive reformulation of policy that took place between 1979 and 1980. In other words, the American leadership was uncertain and hesitant in charting its approach toward the local context but was able, with much less difficulty, to redefine its global posture in the aftermath of the crisis. This contrast unveils an important characteristic of US foreign policy. As a result, the Iranian debacle becomes particularly significant in understanding America's more general exercise of its global power.

The shah's leadership had, for decades, been able (and willing) to guarantee the defense of vital American and Western interests. For this reason, US relations with Iran gradually became identified with the relationship with the shah. After the turning point represented by Nixon's 1972 visit, the shah's Iran became the reference point for America's entire security framework in the Persian Gulf. It is not surprising, therefore, that the reports on the instability of the Pahlavi regime, together with those pointing to the potentially negative repercussions of such high American visibility in Iran, were constantly and repeatedly disregarded. The US leadership wanted and needed to rely on the shah. In this, the Carter administration's position was by no means different from that of the Nixon and Ford presidencies.

At the same time, the importance of Iran as an anti-Soviet asset in the region distorted America's capacity to acutely assess the complex internal grievances against the rule of the shah. The religious opposition, that ultimately provided the gravest challenge for the survival of the regime, was clearly an inscrutable reality for the American leadership. Despite the studies which pointed against evidence of communist infiltration, the prevailing vision in Washington was that if Khomeini's movement were to succeed, then Iran would be open to the advancement of Soviet influence.[85]

---

[85] For example, a CIA assessment of January 1979 stated that "the religious leadership still appears to exercise the greatest degree of influence, but it is certain that radical leftists and the Tudeh Party will make every effort to take advantage of the situation to improve their position. The longer the current crisis continues the more likely it becomes that the radicals will gain in influence"; Intelligence Memorandum, CIA National Foreign

In other words, the Islamist fundamentalist threat was unknown to the United States. The recognized and recognizable enemy was and remained the Soviet Union. The only accepted notion was one of a bipolar world – in which there were two, not more, geopolitical entities.

One particular example illustrates, with emblematic clarity, the overall predisposition of American foreign policy, by no means characteristic only of the Carter administration. In September 1970 (and, curiously, on the same day, September 2nd) Henry Kissinger received two memorandums from the then director of central intelligence Richard Helms. In one memo, Helms forwarded to Kissinger a copy of an August 1970 CIA study on "Student Unrest Abroad" featuring a chapter on Iranian domestic disorder. A note on the attached routing slip read: "There seems no reason for HAK [Kissinger] to read or reply to this. It is much like *Time* and *Newsweek* cover stories. No action required."[86] In the second memorandum, Helms underlined the crucial importance of US intelligence facilities in Iran that monitored Soviet territory. With reference to the decision on the sales of aircrafts to the shah (which was then pending), Helms requested that no action be taken by the US government that would put these facilities in jeopardy. On the side of this memo, Kissinger wrote: "Make sure that this is followed."[87] The side notes on these memos unequivocally disclose Washington's order of priorities.

The Nixon and Ford administrations' (and Kissinger's in particular) indifference to the internal dynamics of countries has been well emphasized by scholars, even by those less critical of Kissinger. Recently, a review of the book on Kissinger by Alistair Horne (*Kissinger: 1973, The Crucial Year*, Simon and Schuster, 2009) criticized the author for glossing

---

Assessment Center, "Iran: The Radicals in the Opposition," January 12, 1979, CWIHP, "The Carter Administration and the 'Arc of Crisis' 1977–1981," Declassified Documents prepared for A Critical Oral History Conference, The Woodrow Wilson Center July 25–26, 2005. In March 1979, a CIA alert memorandum stated that Moscow was likely to increase its covert efforts and expand contacts with the leftist factions, "while gradually becoming more open in support for Tudeh's claim to the role in the new power alignment. Should the situation degenerate into open civil war, the Soviets are likely to funnel covert support to those elements that appear most favorable to their interests, while processing nonintervention and continuing to warn the US against intervention"; Alert Memorandum, Stansfield Turner to National Security Council, "Iran," March 1, 1979, CWIHP, Ibid.

[86] Memorandum From the Director of the Central Intelligence Agency (Helms) to the President's Assistant for National Security Affairs (Kissinger), September 2, 1970, FRUS, Foreign Relations, 1969–1972, Volume E-4, Iran and Iraq, Doc. No. 84.

[87] Memorandum From Harold Saunders of the National Security Council Staff to the President's Assistant for National Secuirty Affairs (Kissinger), September 2, 1970, FRUS, Ibid, Doc. No. 85.

over Kissinger's treatment of nations like chess pieces, while seeming to respect their leaders only in so far as they could enhance American power.[88] The first part of this book confirms that this criticism of the Nixon-Kissinger-Ford years is well founded. However, the analysis of the Carter administration's initiatives points to the fact that the same basic criticism could, and should, be set forth also for the Carter years. In fact, a constructive reflection on the past should recognize that some of the basic flaws of US policy were not personal, nor were they partisan, but were general and systematic in the basic worldview that shaped American foreign policy toward many areas of the world.

From this standpoint, the Carter administration's failure in Iran emerges as much less surprising. The difficulties in understanding the local reality were (and are) a general characteristic of US policy, despite (or perhaps precisely because of) Washington's global extension. Securing primacy on the world arena was America's priority, not the building of durable domestic structures for the future. This was more than evident in America's reaction to the loss of Iran.

---

[88] *The Economist*, July 11, 2009.

12

Reaffirming Containment

The Carter Doctrine

> Since Harold Brown had gone to the Gulf, in February 1979, we had been working to augment our military power in the region ... Afghanistan and the continuing disorder in Iran were threatening the Persian Gulf security system. There was a danger of a vacuum into which Soviet power would spread toward the Indian Ocean and the Persian Gulf.
>
> Cyrus Vance, *Hard Choices*

> The president's words (the Carter doctrine) represented a formal recognition of a centrally important reality: that America's security had become interdependent with the security of three central and interrelated strategic zones consisting of Western Europe, the Far East, and the Middle East-Persian Gulf area. For me it was a particularly gratifying moment because for more than a year I had been seeking within the US government the adoption of such a policy.
>
> Zbigniew Brzezinski, *Power and Principle*

For the United States, the consequences of the Islamic revolution extended far beyond the borders of Iran. The American strategy in the entire region had been based on the premise that Iran was and would continue to be a strong and stable regional power whose policies would, despite some divergences, essentially converge with those of the United States. This assumption affected decisions on US military deployments in Asia and in Europe, weapons procurements, and long-term planning for force structure and readiness. Moreover, the relationship with Iran was inherently linked to the broad spectrum of US-Soviet relations and was, directly or indirectly, interconnected with other important American policies in the region – such as those toward Israel and the Horn of Africa. In addition, Iran was a crucial supplier of oil. Any disruption in the quantity of Iranian exports would inevitably impact on the price of oil defined by international markets, with severe repercussions particularly on Western Europe. In short, without relying on Iran "nothing less than a full-scale reconstruction of US global policies and assets would suffice."[1]

In fact, America's response to the loss of Iran was, indeed, global and comprehensive. In the months after the departure of the shah, the US position in Iran continued to worsen, making it obvious that there was no possibility of resurrecting the Nixon (and never abandoned) twin pillar strategy for the Persian Gulf. Therefore, the rethinking of America's role, triggered already in early 1979, became the Carter administration's central course of action. Then, in a context in which Washington had already initiated its basic adjustment of policy, the Soviet invasion of Afghanistan confirmed the necessity of guaranteeing the pro-Western orientation of the region. Ultimately, the president returned to place the Soviet Union at the center of US foreign policy, completing the shift initiated in 1978. The more traditional Cold War posture of the administration became public and unequivocal with the proclamation of the Carter doctrine in early 1980.

US-IRANIAN RELATIONS AFTER THE SHAH

The general ambiguity and indecisiveness of Washington's policy toward Iran continued throughout 1979. Confronted with a complex and confused internal political scene, an increasingly divided Carter administration proved unable to chart a policy that would salvage – at least partially – its vital interests in Iran. Consequently, the American leadership assisted practically unarmed in or with the radicalization of the Iranian revolutionary process, with grave long-term repercussions for the United States and, more generally, for Western security interests in the Persian Gulf.

After the departure of the shah, the National Security Council, and Brzezinski in particular, advocated support for a military coup that would reestablish order in Iran and ensure the continuation of a tight and positive relationship with the United States. According to Vance and Sullivan, instead, Washington had to support the moderate forces that had contributed to the fall of the shah. In their view, a new government, if dominated

---

[1] Gary Sick, *All Fall Down. America's Tragic Encounter with Iran* (New York: Penguin Books, 1986), 47.

by liberal and moderate forces, could be in line with US interests, despite a less tight relationship than with the Pahlavi regime.[2] In the end, neither side would be able to influence the evolution of events.

These contradictory positions notwithstanding, a general consensus did develop in Washington on the importance of maintaining the unity and stability of the Iranian military forces, considered one of the main pillars of the Iranian state. The United States feared that the domestic unrest might encourage foreign military intervention (the reference was, of course, to the Soviet Union). Moreover, the Iranian oil production and distribution facilities had to be protected from potential sabotage from either outside forces or internal radicals. In short, Washington believed that only the Iranian military forces could avoid the potential collapse of the entire political and economic infrastructure of the country.[3] Therefore, President Carter decided to send a special envoy to Iran – General Robert Huyser, then the deputy commander in chief of the American forces in Europe – with a twofold mission: "to act as a contact between the Iranian military establishment" and the US government and "to encourage the continued solidarity, readiness and operational effectiveness" of the Iranian military forces. Officially, the report on the so-called Huyser mission stated:

> In the performance of his mission, General Huyser worked toward continued Iranian military support for the legitimate government in Tehran. Until the departure of the Shah, this meant support of the Shah's efforts to structure a responsible, stable and effective civilian government. Following the Shah's departure on January 16, 1979, the legal and duly constituted government was that of Prime Minister Bakhtiar and General Huyser urged members of the Supreme Commander's Staff and other senior Iranian generals to support that administration.[4]

In reality, however, General Huyser was authorized to go much further. His instructions actually consisted of three steps:

1. encourage the Iranian military to support Bakhtiar's civilian government;

---

[2] Kenneth M. Pollack, *The Persian Puzzle. The Conflict between Iran and America* (New York: Random House, 2005), 147–148.

[3] Report, State Department, "The Huyser Mission in Iran: January 4 to February 4 1979," undated, *circa* February 1979, Cold War International History Project (hereafter CWIHP), "The Carter Administration and the 'Arc of Crisis' 1977–1981," Declassified Documents prepared for A Critical Oral History Conference, The Woodrow Wilson Center July 25–26, 2005.

[4] Ibid.

2. plan for possible direct Iranian military action if required to bolster the civilian regime;
3. support a military takeover by Iranian forces if the public order collapsed.[5]

Apart from the questionable wisdom of dispatching a military officer to Iran at the moment of greatest uncertainty of the revolution (Huyser's presence could easily – and rightly – be interpreted in Iran as a US effort to intervene in Iranian affairs), the general's assessments on the Iranian situation proved to be erroneous. Huyser returned to Washington in early February 1979 and reported that the Iranian military leaders were strong and reliable. Although the military officers "could not run Iran's complex government," Huyser believed that "they were capable of restoring order." This could be used as the "starting point in the reestablishment of a functioning government."[6] However, only days after Huyser's conversation with Carter in Washington, the military leadership appointed by the shah withdrew its forces and surrendered, marking the end of the Bakhtiar government. Once again, the United States had misjudged the dynamics of the Iranian domestic reality.

In retrospect, it seems that, once the shah's regime was lost, for Washington it appeared pointless to seriously engage a leadership already perceived as threatening and irrational.[7] Yet, during the first months of the postshah rule, the political scene in Iran was complex, confused, and uncertain.[8] From his exile in Paris, Ayatollah Khomeini had played an important role, exercising an indisputable influence on the unfolding of the revolution. Aided by his widespread and charismatic appeal, he unified the otherwise isolated antishah forces. In fact, since the shah had suppressed all forms of political opposition, the protesters had difficulty in finding a common platform. As a prominent leader of the Shiite establishment (the one opposition group that had been less uprooted by the SAVAK for fear of committing sacrilegious acts), Khomeini found a wide audience when he started to portray the Iranian situation in religious

---

[5] Sick, *All Fall Down*, 163.
[6] Ibid, 178.
[7] Ali M. Ansari, *Confronting Iran. The Failure of American Foreign Policy and the Next Great Crisis in the Middle East* (New York: Basic Books, 2006), 82.
[8] James A. Bill, *The Eagle and the Lion. The Tragedy of American-Iranian Relations* (New Haven, CT: Yale University Press, 1988), 276–277. See also Alesha Jalal, "An Uncertain Trajectory. Islam's Contemporary Globalization, 1971–1979" in Ferguson, Maier, Manela, Sargent (eds), *The Shock of the Global. The 1970s in Perspective* (Cambridge, MA: Belknap Press: 2010), 331.

terms – a world of oppressors versus the downtrodden, while calling for the empowerment of the latter. His message was simple and easily discernible by most Iranians.[9] At his return from exile, he was greeted with widespread popular enthusiasm. However, the Ayatollah's popularity did not immediately translate into unquestioned leadership of the revolutionary process. Although he ultimately did emerge as the most prominent figure of the new regime, the "campaign to gain full control over Iran's levers of power" proceeded slowly.[10]

On February 5, 1979, Khomeini appointed Mehdi Bazargan to succeed Shapour Bakhtiar as prime minister of the Provisional Government. Bazargan, as well as Abol Hassan Bani Sadr, who became Iran's first president in January 1980, were representatives of the moderate opposition to the shah. Both were Western educated politicians, well known also in the United States. Although they had "impeccable anti-shah credentials," they were at the same time seen as promoters of a liberal and democratic transition.[11] A few elements in fact suggest that in the immediate aftermath of the shah's departure, the opportunity for the United States to safeguard its relations with Iran may have existed. On February 14, 1979, a radical left-wing group attacked and seized the US embassy in Tehran. Significantly, when compared to the events of only a few months later, the clergy and Khomeini himself immediately denounced the attack and, subsequently, sponsored the liberation of the American personnel. Both the religious authorities and the Provisional Government acted to end the confrontation and to remove the activists.[12]

In March 1979, the new regime held a referendum asking whether the monarchy should be replaced by an "Islamic Republic" but the precise meaning of this concept was still unknown to the 20 million people that, with a 98 percent vote, responded "yes."[13] In the following months, an assembly of experts was appointed to outline a new constitution, which was then approved in October 1979. In these critical months, during which the moderates may have had a chance to emerge as the leaders of the new Iran, Washington's policy remained ineffective. Hindered by a superficial understanding of the events, the American leadership made

---

[9] Amin Saikal, "Islamism, the Iranian revolution, and the Soviet invasion of Afghanistan" in Leffler and Westad (eds), *The Cambridge History of the Cold War* (Cambridge, England: Cambridge University Press, 2010), 119.
[10] Pollack, *The Persian Puzzle*, 152.
[11] Bill, *The Eagle and the Lion*, 263–270.
[12] Ansari, *Confronting Iran*, 84.
[13] Pollack, *The Persian Puzzle*, 152–153.

some unfortunate decisions that, in essence, contributed to plummeting US-Iranian relations to a point of no return.

Between the spring and the fall of 1979, the United States did establish contacts with the members of the Provisional Government and discussed the possibility of improving relations with high-level Iranian officials. For example, in April 1979, the outgoing chargé d'affaires of the US embassy in Tehran, Charles Naas, met with the Iranian deputy prime minister, Ibrahim Yazdi, to convey Washington's "desire to normalize relations" and to "speak frankly" about the problematic state of US-Iranian relations. Naas reported his conversation in a telegram to the State Department:

Yazdi responded that one great obstacle to normalizing Iran-US ties was indeed quote your deep involvement with the previous regime unquote. He moved swiftly to more positive tack, noting that the [Iranian provisional] government is ready to normalize when US quote degree of responsiveness to correct problems of past unquote was clear. Past is past he said and Iranians are pragmatic.

The Iranian deputy prime minister also stated that the nomination of a new US ambassador (Sullivan had left Iran in April 1979) would be a very positive step, especially if he was "someone who understands the new government and the Iranian revolution." Yazdi then concluded that if some basic steps were taken, "cabinet and religious leaders, including Khomeini" would be ready for normalization.[14] During the same months, American embassy officials, on various occasions, met also with Prime Minister Bazargan.[15] The intention of improving relations was in principle stated by both sides. In reality, however, the process stalled. The Iranians expressed disappointment because "US promises had not been backed up by actions." In particular, Bazargan called for "concrete acts" on America's part to demonstrate "goodwill towards Iran."[16]

Also the new US chargé d'affaires, Bruce Laingen (who took office after Sullivan's departure and was the top US official in the absence of

---

[14] Cable, Charles Naas to State Department, "Meeting with Deputy Prime Minister Yazdi," April 25, 1979, CWIHP, "The Carter Administration and the 'Arc of Crisis' 1977–1981," Declassified Documents prepared for A Critical Oral History Conference, The Woodrow Wilson Center July 25–26, 2005.

[15] Cable, Charles Naas to State Department, "Meeting with Prime Minister Bazargan," May 6, 1979, Ibid. It is important to note that ambassador Sullivan left Iran in April 1979. Bruce Laingen then took office as the chargé d'affaires (and remained the top US official until and during the hostage crisis).

[16] Cable, Bruce Laingen to State Department, "Meeting with PM Bazargan," August 12, 1979, Ibid.

an ambassador), expressed frustration and preoccupation regarding Washington's hesitance. He realized that the United States could not remain passive and had to convey understanding and respect for the Iranian transition. For this reason, he exhorted Washington to "speak publicly and positively" about having accepted the change in Iran. "This is not to say that we have to publicly embrace and endorse Khomeini," he wrote. "What we need to say, in ways that we have not yet done, is that we have long-term interests in Iran that continue and which we believe can be preserved in an Islamic Iran." Moreover, Washington had to clearly state that it had no "interest in or intention of imposing any regime, monarchy or otherwise on Iran."[17] These recommendations were never followed.

The hesitant and inept US policy was motivated by various factors. First, as already pointed out, in Washington the overall understanding of Iranian internal dynamics was extremely limited. In July 1979, Henry Precht at the State Department once again alarmingly underlined the absence of reliable information on Iran's internal dynamics. "We simply do not have the bios, inventory of political groups or current picture of daily life as it evolves at various levels in Iran," he wrote in a letter to the US embassy in Tehran. "Ignorance here of Iran's events is massive,"[18] he added. This made it very difficult for Washington to chart effective policies in the complex Iranian scene. Secondly, the US position was complicated by the escalation of radical anti-American sentiments. A strong "undercurrent of anti-Americanism ran through revolutionary Iran," which had been fed by decades of close association with the shah. While the intensity of the feeling differed from faction to faction, it was generally present and palpable. Consequently, the "situation in Iran after the revolution was extremely sensitive and required a delicate and creative diplomatic approach."[19] A delicacy and creativeness that the US policy-makers clearly lacked.

The situation, therefore, was objectively difficult. However, the United States continued to make grave miscalculations that were to seriously worsen an already compromised position. Although the contacts with the moderate members of the Provisional Government were numerous and continuous, no links were established with the religious establishment.

---

[17] Cited in Ansari, *Confronting Iran*, 85–86.
[18] Letter, Henry Precht to Bruce Laingen, July 20, 1979, CWIHP, "The Carter Administration and the 'Arc of Crisis' 1977–1981," Declassified Documents prepared for A Critical Oral History Conference, The Woodrow Wilson Center July 25–26, 2005.
[19] Bill, *The Eagle and the Lion*, 276.

The Shiite leaders and Khomeini himself were clearly anti-American and intransigent.[20] Nevertheless, as some US officials in Washington and in Tehran pointed out, the absence of contacts with the leaders of the revolution was a serious shortcoming. In September 1979, Assistant Secretary of State Harold Saunders wrote to Cyrus Vance alarmingly stressing that Washington had "no direct contact" with the man who remained "the strongest political leader in Iran." While conceding that Khomeini's hostility toward the United States was unlikely to abate significantly and that the first contact risked being a "bruising affair," Saunders underlined that only a meeting with the Ayatollah would signal a definitive acceptance of the revolution.[21] A month later, in October 1979, Bruce Laingen cabled Washington and stressed the same basic point: America had yet to "demonstrate convincingly" that it had accepted the revolution. "No progress in building a new relationship" with Iran could be made unless the United States made concrete steps in that direction.[22] Ultimately, however, Washington never conveyed the signals that the Iranian moderates expected – no public statement of acceptance of the revolution, no admittance of past errors, no meeting with Ayatollah Khomeini and no agreement regarding the contracts for military spare parts pending at the time of the revolution (a point repeatedly raised by the Provisional Government). Yazdi would later state that the United States "never really supported us (the moderate rule). They did not give us one thing. Nothing."[23]

Moreover, in a context in which the future of US-Iranian relations remained uncertain, Washington made the decision, today considered as a grave error, of admitting the exiled shah to the United States for medical treatment. This – directly or indirectly – led to the takeover of the US embassy and to the ensuing crisis that would last until the end of the Carter administration.[24] During the 444-day-long hostage crisis

[20] Bill, *The Eagle and the Lion*, 279; Sick, *All Fall Down*, 176.
[21] Cited in Bill, *The Eagle and the Lion*, 281–282.
[22] Cable, American Embassy Tehran to State Department, "Yazdi in New York: Where Now?" October 12, 1979, CWIHP, "The Carter Administration and the 'Arc of Crisis' 1977–1981," Declassified Documents prepared for A Critical Oral History Conference, The Woodrow Wilson Center July 25–26, 2005.
[23] Interview with Ibrahim Yazdi, cited in Bill, *The Eagle and the Lion*, 282.
[24] The decision to admit the shah was based on humanitarian grounds – the former Iranian leader was seriously ill and would die of cancer in July 1980 – and on the fact that for many years he had been a close ally of the United States. However, the US leadership had been "warned" that the decision to let the shah enter the United States would create some problems for American interests in Iran. On this see, for example, Laingen's cables to Washington: Telegram, Bruce Laingen to Cyrus Vance, "Shah's Desire to Reside in the

the more radical revolutionary factions strengthened their stance while irrevocably weakening the moderates.[25] Khomeini himself, unlike in February 1979, endorsed the takeover. He publicly implicated America in the decades of "reign of terror" of the shah and found it morally justifiable and politically useful to denounce the United States as the "Great Satan." With the hostage crisis, Khomeini successfully humiliated the United States and kept the Iranian public mobilized under his leadership. He inaugurated a combative phase of the revolution, aimed at transforming Iranian politics and society according to his political Islamist vision (this phase dominated the first few years of the Islamic Republic and cost thousands of lives).[26]

In the United States, the emotional shock and public condemnation of the hostage crisis made the pursuit of improved relations with Iran extremely difficult (then and for many years to follow). In essence, the hostage crisis ended any realistic prospect of engagement with the new Iranian regime.[27] Could different American policies in the months preceding the embassy takeover have changed the course of events in Iran? This is a question that, for obvious reasons, will remain unanswered. However, the study of the choices – or nonchoices – made in Washington between February and November 1979 does convey the sense of a potential opportunity prematurely, and irrevocably, lost.

By late 1979, the Islamic character of the revolutionary process in Iran had clearly emerged. Nevertheless, influential members of the Carter administration still remained predominantly focused on the Soviet Union. On November 9, 1979 (i.e., five days after the embassy takeover and the beginning of the hostage crisis), NSC member Paul Henze wrote to Brzezinski:

I have no original thoughts to offer on how we get the hostages released and our Embassy back, but it is important to think beyond the current imbroglio and not let emotions generated during it undermine our longer-term interests in this part

---

U.S.," July 26, 1979 and Cable, American Embassy Tehran to State Department, "Shah's Illness," October 21, 1979 in CWIHP, "The Carter Administration and the 'Arc of Crisis' 1977–1981," Declassified Documents prepared for A Critical Oral History Conference, The Woodrow Wilson Center July 25–26, 2005.

[25] Pollack, *The Persian Puzzle*, 158.
[26] Saikal, "Islamism, the Iranian revolution and the Soviet invasion of Afghanistan," 121.
[27] Ansari, *Confronting Iran*, 90. On the hostage crisis: Mark Bowden, *Guests of the Ayatollah: The First Battle in America's War against Militant Islam* (New York: Atlantic Monthly Press, 2006); David Farber, *Taken Hostage. The Iran Hostage Crisis and America's First Encounter with Radical Islam* (Princeton, NJ: Princeton University Press, 2005).

of the world. If there is a leftist and/or Soviet input, directly or indirectly, into the Embassy takeover, the aim can only be to make it impossible for us to have any relations with Iran over an extended period of time.... It is in the long-term interest of the left, much more than that of the religious fanatics, to have us out of Iran entirely; but it is very convenient for the left (whether they are manipulating or influencing the situation or not) to have the religious fanatics doing their work for them.[28]

Henze's views are symptomatic of the overall Soviet-centric viewpoint of the administration. Although Moscow's role was only supposed, the American leadership assessed the events in Iran in terms of the potential for Soviet advancement. President Carter himself doubted Moscow's expressions of goodwill. In December 1979, Ambassador Dobrynin stressed that the Soviet Union's "clear and unequivocal position in connection with the conflict existing between the United States and Iran" was one which advocated a just settlement to the "mutual satisfaction of both sides." On the side of the message, Carter wrote "this is B.S."[29]

The focus on the Soviet Union had influenced the American stance throughout the entire crisis and after the departure of the shah it triggered plans on a comprehensive reaction. This may have contributed to the paralysis and ineptitude of Carter's Iran policies even after the departure of the shah. In any case, the Carter administration was far more successful in charting its global response than in responding locally to the radicalization of the revolutionary process in Iran.

THE MAKING OF THE CARTER DOCTRINE

As illustrated in Chapter 11, between February and March 1979, while the outcome of the revolution in Iran was still uncertain, in the United States the basic shift of approach had already taken place. Brzezinski in particular advocated the need for a wide-ranging US strategy to counter the Soviet Union's potential advancement into the region. In March 1979, the NSC adviser wrote (in addition to the report cited in the previous chapter) another memorandum proposing a "Consultative Security Framework for the Middle East." He underlined that the fall of the shah had added a new and dangerous dimension to the preexisting problems

---

[28] Memorandum, Paul Henze to Zbigniew Brzezinski, "Thoughts on Iran," November 9, 1979, CWIHP, "The Carter Administration and the 'Arc of Crisis' 1977–1981," Declassified Documents prepared for A Critical Oral History Conference, The Woodrow Wilson Center July 25–26, 2005.

[29] Letter, Anatoly Dobrynin to President Carter, December 4, 1979, Ibid.

in the region, creating a vacuum open to Soviet expansion. This posed a serious challenge to the United States. According to Brzezinski, the situation was as grave as in the aftermath of World War II. "Then too," he stated, "a strategically vital region faced external threat, intra-regional conflicts, socio-economic privation, and local radicalism for which US power, wealth, and leadership toward unity were the remedy."[30] He thus called for a new security framework in the Middle East in which the United States would play a leading role. This entailed a greater commitment to the region's defense, more extensive security guarantees and an increased military presence. Moreover, this shift in policy had to be unequivocal:

> To explain our new strategy toward the Middle East to friends in the region, allies, and to our own public will at some early point require a major Presidential pronouncement ... Such a statement should follow, not precede, tangible steps which demonstrate the viability of this approach."[31]

The first of the "tangible steps" that demonstrated a more assertive US role had, in effect, already been taken. In late February 1979, Carter had approved – once again contradicting the commitment to reduce arms transfers – an aid package for North Yemen designed to counter the Soviet-backed aggression of the South (the PDRY).[32] This decision was clearly linked to the departure of the shah and to the unfavorable (from the US point of view) developments in Iran.[33] Gradually, the American policy in the entire region became linked to the Iranian crisis and to the perception of a looming Soviet threat. The shift of policy toward Somalia was the most tangible sign of Washington's change of stance. The restraint in intervening directly in the Horn of Africa, which had characterized Carter's approach until 1978 (see Chapter 9), disappeared after

---

[30] Memorandum from Zbigniew Brzezinski, "Consultative Security Framework for the Middle East," March 3, 1979, Ibid.
[31] Ibid.
[32] Carter's decision to approve arms sales to Yemen by bypassing Congress on the grounds of a serious and urgent national security threat conveys the sense of crisis of the time. The legitimacy of this decision was seriously questioned by Arthur Schlesinger Jr. in the article "Arms for Yemen, Qualms for US" in the *New York Times* on April 9, 1979.
[33] Jeffrey A. Lefevbre, *Arms for the Horn. U.S. Security Policy in Ethiopia and Somalia 1953–1991* (Pittsburgh, PA: University of Pittsburgh Press, 1991), 199; Raymond Garthoff, *Détente and Confrontation. US-Soviet Relations from Nixon to Reagan* (Washington DC: The Brookings Institution, 1994), 723; Carol R. Saivetz, "Superpower Confrontation in the Middle East and the Collapse of Détente" in Odd Arne Westad (ed), *The Fall of Détente. Soviet-American Relations during the Carter Years* (Oslo, Norway: Scandinavian University Press, 1997), 84.

the shah's departure from Iran. The strategic location of Somalia became increasingly important for the United States. The globalist views – that advocated an agreement with Somalia both to counter the Soviet presence in Ethiopia and to eventually access the port and airfields at the base in Berbera – prevailed over the regional specialists from the Africa Bureau that pointed to the potential negative consequences of "entering Somalia."[34] The concerns regarding continued Somali incursions into the Ogaden subsided and no longer seriously hindered America's relations with Somalia.[35] Moreover, in the summer of 1979, President Carter authorized the CIA to supply assistance to the rebels fighting against the Soviet-backed government in Afghanistan.[36] This definitely confirmed America's more active engagement along the entire arc of crisis.

In parallel with aid packages to various countries (or factions) to oppose Moscow's alleged expansionist drive, Washington also started to plan its own direct intervention capabilities and to consider the logistical means to sustain them. While the discussion on a "reaction force" able to respond to crises had been initiated already in 1977, the actual planning for the force (which was to become the Rapid Deployment Force, or RDF) started only after the realization of US geostrategic vulnerability following the fall of the shah.[37] In the summer of 1979, the Pentagon staff completed a document entitled "Capabilities for Limited Contingencies in the Persian Gulf," which, pointing to the devastating consequences for the United States of Soviet advances in the region, exhorted the administration to place the Persian Gulf at the center of US foreign policy interests.[38]

---

[34] Lefevbre, *Arms for the Horn*, 216.
[35] As the US started negotiating with Said Barre, the Somali presence in the Ogaden remained; Ibid, 203–217.
[36] Steve Coll, *Ghost Wars. The Secret History of the CIA, Afghanistan, and Bin Laden, from the Soviet Invasion to September 10, 2001* (New York: Penguin, 2004), 46.
[37] Zbigniew Brzezinski, *Power and Principle. Memoirs of the National Security Adviser, 1977–1981* (New York: Farrar, Straus and Giroux, 1983), 456. On the perception of US vulnerability after the fall of the shah: Raymond Garthoff, *Détente and Confrontation*, 728–731.
[38] James Mann, *Rise of the Vulcans. The History of Bush's War Cabinet* (New York: Viking Penguin, 2004), 79. The centrality of the Persian Gulf for US foreign policy is confirmed also by the attention dedicated by scholars and commentators of the time to developments in the area. In the spring of 1979, for example, *Foreign Affairs* published two articles on the topic by renowned scholars George Lenxzowski ("The Arc of Crisis: Its Central Sector") and R. K. Ramazani ("Security in the Persian Gulf"); *Foreign Affairs*, Vol. 57, No. 4.

Then, with the hostage crisis in Iran, the implementation of the RDF became a concrete reality. At the NSC meeting on December 4, 1979 (i.e., before the Soviets entered Afghanistan), President Carter decided to seek access to military facilities in Kenya, Oman, and Somalia in order to provide the necessary operational support for the effectiveness of America's rapid deployment force.[39] In this way, the administration tried to counter the by then widespread perception of American vulnerability in the area. The events in Iran had struck a definite blow to the US position in the region. A few weeks later, the Soviet invasion of Afghanistan further exposed the United States, adding urgency to the public announcement of America's renewed and more assertive posture.

By the end of 1979 the public opinion of the Carter administration's performance reached an all-time low point. The commentaries of the time focused on the superpower rivalry in the Third World and underlined the weak and ineffective US response in countering Soviet advances (that were then considered numerous and in rapid sequence – in Africa, Latin America, Southeast Asia, and, potentially, in Iran).[40] These events created the impression of an inexorable decline of American power.[41] Moreover, the Carter administration's failures were seen as graver because so great had been the promise of rebirth and reinvigoration. As the Soviets advanced into yet another country – Afghanistan – and while the hostage crisis in Iran dragged on with no solution in sight, Carter was increasingly labeled as a "crisis president."[42]

THE SOVIET INVASION OF AFGHANISTAN

Afghanistan, a country neighboring both Iran and the Soviet Union, had witnessed growing political instability since 1973 when a successful (and nonviolent) coup led by Mohammad Daoud Khan ended the more than two-hundred-year-long monarchy. Daoud established a republic and tried to consolidate his rule by playing the Pashtun nationalist card, thus renewing Afghanistan's long-standing claims on the northwestern parts of Pakistan. This alarmed the Pakistani leadership, that responded by increasing covert support for Islamist militias fighting against Daoud.

---

[39] Lefebvre, *Arms for the Horn*, 199–200; Brzezinski, *Power and Principle*, 446.
[40] Robert Legvold, "The Super Rivals: Conflict in the Third World" in *Foreign Affairs*, Vol. 57, No. 4, 1979.
[41] Robert W. Tucker, "America in Decline" in *Foreign Affairs*, Vol. 58, No. 3, 1979.
[42] "On Iran and Afghanistan" in the *New York Times*, Jan. 8, 1980.

Nationalist and tribal rivalries, when coupled with Daoud's failed attempts to carry out sorely needed economic and social reforms, led to chronic political instability and internal power struggles, with an increasing influence of the Marxist inspired (and Soviet-sponsored) factions.[43]

In April 1978, Daoud was killed and replaced by Noor Mohammed Taraki, the leader of the pro-Soviet People's Democratic Party of Afghanistan (PDPA). The new government declared Afghanistan a democratic republic with fraternal ties to the Soviet Union. Moscow promptly recognized the new regime and fully supported it, dramatically increasing the number of Soviet military and nonmilitary advisers dispatched to Afghanistan. These developments were assessed in Washington as confirmation of the rising instability along the arc of crisis. Then, as the links between Taraki's government and the Soviet Union were strengthened, leading to the Treaty of Friendship signed in December 1978, the United States considered Moscow's involvement in Afghan affairs another demonstration of its increased assertiveness in the region.

In the fall of 1979, the rivalry and ensuing power struggle between Taraki and Hafizullah Amin led to a counter coup and to the emergence of the latter, much less dedicated than his predecessor to maintaining strong ties with the Soviet Union. In late December 1979, Moscow decided on the necessity to prevent the prospected destabilization of its strategically situated neighbor by intervening directly. Soviet troops occupied Kabul and all other major cities, as well as most strategic lines of communication. Special units eliminated Amin and his colleagues and reinstituted a "friendly" government (led by Babrak Karmal). The Kremlin justified its intervention by claiming it had dispatched a "limited contingent" of troops at the invitation of the PDPA's leadership in order to save Afghanistan from being overrun by imperialist-backed counterrevolutionary forces.[44]

---

[43] Jalal, "An Uncertain Trajectory," 324. Saikal, "Islamism, the Iranian Revolution and the Soviet Invasion of Afghanistan," 125–126.

[44] For reference on the internal situation in Afghanistan in the late 1970s, from the coup against Daoud to the rivalry between Taraki and Amin, and for background information on the events leading to the Soviet invasion: Alvin Z. Rubinstein, *Soviet Policy Toward Turkey, Iran and Afghanistan* (New York: Praeger Publishers, 1982), 150–174; Saikal, "Islamism, the Iranian Revolution, and the Soviet Invasion of Afghanistan," 121–129. For a complete and comprehensive account of the Soviet experience in Afghanistan see Rodric Braithwaite, *Afgantsy. The Russians in Afghanistan 1979–1989* (London: Profile Books, 2011). For Ambassador Dobrynin's account and background on the Soviet decision to intervene: Anatoly Dobrynin, *In Confidence. Moscow's Ambassador to America's Six Cold War Presidents* (New York: Times Books, 1995), 435–454.

The reaction in Washington (and in most of the international community) was immediate. The Kremlin's justification that it had intervened on the basis of the "urgent request" of the Afghan government, under Article 4 of the 1978 Treaty, was unacceptable for the United States. On December 28, 1979, President Carter wrote to Leonid Brezhnev:

> My Government can in no way accept the Soviet Government's explanation ... that Soviet military forces were sent into Afghanistan at the request of the leadership of that country. The facts of the matter clearly show that these same Soviet forces were employed to overthrow that established government and to impose a new government.[45]

In Washington, the Afghan crisis was immediately linked to the turmoil in Iran. From the American point of view, the two situations were intrinsically related because of the potential advancement of the Soviet Union into the Persian Gulf. In the immediate aftermath of the Soviet invasion, Brzezinski wrote to the president:

> Both Iran and Afghanistan are in turmoil, and Pakistan is both unstable internally and extremely apprehensive externally. If the Soviets succeed in Afghanistan, and if Pakistan acquiesces, the age-long dream of Moscow to have direct access to the Indian Ocean will have been fulfilled.[46]

---

[45] Letter from Carter to Brezhnev, December 28, 1979, Jimmy Carter Library (hereafter JCL), Donated Historical Material – Brzezinski Collection (hereafter DHM-BC), Geographic file, box 18, folder USSR – Carter/Brezhnev Correspondence (9/79–2/80). In his response, the Soviet leader defined "the attempt taken in your message to cast doubt on the very fact of the request itself of the government of Afghanistan" as strange. Brezhnev further defended his position: "It is impermissible, and not in conformity with actuality, the claim (accusation), which appears in your message that the Soviet Union allegedly did something to overthrow the Government of Afghanistan. I must with all certainty stress that the change in the Afghanistani Government was the result of the Afghanistanis themselves and only by them," Letter from Brezhnev to Carter, December 29, 1979, JCL, DHM-BC, Geographic file, box 18, folder USSR – Carter/Brezhnev Correspondence (9/79–2/80). The degree of Soviet deception in these statements emerges with evidence when juxtaposed to the Soviet documents that reveal the motivations leading to intervention, which the Politburo had been discussing since March 1979. For insight into the Soviet motivations and for the reconstruction of events from the Soviet point of view: Odd Arne Westad, *Concerning the Situation in "A": New Russian Evidence on the Soviet Intervention in Afghanistan* in *Cold War International History Project Bulletin*, Issues 8–9, Woodrow Wilson International Center for Scholars, Washington DC, Winter 1996–1997, 128–132. Also in the *Bulletin* are the translations of Soviet documents related to the decision to intervene in Afghanistan: *The Soviet Union and Afghanistan, 1978–1989: Documents from the Russian and East German Archives*, 133–184.

[46] Memorandum for the President from Zbigniew Brzezinski, "Reflections on Soviet Intervention in Afghanistan," December 26, 1979, JCL, DHM-BC, Geographic file, box 17, folder Southwest Asia/Persian Gulf – Afghanistan (12/26/79–1/4/80).

The British presence in the Gulf before, and the American-backed Iranian policies after, had constituted a barrier against Soviet expansionism, but the end of the shah's regime had led to "the collapse of the balance of power in Southwest Asia." This theoretically opened the way for a Soviet presence "right down on the edge of the Arabian and Oman Gulfs."[47] In analyzing the grave challenges posed to the United States by the Soviet invasion of Afghanistan, the members of the NSC (by then most influential in determining Carter's outlook) repeatedly focused on Iran. This confirmed the dimension of the setback caused by the revolution in Tehran, its negative impact in Washington, and its centrality in the reshaping of America's regional policy.

In early January 1980, an NSC internal memorandum made references to an unconfirmed report that a Soviet division comprising at least 10,000 troops had taken up position along Afghanistan's border with Iran, within striking distance of the oil fields. This raised questions on Moscow's "real" intentions.[48] A few months later, NSC staffer Paul Henze went a step further, underlining that the possibility of a Soviet move into Iran was not inconceivable:

> I am concerned about the evidence we continue to get of steady, quiet buildup in the Transcaucasus for a Soviet military move into Iran. While I do not question current intelligence assessments that there is no indication that the Soviets are actually preparing to move, I am fearful that we are in danger of wishfully turning this rational assumption into a conviction that they will not move. I worry about the kind of mind-sets that afflict intelligence estimators and comfort policymakers and which led to conclusions, e.g. that the Soviets were not putting nuclear weaponry into Cuba in 1962 or that the dynasty was secure in Iran in 1978.[49]

The Soviet invasion of Afghanistan, therefore, further complicated the already extremely problematic US-Iranian relationship. And the possibility of direct superpower confrontation could no longer be excluded. The end of the pro-Western regime in Tehran also exposed Pakistan to greater pressure, which the United States had to counter. By reviewing its policy toward Islamabad, Washington could channel increased aid in support

---

[47] Ibid.
[48] Memorandum for Zbigniew Brzezinski from Jerry Schecter, "SCC Working Group on Iran and Afghanistan: Public Posture," January 14, 1980, CWIHP, "The Carter Administration and the 'Arc of Crisis' 1977–1981," Declassified Documents prepared for A Critical Oral History Conference, The Woodrow Wilson Center July 25–26, 2005.
[49] Memorandum for Zbigniew Brzezinski from Paul B. Henze, "Iran and the Soviets," April 11, 1980, Ibid.

of the Afghan resistance actively fighting against the Soviet Union.[50] The Carter administration therefore dropped all sanctions against Pakistan and embraced an alliance with General Zia's dictatorship, despite the (by then set aside) public commitment to human rights and democracy. Moreover, the United States backed the use of Islam as an ideology of resistance against the Soviet occupation. In fact, the CIA was authorized to organize a network of material and human support for the Afghan Islamic resistance.[51]

The Soviet move into Afghanistan was, in itself, extremely preoccupying. Moscow had not mobilized its forces for direct intervention in another country since the invasions of Hungary and Czechoslovakia. And Afghanistan was a previously nonaligned state situated outside the Soviet sphere of influence. For Washington, these developments further confirmed the need for a strong reaction. In early January 1980, Brzezinski again set forth his idea of a regional security framework:

> We have to move deliberately to fashion a wider security arrangement for the region, lest Soviet influence spread rapidly from Afghanistan to Pakistan and Iran. I cannot emphasize strongly enough the strategic consequences of such a development. It would place in direct jeopardy our most vital interests in the Middle East.[52]

The creation of a new and more effective regional policy required engaging all countries committed to resisting Soviet expansionism. According to Brzezinski, these included China, Egypt, and Saudi Arabia. Toward China, the terminology on arms sales had to shift from "we will not sell arms to China" to "we will not sell offensive arms to China." This would permit the initiation of a defense arrangement that could involve Beijing in America's new policies toward the Persian Gulf. Regionally, the Egyptians and the Saudis had to be reassured that Washington was prepared to assert its power and defend Western interests. In concluding his memorandum to the president, Brzezinski wrote:

> The above recommendations require major decisions by you, but I believe that a major historical turning point has been reached. You have the opportunity to

---

[50] Ibid.
[51] Saikal, "Islamism, the Iranian Revolution and the Soviet Invasion of Afghanistan," 129–130.
[52] Memorandum for the President from Zbigniew Brzezinski, "Strategic Reaction to the Afghanistan Problem," January 3, 1980, JCL, DHM-BC, Geographic file, box 17, folder Southwest Asia/Persian Gulf – Afghanistan (12/26/79–1/4/80).

288   *Rethinking the Fall of Détente, 1977–1980*

do what President Truman did on Greece and Turkey, and I believe that this is desirable both for domestic and international reasons.⁵³

Brzezinski's recommendations translated into policy with the president's State of the Union address of January 23, 1980. The American commitment to the defense of the region was made explicit with the key phrase: "An attempt by any outside force to gain control of the Persian Gulf region will be regarded as an assault on the vital interests of the United States of America, and such an assault will be repelled by any means necessary, including military force."⁵⁴ This statement – labeled as the Carter doctrine – made the shift in US policy initiated almost a year earlier public and unequivocal.

The American determination to invest in the regional security of the Persian Gulf explicitly emerged in the following months with the finalization of the agreements to access facilities in Egypt, Oman, Kenya, Diego Garcia, and Somalia.⁵⁵ In this way, the United States tried to secure a credible capability to respond to contingencies with the introduction of additional American military power into the region and by acquiring an adequate knowledge of the operational environment. From that moment onward, the Persian Gulf was positioned at the center of US foreign policy interests also from a military (and not only economic and political) point of view – a shift in policy that endures to the present day.⁵⁶

By mid-1980, the Carter administration had broadly redefined the American posture in the Persian Gulf, not merely as a contingent reaction, but as a longer-term strategy. In the fall of 1980, Brzezinski emphasized the importance of the president's choices:

Your "presence" decision on our military forces in the region allowed us to have the largest naval force near the mouth of the Strait of Hormuz as the Iran-Iraq hostilities started.⁵⁷

---

⁵³ Ibid.
⁵⁴ State of the Union address, 1980; www.jimmycarterlibrary.org/documents/speeches.
⁵⁵ Memorandum for the President from Zbigniew Brzezinski, "SCC Summary of Conclusions on Next Steps in Improving our Access to Indian Ocean Facilities," January 31, 1980, JCL, DHM-BC, Subject file, box 32, folder Meetings – SCC 264A: 1/30/80.
⁵⁶ It is important to note that before Carter's decisions on the RDF, the United States did not have a military command dedicated to coordinating operations in the Persian Gulf (the closest to the area was in Europe). Carter's decisions on the RDF were at the basis of the subsequent creation of CENTCOM – the US central command (operational to this date) for the Persian Gulf.
⁵⁷ Memorandum for the President from Zbigniew Brzezinski, "The Security Framework for the Persian Gulf" and attached talking points, October 8, 1980, JCL, DHM-BC, Geographic file, box 16, folder Southwest Asia/Persian Gulf – (10/6/80–10/31/80).

While acknowledging that "a security framework for the region could not be only or primarily a military structure," Brzezinski defined the military component as "critical" in presenting the Soviet Union with a credible deterrent. The negotiations for the use of facilities in the area were fundamental in this context, demonstrating the new direction of US policy:

> These arrangements have reversed a significant trend. Instead of receding, American military power can actually grow and provide the needed security to the region, if the occasion should arise.[58]

These words convey the dimension of the change the Carter presidency had undertaken in the course of its four years in office: from the emphasis on negotiation, and the criticism of excessive Cold War biases, to the reaffirmation of American strength and a renewed priority assigned to the containment of Soviet expansionism. At the time, newspaper headlines such as "Roaring into the 50s"[59] and "The Second Cold War"[60] seemed to put the word "end" to the era of US-Soviet détente.

SALT AFTER AFGHANISTAN

The events of 1979 indisputably contributed to the return of a climate of tension between the superpowers that contrasted sharply with the rhetoric and the high-level summit meetings of the Nixon era of détente. The general impression of a return to the Cold War was validated by the countermeasures adopted by Washington in the aftermath of the Soviet invasion of Afghanistan: the suspension of the SALT II ratification process; the president's firm statement on the commitment to secure the pro-Western orientation of the Persian Gulf; the reduction of grain exports to the Soviet Union; and the boycott of the 1980 Olympic Games. By the end of 1980, US-Soviet relations seemed, indeed, to enter a Second Cold War. Washington and Moscow exchanged hostile words daily, the bilateral economic exchanges reached an all-time low, domestically in the United States citizens were again increasingly concerned about the escalation of the military competition with the Soviet Union, and America's alleged weakness in the face of renewed Soviet assertiveness.

---

[58] Ibid.
[59] James Reston, "Roaring into the 50s" in the *New York Times*, Jan. 27, 1980.
[60] William Safire, "The Second Cold War" in the *New York Times*, Jan. 10, 1980.

However, despite the generally perceived exacerbation of US-Soviet relations and the seemingly total collapse of superpower détente, it is important to underline that the American interest, and parallel necessity, of defending the SALT II Treaty persisted even after the Soviet invasion of Afghanistan. On December 29, 1979, in one of the first memos sent to the president after the Soviet intervention, Brzezinski, though clearly advocating a firm response, at the same time stated that the efforts to achieve SALT II ratification should continue.[61] In early 1980, Carter himself confirmed the importance still assigned to SALT II. While claiming that Moscow's actions in Afghanistan were a "fundamental turning point" in US-Soviet relations, the president also affirmed that as soon as the political climate permitted he would "press for the ratification of SALT II."

Significantly, in January 1980 – that is, in parallel with the proclamation of the Carter doctrine – the president wrote to Brezhnev and declared that the United States would continue to abide by the provisions of the SALT II agreement and would not take any action that could contradict the purpose of the treaty, as long as the Soviet Union reciprocated.[62] A month later the president again underlined the importance of maintaining the momentum of the arms control negotiations and repeated that "the ratification of SALT II continues to have top priority on my agenda."[63] These letters (and draft letters) signal Carter's intention of pursuing SALT despite the heightened tension caused by the events in Afghanistan. In fact, the firm response to the perceived Soviet geostrategic advancement and the determination to ratify SALT II coexisted in the president's prospected policy choices.

Accordingly, in June 1980, the summary of the conclusions of the SCC meeting on SALT and Afghanistan stated:

We will proceed to prepare a policy statement on SALT and Afghanistan which will provide the basis for drafting a platform plank on these issues. The statement will stress that our interest in SALT II ratification and a strong response to the

---

[61] Memorandum for the President from Zbigniew Brzezinski, "Our Response to Soviet Intervention in Afghanistan," December 29, 1979, JCL, DHM-BC, Geographic file, box 17, folder Southwest Asia/Persian Gulf – Afghanistan: (1/5/80–10/1/80).

[62] Draft letter from Carter to Brezhnev, January 26, 1980, JCL, DHM-BC, Geographic file, box 18, folder USSR – Carter/Brezhnev Correspondence (9/79–2/80).

[63] Draft letter from Carter to Brezhnev, February 29, 1980, JCL, DHM-BC, Geographic file, box 18, folder USSR – Carter/Brezhnev Correspondence (9/79–2/80).

Reaffirming Containment: The Carter Doctrine

Soviet invasion of Afghanistan are not incompatible – and that this is not a new statement of administration policy.[64]

The point paper titled "Restarting SALT Without Soviet Withdrawal from Afghanistan" prepared by Secretary of Defense Brown reveals analogous intentions. The paper outlined a plan to win congressional approval for SALT II ratification, despite the continued presence of Soviet troops in Afghanistan. The central premise was to make clear that SALT was valuable to the United States in the management of its adversarial relationship with Moscow, not only, or chiefly, as a sign of cooperation. The treaty limited the Soviet Union's force levels to aggregates inferior to those it could attain in its absence, therefore enhancing American security. The US Senate had to be convinced that America's capacity to effectively compete with the Soviets would be greater with the limits imposed to the respective strategic arsenals. In short, the treaty was even more clearly in the US interest after the Soviet-caused increase of tension. In concluding the paper, Brown looked to the future:

> In a less charged political atmosphere we will be able to make the case that, despite Afghanistan, SALT should be ratified on the merits of our own long-term security interest, not reviewed as a favor to the Soviets.[65]

The idea that SALT aided the United States in the management of its competitive relationship with the Soviet Union – which had been characteristic of the Nixon administration's initial pursuit of the arms control process – therefore resurfaced with clarity. The request to suspend consideration of SALT II in early 1980 had been an immediate reaction to the invasion of Afghanistan in order to convey to the Soviets that from Washington's point of view their action was unacceptable. However, it never reflected the administration's actual intention of abandoning the strategic thinking behind the treaty. SALT II was perceived as a necessity and was clearly in the American longer-term interest. The basic motivations that had triggered the pursuit of SALT I a decade earlier, in essence,

---

[64] Special Coordination Committee Meeting June 6, 1980, "SALT and Afghanistan," 9:30–10:35 A.M., The White House Situation Room, JCL, DHM-BC, Subject file, box 33, folder Meetings – SCC 319: 6/6/80.

[65] Point Paper on Restarting SALT Without Soviet Withdrawal from Afghanistan attached to Memorandum for Mr. L. Paul Bremer, Deputy Executive Secretary of the Department of State, Colonel Leslie G. Denend, Special Assistant to the President for National Security Affairs, July 7, 1980, "SALT," JCL, DHM-BC, Subject file, box 23, folder Meetings – Muskie/Brown/Brzezinski: 7/80–9/80.

persisted. Carter's statement on the intention to abide by the limits of the un-ratified treaty confirmed its crucial importance for the protection of American security.

Even in late 1980, as US-Soviet relations seemed to enter a new phase of the Cold War, American foreign policy was shaped by the determination to firmly respond to Soviet geopolitical challenges while at the same time securing the advantages of arms control. The 1970s had ended. The dual-track policy had not.

Conclusion

During his last year in office President Carter struggled to counter the widespread perception of American vulnerability and decline. The shadow cast by the Vietnam War seemed to still hinder the making of foreign policy, with an overall reluctance to project military power abroad and a pervasive (though, as we now know, exaggerated) feeling of US weakness. The president tried to address these sentiments by initiating a military buildup (that would then escalate under Ronald Reagan) and providing concrete implementation to the Carter doctrine. However, within the Cold War paradigm that continued to dominate the American worldview, the Soviet advances simply could not be ignored. In Washington, they appeared as a series of well-orchestrated and deliberately staged humiliations. Setbacks in the Horn of Africa and Afghanistan (as well as in Nicaragua and El Salvador) were compounded by the day to day chronicle of "America held hostage" by the radical regime of the ayatollahs in Iran.

The sensation of American powerlessness climaxed in April 1980 when the president cancelled an operation that had been underway to free the hostages, held captive on the US embassy grounds in Tehran since November 4, 1979. The photos of the crushed helicopters of the failed rescue mission deeply shook the American public consciousness and became the symbol of the collapse of US power and prestige. These images evoked those of the defeated Americans lining up to board the helicopter on the roof of the US embassy in Saigon in April 1975. Had American power really receded in the face of an expansionist and increasingly global Soviet Union?

In this context, during the 1980 presidential campaign Ronald Reagan's discourse on the restoration of American power resonated widely. The American public wanted and needed a renewed, strong leadership. When Reagan entered the White House in January 1981 he promised not to acknowledge or manage the decline of US power but to reverse it, reasserting American strength and determination worldwide. Disappointed with the image of the United States during the Carter administration and with the sense of decline and impotence associated with those years, the incoming president wanted to "bring America back." His campaign rhetoric had recalled the themes of the early 1950s when, at the height of the Cold War, America had been the overwhelmingly dominant military and economic power. Emblematically, the special election edition of *Time* magazine in November 1980 featured Ronald Reagan and was titled "A Fresh Start."[1] Accordingly, the Reagan administration's initial approach to foreign policy brought an abrupt rupture from the recent past. The even partial cooperation with the Soviet Union of the détente years was set aside in favor of an unequivocally hard-line and hawkish Cold War posture. Some scholars have, in fact, defined the phase initiated in the early 1980s as the Second Cold War.[2]

Reagan asserted that while the United States had allowed its military capabilities to deteriorate, the Soviet Union had been engaging in a massive military buildup which was, by nature, offensive. In response, the new president supported the largest peacetime rearmament program in the history of the United States. The first defining feature of the Reagan administration was, in fact, the restructuring of American defense programs in order to rebuild US military strength after a decade of post-Vietnam retrenchment. Less than two weeks after entering office, Reagan approved an immediate increase of 32.6 billion dollars in the defense budget over the $200.3 billion already requested by Carter during his last year in office. Such a massive increase in the budget was approved by Congress and, most significantly, was decided before obtaining requests from the military (creating the unusual circumstance in which the decision on the increase was taken before determining how to spend it). This decision signaled the Reagan administration's determination to rebuild US military strength. Incoming secretary of defense Casper Weinberger

---

[1] *Time* magazine cover, November 17, 1980.
[2] See, for example Fred Halliday, *The Making of the Second Cold War* (London: Verso, 1986 – Second edition), 225–261 and Raymond L. Garthoff, *The Great Transition. American-Soviet Relations and the End of the Cold War* (Washington DC: The Brookings Institution, 1994), 7–54.

supported the president's mission to "rearm America" and, over three years, the administration planned to increase the military budget share of federal spending from one quarter to one third. Particular stress was given to expanding the US Navy and to implementing Carter's directives on the Rapid Deployment Joint Task Forces. In 1983, these were expanded and institutionalized with the creation of the US Central Command, which was given the responsibility for coordinating US (and allied) military operations in the entire Southwest Asian-Persian Gulf area. In the same year, President Reagan also introduced SDI (Strategic Defense Initiative) – a research program that envisioned a space-based system that would intercept and destroy Soviet nuclear missiles headed toward the United States. The rationale behind SDI was to break the balance of MAD and create a so-called fortress America, which in essence meant reintroducing the invulnerability from a nuclear attack that the United States had enjoyed during the early Cold War years.[3]

A second aspect of the Reagan administration's more muscular approach was the restructuring of US foreign aid programs, which refocused almost exclusively on security (US economic assistance declined during the first Reagan administration while military assistance increased by 600 percent).[4] According to the White House, the countries of the Third World were simply the stage on which the US-Soviet rivalry played out. Reagan believed that the Soviet Union instigated the unrest in these countries and that Moscow was engaged in a game of dominoes, turning peripheral areas of the globe into hot spots for the superpower rivalry. Therefore, the president's approach to regional disputes was also extremely confrontational. He wanted to apply pressure on the Soviets around the globe and ensure that Moscow would remain tied down in long and costly disputes. In 1983, the president approved National Security Decision Directive 75 – a document that spelled out the various components of US policy toward the Soviet Union. The primary focus of American policy remained "to contain and over time reverse Soviet expansionism." In the Third World, the document stated that the United States had to "rebuild the credibility of its commitment to resist Soviet encroachment

---

[3] Raymond Garthoff, *The Great Transition*, 33–42. For an inside view of the time and an explanation of the motivations of the Reagan administration's military buildup: Lawrence J. Korb (then assistant secretary of defense) and Linda P. Brady (then at the Office of the Assistant Secretary of Defense), "Rearming America. The Reagan Administration Defense Program" in *International Security*, Vol. 9, No. 3 (Winter, 1984–1985), 3–18.
[4] Terry Diebel, *Presidents, Public Opinion and Power. The Nixon, Carter and Reagan Years*, Foreign Policy Association, Headline Series, No. 280, April 1987, 49–50.

on US interests and those of its Allies and friends, and to support effectively those Third World states that are willing to resist Soviet pressures or oppose Soviet initiatives hostile to the United States, or are special targets of Soviet policy."[5] This document was the basis for the development of the Reagan doctrine and the channeling of covert assistance to sponsor anti-Soviet factions engaged in fighting against Moscow's presence and influence (most notably in Nicaragua and in Afghanistan).

A third characteristic of Reagan's initial attitude toward the Soviet Union was his uncompromising rhetoric. The president's anticommunism was outspoken and ardent. In 1981, he stated that "the West won't contain communism, it will transcend communism. It will dismiss it as some bizarre chapter in human history." A few years later, Reagan famously denounced the Soviet Union as "the evil empire."[6] Equally important to his efforts to project the image of American power was the reconstruction of the role of an assertive president domestically. Breaking the trend started in the mid-1970s of increased power and influence of the US Congress on the making of foreign policy, Reagan reasserted an "imperial presidency." He wanted to convey the image of a strong and determined leader, who knew what he wanted and how to achieve it. In contrast to the decline and seeming impotence of the Carter years, America had to again be seen as a powerful country, unwilling to be toyed with and bullied.

Such hawkish posture had a deep impact on US-Soviet relations. The tough talk fueled Soviet propaganda and exacerbated the relationship, while strategic arms control negotiations – the crucial barometer of the state of the bilateral tension – stalled due to unilateral American proposals (to pass from strategic arms limitation talks to strategic arms reduction talks). The United States, evidently, wanted to delay the talks in order to regain a position of strength before reentering serious negotiations. By the fall of 1983, the superpower relationship was more hostile than at any period since the Cuban missile crisis.[7] It seemed impossible for Washington and Moscow to reinitiate any kind of dialogue, and agreements and high-level summits were even less foreseeable. Had the policies of the 1970s definitely ended, leaving no trace? Was détente finished and buried under the renewed confrontation of the early 1980s? The answer

[5] National Security Decision Directive 75, January 17, 1983, Appendix A to Norman A. Bailey, *The Strategic Plan that Won the Cold War. National Security Decision Directive 75* (McLean, Virginia: The Potomac Foundation, 1998).
[6] Quoted in Beth A. Fischer, "US Foreign Policy under Reagan and Bush" in Leffler and Westad (eds), *The Cambridge History of the Cold War. Volume III* (Cambridge: Cambridge University Press, 2010), 269–270.
[7] Ibid., 272.

depends on how one assesses the 1970s, the consequences of the policy of US-Soviet détente and its meaning and implications for the overall exercise of American international power.

A GEOPOLITICAL BATTLE?
Reinterpreting Superpower Détente

When the Nixon administration entered office in 1969 the relative decline of the United States in the face of the Soviet attainment of nuclear parity imposed an unprecedented acknowledgment of the limits of American power. The main thrust behind Nixon's call for "an era of negotiation" was the need to limit the growth of the Soviet Union's nuclear arsenal. Moscow and Washington had both understood that in the thermonuclear era the arms race had to be regulated in order to maintain the credibility of deterrence, a central feature of the Cold War. Consequently, SALT came to be perceived by both sides as a necessity and as a means to guarantee strategic stability. The different equilibrium of forces between the United States and the Soviet Union, with the Soviets much closer to the American nuclear-strategic capabilities than ever before, provided Washington with a continued and potent incentive for negotiating with the Soviets. In order to induce Moscow's cooperation in SALT, Nixon and Kissinger tried to engage the Soviets in economic, technological, and cultural transactions. Within a few years, the climate of the bilateral relationship totally changed, with high-level summit meetings and an unprecedented level of communication and exchanges between the United States and the Soviet Union. As the Cold War tension seemed to subside, Nixon started invoking a "new structure of peace." But had US policy toward Moscow fundamentally changed, as the atmospherics seemed to suggest? Did Washington really shift its emphasis away from American containment of Soviet expansionism to induce Soviet "self-containment"? Were Nixon and Kissinger actually committed – as some scholars have asserted – to restraint and to preserving the status quo in international affairs?[8] The reading set forth in this book (in Chapters 2 to 5) points to the opposite.

---

[8] The emphasis on restraint and on inducing Soviet "self-containment" as the main objectives of détente is the view set forth by Olav Nolstad in "The collapse of superpower détente, 1975–1980" in Leffler and Westad (eds), *The Cambridge History of the Cold War. Volume III* (Cambridge: Cambridge University Press, 2010), 137. Nolstad refers to such scholars as Stanley Hoffman in *Dead End* (Cambridge: Ballinger, 1983), 90 and Mike Bowker and Phil Williams in *Superpower Détente: A Reappraisal* (London: Sage, 1988), 54–55.

The recognition of Soviet strength and superpower status that the SALT negotiations implied was, in fact, accompanied by a greater emphasis on the geopolitical dimension of the Cold War. While this had obviously been a part of the bipolar competition from its outset, during the détente years it progressively became the main parameter through which the United States sought to more effectively pursue the same long-standing objective: containing Soviet expansionism. Despite the negotiations on arms control – or, perhaps, precisely because of these – Washington and Moscow both continued their quest to expand their influence worldwide. From the beginning, Nixon's innovative management of the adversarial relationship with the Soviet Union evolved around the dual track of cooperation (in SALT) and competition (elsewhere).

Between 1969 and 1972 the ambivalence of American policy emerged in the parallel unfolding of the administration's China policy and of SALT. Nixon and Kissinger's triangular diplomacy was mainly a bargaining chip: Washington used the "China card" to strengthen its strategic position while negotiating with Moscow. The Sino-American opening was made possible by a deemphasis on ideology and by a pragmatic view of the international balance of power, coupled with a shrewd analysis of national interests. With the deterioration of Sino-Soviet relations, China developed the idea that the Soviet Union was the major threat to its national security. Therefore, after decades of hostility and isolation, the common perception of the Soviet challenge brought the United States and China together. The July 1971 and February 1972 conversations in fact confirm the centrality of the Soviet Union in the discussions between the Americans and the Chinese. The "antihegemonic clause" of the Shanghai Communiqué formally sanctioned the direction and scope of the nascent relationship, firmly grounded on the security interests of both sides. With the China opening, Washington successfully engaged Beijing in the geopolitical containment of the Soviet Union.

The Nixon administration's ambivalent policy again surfaced during the spring of 1972 in the interrelationship between the escalation in Vietnam and the first Nixon-Brezhnev summit. In April 1972, Kissinger grasped the inherent possibility for the United States to firmly respond in the Vietnamese context, without giving up the summit. Considering Brezhnev's willingness to discuss SALT regardless of the American bombings, Kissinger proceeded on the dual path, securing the summit but not yielding in Indochina. Nixon then confirmed the twofold purpose of American policy by ordering the mining of Haiphong only days before his scheduled departure for Moscow. If détente was about inducing restraint, then why did Nixon escalate the bombings in Vietnam, demonstrating firm opposition to Soviet-backed aggression? The events of April and May 1972 suggest that détente was about both negotiating and competing. The Soviets, in fact, did not cancel the summit. The course seemed set for a different management of the Cold War bipolar relationship.

The competitive aspect of the superpower relationship, which generally remains in the shadow of the overemphasized "era of negotiations," was, instead, central in the shaping of US policy even at the height of détente. While the signing of the SALT I agreements codified the continued reliance on deterrence (an aspect that inherently confirmed the enduring Cold War mind-set of the superpowers), Washington demonstrated that it would not remain idle in the face of Soviet, or Soviet-sponsored, challenges. As Kissinger stated, "third areas" were increasingly becoming the "real sources of tension."

The fact that for Washington détente was not primarily about restraint emerges fully when assessing the Nixon administration's relationship with Iran. The motivations that led to the strengthening of the ties between Nixon and the shah were, in fact, directly linked to the broader context of US-Soviet relations. Iran had been decisive in the shaping of Nixon's regional strategy from the beginning of the administration because of its strategic location and its particular characteristics, which made it the ideal country for the application of the Nixon doctrine in the Middle East. However, despite the importance of the US-Iranian relationship, the shah's requests on weapons procurement were initially only partly satisfied. The shift in policy, and the definitive strengthening of the bond with the shah, occurred only during Nixon's May 1972 trip to Tehran. After the meetings with the Soviet leadership, Washington had to tangibly demonstrate that the support for its allies was unaltered, if not increased. From this perspective, the symbolic impact of the resolute strengthening of a de-facto anti-Soviet alliance, while practically at the same time signing agreements in Moscow must be underlined. Nixon's decisions in Tehran, their motivations and timing, substantiate the dualistic notion of détente, with its simultaneous cooperative and competitive drives.

The nascent relationship with the People's Republic of China, the Vietnam-SALT I interrelationship, and the strengthening of the ties with Iran demonstrate the importance the Nixon administration assigned to the definition of a wide-ranging global policy to counter Soviet expansionism. The analysis of these initiatives alters the understanding of the first years of détente (1969–1972), adding another layer to the debate on its objectives. The idea that surfaces is that the Nixon policies did not represent a shift from American containment of Soviet expansionism, but rather a different way of implementing it.

With the 1973 October War in the Middle East the underlying tension between the cooperative aspects of détente and the superpowers' determination to respectively maintain, or enhance, their spheres of influence worldwide – which had been present from the outset – openly emerged. In Washington, the conflict in the Middle East – like all the other policies studied here – was viewed almost exclusively in terms of its broader repercussions on the competition with the Soviet Union. During the critical phase of the conflict, the United States firmly opposed the introduction of a Soviet presence into the region. Whether Brezhnev's letter on unilateral action represented a credible threat or was misinterpreted in Washington, the decision on the nuclear alert unequivocally conveyed the American unwillingness to compromise. The contacts with Egypt before and during the war, together with the diplomatic campaign to reduce the potentially adverse effects in the Arab world of the US airlift to Israel, revealed America's longer-term strategy (pursued by Kissinger in Moscow as he separated the discussions on the cease-fire from those on a political settlement). The United States gradually – and successfully – worked to secure for itself the role of sole mediator in the postwar negotiations, therefore permanently excluding the Soviet Union from the Middle East and from high-level diplomacy in the region.

While "improved relations" with Moscow were still openly proclaimed to be the central objective, the policies pursued by the Nixon administration in the Middle East confirmed that détente did not, and would not, signify yielding to Soviet advances, even if only potential. Moscow reacted by strengthening its ties in Iraq, South Yemen, Syria, and Somalia. This polarized the shift between moderates and radicals in the Arab world – a long-term negative consequence of the superpower rivalry in the region, overlooked at the time of Kissinger's diplomatic successes.

Between 1972 and 1973, as Nixon tried to continue implementing his innovative management of the superpower relationship, domestically the administration's policies were increasingly under attack. Although détente was characterized by both cooperative and competitive aspects, initially – also for domestic political calculations – the emphasis was put on the novelty of cooperation. As Nixon later acknowledged "the creation of willowy euphoria is one of the dangers of summitry. During my administration excessive euphoria built up around the 1972 Peking and Moscow summit meetings. I must assume a substantial part of the responsibility for this. It was an election year and I wanted the political credit."[9]

Nixon and Kissinger had never comprehensively explained the complex design of détente to their domestic constituency. This generated unrealistic expectations on the part of the American public, as the "era of negotiations" became erroneously identified with the pursuit of a generalized and unspecified "lasting structure of peace." The lack of domestic understanding of the innovative approach toward the Soviet Union led to the crisis and eventual fall of détente. Its central aspect, the SALT negotiations, resulted from the Soviet attainment of parity in the nuclear field. But for decades the Cold War posture maintained by the United States had never conceded an acknowledgment of limits. Moreover, throughout the history of the Cold War, America's battle against communism had always been justified on the basis of an idealistic moral crusade. For these reasons, it was difficult to explain the intrinsic *realpolitik* behind the pursuit of détente (which was, instead, concealed).[10]

As Kissinger asserts, many "misconceived" the administration's design and "misinterpreted" its purpose. However, neither the design, nor the purpose had been explained to the American public, not ready for, and not used to, policies based on a realistic and pragmatic assessment of the national interest. Therefore, as the competitive aspect of détente openly surfaced in the aftermath of the October War, and the ideal of a "lasting peace" revealed its limits, the fragile domestic equilibrium upon which the administration's policies rested started to vacillate. The inaccurately interpreted détente was attacked from all sides: by the conservatives, criticizing the terms of the Interim Agreement; and by the liberals, with the emergence of the Jewish emigration issue.

While under normal circumstances a strong president in his second term, after an overwhelming victory in the elections, might have sustained his ambitious foreign policy also in the face of such serious domestic challenges, the Watergate scandal deprived Nixon of the authority and strength needed to defend his course. The decline of détente was the consequence of the particular combination of its innate fragility and the crisis

---

[9] Richard Nixon, *The Real War* (New York: Warner Books, 1980), 237.
[10] On the failure of Nixon and Kissinger to legitimate their grand design domestically and on the unwillingness of the American Congress and public to support a foreign policy based on "the maximization of power rather than the promotion of principles and ideals" see Dan Caldwell, "The Legitimation of the Nixon-Kissinger Grand Design and Grand Strategy" in *Diplomatic History*, Vol. 33, No. 4 (September 2009).

that led to Nixon's resignation. However, while undeniably détente was *domestically* criticized, did the US *foreign policy* lines shift accordingly?

During the Ford administration, the American policy toward the Soviet Union did not significantly change. The incoming president, for obvious reasons, endorsed continuity. The Vladivostok agreement demonstrated the unrelenting importance of arms control. At the same time, the American leadership focused on Angola. Not because of its "intrinsic importance" but because of "the implications for Soviet policy." Yet another local conflict was, therefore, viewed in Washington in terms of its repercussions on the competition with the Soviet Union. US-Soviet relations continued to proceed on the dual track of negotiation and competition.

While in Angola the US leadership searched for means to counter the Soviet-Cuban presence, President Ford sent Kissinger to Moscow to discuss SALT. The analogy between the January 1976 and the April 1972 trips to Moscow rests in the circumstances under which Kissinger negotiated, but not in the results. On both occasions, a high-level representative of the American president (with undisputable authority) negotiated in the Soviet capital on important issues related to SALT while in a regional conflict the United States and the Soviet Union were struggling to obtain geopolitical advantages. In 1976, the US domestic disarray prevented both the definition of a unified SALT position and the possibility to bolster the anticommunist factions in Angola. But the twofold motivations on the administration's part existed: securing the SALT treaty and responding to the Soviet challenge in Angola. This demonstrated that the framework for the management of the US-Soviet relationship introduced by Nixon persisted. The pattern that had emerged from the policies of the early 1970s – the search for negotiations with the Soviet Union on arms control and the simultaneous continued, and at times exacerbated, competition in areas of the periphery considered strategically important – seemed to remain a reference point in the making of US foreign policy, despite the domestic crisis of détente.

MORE CONTINUITY THAN CHANGE?

Rethinking the Carter Administration's Foreign Policy

Jimmy Carter entered office with the declared intention of breaking from the policies of the past, criticizing the *realpolitik* and the excessively Soviet-centric views of the previous administrations. The incoming president seemed to share Secretary of State Cyrus Vance's view that the major flaw in America's foreign policy was "that it was too narrowly rooted in the concept of an overarching US-Soviet 'geopolitical' struggle. Obviously, such a conflict did exist and it was of major dimensions" but American "national interests encompassed more than US-Soviet relations." Therefore, Carter intended to place other issues and more moral values at the center of American foreign policy making. This initial attitude shaped, for example, the administration's policies toward the Third World, with the emphasis on the respect for local dynamics and realities, and the "deep cuts" approach to strategic arms limitation, proposed by Vance to the Soviets in March 1977.

However, already by the end of his first year in office, Carter started to move away from his proclaimed intentions. Then, between 1978 and 1979, the interconnection of the policies toward the Horn of Africa and China, and the continued pursuit of SALT II, revealed a remarkable and not always unintended continuity with the pattern outlined during the Nixon/Ford years. As the crisis unfolded in the Horn of Africa, the Carter administration in fact focused more on the potential for Soviet expansionism than on the complex local grievances that motivated the war between Somalia and Ethiopia. Although no direct intervention to match Moscow's involvement in the Horn was deemed necessary, Carter's attitude shifted to a refocus on US-Soviet relations and on the geopolitical dimension of the superpower rivalry. The president reacted to the perception of an increased Soviet threat within the diplomatic framework of options available to the United States – options that he had inherited from the Nixon administration: the reliance on the two "pillars" of US regional policy, Iran and Saudi Arabia (with Iran clearly representing the regional stronghold); and the use of the "China card" as a means to put pressure on Moscow.

The decision to signal America's readiness to move toward normalization of relations with the People's Republic of China and the increased influence of Brzezinski's hawkish Soviet-centric views reflected the change in Carter's perception of the Soviet Union. The May 1978 trip to Beijing was clearly a signal to Moscow, which had to be "reminded that the United States, too, could effectively compete geopolitically." As the restating of the antihegemonic clause of the Shanghai Communiqué unequivocally suggested, the common assessment of the Soviet threat was placed at the center of the diplomatic normalization between the United States and the People's Republic of China. Carter's China policy was therefore strikingly similar to Nixon's: It had a distinct anti-Soviet connotation, it had been managed directly (and secretly) by the White House, and human rights considerations never interfered with the process of rapprochement. The tacit aim of the normalization process was the eventual creation of a security relationship with Beijing, therefore enlisting Chinese support in America's global competition with Moscow.

The rivalry with the Soviet Union clearly shaped President Carter's Horn of Africa and China policies. At the same time, the determination to conclude the SALT II Treaty also remained a priority for the administration. After the failure of the Vance mission in 1977, the negotiations returned to the framework established in Vladivostok. Arms control continued to be the central area of US-Soviet negotiations. The parallel evolution of the normalization with China and the dialogue in SALT confirmed the persisting ambivalence of American policy. The pattern was one of competition and cooperation. As noted by Brzezinski, "Plus ça change, plus c'est la même chose!"

Therefore, even before the crises of 1979, the initiatives analyzed in Chapters 9 and 10 – the focus on the Soviet Union's role in the Horn of Africa, and not on local dynamics; the reliance on regional allies to contain Soviet expansionism; the use of the China card to exercise pressure on Moscow; and the parallel, continued pursuit of SALT amid the escalating geopolitical competition – resemble the policies that had been outlined by Nixon. But what is the meaning and implication of this link between Carter's policies and those of his so bitterly criticized predecessor?

This inherent – though never acknowledged – continuity is all the more evident in America's unrelentingly tight relationship with Iran. Carter's support for the shah overlooked the principles and values that he had promised to pose at the center of American foreign policy. It revealed, instead, the continued reliance on one of the fundamental elements of Nixon's strategy of containment in the Persian Gulf. Carter evidently shared the assessment on the vital importance of Iran in guaranteeing the pro-Western orientation of the region, in the interest of the United States and of the entire free world. Despite a "sketchy" knowledge of the internal dynamics of the Iranian society, in December 1977 Carter publicly lauded the shah's Iran as "an island of stability" – therefore using the *same* expression repeatedly used by Kissinger in his memorandums to Nixon.

The unfolding of the Iranian crisis dramatically revealed the US incapacity to understand the complex local reality. Washington – firmly locked in a Cold War mind-set – failed to foresee the emergence of an entirely different type of challenge to the position of the United States. The Iranian internal upheavals – that eventually led to the overthrow of the shah – were constantly and almost exclusively assessed in terms of the potential for Soviet penetration. The American inability to formulate effective policies to respond to the local crisis was manifest, both before and after the shah's departure from the country.

On a global level, instead, the United States promptly reacted. The Iranian revolution was perceived as a grave setback, as the "loss" of a long-standing strategic barrier against Soviet expansionism. Consequently, Washington started to rethink its role in the region, foreseeing a direct commitment to its defense. The Carter doctrine was therefore a response to the vulnerability posed by the Iranian revolution, before Moscow's invasion of Afghanistan. It was a necessary adjustment of policy – a consequence of events which proved to be beyond American control – and not a rupture from the past. As the strengthening of the Nixon-shah relationship had demonstrated in 1972, the geopolitical containment of the Soviet Union had become more, and not less, important for the United States during the era of détente. Carter's crucial statement pronounced in January 1980 connected to "classic" Cold War doctrines – Truman and Eisenhower – and defined an always greater area of direct American commitment around the perimeter of the Soviet Union: first the immediate "northern tier" nations of Greece and Turkey, followed by the Middle East, and then the Persian Gulf. Although differentiating itself from the Nixon doctrine, because the reliance on local powers was no longer sufficient to defend American interests, the Carter doctrine was directly linked to Nixon's policy because it emerged as a consequence of the "loss" of Iran – a country considered by both administrations as vital for the implementation of US policy.

While the administration's intrinsic, albeit denied, Cold War mentality had previously remained concealed, in the aftermath of the Soviet invasion of Afghanistan the emphasis on the Soviet threat openly and publicly shaped Carter's posture. The depth of the change undertaken, from the intentions initially proclaimed to the policies then actually pursued, was evident. But contrary to the public pronouncements, the Soviet invasion did not signify a complete abandonment of the SALT II Treaty, nor a refusal to further cooperate with the Soviet Union on arms control. The administration decided that it would continue to pursue the ratification of the treaty, notwithstanding the presence of the Soviet troops in Afghanistan. The Carter administration had come to the conclusion that SALT was in the American interest, that it was not a favor granted to the Soviets and that, in line with what had been Kissinger's approach, it helped to more effectively manage the adversarial relationship with the Soviets (as had been the case, for example, in April/May 1972). Therefore, SALT was even more vital in a period of increased tension. This not only confirms the continued inherent ambivalence of American policy, but also a certain institutionalization of a different management of the superpower relationship. The significance of the interrelationship between Carter's and Nixon's policies in fact lies in the persistence of the dual pattern of negotiations with Moscow – motivated by the need to curtail or reduce the arms race – and a continued, but more geopolitically driven Cold War mind-set. Far from being just an elusive design, described as having "changed the climate of US-Soviet relations but not much else,"[11] the détente years transformed the way in which the United States positioned itself toward its global rival, the Soviet Union. And the coming of the Second Cold War did not necessarily render this transformation irrelevant.

Despite the acrimony and tough anti-Soviet rhetoric, sustained by a massive military buildup, only a few years after entering office even the Reagan administration started to search for cooperation with Moscow. In the spring of 1982, efforts at reinitiating arms control talks stood at the center of the administration's agenda and these were accompanied by more conciliatory tones toward the Soviet Union. In May 1982, for example, Secretary of State Alexander Haig addressed the US Chamber of Commerce and stressed the need for a political dialogue with Moscow. During the same month, President Reagan announced that the Soviet behavior in Afghanistan was no longer an obstacle for initiating arms negotiations. While these overtures might have been hesitant and tentative, they were enough to alarm the neoconservative and hard-line anti-Soviet ideologues who started to criticize Reagan for not following up with policies the promises made at the offset of the administration.[12] Nevertheless, pressured by some of his advisers on the need to reengage the Soviets and by his own aversion toward nuclear weapons, Reagan outlined a plan to pass from SALT to START. The proposed phased reductions mainly targeted land-based ICBMs and would have therefore had a

---

[11] Olav Nolstad, "The collapse of superpower détente, 1975–1980," 155. Nolstad refers to the main argument made by Jussi Hanhimäki in *The Flawed Architect. Henry Kissinger and American Foreign Policy* (New York: Oxford University Press, 2004), 486–91.

[12] Norman A. Graebner, Richard Dean Burns, Joseph M. Siracusa, *Reagan, Bush, Gorbachev. Revisiting the End of the Cold War* (Westport, CT: Praeger Security International, 2008), 36–37.

much deeper impact on the Soviet arsenal than on the American one. The proposal was thus rejected as one-sided by Moscow and the negotiations predictably stalled. President Reagan's interest in arms control and in reducing nuclear weapons was, however, evidently surfacing.[13]

In February 1983, Reagan met Soviet ambassador Dobrynin for the first time and discussed improving US-Soviet relations. While the Kremlin was not prepared to take the American overtures seriously, Reagan's shift in approach was clearly in the making. Even as the superpower relationship continued to remain tense throughout 1983, the administration under the growing influence of the new secretary of state, George Shultz, was moving toward a more moderate posture. After his famous "evil empire" speech in March 1983, Reagan assured a British correspondent that "he sought only to dramatize the differences between the United States and the Soviet Union in order to create the bases of realistic negotiations." In the following months, the president began exchanging messages with Soviet leader Yuri Andropov (who had succeeded Brezhnev) in which he stressed the superpowers' responsibility in maintaining peace and the need to engage in nuclear arms negotiations.[14]

By the fall of 1983 President Reagan had established an advisory group to chart a course of "constructive cooperation" with the Soviet Union.[15] This new approach was unveiled in January 1984 during a major speech on superpower relations. "We are prepared," stated Reagan, "to deal with our differences peacefully and through negotiations ... together we can strengthen peace, reduce the level of arms, and know that in doing so we have helped fulfill the hopes and dreams of those we represent and, indeed, of peoples everywhere. Let us begin now."[16] Although the aging Soviet leadership was not prepared to respond to these overtures,

---

[13] On SALT and START see, for example, Garthoff, *The Great Transition*, 553–558.

[14] Graebner, Burns, Siracusa, *Reagan, Bush, Gorbachev*, 58–59.

[15] Fischer, "US Foreign Policy under Reagan and Bush," 272. See also George P. Shultz, *Turmoil and Triumph. Diplomacy, Power and the Victory of the American Ideal* (New York: Touchstone, 1993), 159–171. It is important to notice that even in NSDD 75 of January 1983 Reagan called for negotiations with the Soviet Union when in the interest of the United States (specifically mentioning arms control) and ends the document – which according to some was a strategy designed to bring down the Soviet Union – by stating: "the US must demonstrate credibly that its policy is not a blueprint for an open-ended, sterile confrontation with Moscow but a serious search for a stable and constructive long-term basis for US-Soviet relations"; National Security Decision Directive 75.

[16] Address on US-Soviet relations, January 16, 1984, *Public Papers of the Presidents: Ronald Reagan, 1984, I* (Washington, DC: Government Printing Office, 1986), 42.

the president proceeded on his new course. Throughout 1984 – influenced also by domestic political calculations connected to the upcoming presidential election – Reagan publicly underlined that the United States and the Soviet Union had never been at war, and they never should be. The great challenge for them both was to reduce the risk of nuclear war because "a nuclear war cannot be won and must never be fought."[17] The first and principal objective of improved US-Soviet relations was, in fact, to reengage in productive negotiations on reducing nuclear weapons.

Assessing the reasons behind Reagan's shift in attitude goes well beyond the scope of this book. But three elements do need to be underlined: that Reagan's initial confrontational approach toward the Soviet Union did not endure; that the shift in his posture was initiated before the change in the Soviet leadership and the emergence of Mikhail Gorbachev; and that the dominant motivation for Reagan's search for a dialogue with Moscow was to negotiate on arms control and on the reduction of nuclear weapons. The necessity to curb the arms race – boosted by Reagan's personal quest to abolish nuclear weapons – was, therefore, once again placed at the center of the US-Soviet dialogue. Once Gorbachev came to power in the Soviet Union, the shift in Reagan's posture paved the way for another era of high-level summits: Geneva (1985), Reykjavik (1986), Washington (1987 – when the Intermediate Nuclear Forces Treaty was signed, which brought the first actual reduction in the nuclear arsenals of the superpowers), and Moscow (1988). Although the START negotiations remained stalled and were signed under different circumstances in 1991 (during the Reagan years the Soviets continued to subordinate the signing of the treaty to the US abandonment of SDI), the Reagan-Gorbachev détente – much like the Nixon era of détente – was unquestionably characterized by the dialogue on nuclear arms control.

At the same time, however, by 1985 – when the strategic dialogue started to produce the first results and would initiate a new era of US-Soviet summit diplomacy – the Reagan crusade in support of anti-communist guerrilla forces around the world evolved into the Reagan doctrine. The president committed his administration to aid popular insurgencies against communist domination. In his February 1985 State of the Union Address, Reagan stated:

We must stand by all our democratic allies. And we must not break faith with those who are risking their lives – on every continent, from Afghanistan to

---

[17] Quoted in Graebner, Burns, Siracusa, *Reagan, Bush, Gorbachev*, 59.

Nicaragua – to defy Soviet-supported aggression and secure rights which have been ours from birth.... Support for freedom fighters is self-defense ...[18]

Unlike previous Cold War doctrines, which justified interventions in defense of governments threatened by communist expansion, Reagan proclaimed the right to subvert existing communist regimes. With a revised version of the 1950s' call to "roll back" the Soviet Union, the Reagan administration engaged in a fierce geopolitical war by proxy to fight against Soviet influence in countries like Nicaragua, Afghanistan, Cambodia, Ethiopia, and Angola. Although more aggressive in tone and allegedly committed to counter, and not only resist, Soviet expansionism, the Reagan doctrine and its support for "freedom fighters" was, in essence, a continuation of the geopolitical fight against the Soviet Union already initiated in the 1970s. And, most significantly, it was proclaimed and officially endorsed while at the same time Washington was engaging Moscow to negotiate on arms control. At the highest level Reagan and Gorbachev met in successive summits and discussed the limitation and reduction of the nuclear arsenals, while in Afghanistan, for example, US-armed militias were killing Soviet soldiers and draining Moscow's resources. Was this not a return to the dual-track policy of engagement in arms control while competing for influence geopolitically?

A real answer to this question would require a more in-depth study of the Reagan administration's policies than the relatively cursory assessment proposed in these paragraphs. But the purpose here is to suggest that the policies of the 1970s may have remained a reference point for US foreign policy making until the end of the Cold War.

THE LEGACY OF THE 1970S

The Transformation of American International Power and Its Consequences

The pattern introduced by Nixon and Kissinger during the era of détente rotated around the necessity of arms control notwithstanding a continued, and at times escalating, geopolitical competition. On the basis of this interpretation, their policies set the stage for the following years, with continued arms control negotiations with the Soviet Union – considered

---

[18] Ronald Reagan's Address before a Joint Session of Congress on the State of the Union, February 6, 1985 (transcript available at: http://reagan2020.us/speeches/state_of_the_union_1985.asp).

by many as having contributed to the beginning of the end of the Cold War – and an increasingly global presence of the United States, which ultimately prevailed over Soviet influence worldwide.

Until the collapse of the Soviet Union, the United States would never return to the dominant position of the early Cold War years. But the transition "from dominance to leadership" called for by Henry Kissinger was charted successfully. Washington *did* redefine its leadership and transform its foreign policy, adjusting it to the increased Soviet nuclear power while maintaining or reasserting the US global presence. American partnerships or influence was secured in key areas of the world – in China and in the Middle East/Persian Gulf – areas that remain of vital strategic importance today. The foundations for the post–Cold War era of American leadership had thus been laid.

However, while the 1970s witnessed the successful transformation of American international power, the policies pursued throughout the decade – and beyond – brought a whole series of unintended consequences that endure to the present day. For this reason, the study of the 1970s is relevant and important also for current debates on how to reorient American foreign policy in an era of setbacks and (arguably) decline. The intervention of the United States in places like Angola and Somalia, exclusively motivated to counter the expansion of Soviet influence, exacerbated the already deep divisions within these countries, leaving them torn apart, in desperate poverty, and with little possibility for autonomous development. The Angolan civil war lasted for decades (the cease-fire between the MPLA and UNITA only came in 2002). In Somalia, US-sponsored dictator Said Barre held on to his undemocratic military rule but, as the Cold War strategic interest in the country progressively diminished, chaos and civil war erupted. Today, Somalia remains one of the most unstable, divided, and poor countries in the world.

Likewise, Washington's excessively Soviet-centric worldview, though justified by the necessities of the Cold War, led to overlooking the complex local reality in a country of vital strategic and economic importance such as Iran. The US stubborn and one-sided support for the shah (from Nixon to Carter) eventually led to one of the gravest setbacks in the history of US foreign policy, followed by a more than thirty-year-long animosity that continues today to hinder the making of effective long-term American policies toward Iran and the entire Southwest Asian region. Moreover, the United States failed to understand the emergence of a "third way" – a different kind of challenge – represented by the rise of political Islam. Locked in a Cold War mind-set, Washington remained focused on the Soviet Union. Despite the specificity of the Iranian revolution, the overthrow of a pro-Western government and the establishment of an Islamic state (even if it saw the triumph of the minority Shia version of Islam) were viewed as examples to follow in the Islamic world. Anti-Americanism emerged as a deeply rooted, clear-cut policy and, from Iran, spilled over to other states in the region, regardless of other policies pursued by Washington (some that could be seen as favorable to various Islamic states, such as the support for Iraq and the relationship with Egypt).

At the same time, the Soviet invasion of Afghanistan was assessed in Washington as the confirmation of Moscow's intention to expand its influence in the area. This led the US leadership to embrace the Afghan insurgency fighting against the Soviets. Initially supported indirectly by Carter and then openly endorsed as "freedom fighters" by Reagan, these fighters were animated by some of the same anti-Western sentiments as the radicals in Iran. Oversimplifying the Sunni-Shia division, while exclusively focused on countering the Soviet Union, America was both ally and adversary to the new, potent Islamic forces taking hold in the region. How did this dichotomy place the United States in the face of the rise of militant Islam? Charges of inconsistency, opportunism, and cultural insensitivity inevitably tarnished the image of the United States in the region. When the Cold War ended, Afghanistan lay in ruins and – amid the disinterest of America and the West – the forces that Washington had helped coalesce escalated their political Islamic battle. Many of these developments were hardly foreseeable in the 1970s, but the long-term consequences of a consistently and persistently Soviet-centric bias must be underlined. The Nixon-Kissinger – and never truly abandoned by Carter – approach to regional conflicts was inherently flawed. Assessing these shortcomings from the standpoint that they were neither personal (as many have argued, for example, against Henry Kissinger) nor partisan, but systematic in Washington's basic worldview, would lead to a constructive reflection on the lessons of history. And considering the ongoing crises in many of the same hot spots of the 1970s, such a reflection seems sorely needed.

Pointing to the continuity of American foreign policy despite such different presidencies as Nixon's and Carter's is therefore important for both historians and policymakers. One of the major debates among Cold War historians revolves around the "causes" of the end of the Cold War and who deserves the greatest "credit" for having brought the bipolar division of the world to an end. Schools of thought vary from the "triumphalists" – who contend that the Reagan administration deserves the greatest credit for having hastened or even caused the collapse of the Soviet Union – to the opposite view – that President Reagan and President Bush were both almost irrelevant to ending the Cold War, which was brought about practically singlehandedly by the policies pursued by Mikhail Gorbachev.[19] However, the debate seems to focus almost exclusively on the last decade of the Cold War, while an assessment of previous policies and their influence on the events of 1989–1991 remains outside the scope of the discussion. Instead, in addition to the dialogue on arms control, which is an essential element of the Reagan-Gorbachev era that clearly originated during the 1970s, also the policies toward the "arc of crisis," which are considered to have played a crucial role in bringing the Cold War to an end, can be assessed in terms of overall continuity. The Reagan administration is, in fact, often credited for its policy toward Afghanistan, aimed at drawing Moscow into a protracted struggle that drained limited Soviet resources and accelerated the demise of the Soviet Union.[20] But did this American foreign policy goal predate the Reagan presidency?

The analysis of US policy in 1978–1979 unveiled that President Carter initiated such policies as the creation of an American force to be stationed in the Gulf – the Rapid Deployment Joint Task Force (RDJTF); the negotiation to access strategically located naval bases in Somalia, Kenya, and Oman; and the support for Afghan factions fighting against Soviet influence in Afghanistan. These decisions set the stage for the policies developed by the Reagan administration throughout the 1980s, such as the evolution of the RDJTF into CENTCOM (US Central Command for the Persian Gulf); the escalation of the US naval presence in the region;

---

[19] Fischer, "US Foreign Policy under Reagan and Bush," 269–267. For a typically "triumphalist" view, according to which Reagan "adopted, designed and successfully implemented an integrated set of policies, strategies, and tactics specifically directed toward the eventual destruction (without war) of the Soviet Empire and the successful ending of the Cold War with victory of the West" see Norman A. Bailey, *The Strategic Plan that Won the Cold War. National Security Decision Directive 75* (McLean, Virginia: The Potomac Foundation, 1998). For a recent appraisal of Ronald Reagan's policies and their impact on the end of the Cold War: James Mann, *The Rebellion of Ronald Reagan. A History of the End of the Cold War* (New York: Penguin Books, 2009).

[20] On Reagan's policies in support of the *mujahideen* in Afghanistan: John Patrick Diggins, *Ronald Reagan. Fate, Freedom and the Making of History* (New York: W.W. Norton & Company, 2007), 227–234. On the continuity of Carter's and Reagan's policies toward Afghanistan, see the first part of Steve Coll, *Ghost Wars, The Secret History of the CIA, Afghanistan, and Bin Laden, from the Soviet Invasion to September 10, 2001* (New York: Penguin, 2004).

and the support for the *mujahideen* in Afghanistan, famously endorsed by President Reagan as "freedom fighters" in 1985. But if the roots of the policies developed by Reagan can be traced to the decisions leading to the Carter doctrine, which in turn can be linked to previous policies pursued by Nixon, this would set the stage for major reinterpretations on the end of the Cold War. In particular, the decisions made by the United States toward the arc of crisis during the 1970s would, at a minimum, acquire a much greater importance.

Although the debates on the end of the Cold War are definitely crucial for historians and for historiography, they appear somewhat less significant when compared to the long-term implications of the policies studied in this book. The adjustments of the 1970s and the effective transformation of American international power left a powerful but problematic legacy, which can be summarized in three broad considerations. First, the emphasis on the geopolitical dimension of power introduced by Nixon and Kissinger led the United States to expand (or strengthen) its outreach to complex, remote countries (in Africa, Afghanistan, and Iran) and to previous enemies (China). In order to respond to the alleged decline of American power, the Nixon, Ford, and Carter administrations did not retreat, but conceived different and more innovative means to enhance US influence while countering Soviet expansionism. Although not always successful, the initiatives pursued by the presidents of the 1970s were *not* passive acceptance of the post-Vietnam retrenchment as is often portrayed. The drive to reassert global primacy thus emerges as a constant feature of US foreign policy, particularly in moments of perceived relative decline of American power.

Second, the shortcomings and grave consequences of the limited, Soviet-centric vision of American policymakers have already been underlined. But beyond these, the real dilemma which potently surfaced throughout the 1970s is precisely *how* to reconcile America's need (and sometimes obligation) to assess and respond to global challenges while not overlooking local realities and regional dynamics. For Nixon, Ford, and Carter the Soviet Union was the global enemy, and the relationships with Angola, Somalia, Iran, and even China were subordinated to that overriding dominant concern. Decades later, when the terrorist threat dramatically emerged on the world scene after the September 11, 2001, attacks in New York and Washington, America (yet again a bipartisan America, from President Bush to President Obama) seems to have substituted the Soviet threat with the radical Islamic threat, engaging in the Iraq War and intervening (or remaining) in Afghanistan. While undeniably the terrorist challenge is of global concern, the regional contexts are just as, if not more, important. America's global bias still hampers the making of longer-term, sustainable policies in complex regional contexts, such as Iraq and Afghanistan. A more balanced approach – which seeks to more comprehensively reconcile global concerns and local dimensions – has yet to be conceived even in contemporary American policies.

A third and final consideration that emerges from the study of continuity throughout the 1970s notwithstanding the repeated calls for new beginnings or fresh starts is the absolute centrality of the American national interest in the making of US foreign policy. Whether it was Kissinger's *realpolitik* or Carter's human rights-focused approach, a perceived threat to America's vital security interests triggered the same, forceful reactions. The 1970s confirm – perhaps better than any other Cold War period – that even very different administrations are eventually compelled to follow the same pattern when confronted with what they perceive as vital security challenges. Despite America's traditional value-based and idealistic foreign policy, in the area of US-Soviet relations – the dominant aspect of Washington's foreign policy for decades – national security seems to *always* have prevailed over the promotion of human rights and democracy. The relationship with China is in this regard emblematic – because it started, endured, and developed for strategic (and economic) reasons despite the constant abuses of human rights and absence of political openings by the Chinese leadership. For a great power such as the United States, this is neither too surprising, nor excessively deplorable. But it is a fact often overlooked by many, particularly outside the United States and around the world, who often turn to Washington in search of a global defender of freedom, Western ideals, and values. Although American leadership on the world scene even throughout the difficult 1970s is hardly disputable, the often flagged "exceptionalism" of US foreign policy fades away in the face of the motivations and justifications of the choices made during those turbulent years. In Henry Kissinger's words, in the end America did take on a role that was novel in its history and prevented "the accumulation of seemingly marginal geopolitical gains which, over time, would overthrow the balance of power."[21] In this Washington was, ultimately, very successful. But in the process, America increasingly positioned itself on the world scene as a traditional, self-serving great power rather than the idealistic, inherently more "moral" and value-based nation it claims to be.

---

[21] Henry Kissinger, *Diplomacy* (New York: Simon & Schuster, 1994), 751.

Selected Bibliography

Archives

National Archives, College Park, Maryland, Nixon Presidential Materials

National Security Council Files
- ABM/MIRV
- Country Files – Europe (USSR)
- Country Files – Middle East
    Egypt
    Iran
    Middle East General
    Middle East War
For the President's Files
HAK Office Files
SALT
Subject Files
The President's Trip Files

Gerald R. Ford Presidential Library, Ann Arbor, Michigan

National Security Adviser Files
- Kissinger Reports on USSR, China and the Middle East
- Memoranda of Conversations, 1973–1977
- National Security Study and Decision Memoranda, 1974–1977
- NSC Meeting File, 1974–1977
- Presidential Country Files for Africa
- Presidential Country Files for East Asia and Pacific
- Presidential Country Files for Europe and Canada (USSR)
- Presidential Country Files for the Middle East and South Asia (Iran)

Jimmy Carter Presidential Library, Atlanta, Georgia

Donated Historical Material – Zbigniew Brzezinski Collection
- Geographic File
    - China (People's Republic of)
    - Ethiopia/Somalia and Iran
    - Southwest Asia/Persian Gulf
    - USSR
- Subject File
    - Alpha Channel
    - Meetings Muskie-Brown-Brzezinski,
    - PRC Meetings
    - SCC Meetings
    - Serial Xs
    - Weekly Reports

National Security Council Files
- Country Files
    - Afghanistan
    - Africa
    - China (People's Republic of)
- Staff Material Horn/Special
- Brzezinski Material Memcons

Published Document Collections

Foreign Relations of the United States, 1969–1976, Volume E-4, Documents on Iran and Iraq, 1969–1972.

Foreign Relations of the United States, 1969–1976, Volume XVII and XVIII (China).

Foreign Relations of the United States, 1969–1976, Volume XII and XIII (Soviet Union).

Setting the Course: The First Year. Major Policy Statements by President Richard Nixon. New York: Funk and Wagnalls, 1970.

Soviet-American Relations. The Détente Years, 1969–1972. Washington DC: United States Government Printing Office, 2007.

The Cold War International History Project Bulletin, Issues 8–9 "The Cold War in the Third World and the Collapse of Détente in the 1970s," Washington DC, Woodrow Wilson Center for Scholars, Winter 1996/1997.

The Carter Administration and the "Arc of Crisis" 1977–1981, Declassified Documents prepared for a Critical Oral History Conference, The Woodrow Wilson Center July 25–26, 2005.

Articles and Books

Aitken, Jonathan. *Nixon. A Life*, Washington, DC: Regnery Publishing Inc, 1993.

Ambrose, Stephen E. *Nixon: The Triumph of a Politician 1962–1972*. New York: Simon and Schuster, 1989.
   Nixon: Ruin and Recovery, 1973–1990. New York: Simon and Schuster, 1991.
Andrew, Christopher. *For the President's Eyes Only. Secret Intelligence and the American Presidency from Washington to Bush*. London: Harper Collins, 1996.
Andrew, Christopher and Mitrokhin, Vasilij. *The World Was Going Our Way. The KGB and the Battle for the Third World*. New York: Basic Books, 2005.
Andrianopoulos, Gerry A. *Kissinger and Brzezinski. The NSC and the Struggle for Control of US National Security Policy*. London: Macmillan, 1991.
Arbatov, Georgi. *The System. An Insider's Life in Soviet Politics*. New York: Random House, 1992.
Ball, Desmond. *Developments in the U.S. Strategic Nuclear Policy Under the Carter Administration*. ACIS Working Paper No. 21. University of California, Los Angeles: Center for International and Strategic Affairs, 1980.
Bell, Coral. *The Diplomacy of Détente: The Kissinger Era*. New York: Cambridge University Press, 1977.
   "Virtue Unrewarded: Carter's Foreign Policy at Mid-term," *International Affairs*, October 1978.
Berman, Larry. *No Peace, No Honor. Nixon, Kissinger and the Betrayal in Vietnam*. New York: Touchstone, 2002.
Bill, James A. *The Eagle and the Lion. The Tragedy of American-Iranian Relations*. New Haven, CT: Yale University Press, 1988.
Bohlen, Avis. "The Rise and Fall of Arms Control," *Survival*, Vol. XLV, No. 3, Autumn 2003.
Brinkley. Douglas. *Gerald R. Ford*. New York: Times Books, 2007.
Brown. Seyom. *The Faces of Power. Constancy and Change in United States Foreign Policy from Truman to Reagan*. New York: Columbia University Press, 1983.
Brzezinski, Zbigniew. *Power and Principle. Memoirs of the National Security Adviser, 1977–1981*. New York: Farrar, Straus and Giroux, 1983.
Bundy, William. *A Tangled Web: The Making of Foreign Policy in the Nixon Presidency*. New York: Hill & Wang, 1998.
Burr, William. *The Kissinger Transcripts: The Top Secret Talks with Beijing and Moscow*. New York: The New Press, 1999.
Cahn, Anne Hessing. *Killing Détente. The Right Attacks the CIA*. University Park, PA: The Pennsylvania State University Press, 1998.
Carter, Jimmy. *Keeping Faith. Memoirs of a President*. Fayetteville, AK: The University of Arkansas Press, 1995.
Catudal, Honoré M. *Soviet Nuclear Strategy from Stalin to Gorbachev*. West Berlin: Berlin Verlag Arno Spitz, 1988.
Cohen, Warren I. *America's Response to China. A History of Sino-American Relations*. New York: Columbia University Press, 2000.
Cold War History, Special Issue: Détente and its Legacy, Volume 8, Number 4, November 2008.

Coll, Steve. *Ghost Wars. The Secret History of the CIA, Afghanistan, and Bin Laden, from the Soviet Invasion to September 10, 2001.* New York: Penguin, 2004.
Collins, John. *American and Soviet Military Trends since the Cuban Missile Crisis.* CSIS, Washington, DC: Georgetown University Press, 1978.
Craig, Gordon A. and Francis L. Loewenheim (eds). *The Diplomats 1939–1979.* Princeton, NJ: Princeton University Press, 1994.
Dallek, Robert. *Nixon and Kissinger: Partners in Power.* New York: HarperCollins, 2007.
Deibel, Terry L. and John Lewis Gaddis (eds). *Containing the Soviet Union. A Critique of US Policy.* Washington, DC: Pergamon-Brassey's International Defense Publishers, 1987.
  Containment. Concept and Policy. Based on a Symposium Cosponsored by the National Defense University and the Foreign Service Institute, Vol. I and II. Washington, DC: National Defense University Press, 1986.
De Tinguy, Anne. *US-Soviet Relations during the Détente.* New York: Columbia University Press, 1999.
Del Pero, Mario. *The Eccentric Realist. Henry Kissinger and the Shaping of American Foreign Policy.* Ithaca, NY: Cornell University Press, 2010.
Dobrynin, Anatoly. *In Confidence: Moscow's Ambassador to Six Cold War Presidents (1962–1986).* New York: Random House, 1995.
Dumbrell, John. *The Carter Presidency. A Re-evaluation.* Manchester and New York: Manchester University Press, 1993.
Edmonds, Robin. *Soviet Foreign Policy: The Brezhnev Years.* New York: Oxford University Press, 1983.
Feinberg, Richard E. *The Intemperate Zone. The Third World Challenge to U.S. Foreign Policy.* New York: W.W. Norton & Company, 1983.
Foot, Rosemary. *The Practice of Power: U.S. Relations with China since 1949.* Oxford: Oxford University Press, 1995.
Ford, Gerald R. *A Time to Heal.* New York: Harper and Row Publishers, 1979.
Fosdick, Dorothy (ed). *Staying the Course: Henry M. Jackson and National Security.* Seattle, WA: University of Washington Press, 1987.
Foster, William C. "Prospects for Arms Control," *Foreign Affairs*, April 1969.
Froman, Michael B. *The Development of the Idea of Détente: Coming to Terms.* London: Macmillan, 1991.
Gaddis, John. *Strategies of Containment: A Critical Appraisal of Postwar American National Security Policy.* New York: Oxford University Press, 1982 (revised and updated 2005).
  We Now Know. Rethinking Cold War History. New York: Oxford University Press, 1997.
  "Containment: A Reassessment," *Foreign Affairs*, July 1977.
Garthoff, Raymond. *A Journey Through the Cold War. A Memoir of Containment and Coexistence.* Washington, DC: The Brookings Institution, 2001.
  Détente and Confrontation: American Soviet Relations from Nixon to Reagan. Washington, DC: The Brookings Institution, 1994.
  The Great Transition: American-Soviet Relations and the End of the Cold War. Washington, DC: The Brookings Institution, 1994.

Gates, Robert M. *From the Shadows. The Ultimate Insider's Story of Five Presidents and How They Won the Cold War.* New York: Simon and Schuster, 1996.
Genovese, Michel A. *The Nixon Presidency. Power and Politics in Turbulent Times.* New York: Greenwood Press, 1990.
George, Alexander L., Philip J. Farley, and Alexander Dallin (eds). *U.S.–Soviet Security Cooperation. Achievements, Failures, Lessons.* New York: Oxford University Press, 1988.
Gleijeses, Piero. *Conflicting Missions: Havana, Washington, and Africa, 1959–1976.* Chapel Hill, NC: University of North Carolina Press, 2002.
  "Moscow's Proxy? Cuba and Africa 1975–1988," *Journal of Cold War Studies*, Vol. 8, No. 4, Fall 2006.
Golan, Galia. *Soviet Policies in the Middle East from World War II to Gorbachev.* Cambridge: Cambridge University Press, 1990.
Greene, John Robert. *The Presidency of Gerald R. Ford.* Lawrence, KS: University of Kansas Press, 1995.
  The Limits of Power: The Nixon and Ford Administrations. Bloomington, IN: Indiana University Press, 1992.
Guderzo, Max and Bruna Bagato (eds). *The Globalization of the Cold War. Diplomacy and Local Confrontation, 1975–1985.* London: Routledge, 2010.
Haig, Alexander M. Jr. *Inner Circles. How America Changed the World.* New York: Warner Books, 1992.
Halliday, Fred. *The Making of the Second Cold War.* London: Verso, 1986.
Hammond, Thomas T. *Red Flag Over Afghanistan. The Communist Coup, The Soviet Invasion and the Consequences.* Boulder, CO: Westview Press, 1984.
Hanhimäki, Jussi M. *The Flawed Architect: Henry Kissinger and American Foreign Policy.* New York: Oxford University Press, 2004.
  The Rise and Fall of Détente. Dulles, VA: Potomac Books, 2013.
  "'Dr. Kissinger' or 'Mr. Henry'? Kissingerology, Thirty Years and Counting," *Diplomatic History*, Vol. 27, No. 5, November 2003.
Hanhimäki, Jussi M., Benedikt Schoenborn and Barbara Zanchetta. *Transatlantic Relations Since 1945: An Introduction.* London: Routledge, 2012.
Hargrove, Erwin. *Jimmy Carter as President: Leadership and the Politics of the Public Good.* Baton Rouge, LA: Louisiana State University Press, 1988.
Hartman, Robert T. *Palace Politics. An Inside Account of the Ford Years.* New York: McGraw-Hill, 1980.
Harvey, Robert. *Comrades. The Rise and Fall of World Communism.* London: John Murray Publishers, 2003.
Helms, Richard. *A Look over My Shoulder. A Life in the Central Intelligence Agency.* New York: Ballantine Books, 2003.
Herring, George. *America's Longest War. The United States and Vietnam, 1950–1975* (4th edition). New York: Mc-Graw-Hill, 2001.
Hersh, Seymour. *The Price of Power: Kissinger in the Nixon White House.* New York: Summit Books, 1983.
Hoff, Joan. *Nixon Reconsidered.* New York: Basic Books, 1994.

Hoffman, Stanley. *Primacy of World Order. American Foreign Policy since the Cold War*. New York: McGraw-Hill, 1980.
Hogan, Michael J. (ed). *America in the World. The Historiography of American Foreign Relations since 1941*. New York: Cambridge University Press, 1995.
Holdridge, John H. *Crossing the Divide. An Insider's Account of the Normalization of U.S.-China Relations*. New York: Lanham, Rowman & Littlefield, 1997.
Holsti, Ole R. *Public Opinion and American Foreign Policy*. Ann Arbor, MI: University of Michigan Press, 1997.
Hunt, Michael H. *Ideology and U.S. Foreign Policy*. New Haven, CT: Yale University Press, 1987.
Hyland, William G. *Mortal Rivals: Superpower Relations from Nixon to Reagan*. New York: Random House, 1987.
Isaacson, Walter. *Kissinger*. New York: Simon & Schuster, 1992.
Israelyan, Victor. *Inside the Kremlin during the Yom Kippur War*. University Park, PA: Pennsylvania University Press, 1995.
Jian, Chen. *Mao's China and the Cold War*. Chapel Hill, NC: The University of North Carolina Press, 2001.
Johnson, Robert David. "Congress and the Cold War," *Journal of Cold War Studies*, Vol. 3, No. 2, Spring 2001.
Kaufman, Burton I. *The Presidency of James Earl Carter*. Lawrence, KS: University Press of Kansas, 1993.
Kaufman, Robert G. *Henry M. Jackson: A Life in Politics*. Seattle, WA: University of Washington Press, 2000.
Kaufman, Scott. *Plans Unraveled. The Foreign Policy of the Carter Administration*. DeKalb, IL: Northern Illinois University Press, 2008.
Kanet, Roger E. "The Superpower Quest for Empire: The Cold War and Soviet Support for 'Wars of National Liberation,'" *Cold War History*, Vol. 6, No. 3, August 2006.
Kimball, Jeffrey. *Nixon's Vietnam War*. Lawrence, KS: University Press of Kansas, 1998.
Kissinger, Henry. *Crisis. The Anatomy of Two Major Foreign Policy Crises*: New York: Simon & Schuster, 2003.
   White House Years. London: Phoenix Press, 2000.
   Years of Upheaval. London: Phoenix Press, 2000.
   Years of Renewal: London: Phoenix Press, 2000.
   Diplomacy. New York: Simon & Schuster, 1994.
   Observations. London: Michael Joseph and Weindenfeld and Nicolson, 1985.
Kinzer, Stephen. *All the Shah's Men. An American Coup and the Roots of Middle East Terror*. Hoboken, NJ: Wiley, 2003.
Kotkin, Stephen. *Armageddon Averted. The Soviet Collapse, 1970–2000*. New York: Oxford University Press, 2001.
Kuisong, Yang. "The Sino-Soviet Border Clash of 1969: From Zhenbao Island to Sino-American Rapprochement," *Cold War History*, Vol. 1, No. 1, August 2000.
Kupchan, Charles A. *The Persian Gulf and The West. The Dilemmas of Security*. Boston, MA: Allen &Unwin, 1987.

Kurzman, Charles. *The Unthinkable Revolution in Iran.* Cambridge, MA: Harvard University Press, 2004.
Lafeber, Walter. *America, Russia, and the Cold War, 1945–2000.* New York: McGraw-Hill, 2002.
Laird, Melvin R. *The Nixon Doctrine.* Washington, DC: American Enterprise Institute for Public Policy Research, 1972.
Laird, Robbin F. and Dale R. Herspring. *The Soviet Union and Strategic Arms.* Boulder, CO: Westview Press, 1984.
Lefebvre, Jeffrey A. *Arms for the Horn. US Security Policy in Ethiopia and Somalia 1953–1991.* Pittsburgh, PA: University of Pittsburgh Press, 1991.
Leffler, Melvyn P. and Odd Arne Westad (eds). *The Cambridge History of the Cold War. Volume II: Crises and Détente.* Cambridge: Cambridge University Press, 2010.
  The Cambridge History of the Cold War. Volume III: Endings. Cambridge: Cambridge University Press, 2010.
Light, Margot (ed). *Troubled Partnerships: Moscow's Third World Ventures.* London: Macmillan, 1993.
Litwak, Robert S. *Détente and the Nixon Doctrine: Foreign Policy and the Pursuit of Stability.* Cambridge: Cambridge University Press, 1984.
Logevall, Frederick. *Choosing War: The Lost Chance for Peace and the Escalation of War in Vietnam.* Berkeley, CA: University of California Press, 1999.
Logevall, Frederick and Andrew Preston (eds). *Nixon in the World: American Foreign Relations, 1969–1977.* New York: Oxford University Press, 2008.
MacFarquhar, Roderick and Michael Schoenhals. *Mao's Last Revolution.* Cambridge, MA: Harvard University Press, 2006.
MacMillan, Margaret. *Nixon and Mao: The Week That Changed the World.* New York: Random House, 2007.
Mann, James. *About Face. A History of America's Curious Relationship with China, from Nixon to Clinton.* New York: Vintage, 1998.
  Rise of the Vulcans. The History of Bush's War Cabinet. New York: Viking Penguin, 2004.
Mason, Robert. *Richard Nixon and the Quest for a New Majority.* Chapel Hill, NC: The University of North Carolina Press, 2004.
Mastny, Vojtech, Sven G. Holtsmark, and Andreas Wenger (eds). *War Plans and Alliance in the Cold War. Threat Perceptions in the East and West.* London: Routledge, 2006.
Mastny, Vojtech and Malcolm Byrne (eds). *A Cardboard Castle? An Inside History of the Warsaw Pact.* Budapest: Central European University Press, 2005.
Maxwell, Neville. "The Chinese Account of the 1969 Fighting at Chenpao," *The China Quarterly,* No. LVI, October–December 1973.
Mitchell, Nancy. "Tropes of the Cold War: Jimmy Carter and Rhodesia," *Cold War History* 7:2 (May 2007), 263–283.
Morris, Benny. *Righteous Victims. A History of the Zionist-Arab Conflict, 1881–2001.* New York: Vintage Books, 2001.
Morris, Kenneth E. *Jimmy Carter: American Moralist.* Athens, GA: University of Georgia Press, 1996.

Nelson, Keith L. *The Making of Détente: Soviet-American Relations in the Shadow of Vietnam*. Baltimore, MD: Johns Hopkins University Press, 1995.

Newhouse, John. *Cold Dawn. The Story of SALT*. New York: Holt, Rinehart and Winston, 1973.

Nitze, Paul H. *From Hiroshima to Glasnost. At the Center of Decision. A Memoir*. New York: Grove Weidenfeld, 1989.

Nixon, Richard M. *RN: The Memoirs of Richard Nixon*. New York: Touchstone, 1990.

Njolstad, Olav. "Shifting Priorities: The Persian Gulf in US Strategic Planning in the Carter Years," *Cold War History*, Vol. 4, No. 3 (April 2004).

Odom, William E. *On Internal War: American and Soviet Approaches to Third World Clients and Insurgents*. Durham, NC: Duke University Press, 1992.

Olson, Keith W. *Watergate: The Presidential Scandal That Shook America*. Lawrence, KS: The University Press of Kansas, 2003.

Onslow, Sue (ed). *Cold War in Southern Africa: White Power, Black Liberation*. London: Routledge, 2009.

Ouimet, Matthew J. *The Rise and Fall of the Brezhnev Doctrine in Soviet Foreign Policy*. Chapel Hill, NC: University of North Carolina Press, 2003.

Parmet, Herbert S. *Richard Nixon and His America*. Boston, MA: Little Brown and Company, 1990.

Perlstein, Rick. *Nixonland: The Rise of a President and the Fracturing of America*. New York: Scribner, 2008.

Pollack, Kenneth M. *The Persian Puzzle. The Conflict between America and Iran*. New York: Random House, 2005.

Preston, Andrew. *War Council: McGeorge Bundy, the NSC, and Vietnam*. Cambridge, MA: Harvard University Press, 2010.

Quandt, William B. *Peace Process: American Policy Toward the Arab-Israeli Conflict*. Berkeley, CA: University of California Press, 1984.

Reeves, Richard. *President Nixon. Alone in the White House*. New York: Simon and Schuster, 2001.

Ross, Robert S. *Negotiating Cooperation. The United States and China 1969–1989*. Stanford, CA: Stanford University Press, 1995.

Rubinstein, Alvin Z. *Soviet Policy Toward Turkey, Iran, and Afghanistan. The Dynamics of Influence*. New York: Praeger Publishers, 1982.

  Moscow's Third World Strategy. Princeton, NJ: Princeton University Press, 1989.

Schmitz, David F. and Vanessa Walker. "Jimmy Carter and the Foreign Policy of Human Rights: The Development of a Post-Cold War Foreign Policy," *Diplomatic History*, Vol. 28, No. 1, January 2004.

Schulz, Mathias and Thomas Schwartz (eds). *Strained Alliance: US-European Relations from Nixon to Carter*. Cambridge and New York: Cambridge University Press, 2010.

Schulzinger, Robert. *American Diplomacy in the Twentieth Century*. New York: Oxford University Press, 1990.

  Henry Kissinger: Doctor of Diplomacy. New York: Columbia University Press, 1989.

Sick, Gary. *All Fall Down: America's Tragic Encounter with Iran*. London: I. B. Tauris, 1985.
Small, Melvin. *At the Water's Edge: American Politics and the Vietnam War*. Chicago, IL: Ivan R. Dee, 2005.
  The Presidency of Richard Nixon. Lawrence, KS: University of Kansas Press, 1999.
Smith, Gaddis. *Morality, Reason and Power. American Diplomacy in the Carter Years*. New York: Hill and Wang, 1986.
Smith, Gerard C. *Doubletalk: The Story of the First Strategic Arms Limitation Talks*. Garden City, NY: Doubleday, 1980.
Stone, Jeremy J. "When and How to Use SALT," *Foreign Affairs*, January 1970.
Strong, Robert A. *Working in the World: Jimmy Carter and the Making of American Foreign Policy*. Baton Rouge, LA: Louisiana State University Press, 2000.
Sulzberger, C. L. *The World and Richard Nixon*. New York: Prentice Hall Press, 1987.
Suri, Jeremi. *Power and Protest: Global Revolution and the Origins of Détente*. Cambridge, MA: Harvard University Press, 2003.
  Henry Kissinger and the American Century. Cambridge, MA: Harvard University Press, 2007.
  "The Cold War, Decolonization and Global Social Awakenings: Historical Intersections," *Cold War History*, Vol. 6, No. 3, August 2006.
Talbott, Strobe. *EndGame. The Inside Story of SALT II*. New York: Harper Colophon Books, 1980.
Thornton, Richard C. *The Carter Years: Toward A New Global Order*. New York: Paragon Press, 1992.
  The Nixon-Kissinger Years: Reshaping America's Foreign Policy. New York: Paragon House, 1989.
Tompson, William. *The Soviet Union under Brezhnev*. London: Pearson, 2003.
Trofimenko, Henry. "The Third World and the U.S. – Soviet Competition: A Soviet View," *Foreign Affairs*, Summer 1981.
Tucker, Nancy Bernkopf. *China Confidential: American Diplomats and Sino-American Relations, 1945–1996*. New York: Columbia University Press, 2001.
Tyler, Patrick. *A World of Trouble: The White House and the Middle East – from the Cold War to the War on Terror*. New York: Farrar, Straus and Giroux, 2009.
  A Great Wall. Six Presidents and China: An Investigative History. New York: Century Foundation, 1999.
Ulam, Adam B. *Dangerous Relations. The Soviet Union in World Politics, 1970–1982*. New York: Oxford University Press, 1983.
Vance, Cyrus. *Hard Choices. Critical Years in America's Foreign Policy*. New York: Simon and Schuster, 1983.
Westad, Odd Arne. *Reviewing the Cold War. Approaches, Interpretations, Theory*. London: Frank Cass Publishers, 2000.
  The Global Cold War. Third World Interventions and the Making of Our Times. New York: Cambridge University Press, 2005.

    Brothers in Arms: The Rise and Fall of the Sino-Soviet Alliance, 1945–1963. Washington, DC: Woodrow Wilson Center Press, 1998.

    The Fall of Détente. Soviet–American Relations during the Carter Years. Oslo, Norway: Scandinavian University Press, 1997.

Wohlforth, William. "Superpowers, Interventions and the Third World," *Cold War History*, Vol. 6, No. 3, August 2006.

York, Herbert F. *Salt I and the Future of Arms Control and Disarmament.* California: Arms Control and Foreign Policy Seminar, 1973.

Zakaria, Fareed. *The Post-American World and the Rise of the Rest.* New York: Penguin, 2009.

Zubok, Vladislav. *The Failed Empire: The Soviet Union in the Cold War from Stalin to Gorbachev.* Chapel Hill, NC: University of North Carolina Press, 2007.

Index

Aaron, David, 216
ABM (Anti-Ballistic Missile), 62, 63, 65, 68, 69, 83, 146
Acheson, Dean, 20
Agnew, Spiro, 148
Agreement on the Prevention of Nuclear War (PNW), 121
Amin, Hafizullah, 284
Andrew, Christopher, 206
Andropov, Yuri, 307
Angola
  and CIA, 163, 164, 169
  and Soviet-Cuban intervention, 168
  Chinese involvement in, 161
  factions competing in, 159
Armacost, Mike, 237

Backfire
  code-name of Soviet bomber, 167, 175, 176, 234, 240
Bakhtiar, Shapour, 273, 274, 275
Ball, George W., 258, 259
Bani Sadr, Abol Hassan, 275
Bazargan, Mehdi, 275, 276
Begin, Menachem, 195
Berlin Agreements, 61, 65
Bill, James, 246, 259
Brezhnev doctrine, 40
Brezhnev, Leonid, 153, 285
  background of, 11
  and his views on China, 122, 138, 147, 151
  and his views on the Middle East (1973), 123
  and protests against Israel's stance, 127
  and reaction to US opening to China, 82
  and SALT I agreements, 70
  and US normalization of relations with China, 232
  and Vietnam (1972), 77
Brown, George S., 172
Brown, Harold, 201, 238
Brzezinski, Zbigniew, 10, 199
  and Afghanistan, 285
  and China, 223, 225
  and Horn of Africa, 219
  and Iran, 261, 263–264, 272, 280
  and May 1978 trip to China, 226–230
  and relationship with Brown, 201
  and relationship with the First Lady, 201
  and Somalia, 209, 212
Buchen, Philip, 148
Bush, George, 177, 217

Cambodia
  and 1970 coup, 46
  and American incursion in, 46
Camp David Accords, 193, 195
Carter doctrine, 263, 266, 272, 288, 290, 293, 305, 313
Carter, Jimmy, 4, 6, 115, 156, 189, 190, 191, 192, 244, 248, 250, 302, 319, 321, 322, 323
  and Afghanistan, 282, 285
  background of, 8, 189–191
  and criticism of Nixon, 192

Carter, Jimmy (*cont.*)
    and curbing arms transfers, 198
    and hostage crisis, 280
    and human rights, 196, 214, 219
    and Iran, 247, 250, 263
    and reestablishing triangular diplomacy, 238
Carter, Rosalynn, 201
Castro, Fidel, 211
Cheney, Richard (Dick), 149, 177
Chiang Kai-shek, 35
China opening
    and "Pakistani channel," 44
    and Ping-Pong diplomacy, 47
    and Vietnam, 52–53
    and Warsaw meetings, 38, 44–45
Colby, William, 177
CPSU (Communist Party of the Soviet Union), 10
Crisis (Henry Kissinger), 128
CSCE (Conference on Security and Cooperation in Europe), 165, 168, 196
Cuban missile crisis, 62, 129, 296
Cultural Revolution, 153

Daoud Khan, Mohammad, 283
Davis, Nathaniel, 164
Dobrynin, Anatoly, 32
    and Carter's human rights policy, 196
    and his view of Kissinger's strategy in the Middle East, 136
    and the beginning of SALT, 64
    and the Horn of Africa, 217
    and view of US opening to China, 82
    and view on US desire for strategic superiority, 83
Douglas, Helen, 29

Eisenhower, Dwight, 6, 19, 29, 30, 33, 36, 89, 90, 252, 305
Enlai, Zhou, 12, 40, 44, 46, 48, 50, 52, 53, 54, 57, 153, 154, 224
Evening News, 42

Ferguson, Niall, 1
FNLA (National Liberation Front of Angola), 159, 160, 161, 162, 163, 164
Ford, Gerald, 6, 8, 115, 147, 148, 177, 245
    and 1975 visit to China, 181–183
    background of, 8, 147

Forty (40) Committee, 32, 163
Forward Based-Systems (FBS), 152
Fulbright, William, 3

Garthoff, Raymond, 239
Gorbachev, Mikhail, 308, 312
Guofeng, Hua, 224

Haig, Alexander, 39, 148, 306
Halperin, Morton, 31
Hanhimäki, Jussi, 58, 120
Hartmann, Robert, 148
Helms, Richard, 100, 244, 269
Henze, Paul, 209, 279, 286
Hiss, Alger, 29
Holbrooke, Richard, 230, 237
Hongqi, 37
Hopkins, Harry, 33
Horne, Alistair, 269
hostage crisis (in Iran), 278, 279
Howe, Jon, 126
Humphrey, Hubert, 29, 199
Huntington, Samuel, 2
Huyser, Robert, 273
Hyland, William, 32, 138

ICBM (Intercontinental Ballistic Missiles), 62, 63, 68, 180, 234, 240
Ismail, Hafiz, 132
Izvestia, 235

Jackson, Henry, 118, 155
JCS (Joint Chiefs of Staff), 101, 118, 167, 172, 176
Johnson, Lyndon, 20, 28, 36, 37, 65, 91, 199, 201, 253

Karmal, Babrak, 284
Kaufman, Scott, 202
Kennedy, Edward (Ted), 190
Kennedy, John F., 20, 29, 31, 36, 91, 199, 201, 253
Kennedy, Robert, 20
Khan, Yahya, 44
Khomeini, Ruhollah (Ayatollah), 253, 258, 259, 260, 267, 268, 274, 275, 276, 277, 278, 279
Khrushchev, Nikita, 10, 40
King, Martin Luther Jr., 20
Kissinger, Henry, 4, 6, 7, 8, 9, 12, 22, 31, 82, 149, 177, 195, 199, 310, 311, 314

and "linkage," 72
and Angola's global significance, 171, 172
and anti-Soviet strategy in the Middle East (1973), 126, 130, 132
and April 1972 secret trip to Moscow, 79
and back-channel meetings with Dobrynin, 43
and disagreement with Nixon over Middle East, 134
and domestic criticism of detente, 144
and 'emergency' visit to Moscow Oct. 1973, 127, 133
and Feb. 1973 trip to China, 120–121
and Iran as "an island of stability," 98
and Jan. 1976 trip to Moscow, 174–177
and July 1971 secret trip to China, 49–52, 55–56
and no more limits toward Iran, 112
and purpose of Nixon's visit to Iran, 110
and shah of Iran, 247
and shuttle diplomacy, 23, 136
and upheavals in Iran, 269
and urging Nixon to visit Iran, 106
and Watergate, 119
Kupchan, Charles, 1

Laingen, Bruce, 276, 278
Laird, Melvin, 31, 131
Lin Biao, 45, 46
Litwak, Robert, 23

MacArthur, Douglas, 96, 99, 254
MAD (Mutual Assured Destruction), 66, 69, 83
Maddox, Lester, 190
Mansur, Hassan Ali, 253
McCoy, Alfred, 1
McNamara, Robert, 31
Mengistu, Haile Mariam, 207, 213
MFN (Most Favored Nation), 118, 142, 145, 146, 150, 156
Middle East war (1973)
and US nuclear alert (DEFCONIII), 130
MIRV (Multiple Independently-targeted Re-entry Vehicle), 63, 65, 70, 117, 121, 176
Mitchell, Nancy, 218
Mondale, Walter, 202
Mossadeq, Mohammed, 89

MPLA (Popular Movement for the Liberation of Angola), 159, 160, 161, 162, 168, 169, 185, 310
Mugabe, Robert, 195

Naas, Charles, 276
neoconservatives
and criticism of US-Soviet détente, 155–156
New York Times, 140, 196, 250
Nixon doctrine, 7, 28, 87, 95, 97, 101, 108, 243, 299, 305
Nixon, and realism, 7
Nixon, Richard, 4, 6, 20, 22, 36, 147
and airlift to Israel, 126
background of, 7, 28–30
and centrality of the White House, 30
and China summit, 52, 57
and Haiphong bombing, 79–81
and no more limits toward Iran, 108, 112
and response to Sadat, 128
and restraint toward Iran, 97, 104
and SALT I, 61–64

Ogaden War
and Soviet involvement, 215
Oksenberg, Michel, 226, 237

Panama Canal Treaties, 193, 196
Pentagon, 167
People's Republic of China, 21, 23, 26, 33, 42, 46, 60, 65, 82, 151, 153, 221, 222, 238, 243
Petrov, Vasilii I., 215
Pisar, Samuel, 196
Pravda, 42
Precht, Henry, 258, 260, 277

Qiao Guanhua, 53
Qing, Jiang, 181

RDF (Rapid Deployment Force), 282, 283
Reagan doctrine, 296, 308, 309
Reagan, Ronald, 4, 83, 155, 178, 181, 293, 294
realpolitik, 7, 9, 26, 58, 119, 136, 154, 192, 301, 302, 314
Red Star over China (Edgar Snow), 38
Renmin ribao, 37
Rockefeller, Nelson, 149
Rogers, William P., 30

Roosevelt, Franklin, 33
Rumsfeld, Donald, 148, 172, 177

Sadat, Anwar, 12, 195
  and request for Soviet and American troops, 127
Said Barre, Muhammad, 208, 212
Saigon
  fall of, 5, 156
Sakharov, Andrei, 196
SALT (Strategic Arms Limitation Talks), 5, 12, 61, 64
SALT I, 32, 60, 61, 66, 68, 71, 72, 73, 83, 118, 144, 153, 178, 241, 291
  and content of agreements, 69
SALT II, 83, 117, 121, 140, 152, 155, 160, 165, 167, 173, 178, 180, 196, 198, 222, 233, 236, 239, 289, 290, 291
SALT II Treaty
  content of, 240–241
Saunders, Harold, 278
Schlesinger doctrine, 145
Schlesinger, James, 144, 149, 177, 246
Schulzinger, Robert, 4, 71
Scowcroft, Brent, 126, 177
SDI (Strategic Defense Initiative), 295
Selassie, Haile, 207
Shanghai Communiqué, 53, 57, 58, 181, 222, 228, 231, 298
Shultz, George, 307
Sick, Gary, 249, 261
Siedman, William L., 148
Sino-Soviet split, 3, 5, 22, 40
SLBM (Submarine Launched Ballistic Missiles), 62, 63
Smith, Gaddis, 193
Snow, Edgar, 38, 47
Sonnenfeldt, Helmut, 32, 61
Soviet Union
  and possible attack on China, 42
  and SALT, 64, 67–68
START (Strategic Arms Reduction Talks), 306
Sullivan, William, 258
Suslov, Mikhail, 206

Taraki, Noor Mohammed, 284
Time (magazine), 47, 86, 294
triangular diplomacy, 39, 47, 151, 154, 239, 298

Truman, Harry, 20, 148, 288, 305, 317
Tunney Amendment
  and Angolan civil war, 171, 177

UNITA (National Union for Total Independence of Angola), 159, 162, 310
US-Iran relations
  and 1953 coup, 89–90
  and 1959 Treaty, 91, 252
  and 1968 Memorandum of Understanding, 97
  and Carter's Dec. 1977 trip to Tehran, 251
  and Nixon's May 1972 visit to Tehran, 108–115
  and the "arc of crisis," 264, 265, 282, 284, 312, 313
  and the shah's Nov. 1977 trip to the US, 250
  and the shah's Oct. 1969 trip to the US, 94–96
  origins of, 88–91
US-Soviet relations
  and 1974 summit, 139, 146–147
  and Jackson-Vanik amendment, 118
  and June 1973 summit, 121–124
  and Moscow summit, 117
  and Trade Bill, 142, 145, 156
  and Vienna summit, 240
  and Vladivostok summit, 150–153
Ussuri River, 39, 41

Vance and Brzezinski
  different views of, 199–201, 216
Vance, Cyrus, 10, 199, 200, 256, 278, 302
  and "deep cuts" proposal in SALT, 235
  and August 1977 trip to China, 224
  and China, 223
  and Iran, 267, 272
  and May 1977 trip to Tehran, 249
Verification Panel, 32
Vietnam War, 3, 15, 22, 26, 36, 41
  and China opening, 46
  and Easter Offensive, 61, 73
  and Haiphong Harbor, 74, 77
  and interconnection with Moscow summit, 80
  and mining of Haiphong harbor, 61
  and Tet Offensive, 20

Vietnamization, 28
Vladivostok summit, 12

war on terror, 4
Washington Post, 153
Washington Special Actions Group, 32
Watergate
    scandal and/or affair, 8, 9, 12, 31, 117, 119, 120, 130, 142, 143, 145, 146, 149, 189, 190, 191, 196, 301, 322
Weinberger, Casper, 294
Westad, Odd Arne, 210, 321
Western Europe, 3, 5, 20, 65, 67, 138, 194, 200, 212, 218, 227, 272

Wheeler, Earle, 101
Wilson, Woodrow, 7, 29, 33, 323
Woodcock, Leonard, 230

Xiaoping, Deng, 12, 153, 154, 181, 182, 224, 227, 239

Yazdi, Ibrahim, 276, 278
Young, Andrew, 205

Zakaria, Fareed, 2
Zedong, Mao, 12, 35, 45